Ch'orti'-Maya Survival in
Eastern Guatemala

Ch'orti'-Maya Survival in Eastern Guatemala

Indigeneity in Transition

Brent E. Metz

University of New Mexico Press Albuquerque

YEAR   PRINTING
10 09 08 07 06   1 2 3 4 5

LIBRARY OF CONGRESS CATALOGING-IN-PUBLICATION DATA

Metz, Brent E.
Ch'orti'-Maya survival in eastern Guatemala : indigeneity in transition /
Brent E. Metz.
p. cm.
Revision of thesis (Ph. D.)—State University of New York at Albany, 1995.
Includes bibliographical references and index.
ISBN-13: 978-0-8263-3880-8 (PBK. : ALK. PAPER)
ISBN-10: 0-8263-3880-1 (PBK. : ALK. PAPER)
1. Chorti Indians—History.
2. Chorti Indians—Social conditions.
3. Chorti Indians—Politics and government.
4. Guatemala—Social life and customs. I. Title.

F1465.2.C5M48 2006
972.8100497'428—dc22

2005027958

Book design and type composition:
Kathleen Sparkes

This book is typeset using Utopia 9.5 / 13.5; 26P
Display type is Berthold Akzidenz Grotesk

Contents

Acknowledgments

With the completion of a book as drawn out and overdue as this one, I am not sure whether to thank or apologize to all the people I leaned on along the way. I would not be publishing this book, much less continue to survive in academics, if it were not for the combined support of the following generous people. To Gwynne Jenkins, who suffered through this in its dissertation stage and then two major revisions, I am sorry and thank you for all your saintly patience and your thoughtful commentary over the years. Oscar Horst introduced me to Guatemala in 1984, and his enthusiasm for Guatemala has lit a fire of curiosity that has burned in me ever since. My appreciation for John Watanabe's mentorship grows as my academic experience deepens. John's patience with a very green and talkative grad student like me at the University of Michigan was magnanimous, and he probably never suspected that he would be writing letters of recommendation for me nearly two decades afterward. I have come a long way under his tutelage. I was also fortunate to study at the University of Albany under John's first anthropology professor, Gary Gossen. There may be equals to Gary in knowledge of Mesoamerican worldview, but there are none better. As my professor, dissertation cochair, friend, and idol, Gary has also shown tremendous patience and loyalty. My other cochair, Robert Carmack, has been such a fatherly, guiding presence in my fieldwork and theoretical orientation that I find it difficult to address him other than "Dr. Carmack." His incredibly broad range of expertise on Central American indigenous peoples, his fieldwork record, and his professionalism have set an example that lesser mortals like me could never attain. Liliana Goldin has not only been very patient and generous over the years, but also provided me the invaluable experience of copublishing my first article on Guatemala. With moments of burnout, failed grant and job applications, and publication rejections over the years, having the emotional, intellectual, and temporal support of these scholars has been vital.

Julián López García, coauthor of our book *Primero Dios*, has shared so much information with me since our chance meeting in Jocotán in 1992 that he is indirectly coauthor of this book as well. Other colleagues who have given me valuable insights and collaboration in the field include Johanna Kufer, Lincoln Vaughn, Felipe Girón, Jim Dugan, Claudia Dary, John Durston, Sofie de Broe, Christa Little-Siebold, Otto Schumann, Kerry Hull, Alfonso La Cadena, Alfonso Morales, Cameron McNeil, Michelle Moran-Taylor, and Debra Rodman. I have also had the high honor that Christine Eber, Richard Adams, Kay Warren, and John Hawkins—a veritable Mesoamerican "hall of fame"—have reviewed previous manuscript versions and provided me critical commentary. The book has come a long way due to their input. The University of Oklahoma Press and the University of Texas Press had earlier versions of this book painstakingly reviewed and provided helpful evaluations. I can highly recommend them to any aspiring author concerned with professionalism and cordiality. Obviously, then, I cannot say enough for the patience, friendliness, advice, and professionalism of David Holtby and the University of New Mexico Press. David has been nothing if not encouraging, and I am honored to have worked with him. Elizabeth Kuznesof of the University of Kansas Center of Latin American Studies has also provided key advice about management of the manuscript, and the Center offered a terrific context and support for finishing the book.

Like most ethnographic fieldwork, mine relied on particularly generous, friendly, and often intellectually curious people, as well as those who have self-interest in reciprocating with the ethnographer. Those who fall in the former category are many, but the most notable include the families of Ch'orti's Teodoro Ramírez, Raimundo García, Gregorio García, Saturnino Ramírez, Isadora Pérez, and Gabriel Pérez. From Jocotán, I thank especially the families of Celeste Ramírez and Hector Peña, Julió and Olfania Paz, doña Tonia Guerra, Yolanda Pérez, and the Brínguez family. Generally, these people are exceptions to the negative patterns and structures that I will uncomfortably but frankly lay out below. In Guatemala City, Linda Asturias, Arturo Duarte, and Primina Mendizabol provided me intellectual stimulation, key social contacts, and room and board. Among the most important collaborating organizations in Guatemala are Ch'orti' Maya

Coordination (COMACH), especially President Rigoberto Ramírez; PRO-CHORTI, especially George Grunberg and Director Carlos Bonilla; the Academy of Maya Languages, especially Federico García; the Catholic parishes of Jocotán and Olopa, especially Padre Juan Boxi; the Lubeck family (formerly of Wycliffe Bible Translators); the Spanish Cooperation for Development; the Movimiento para la Paz, Desarmamiento, y Libertad, especially Andrea Mallo; and the Hospital Betania, especially Dr. Carlos Arriola. I reserve special thanks for Peace Corps volunteers Carol Findlay, Beatrice Adler, and Phil and Linda Miller. Carol, who retired in Olopa, was my host, collaborator, critic, occasional chef, and icon of selflessness, and all who care about Olopa miss her dearly, whether they met her or not. Finally, I thank my parents, Julie Metz, Dennis Metz, and Lyla Metz, for their patience and support. If there's another book, I promise that it will be quicker, and easier.

Grant support from the University of Albany Institute of Meso-american Studies Christopher Decormier Award, the State University of New York Benevolent Foundation, Grinnell College, and the Fulbright-Hays Faculty Research Abroad Grant greatly facilitated the research behind this book. I also thank the University of Kansas Hall Center for the Humanities, particularly Kathy Porsch, for assisting me with grant writing and thoughts about restructuring the book.

MAP 1: *Areas of Maya Cultural Concentration.*

INTRODUCTION

What's Indigenous, What's Maya?

In August 2001, Guatemala's little-studied eastern Department of Chiquimula emerged from the shadows when international headlines reported ghastly scenes of a Central American famine. Dozens of international reporters invaded a local hospital and scoured the countryside in search of horrific cases of starvation. They were not disappointed. Well into 2002 they described mass starvation, hundreds of children dead, and thousands more in peril if aid did not arrive soon (e.g., Brosnan 2001, 2002; Hadden 2002; Williams 2002; Planet Ark 2002). The "famine" is ongoing to this day (2004) and has been explained as a convergence of low coffee prices, on which the campesinos (subsistence farmers) depend for wages, and irregular rainfall, on which they rely for corn and beans agriculture. Local health records, however, document malnutrition and other maladies of the poor for forty years, and malnutrition has certainly been endemic to the region since I began ethnographic fieldwork there in 1991, especially among the little recognized Maya population.

How could reporters mistake chronic malnutrition among Mayas for a punctuated famine among "the poor" in a country spotlighted for its Maya heritage? Scholars and even western Guatemalan Mayas have generally characterized the Oriente (eastern Guatemala) as "Ladino" or nationalized and non-Indian. Ch'orti' Mayas of Chiquimula were presumably long acculturated to the Guatemala Ladino nation. Absent are obvious indigenous markers exhibited by Mayas of western Guatemala, Chiapas, and the Yucatán Peninsula of Mexico. Only a fraction still speak Ch'orti', most no longer wear distinctive dress, and civil-religious community organizations have long been abandoned. While an army-led scorched-earth campaign in the 1980s has drawn international attention to the Occidente Mayas, the political violence in the Oriente from the 1960s to 1980s, if acknowledged at

1

all, is whitewashed as nonethnic. The most recent academic focus in Guatemala, the Maya Movement, is also thought to be active only in Guatemala City and the Occidente, and the Maya organization that influenced the Ch'orti' region the most, Majawil Q'ij, was labeled leftist or "popular" and not "culturally" Maya. Only on national maps that exaggerate the extent of Maya linguistic "territories" does Ch'orti' ethnicity tend to be recognized (Vaughn 2002). Consequently, despite a veritable academic industry of Guatemalan Maya studies, which has produced more ethnographies than all the rest of Central America combined (Bolanos and Adams 1994), no major English-language monograph has been published on the Oriente for a half century.

This raises the question of what criteria are being used to define indigeneity (indigenous-ness) and Maya-ness. Some academics claim that they do not define indigeneity or indigenous identity; they study it. Nevertheless, they cannot help but make judgments about what qualifies as "indigenous" and "Maya"; otherwise, someone would have published an English-language monograph on the self-proclaimed Ch'orti' Mayas since 1940. In the very application of terms like "indigenous" or "Maya," including to such things as ethnic maps and coverage in edited volumes, judgments are made about who and what is and is not indigenous. No one puts quotations around Indian, indigenous, Maya, etc., or uses the qualifier "so-called" all the time. The concept of indigeneity is maintained by ongoing conscious and subconscious social reproduction.

The problem of identifying "the indigenous" is far from new in Mesoamerica.[1] At the start of the twentieth century, anthropologists studied indigenous cultural survivals to shed light on the ancient Mesoamerican past (e.g., Tozzer 1907; Gann and Thompson 1931; Girard 1949; Roys 1965). Native American civilization was being abandoned, or contaminated, as Western civilization advanced, and the progression from Indians to peasants to civilized city dwellers was the subject of Redfield's and Tax's acculturation models in the 1930s–50s (e.g., Redfield 1941, 1953; Tax 1952). For Redfield,

---

1. Mesoamerica is itself a contentious term that encompasses the "great civilizations" of the Mayas and the Aztecs, among several other large-scale, literate societies of central and southern Mexico, Guatemala, Belize, El Salvador, western Honduras, western Nicaragua, and northwestern Costa Rica. Among the characteristics that unify the cultures of this area are highly complex and stratified social organizations, similar linguistic structures and poetics, a strong dependence on maize and beans agriculture, and similar cosmologies and literary traditions (Carmack, Gasco, and Gossen 1996).

distinguishing Indians from Westerners was futile because entirely new societies and cultures were forged after the Spanish Conquest, such that traits must be understood as integral parts of contemporary social systems, not isolated remnants from the past. For example, the meanings and functions of Mesoamerican rain god beliefs today are qualitatively different than they were for pre-Columbian societies.

The more scholars learned about the "heritage of conquest" and the massive changes endured by Mesoamerican populations over the centuries, the more the idea of continuity from the pre-Hispanic past was de-emphasized. Wolf (1957) in particular demonstrated how contemporary "closed corporate peasant communities" were actually reactions to exploitation rather than primordial indigenous organizations. By the 1960s and 1970s Marxian scholars were arguing that Indian ethnicity was not indigenous at all but a mystifying palliative imposed by the ruling classes. In other words, the Spanish invented the category "Indian" to create a class of servants, who in turn embodied their inferior Indian status and unwittingly facilitated their own exploitation (e.g., Martínez Paláez 1970; Friedlander 1975; cf. Warren 1989). At the other extreme, Levi-Straussian structuralists excavated "deep" generative mental structures that presumably endured across the generations, digesting ongoing major historical events but not being altered by them (Vogt 1976; Hunt 1977; Bricker 1981).

Starting in the 1970s and accelerating in the 1980s, the Marxist ethnicity-as-exploitation paradigm and the structuralist primordial paradigm were tempered by more ethnicity-based approaches emphasizing counterhegemony and cultural resistance. In an era when the indigenous suffered horrific repression, to depict them as unwitting dupes to class exploitation or to emphasize detached deep structures seemed not only inaccurate but also cruel. For a rising group of cultural survivalists, the question now became, how have indigenous cultures enabled their practitioners to survive centuries of repression and exploitation (e.g., Burgos-Debray and Menchú 1984; Lovell 1988; Watanabe 1992; Carlson 1997). Though rarely stated explicitly, defining indigeneity was a thorny problem best left unresolved, because it would inevitably exclude some people and call the concept of indigeneity itself into question. As some indigenous colleagues have said of the apparently neo-indigenous, "if they want to be indigenous, welcome!" Nevertheless, cultural survivalists, including indigenous leaders, do regard indigeneity as having certain criteria, such as being colonized, having a unique identity, practicing animism, valuing communalism, and exhibiting distinctive languages and dress.

Social deconstructionists, like the cultural survivalists, cede constructive agency to all social strata, including indigenous peoples, not just the ruling class. Unlike the cultural survivalists, however, they, like Redfield, argue that indigeneity is not historically "deep" or rooted because it is perpetually redefined and reconstructed through social engagement. New contexts, new meanings, new cultures (e.g., Warren 1989, 1998; Nelson 1999; Yashar 1998; Harris 1995; Hervik 1999; de la Cadena 1995; Rodas 1995:63 in Girón 2001:4; Conklin 1997; Rogers 1998). Ethnic boundaries are constantly being socially renegotiated and reconstructed such that authenticity is nothing more than a charade, and defining and fixing "real" indigeneity is hopelessly misguided and primordialist. Anyone purporting to be a "real" anything—Native American, European, Jew, African American, etc.—is practicing a politics that can be deconstructed, leaving one to wonder whether to put all proper nouns in quotations. Not only should indigeneity not be defined, but it cannot be defined in any lasting sense.

My attempt to pin down indigeneity in eastern Guatemala then, is confused, outdated, and even dangerous. Rather, I should leave the issue open, à la the cultural survivalists, or recognize as do the social constructionists that self-proclaimed Ch'orti's are playing identity politics, knowing that political and economic capital lies in catering to Western exoticism and essentialism. When powerful Western institutions demand indigenous essentialism, it is no mystery why indigenous peoples are strategically essentialist (Warren 1992; Dover and Rappaport 1996:8).

On the other hand, largely illiterate, localistic, "indigenous" societies need no training in essentialism (e.g., Navinguna 1996:18–19), as the very name that most apply to themselves is often something like "the real people," "speakers of the real language," or "God's chosen people." Ch'orti' speakers refer to their language as "the first" or principal language, because God placed their "race" first on Earth. These seem to be identities rooted in traditions deeper than tactical, conscious play. No doubt some "indigenous" leaders have been influenced by Western scholarship and tourism, and some evoke a timeless Indian trope for purposes of power (e.g., Briggs 1997; Hervik 1999), but framing indigeneity strictly in terms of "identity politics" is simplistic and hostile (Watanabe 1995).

Recognizing "indigenous" as a valid or authentic historical category is important because the term is ultimately about justice. Just a few decades ago the people now referred to as indigenous were being called savages, primitives, natives, Indians, and other terms with implicitly derogatory connotations. The turn to the term "indigenous" marks a concern for inverting an aggressively modernist stance with one more respectful of cultural differences and human rights. One can debate why the global powers that be are positively recognizing indigeneity (e.g., to cynically divert attention from class issues or from a genuine concern for human rights), but for indigenous peoples themselves, the movement emerges from cultural and identity crises. Faced with discriminatory political violence, the erosion of subsistence economies, new consumer markets, and the neoliberal retraction of already weak state services and institutions, indigenous peoples have, with the help of cosmopolitan allies, organized beyond the local community to seek to "preserve" or "recover" their indigenous traditions by demanding protection from encroachment, remuneration for lost resources, and greater self-determination (e.g., Díaz Polanco 1997; Brysk 2000; Kleymeyer 1994; Friedman 1994; Fisher and McKenna-Brown 1996).

To identify the "indigenous," then, is to often identify generations of people who have been wronged by colonialism. Political and legal justice in this regard demands some definitional coherence and fixity, which in turn have relied on both experts, like academics, and popular perceptions. Academics, in their selective application of "indigenous," cannot escape from being political (Friedman 1994; Watanabe 1995).

If indigenity has become a source of positive identity and is even competed over, then what criteria are used to distinguish indigenous peoples from others? The European Union (1998), the United Nations Development Programme (2003), the International Labor Organization (2003), and the World Bank (2001) have all found it necessary to define "indigenous" operationally, but they, like other international donors, international regulatory bodies, transnational banks, governments, and scholars have done so rather loosely (Cojtí 1997; Rappaport and Dover 1996; Briggs 1997; Watanabe 1995; Warren 1998; Nelson 1999). Most restrictive was the World Bank's working draft (4.10) listing: 1) close attachment to ancestral lands; 2) customary social and political institutions; 3) subsistence economies; 4) indigenous languages; and 5) general societal recognition of a people's indigeneity (Downing 2001:23–24). This, of course, received a lot of criticism. Almost all definitions, institutionally and popularly, apply "indigenous" generally to the original inhabitants (and descendents) of a territory whose unique cultures are so threatened by more technologically powerful, colonizing societies, that they become vulnerable to ethnocide (Kizca 1993:xi; Kearney 1996; Niezen 2003:12). Thus, two basic ingredients of indigeneity are cultural distinctiveness and the historical experience of colonialism. As newly identified "indigenous peoples" have garnered important political, economic, and symbolic capital and made remarkable strides in gaining national and international recognition for their group rights, debates about indigeneity have heated up. What counts as culturally distinctive and suffering from a legacy of colonialism? Must one continue to practice the exact traditions of one's precontact ancestors to be considered culturally unique and culturally dominated?

Concern about indigenous authenticity in the market is nothing new, as the value of certain prized commodities rests almost entirely on whether they are really indigenous or not (Evans-Pritchard 1987; King 1997), but now people compete over political capital as well. When people who did not claim to be "Indian," native, or aboriginal before now embrace indigeneity and the capital it commands, there will be internal competitions for power and external accusations of artificiality. The power wielded by Guatemalan Maya organizations has sparked contentious debates about indigeneity and Maya-ness. Some non-Maya nationalists have argued, à la Redfield and the social constructionists, that "Maya" indigeneity is inauthentic because all Guatemalans are best thought of as culturally and biologically mestizo (Nelson 1999:321; Casaús 2001:224; Warren 1998:42). Some use the facile argument that because Mayas did not refer to themselves as such until recently, they are disqualified from being authentic Mayas, thus placing complete emphasis on conscious identity and ignoring culture and social position. From the Maya side, Maya demographer Leopoldo Tzian (1994) concluded that Mayas comprised 68% of the population, whereas the National Statistical Institute (Instituto Nacional de Estadística [INE] 1996) recorded 42% in its census based strictly on identity.[2] Among the Maya themselves, there are debates about who or what is more Maya, including matters of gender and political action.

When I set out to do research among the Ch'orti's, I hypothesized that cultural indigeneity would involve a worldview that motivated people morally to oppose integration into the capitalist individualistic, acquisitive market culture. I planned to investigate whether both the Protestant and Catholic assaults on this worldview led Ch'orti's to accept the materialistic market culture. The eminent German sociologist Max Weber had theorized a century earlier that Protestantism reinforced the cultural hallmarks of

2. In this same 1994 census, INE recorded one-third of the population in the Ch'orti' area as indigenous, while many Guatemalans, including those in the Oriente, categorize the region as completely non-Indian.

modern capitalism, including rationalism, entrepreneurialism, personal sacrifice, and individualistic acquisitiveness. In the 1880s Guatemalan liberal (in the sense of liberal capitalism and positivism, which placed individual rights over communal ones and promoted science, technology, foreign investment, and white immigration as means to development) elites invited Protestant missionaries from the United States to overcome the Mayas' closed, communalistic cultures and convert them to docile laborers. From the 1920s on, the Catholic Church responded with an evangelical crusade of its own, which became particularly effective when it combined liberation theology (put simply, a theology regarding gross inequality, exploitation, and oppression as sins to be overcome, rather than ordained conditions to be piously endured) and development programs in 1960–80. Were such Western religious influences inspiring Ch'orti's to buy, sell, and work more in the market for personal gain?

The Ch'orti's were a suitable population in which to study such issues because an ethnographic study in the 1930s found them to be almost entirely self-subsistent and religiously independent, to the extent that money was considered to hold an unnatural and mysterious power. Ch'orti's did not consider Ladinos their ipso facto superiors, and they responded to their ethnic slurs with insults of their own. I was soon to discover that by the early 1990s, campesinos in the region exhibited few obvious indigenous markers and many were phenotypically indistinguishable from Ladinos. They held little more than a tacit indigenous identity, preferring to call themselves "people of the countryside" (*gente de las aldeas*) because "Indian," "indigenous," and any other directly ethnic term had negative connotations. My questions now became, what caused this profound transformation, and in what senses should these campesinos continue to be regarded as indigenous?

Over twenty-two months from 1991 to 1993 I investigated these issues by living with three Ch'orti'-speaking families of different communities, learning the Ch'orti' language, and carrying out a three-step research plan consisting of: 1) informal interviews; 2) a household survey; and 3) extended, tape-recorded interviews about perceptions of historical change (see next chapter). This was a pivotal period in Guatemalan history. Guatemala hosted the Second Encounter of Five Hundred Years of Resistance with tens of thousands of international indigenous activists in attendance, K'iche Maya Rigoberta Menchú was the first Native American to win the Noble Peace Prize, an army-backed coup was thwarted by massive popular mobilization and pressure from the Clinton administration, and the peace process was set on track with input from Guatemala's civil sectors (business leaders, church officials, press, educators, and Mayas). The Maya Movement reached the Ch'orti' area, and I gained privileged access to movement activities via my host families and my fluency in Ch'orti'. I have continued to collaborate with and study Ch'orti' Maya organizations annually ever since. In 2000 I was invited to be an assessor for a Ch'orti' ethnodevelopment project (PROCH'ORTI') that continues to promote ethnic revival to motivate campesinos to procure communal lands titles and thereby preserve the last stands of forests.

Attention to questions of ethnic identity in the Oriente challenges ideologically driven narratives about Guatemala's civil war, the Maya Movement, and the conditions behind them. Most agree that in the thirty-six-year civil war (1960–96), two hundred thousand people, mostly Maya civilians, were killed, overwhelmingly at the hands of the army, but the causes and solutions of the war are contested. The Right claims that Guatemalan society was doing just fine, that the poor Indian majority was content in its poverty and even practiced a culture that reproduced it. Then, Cuban-backed guerrilla agitators stirred up Maya rebellion and compelled the army to take drastic measures in defense of the country. Hundreds of thousands of campesinos, students, labor union members, politicians, and other social reformers were forced to take sides, and those siding with the resistance necessarily became legitimate army targets. If any excesses were committed, well, that's what happens in war, unfortunately. Leftists, on the other hand, argue that Guatemala's extreme socioeconomic inequality, inhuman repression, and the army's closure to any democratic means of reform called for resistance, including armed revolt.

For Mayanists, "the war" is better named "the violence," "the massacres," and "the ruins," (*las ruinas*) as the army regime butchered any conceivable dissenter. Neither the Right nor the Left represented their interests, and in fact both opposed Maya self-determination. The modernist Right saw the Indians and their culture as an anachronism and hindrance to development, and the orthodox Marxist Left condescendingly believed that to put ethnic struggle ahead of or on par with class struggle was false consciousness. The Maya Movement has had a greater affinity with the Left than the Right, but only because the Right has treated Mayas so horribly. Accusations abound that the Left has been trying to appropriate the Maya Movement. The story of the Ch'orti's, who suffered disproportionately in eastern Guatemala, enlightens the strengths and weaknesses of these three arguments—those of the Right, the Left, and the Mayanist.

Chapter Outline

I review my introduction to the Ch'orti' region and thereby reveal the limitations of my fieldwork in chapter 1. In confessional ethnographic fashion (Van Maanen 1988), I relate how miserable conditions eventually improved to the point where I could work, live, and learn in eastern Guatemala.

In chapters 2 and 3, I retrace the historical foundations of Ch'orti' indigeneity. The Ch'orti' experience of Spanish colonialism was especially harsh compared to western Guatemala due to frequent catastrophes, greater market activity, and a higher proportion of non-Indian settlers to "Indians." Mayas made a demographic recovery in the late seventeenth and early eighteenth centuries, only to suffer a reversal when the Spanish Crown carried out its Bourbon Reforms in the second half of the eighteenth century. By the end of the colonial period, chronicles reported unrestrained exploitation and precipitous Ch'orti' population declines. After Guatemalan independence from Spain in 1821, more Ladino settlers moved into the area and both they and Ch'orti's began producing coffee for the market, which in turn resulted in the destruction of forests and forced conscription of Ch'orti' labor. The protracted "era of slavery" ended with the fall of the US-backed Ubico dictatorship in 1944, when a democratic revolution ushered in import substitution and land and labor reforms. These were decisively reversed by a Central Intelligence Agency (CIA) orchestrated coup and the United States' imposition of the National Security Doctrine during the Cold War. Although guerrillas were never strongly present in the Ch'orti' region, from 1950s to 1980s the Guatemalan army and associated death squads massacred countless of Ch'orti's for economic and political reasons.

Chapter 4 introduces what remains distinctive about campesino traditions in the Ch'orti' area today. As Ch'orti's are largely excluded from national society, they produce and reproduce cultures that are uniquely their own. Their subsistence economy and corresponding family life, morality, rhythm of life, supernatural beliefs, humor, sexuality, music, and dances distinguish them from the town-dwelling Ladino population.

Standards of poverty are relative, especially between indigenous and modern societies, but in chapter 5 I argue that Ch'orti' campesinos are poor even according to their own low standards. Three generations ago Wisdom (1940) reported that their diet was diverse and the land was productive. Today, too many people are trying to grow food on plots that are too small, steep, and eroded. Almost all are malnourished and ridden with intestinal and respiratory infections. Though most Ch'orti's recognize that these maladies are due partly to their subordination to local, national, and international powers, they tend to interpret them as an internal problem. The younger, formally educated generation argues that elders lacked foresight in destroying their environment, while elders blame the youth for loss of respect for God and the old ways. Because subsistence agriculture is withering with material conditions, Ch'orti's are desperate for alternatives, but the market economy offers little hope. Ch'orti' wage labor is cheapened, and Ladino townspeople monopolize most commerce.

In chapter 6, it is seen that far from creating a program of cultural hegemony or building an imagined community, the state[3] has done little to invite "Indians" into the Guatemalan national society, and in many cases has intentionally excluded them. State services are meager, and public health clinics, schools, police, and infrastructure such as water and sewage treatment and power systems are underfunded or nonexistent. The availability of antibiotics has lowered mortality rates, but lack of cultural access to family planning means that campesinos are having more children than they can care for.

In chapters 7 and 8, I explore the possibilities for development. Development projects have transformed the landscape in Ch'orti' communities, but they have not been able to keep up with the growing population. Many have failed due to misunderstanding, mismanagement, and corruption as well as Ch'orti's' own distrust and opportunism. Some unscrupulous Ladinos appropriate much development aid that enters the region, even during crises of cholera and famine. In 1992 the Maya Movement promised a national ethnic transcendence of gender, generational, and class divisions. Though confused by the blend of western Maya and Western academic discourses, many campesino leaders embraced the movement as a source of a positive identity and unification. The movement has been met with several challenges, however, including little organizational experience, semiliteracy, lack of communication, fear of repression, envy, guerrilla influence, and cuts in foreign funding.

3. Nelson (1999:76, 83) points out that the state is often reified and vilified, sometimes for the sake of leveraging handouts, while in reality states or governments are composed of multitudes of people with myriad interests and capacities. When I use "the state" here, I specifically refer to the Guatemalan oligarchy, including the economic and military elites, who have inordinate control over the national economy, political parties, policy, and the use of force.

The conclusion revisits the question of what, if anything, constitutes indigeneity, and whether campesinos in eastern Guatemala can accurately be referred to as indigenous, Ch'orti', and Maya. Ch'orti's are arguably indigenous according to their racial status, their distinctive processes of cultural construction, and their traditions. Ethnodevelopment has pushed the notion of "the Ch'orti'" farther than ever, and its successes and failures illuminate whether ethnic pride can be the basis of reversing the spiral of poverty. Finally, the Ch'orti's and Mayanists immediate affinity for each other reflects the fact that while common use of the term "Maya" might be new, the unity of "Maya" cultures is not completely fabricated. In the conclusion, I revisit the issue of Ch'orti' indigeneity and how there are greater or lesser degrees of cultural indigeneity but firmer foundations in "race" and history. Ch'orti' informants close the book with some reflections on their future.

CHAPTER ONE

In Search of Indigeneity in Eastern Guatemala

O n my first visit to Guatemala as a college student in 1984 I suffered acute culture shock. Stepping out of Aurora Airport into a steamy Guatemala City night, I was overwhelmed by throngs of ragged, dark-skinned children struggling to carry my luggage in exchange for a tip. In my naïveté, I gave them candy. Now in June 1990, returning to Guatemala with an old photographer friend, Erich, to visit eight townships in Guatemala and Belize to find a field site for my dissertation, the children had been replaced by well-groomed men in coveralls performing the same services with equal vigor. Guatemala was modernizing. After a decade of all-out war against any potential dissenters to Guatemala's repressive and highly unequal status quo, the military was cleaning up the nation's image.

That same morning a colleague informed us of a Guatemalan Ministry of Culture seminar on ethnic politics at the national theater at noon. We interpreted "seminar" to mean a relaxed, academic affair in an auditorium of students and professors. We arrived in very casual attire amidst Guatemalan elites dressed to the hilt in three-piece suits, silk dresses, and heels. Rather than finding some academics discussing the intricacies of ethnicity, we entered the national theater to the Guatemalan national anthem as President Cerezo himself took the stage. El Presidente echoed Guatemala's Nobel laureate novelist, Miguel Asturias, depicting Guatemala as a unique, magical nation where two civilizations, the Spanish and the Maya, had harmoniously converged. "Until we decide who we are," he expounded, "we have no direction, no common strategy for resolving the country's problems." Ironically, Asturias (1985) had also adeptly captured

Guatemalan political terror in his novel *El Presidente,* and a few months after the seminar the Presidential Guard (Estado Mayor Presidencial) assassinated anthropologist Mirna Mack for defying the army by her study of hundreds of thousands of Maya internal refugees. The most impressive speaker was Maya scholar Demetrio Cojtí, whose defiant pro-Maya, anticolonial speech roused the audience and signaled that a new era of political openness might be at hand, albeit in fits and starts.

Erich and I were glad to be out of smoggy, congested, dangerous (or so we were often told) Guatemala City and on a bus eastward to the small city of Chiquimula in the Ch'orti' region. As we descended four thousand feet in three and a half hours, the heat and desolation of the Oriente—the stunted trees, cactus, and desert—not to mention the crowded school bus with three to a seat, wore us down. Unlike the mild capital and western highlands, the cities of the east lie in low, hot, windless valleys where the sun is a mortal threat. We wondered why anyone would settle here and erect one-story towns of cement and corrugated sheet metal that doubled as human ovens, but we did notice some cattle, melons, and tobacco along the way. In Chiquimula, we felt like aliens with our backpacks, shorts, and sandals among the well-dressed townspeople clad in pants and skirts. We soon realized that the locals had seen plenty of shabbily dressed gringos[1] like us before, as a steady stream of European, US, Australian, and Israeli travelers trickled through on their way to Copán Ruins, just across the border in Honduras. We found a hotel with prices to our liking, $2 a night per person. That night, after eating Chinese, we walked through the town park and witnessed Guatemalan politics in action: a Caribbean band sponsored by PAN (the oligarchy's National Alliance Party) performed to a crowd of remarkably dispassionate campesinos in sandals, rubber boots, and cowboy hats.

The next morning we started on the wrong foot. The shirt I had left to dry in the window of our room was stolen. I met a Peace Corps volunteer at the end of her service who took it upon herself to inform me that my intended study of the Ch'orti' was hopelessly naive and that I could not possibly be prepared for the poverty I would encounter. After missing our bus to Jocotán, a town in the heart of the Ch'orti' area, because it left a half hour before its scheduled time (buses leave when they are full), I entered

---

1. In eastern Guatemala it is common among campesinos and some poor Ladinos to call someone a gringo without derogatory intent. In fact, for most campesinos this is the only term for a light-skinned foreigner (cf. Nelson 1999:63).

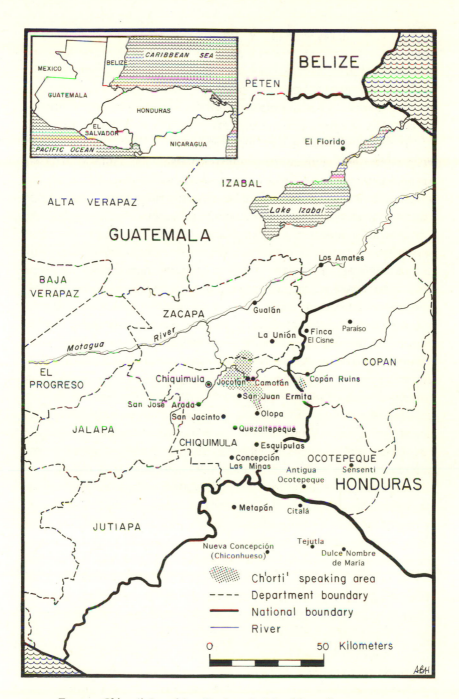

MAP 2: *Former Ch'orti'-Speaking Region. Original base for map courtesy of Amy Henderson.*

the market to interview an old Ch'orti' man, recognizable by his sandals, weathered feet, and distinctive, white pajama-like clothing. I asked him if he spoke Ch'orti' and if there were speakers in Chiquimula. "No," he said, "there are no more *lenguajeros*."

On the way out of Chiquimula, asphalt soon turned to dirt as the old Bluebird school bus to Jocotán climbed the barren mountains. We passed San Juan Ermita, where an ancient church surrounded by palms, banana trees, and humble adobe and palm frond dwellings made it seem like were traveling back centuries in time. Twenty minutes later, when the dusty road turned to rocky streets lined with whitewashed and painted cement houses, we realized we were in Jocotán, a town of about three to four thousand people. A colonial church dominated the small central park, which showcased a bust of the prolific Swiss ethnographer and Ch'orti' aficionado Rafael Girard. We interrupted some police officers in the middle of a checkers game to introduce ourselves and ask about lodging. They were amused with our interest in Ch'orti's, though other townspeople later spoke proudly of "their" Indians. The owner of one of the two local motels, the Pensión Ramírez, proudly loaned me a small collection of books on Ch'orti's: Wisdom's encyclopedic monograph (1940); one of Girard's volumes; a Ch'orti' grammar recently published by Wycliffe Bible Translator and Friend (Quaker) John Lubeck (1989); and the owner's granddaughter's thesis on Ch'orti' architecture. The Francisco Marroquín Linguistic Project in central Guatemala had given me the names of some possible Ch'orti' contacts, one of whom the owner tracked down by word of mouth, as there were no telephones beyond Chiquimula.

My first visit with Pedro[2] was eerie. Standing about 4'10", never looking me in the eye, and speaking in a soft voice, Pedro and I had trouble communicating. After I thought I had finally convinced him that I was neither a Protestant missionary nor a Peace Corps worker, we settled on calling me a linguist, which I failed to realize placed me back in the category of Protestant missionary. That resolved, Pedro kindly invited us to climb thirty-three hundred feet to his home in the *aldea* (rural community) of Pelillo Negro ("fine black hair," from a black tree moss that once grew in

---

2. The sensitivity of some topics discussed poses a dilemma regarding anonymity. Some informants were proud to contribute to the writing of their history and wanted to receive credit or recognition, which makes the use of pseudonyms problematic. For my principal informants I use pseudonyms, but I use the actual first names of all except for those who provided me with information that is potentially dangerous or embarrassing.

the now extinct cloud forest) the next day, although he was concerned about whether we would be able to eat the only fare that his family could afford, beans and tortillas. Erich and I eagerly accepted and looked forward to authentic Ch'orti' cuisine. The motel owner thought we were crazy for even considering the hike into Indian country, not to mention spending a few nights up there, but some gringos just have to learn the hard way.

Pedro arrived the next morning a half hour early, a rare virtue that all good Ch'orti' leaders possess, I later learned. It was Sunday, market day, and he proudly gave us a tour of the congested market that overflowed from the park, through the streets, and down to a roofed meat market swarming with flies and half-starved dogs. Tomatoes, green beans, black beans, corn, potatoes, cabbage, carrots, onions, cilantro, beets, chiles, cucumbers, bananas, plantains, oranges, green peppers, melons, mangos, vegetable pears (*guisquil, ch'iwan, chayote*), avocados, *chuctes* (an avocado-like fruit), coffee, pineapples, pottery, cheap clothing, rubber boots, reed mats (*petates, pojp*), palm frond brooms, hammocks, rope, net bags, burlap bags, cowboy hats, machetes, baskets, and fowl were all laid out on the streets for sale. Vendors included male Ch'orti's dressed in cheap Western clothing, females dressed in their distinctive pleated blouses and dresses (an old Spanish peasant style once used throughout this part of Central America, see for example, photos 4, 6, 18, and 21), and well-dressed merchants from distant parts of northern Central America. Erich and I bore the stares of the thousands of campesinos but felt welcomed when a vendor offered us free coconut milk and another gave us our first *paterna*, a green podlike fruit with a sweet, white interior. Pedro bartered down the prices of two colorful, fiber hammocks from $5 to $4 for our sleeping accommodations in his home. Already by nine o'clock in the morning the searing sun had sent us for the sunscreen. By noon, after we had bought Pedro a lunch of beans, eggs, and tortillas, the sun's intensity was ominous, but we resolutely set off for Pelillo Negro with thirty pounds of fruit, water, and hammocks on our backs.

Passing along the shore of the Jocotán River (or Río Grande) for a half hour, we were relieved that the walk was fairly flat. Then we literally hit "the wall." The Loma Blanca or "white hill" is a fifteen-hundred-foot escarpment with a slope that surpasses sixty degrees in places. We desperately hoped that Pedro was kidding when he said that we had to climb straight up it, no switchbacks. The "hill" and sun brought us to our knees, and like the rest of the surrounding rugged, baked, precipitous landscape, it was mercilessly devoid of trees. In fact, the entire region was devoid of forests except for some scrub on fallow lands and pine stands on poor soil, which were grazed and eroded by cattle. We ran out of our two quarts of water before reaching the top and seriously contemplated an early return. Meanwhile, Ch'orti's of all ages, returning from the market with their purchases, filed past us with smiling encouragement without so much as breaking a sweat. Pedro said the trip was only three hours and that there was a descent ahead, so we persevered in our sweat-soaked clothing, privately cursing the Ch'orti's for considering shorts to be improper attire. After making it to the top, we descended a few hundred feet to a stream, where we rested beneath an old, lonely mango tree that offered fruit and shade. We purified stream water—the local sewer system we later learned—with iodine and continued the ascent, climbing another eight hundred feet or so, high enough to see the Jocotán Valley and a thunderstorm approaching at our altitude. For Erich and me, the rain was a welcome respite from the heat, but Pedro hurriedly shepherded us into an acquaintance's thatch-roofed patio. I was thrilled to finally enter a rural Maya household, constructed completely from natural materials—palm fronds, sticks, grass, and vines—and bustling with movements of dogs, turkeys, and chickens, all crowded under the roof. Women and children spied on us from inside the house. Pedro had trouble explaining to our host what we were up to and kept returning to the Protestant missionary trope.

By the time the storm subsided, our legs had tightened up like jerky, and we were still to climb another eight hundred feet or so. Resenting Pedro for his "three hour" estimation, we trudged up the worn rocky paths, which had become slippery, trickling streams, with all the determination we could muster. Hundreds of thatched roofs came into view, widely dispersed in typical Maya fashion over the vertical slopes, and we realized that we were in the midst of thousands of Ch'orti's. When we passed the community "center"—a run-down two-room schoolhouse and Catholic oratory bordered by a soccer yard whose end lines were cliffs—Pedro said we had only five minutes to go.

Twenty minutes later, and after a five-and-a-half-hour ascent, we arrived exhausted at his thatched hut, only to find that Pedro had scarcely a seat—except for a one-foot-high stool. His terrified wife, mother, three-year-old daughter, and seven-year-old nephew were caught completely by surprise, and the women kept in the shadows, emerging only to give us a stack of tortillas and bowl of beans. Pedro apologized that the tortillas were of *maicillo*, or sorghum, as it was June and his maize store from last

1. *Ch'orti' palm and thatch house and kitchen. Courtesy of Erich Nus.*

year's harvest had run out. Night fell quickly, and with only the illumination of a homemade kerosene wick lamp, Erich and I instinctively looked for a light switch near the door. We chilled in a hurry and our legs itched, probably from our salty sweat, we guessed. We did our best to eat the approximately two and a half pounds of thick, crispy-on-the-outside, doughy-on-the-inside tortillas, chasing them down with lukewarm, weak, sickly sweet, toasted corn "coffee." Before retiring to our hammocks, I naively asked Pedro where one "did one's necessities." Puzzled at first, he eventually realized what I was asking and said "anywhere you want," but his family "did it" in the thicket on the steep slopes below the house yard. After some bathroom acrobatics, wrestling pants, belts, and underwear in a spiny thicket on a dark slope, we returned to sleep in our hammocks among dogs, chickens, turkeys, and Pedro's most prized animal, his cat, as the extended family lay in a pile of old clothes in the corner.

We awoke to the smoke of the cooking fire and slapping sounds of Pedro's wife forming tortillas with her palms. We discovered the hard way that if the days were deathly hot, nights in the mountains were chillingly cold, especially when sleeping in a hammock. Erich, who had biked from

France to Russia and experienced an array of menacing bugs, confidently slept in a sewn sheet that closed around his face like a mummy bag. Not only did he freeze, but in the morning we were horrified to find he had invented the perfect flea hotel. Dozens of fleas hopped inside his blood-speckled bag, and we did our best to rid them from our spotted socks and underwear. For breakfast, another mountain of tortillas and beans, and a hardboiled egg for the guests only. It was a chore getting them down, but we did our best not to offend Pedro and his family. Only much later did I learn that guests are always served the maximum amount of tortillas that they could possibly eat and are not expected to finish them. After all, the kids, the women, and the animals have to eat, too. After breakfast, Pedro showed us his closest plot of land, as his more distant plots were over a half-hour walk away. He proudly presented the beautiful view of Camotán, some ten miles or so below, and his small stand of sugarcane, *jocote* trees, mango trees, banana trees, and sprouting beans and corn. He cut some cane for us, and we gnawed it while watching a group of six men plant corn and beans on a plot of reddish soil so steep that it seemed ninety degrees vertical. I later learned that some men tie themselves to trees while tending their fields to prevent tumbling down the mountain, and one elderly man in fact fell out of his field to his death while I was living there.

The tour continued to the new house he was building. The zinc-laminated roof, despite turning a home into an oven, meant progress for Pedro, but he still needed two thousand pounds of cement mix for the floor of his dream house. The hauling of the cement alone was more than he could afford, because the Ladino owners of four-wheel drive trucks charged about $20 for the treacherous, circuitous four-hour roundtrip to Pelillo Negro, while porters charged about $1.20 to carry a one-hundred-pound sack by headstrap from Jocotán. The rainy season was on us any-way, which meant that trucks would not be able to make the ascent for another five months. Pedro then interrogated me about the prices of pickups in the United States and asked if I could bring one for him and his friends to buy so he could haul the cement himself. The humble peasant had suddenly become a shrewd entrepreneur. When I was hesitant about the truck, he softly demanded again why I wanted to live among them. That I was a student interested in cultural change held no water whatso-ever. I further explained my career requirements in anthropology. Nothing doing. A Protestant himself, he may have secretly wished I were a missionary, as he couldn't seem to escape that assumption. Frustrated, we left it at that. I was still a Protestant linguist. I pulled out a small set of binoculars and handed them to Pedro, and he and a friend laughed in amazement at their ability to bring things closer. They joked about spying on women.

After ashamedly struggling through half of our allotted tortillas for lunch, Erich and I dozed off despite the hushed giggles of gawking children and relentless fleas. When Pedro came back from soccer practice, I assisted him with his math problems for the eighth-grade class he was taking through the Home Teacher (Maestro en Casa) program broadcast over the Catholic-sponsored Radio Ch'orti'. I was relieved at last that we could be of help rather than a burden, as our guilt about draining the family's meager resources reached the point of refusing hospitality from Pedro's silent, overworked wife. During dinner of yet more tortillas and beans, which again Erich and I simply couldn't finish, Pedro asked the sixty-four-dollar Ch'orti' question: How does one migrate to the United States and earn dollars? So much for the Ch'orti' moral subsistence economy. Having worked three summers with the Michigan Migrant Legal Assistance Project, I warned that it was certainly no picnic getting to the United States and finding work, but he was undeterred.

My stomach now was decidedly upset, feeling as if I had swallowed a quart of battery acid and a bowling ball, and it was another cold, flea-infested night, which persuaded Erich and me to decide to leave early the next day. To our surprise, Pedro, rather than celebrating the departure of these massive, hairy, two-legged parasites, was hurt that we were leaving so soon.

At breakfast, I could only choke down one tortilla. Erich took photos of the family after they proudly dressed up in their only set of untattered clothing. Pedro was offended when I gave him one of our hammocks and Q10 for his hospitality,[3] but I quickly tried to cover my faux pas by saying that the money was for postage and materials so he would respond to my letters from the United States. He grudgingly accepted, although, as I discovered later, few Ch'orti's have ever sent a letter in their entire lives. His nephew boastfully paraded us out of the aldea to the stares and chuckles of adults and howling kids.

By this time I was green with a slight fever. My body rejected any water I drank, as I made several stops for vomiting and diarrhea. Dehydrated, I

---

3. From 1991 to 1993 the value of the national currency, the quetzal, varied from Q5.00 to the dollar to Q5.60 to the dollar. In other words, Q1.00 was worth between 18¢ and 20¢. Today it has sunk almost to eight to the dollar.

concentrated on every step down the mountain so as not to stumble and tumble. What had taken five and a half hours to ascend, took us eight hours to descend. Some Ch'orti' men showed concern for my illness and gave me lemons to cool my stomach, the Ch'orti' panacea. Unfortunately, more acid was not what my stomach needed. Another man, teetering drunk and aggressively clutching his machete, blocked my path and demanded to know who we were and what we were doing. As I have done several times with aggressive drunks since, I cautiously sat down, answered all his questions, and bored him into leaving. I don't remember whether or not I resigned myself to telling him that I was a Protestant linguist. By the time we reached the Jocotán River, Erich, ill himself, literally had to drag my desiccated, limp, semiconscious body into town, where I was finally able to hold down some distilled water before immediately passing out for three hours.

We continued our travels to other Maya townships in western Honduras, eastern and northern Guatemala, and Belize, areas where forests still stood and where I didn't get sick. All seemed more livable than the Ch'orti' region of Jocotán. But Belize was less politically interesting than Guatemala, the Hondurans in Copán told us there were no more Ch'orti's there, and most Q'eqchi'- and Poqomchi'-speakers in northern Guatemala, who had suffered land dispossessions and unspeakable massacres in the 1980s, were hostile towards us. Besides, my doctoral committee regarded eastern Guatemala as the most interesting ethnographically and historically, and whatever propensities Pedro had for becoming an amoral capitalist, the Ch'orti's had all the pieces of my research plan: Protestantism, Catholicism, and subsistence agriculture.

In the fall of 1991 I began twenty months of fieldwork by taking a month of Ch'orti' language tutorials at the Francisco Marroquín Linguistic Project in central Guatemala. Though the course provided me with hundreds of words for constructing a Ch'orti' vocabulary, its greatest value was ethnographic. I habitually interrupted Carlos my tutor's monotonous translations of Ch'orti' phrases into Spanish to ask about life in his home community, which happened to be Pelillo Negro. In fact, many other educated Ch'orti' professionals were from Pelillo, which, despite its relative inaccessibility, had been visited by Protestant missionaries, Bible translators, and yes, linguists. We discussed the Ch'orti' diaspora, creation stories, coffee plantations, forest depletion, and tales of cannibalistic gringos, much to our mutual discomfort. We discovered that we shared a similar sense of humor and standards of indecency about the human body and sexuality. Carlos's friendship was something I deeply appreciated, and we shared dreams of someday founding a Ch'orti' educational institute. To my astonishment, however, on our long bus ride to Jocotán at the end of the course, Carlos refused to speak Ch'orti' with me publicly.

During my first night back at the Pensión Ramírez in Jocotán, three young Guatemalan men kindly introduced themselves. They were Protestant World Vision development workers and assumed that I was a new Peace Corps volunteer, someone for whom they had little professional regard but found amusing nonetheless. When I identified myself as an anthropologist and explained my project, their leader, like many well-educated, middle class Ladinos, cited Guatemalan historian Severo Martínez Paláez in proclaiming that "Indian" culture and identity are colonial inventions designed to subordinate poor peasants. Persons adopting an indigenous culture and lifestyle were dupes in their own exploitation, and anthropologists like me were accomplices. Ch'orti's like Pedro had already questioned the utility of my project by being unable to comprehend it, and the condescension of some development workers compounded the sense that I was either hopelessly naive and useless at best, or exploiting the poorest of the poor at worst.

I spent the first six weeks in Jocotán getting acquainted with town life and making short excursions into Ch'orti' rural villages. I was looking for a suitable Ch'orti' family willing to house me for several months, despite the townspeople's insistence that it was foolishly dangerous to live among "the Indians," especially with a cholera epidemic raging in neighboring Chiquimula. But I knew that I would never be able to learn Ch'orti' and gain the campesinos' confidence unless I lived with them. I visited sixteen of Jocotán's stores to see what they had in stock, but after the first few owners gruffly gave me the cold shoulder when I refused to buy, the visits became tests of courtesy. It wasn't until much later, after having witnessed the townspeople's resentment towards backpacking gringos on their way to and from Copán Ruins, that I understood their animosity. Gringo travelers are generally considered ethnocentric, poorly mannered, inarticulate penny-pinchers despite their imagined limitless wealth. Three storeowners were hospitable, especially a seventy-four-year-old owner of a humble one-room store that doubled as her living room. She invited me to sit with her friends and chat for as long as I liked. Strong willed, self-righteous, and unabashed to say what was on her mind, she became a tremendous source of information about Jocotán's past and current townspeople's sentiments towards Ch'orti's. But more than an informant, doña Tonia was a grandmother to me, caring about my health and sharing my concern for Ch'orti's. Though her supplies were limited, I made it a point to visit her regularly.

Of all the Ladino townspeople, the most near and dear to me were the owners of the Pensión Ramírez. They ran a clean motel, and when amoebas made life miserable, they brought me lemon seltzer with rehydration salts, advised rest, and called the health center doctor, their brother-in-law, or sent out for medicine from the wife's brother, one of the town pharmacists. I spent many hours with them discussing local and national politics. They were my trusted family in an area where cheating gringos was as immoral as riding a horse or slaughtering a pig. Besides guarding my office machines and other supplies, they let me recharge my laptop computer batteries without cost. As they ran the best restaurant in town with a television broadcasting the Spanish channel Univision out of Miami (thanks to the owner of a satellite dish who ran his own local cable company), the Pensión Ramírez proved to be one of the hubs of town information. Eventually the señor's generosity and affability would win him the mayor's seat.

Among my favorite diners (*comedores*) was Enmas, whose owners' son, an amicable man of my age, became my friend upon quizzing me on my Ch'orti' vocabulary the first time I ate there. He was the only townsperson I knew who understood more than a few of words of Ch'orti', and his knowledge of US professional sports was extraordinary. I consider myself a moderate sports fan in my own right, but he amazed me with his name-dropping of countless US professional baseball, basketball, and football players, not to mention Spain's and Mexico's soccer leagues. Like other Oriente Ladinos, he wanted to learn English to better understand US television, migrate to the United States, communicate with local tourists, gain prestige, and talk to gringas. He also knew just about everybody and everything happening in Jocotán. He was constantly visiting others or carousing with the men in the park, and seemed unable to stay in one place for more than an hour. He and his family have always been very generous in offering me drinks, ice cream, and meals, and I've had difficulty reciprocating with photos and gifts from the United States. Beyond his fixation on television, he knew quite a bit about the United States from his brother, who was among the hundreds of Jocotecos who have migrated to New Jersey since the 1960s. One of the first migrants made a fortune in restaurants and real estate in New York City and New Jersey and offers employment to fellow Jocoteco Ladinos.

At the first Sunday morning market of my return, almost a year and a half after my fateful trek to Pelillo Negro, I searched for Pedro. I had sent him a letter with his family photos but received no reply. I had difficulty distinguishing him among the sea of glaring Ch'orti' faces in the market and had given up until I heard "Bren Mes" voiced behind my back. I turned around and recognized him immediately and was so happy to see a friendly face that I wanted to hug him. He was amazed to see me and thought he'd never hear from me again, as the postal service had pilfered my mail for the first of many times. Unlike Carlos, Pedro excitedly began to speak Ch'orti' with me in public upon learning of my language training, and in the process attracted a crowd of bemused Ch'orti's. He had wisely built his house with mud and straw rather than rest his hopes on my bringing a truck to haul the cement. He asked me to accompany him while he (unsuccessfully) pressed a landowner to sell twelve *manzanas*[4] of land that he had promised for Q2,000, or about $400. It would have been a great deal considering it was located in the low, hot country (*tierra caliente*) where it is relatively flat and three crops of maize per year are possible with irrigation. Upon his prompting, I treated him to eggs, beans, and tortillas again. Now it was my turn to drop a bomb on him. Could I live in his house compound in Pelillo Negro? He was hesitant, saying he would discuss it with his wife, and instead offered to tutor me in Ch'orti' in town.

A bilingual teacher, Carlos's income enabled him to buy a two-room house on the outskirts of town for his wife and one-year-old daughter. They invited me to dinner, and we spent much time with his brother (a national math champion and one of only a few college-educated Ch'orti's) joking about the differences between Ch'orti's, Ladinos, and gringos. When I decided to take a reconnaissance trip to Quezaltepeque to determine whether Ch'orti' was still spoken there, which for Carlos and Pedro was the true marker of Ch'orti' ethnicity, Carlos offered to accompany me. He was unaware but curious about the geographical extent of Ch'orti', which many Jocotecos proudly but erroneously proclaimed was confined to their municipal borders.

Curiously, in Quezaltepeque not even the town officials knew if and where Ch'orti' was spoken, but a few suspected it might be in the remote highland aldea of Nochán (*noj chan*, "great serpent"). So Carlos and I set off walking there, expecting to return in a few hours. He was impressed

---

4. An acre is 4,840 square yards, or about the size of a football field without the end zones. The Ch'orti's count land in terms of manzanas and tareas. One manzana, or sixteen tareas, is 7,000 square meters, equivalent to 1.73 acres or 8,373 square yards (cf. López and Metz 2002).

with the landscape of Quezaltepeque, rugged and overworked like Jocotán but with many trees, including the incense producing copal shrub. It took four hours to reach the summit of Nochán, and of the many seemingly Ch'orti' campesinos with whom we chatted, no one claimed to speak Ch'orti', but Carlos was certain that they were just ashamed to admit their Ch'orti' fluency.

Nochán is only about an hour and a half walk from the town of Olopa, lying at forty-five hundred feet above sea level, so we continued in that direction, crossing a mountain summit where thick fog, large wooden crosses, shadows of lumbering cows, and our disorientation was haunting. At my insistence, we continued to ask campesinos whether they spoke Ch'orti', but they only chuckled mockingly and said no. Exhausted and in Olopa, we were impressed with the segregation between the light-skinned town and the dark-skinned country, and we interpreted the blatant staring as unfriendly. I knew that Olopa was a site of severe violence during the civil war. When we discovered that we had missed the last bus out of town, we were dismayed to learn that the only hostel charged Q10 (about $2) per bed, more than what we had because we had not intended to stay the night. Carlos decided that we would continue on foot for an hour to the community of Tuticopote to spend the night at his Ch'orti' friend Miguel's house. The next day we would walk another fifteen miles over rugged terrain to Jocotán.

It was getting dark, and despite the arduous walking, we were tired and shivering. Unsure of the trail, we asked some young women from Tuticopote if they would guide us. They giggled, agreed, and dodged us a few hundred yards down the trail. With no moon on an overcast night, I couldn't see my own hand in front of my face. After I stumbled on the steep, rocky trail a few times, Carlos grabbed a stick and followed the barking of a dog to an old woman's house, where she rejected our request to pay for lodging and told us that Miguel's house was five minutes down the trail. Realizing her fright, I waited from a distance when Carlos approached the next house. He returned with a flashlight-wielding old woman who led us down the trail as we tried in vain to explain what we were up to. Her two sons and their dogs relieved her as guide and silently led us through streams and up and down muddy trails for forty-five minutes until we finally reached the house. Miguel's wife, petrified, refused even to peek out of her house to tell us in her high voice that Miguel wasn't home. The only option left was to ask lodging from Miguel's sister, Carmen, yet another five minutes' walk away.

Fifty-five-year-old Carmen, her eleven sons and daughters, and their children welcomed us as if expecting us, and our provisional guides were thrilled with the few *quetzales* I gave them for their invaluable service. She ordered her family to give us stools around a large mud stove, and her daughters quickly prepared tortillas and gave us bananas. It was the first time that I had been offered beans and tortillas since my illness at Pedro's house, but they were surprisingly delicious. While young women slyly stole peeks at me, Carmen and the men stared shamelessly and joked about gringos, especially once the slightly intoxicated Miguel strode in. Miguel compared me to the incomparable "Jaime," or Jim Morris, a Peace Corps volunteer who had endeared Olopa campesinos with his five years of service, his fluency in Ch'orti', and his donning of the traditional white cotton trousers and shirt. He recounted how Jaime had organized a road-building project from Olopa to Jocotán despite townspeople's opposition and accusations that he was a guerrilla. Miguel confirmed that many Olopa Ch'orti's were massacred in the political violence of the 1960s–1960s–80s. He challenged me to become the next Jaime and do fieldwork in Tuticopote, which I took him up on a year later. Despite having hiked about fifteen mountainous miles, Carlos and I didn't get much sleep that night due to our excitement about the day's adventures and the cold, flea-infested stable grounds on which we lay.

As we walked the five hours to Jocotán the next day, Carlos pointed out communities, ox-driven sugarcane presses, and unique house designs with tall roofs reminiscent of those I had seen in Belize and Yucatán, Mexico. He queried me about my religion and was disappointed that I had been raised a Lutheran, skeptical of my plea that Catholicism and Lutheranism are not significantly different when contrasted with Pentecostalism. Later, when Carlos and his wife invited me to dinner and pressed me again on my religious beliefs, I feared they were about to terminate our friendship on religious grounds. Instead, they asked that my soon-to-arrive wife and I act as godparents, or *padrinos*, for their daughter's baptism. I tentatively agreed, though leery of the obligations required of a *compadre*. Carlos explained that godparents customarily purchase the child's outfit, and the parents reciprocate with a basket of roast turkey, sixty to seventy tortillas, rice, and fruit. Since my wife and I were alone, they would take us to a nice dinner in Chiquimula instead. We eventually went through with the baptism in Chiquimula, not realizing that by attending a baptismal mass in a neighboring parish we were accomplices to sponsoring a baptism without the obligatory counsel of the local Jocotán priest.

I now pressed both Carlos and Pedro about a house to rent in Pelillo Negro. Once I made it clear that I was willing to cover the expenses, Carlos offered to build a house on his own land, and Pedro suggested building a room off his house. So I walked to Pelillo Negro to survey the situation, this time leaving at 5:00 AM in the dawn coolness and arriving in only three and a half hours. Various Ch'orti' men welcomed me along the way, and some invited me to visit. In Pelillo, I found Pedro with fifteen men repairing the rugged dirt road annually eroded by the rains. They all joked about me in Ch'orti', as I stood by helplessly, unable to keep up. Pedro saved me by taking me to his new and improved homestead, with a separate cooking house made of thatch and a large (fifteen-by-twenty-five-foot) sleeping house made of wattle-and-daub walls and a zinc-laminated roof. His wife was as shy as ever and said no more than a few words to me, sometimes seeming annoyed with my awkward presence. After I watched the community's afternoon soccer game while being watched myself by dozens of amused men and boys, Pedro, Carlos, Carlos's brother, and I, all embarrassed at my social and linguistic clumsiness, returned to Carlos's father's homestead, just a few steps away from Pedro's. They heatedly argued in Ch'orti' about who could best accommodate me, and somehow it was agreed that I would stay with Pedro, where I would not be isolated and could pay his wife to bring me water from a spring fifteen minutes away. Pedro and I calculated the cost of building the room, including labor in hauling grass, wood poles from the only remaining patch of forest within an hour's walk away, laminated metal, and nails, to be $130. The roof, which included a homemade gutter, was his idea, as it funneled precious rainwater into a barrel. I also begrudgingly loaned Pedro $45 to buy corn for resale to other campesinos. Having won less than $4,000 in grants, I had little choice but to conform to the stereotype of the ungenerous gringo.

After I arranged accommodations in Pelillo and Tuticopote, which are nine hours' walk apart at opposite ends of the Ch'orti'-speaking territory, I scored my third living arrangement in a lowland aldea in between, Pacrén. Three Peace Corps volunteers in Jocotán—two retired early from the Forest Service (ski instructors from Colorado) and one early retired IBM employee from upstate New York—were crucial in setting me up with contacts in Pacrén. Linda's, Phil's, and Beatrice's Peace Corps assignments were the Sisyphean tasks of teaching literacy, the promotion of forest conservation, and respect for wildlife, respectively. The campesinos kill virtually everything that moves because it is considered good to eat, dangerous, an agricultural pest, or has a prized pelt. The volunteers and their colleagues in Olopa, one of whom was a retired chemical engineer, Carole Finlay, who eventually stayed for fourteen years until her death in 2003, were so devoted that they spent their meager Peace Corps salaries on their underfunded projects.

Phil and Linda worked in the aldea Pacrén, which at roughly sixteen hundred feet is only an hour-and-fifteen-minute walk from Jocotán (at one thousand feet). When we visited Pacrén for the first time, the Ch'orti' foreman of the carpentry project, Cresencio, warmly introduced himself and suggested that I learn about the prayer ceremony called *la limosna*, "the alms," at his home on New Year's Eve. He also offered to repair and rent out his old palm house. I was thrilled with this proposition because I had doubts about moving my wife and myself immediately to the more distant Pelillo Negro. A few weeks later, on New Year's Eve, he showed us his altar for la limosna, where at midnight he thanked God for granting another year and prayed for the protection and fertility of his homestead and crops. Days later we moved into his wattle-and-daub, zinc-roofed house (again, his idea) with the help of the four-wheel drive truck of Padre Juan, a Belgian priest who had made great inroads in developing the area and converting Ch'orti's of the Jocotán parish to orthodox Catholicism. Cresencio and his son Paco cautiously charged us Q30 (about $6) a month for rent and the installation of a gravity-driven water spigot, although they dropped the rent as soon as we knew each other better. We in turn felt guilty that they dropped the charge, but I had already learned from Pedro that money can stand in the way of *confianza* among Ch'orti's.

I was now ready to carry out my research plan, but it already seemed simplistic. I had originally hypothesized a link between Western religions and the market economy, and traditional Ch'orti' worldview and subsistence, but it was clear that Ch'orti's were so poor that they had to take whatever economic opportunities presented themselves in the market or in subsistence agriculture, regardless of religion. The best I could do was to gauge how they interpreted and felt about their plight. I already saw their pride in their subsistence skills and stamina, and many regarded subsistence production to be more secure than the market. On the other hand, foreign-made radios, Western-style clothing (jeans, cowboy hats, leather boots, watches, etc.), housewares, and tools were valued as social capital. In fact, they seemed to treat Protestantism and Catholicism as opportunities and status symbols, rather than as avenues to eternal salvation. Most, like Carlos, were ashamed to speak Ch'orti' beyond their aldeas, and even raising the polite term *indígena*, or "indigenous person," made them uncomfortable. How had the Ch'orti's changed so much since Wisdom's study in the early 1930s? Did these people still qualify as indigenous peoples, Ch'orti's, and Mayas? Fortunately, my original three-stage research plan served me well for answering these new questions.

Life among Ch'orti's

As one might expect, the start to my life among Ch'orti's was not a bed of roses. Suspected as a cannibal of children, I was the object of avoidance and extreme fright by some women and children (for Copán, see Schumann de Baudez 1983:204). One woman was so horrified to encounter me on a remote trail that she froze with eyes bulging and mouth agape, and it was many a small child who ran screaming in terror. Some men kept their lips sealed and their machetes ready as well, with a few even spying from the brush as children talked to me. Only over several months was I able to shake perceptions that I was a Protestant missionary, who Catholics consider confrontational, arrogant, and even diabolical.

To make matters much worse, my wife and I were at the end of a troubled marriage. The insanity of working our way through graduate school and my privileging of career over married life finally caught up to us when it was time to move to Pacrén. Within weeks, she left me, Ch'orti' country, and anthropology, and eventually returned to the United States with the World Vision worker who had accused me of being colonialist. The Ch'orti's in my current host community sensed what was happening, and some young men seized the opportunity, peppering me with questions like, "Where is your wife?"

The divorce, though not a surprise, hit me hard because I had little social support, but after a short break riding old Bluebird buses around Central America, I decided to finish the project and convinced myself that any laughter from young Ch'orti' men was either due to their nervousness or competitiveness due to my global, if not local, position of power. I reminded myself that painful and error-ridden incidents were always learning experiences, and that whatever losses I might have were trivial compared to the losses and suffering endured by Ch'orti's. It also helped that soon after my return some Ladinos and foreigners began to show some respect for my work and the sacrifice I made. One project director invited me to dinners in exchange for information on how to improve communication with Ch'orti's, and some religious leaders also interviewed me about what I had learned. Such occasional tokens of respect amidst criticisms and doubts were enough to keep my spirits up.

My bachelorhood in Cresencio's home was awkward, as his wife, three sons, and eight daughters felt uncomfortable watching me do women's work like sweeping and cooking. My zealousness in purging my house of fleas was strange and annoying, as I occupied their clothesline every day to hang my flea-ridden bedding in the sun. They were also disappointed with my occasional refusal of offers of tortillas and beans, which typically occurred after I had already cooked my own dinner on a Coleman camp stove. With my computer, frequent visits to town, and purchases of extravagant foods like spaghetti and peanut butter, I probably was regarded as a scrooge because I jealously guarded all food I carried on my back to the aldea.

Food turned out to be a major issue among Ch'orti's (cf. López 1993, 2003). Among all three host families I became a renowned chef of popcorn and pancakes, which I exchanged for beans, tortillas, and corn gruel on a regular basis. The ethnographic tradition of distributing medicine and medical knowledge was generally appreciated as well, just as I appreciated their spiritual and herbal remedies for me. My photos of them were even more prized. One destitute old man bragged to his wife that not the teachers, the diviners, the sorcerers, the healers, nor even the wisest of rain-callers had their photos taken by foreign scholars. Though I was always a strange gringo among Ch'orti's, we gradually came to understand each other and build a culture. As my Ch'orti' comprehension improved, so did the complexity of our relationships, including the frequent joking. By the time I moved into my third household, that of Carmen and her large family, I was relaxed enough that children felt free to climb all over me. I became a pied piper of sorts, to the point that the kids were menaces at times. In the end, I was never charged for rent and all invited me to important family events. I continue to visit my host families annually as "their gringo."

My stay in each aldea began with two months of participant observation, which involved simply trying to make myself visible and familiar, taking part in activities as varied as planting, house building, playing soccer, and even drinking *chicha*, a popular, illegal sugarcane beer. This enabled me to slowly nurture confianza beyond my host homesteads. Though some hostile men—most of them enemies of my hosts—were intent on either humiliating, physically threatening, or exploiting me for loans they never intended to pay back, others came to appreciate my study once they understood what I was doing. Many new acquaintances invited me to visit or reside in their communities.

In many ways, my personal experiences and research became more rewarding as my hosts and I established confianza. As my Ch'orti' improved, many speakers and envious nonspeakers saw me as proof that the language was not dying but regaining importance. Countless Ch'orti's, from very old to young, continue to be amazed with my colloquial Ch'orti', even though for me Ch'orti' was much easier to learn than Spanish. Many were amused at the arcane words my expert Ch'orti' teachers taught me. Many, including aggressive drunks, took it upon themselves to teach me Ch'orti' vocabulary. When Ernesto, an immigrant to northern Guatemala, heard me speaking, he profusely thanked me, exclaiming that the language was truly undergoing a revival. Some, upon hearing me in Tuticopote, apologized to other speakers because they had abandoned the language, and some young men asked me to teach it. Old men, especially, used me as an opportunity to scold youth for abandoning the language. The Academy of Maya Languages, established in the Ch'orti' area soon after I arrived, invited me to their meetings and offered an honorary membership. When the Maya organization Majawil Q'ij later began holding workshops in Jocotán, my Ch'orti' speaking and aldea residence were enough to assuage doubts that I was attending not just for self-interest or research, but because I truly cared about Ch'orti's and Mayas. Townspeople have also been astonished to hear me speaking it, as many had never heard it spoken openly. Some presume that it is somehow linguistically related to English, which Ch'orti's do nothing to dispel.

My relationships with Ch'orti's have constituted some of the highest highs and lowest lows of my life. Although I, like other ethnographers, worked through illnesses, threats by machete-wielding drunks and military commissioners, and weight loss from 170 to 129 pounds, humor has been a steady part of our relations. As a gringo, I was a frequent target of humor, including my ineptitude at tying slipknots, picking coffee, and cutting and roasting banana leaves for wrapping tamales. Who could help but laugh when I stumbled over backwards and flattened my own goalie in a soccer match, when my rat poison was seemingly so ineffective that mice tore open the package and ate it, when I swept with a family broom that actually was the discarded stub of an old one, and when Pedro sarcastically informed the ethnographer that Ch'orti's are not capable of eating with silverware, but only their hands? Attendants could not contain their mirth when a dog defecated at my side during a Catholic mass, and when toads—symbols for vaginas—congregated outside my house at night as my "lovers." When one young man saw that I had hair on my stomach, he rushed to tell his brothers, who asked whether I had hair on my penis and if it was "standing" (*wa'r*), inciting laughter among the women present. Another friend constructed my bed as sturdily as possible in case I found a woman. In Cresencio's family, three girls constantly teased their three-year-old sister by throwing her into my room for me to devour, running her rapidly past my door in a wheelbarrow, and pressing the cellophane I gave them against her face to make her look like a pig. As my Ch'orti' improved, I learned to direct the humor by joking about my bachelor status, poor cooking abilities, experiences with chicha, and the origins of my Tuticopote nickname *kujtz'* (tobacco), which Miguel had bestowed when he misheard my surname "Metz." When parents were hesitant to give a survey, I broke the ice by interviewing children as if they were adults, matter-of-factly asking them if they were married and how many lovers they had, or declaring that by the number of children in a homestead "no one seems to be getting any sleep around here." One elderly man seriously asked whether I, as a gringo, have sex, and when I told him not enough, he and others howled in delight.

A more formal stage of my research plan consisted of a socioeconomic survey of every household in each aldea—190 in Pacrén, 261 in Pelillo Negro, and 114 in Tuticopote Abajo. The survey data included each occupant's age, sex, marital status, voter registration, place of birth, education, seasonal migration, occupation, religious affiliation, and participation in development projects, as well as general household data about the use of health centers, the practice of key religious ceremonies, sources of water, house construction materials, crops, land ownership, use of chemical fertilizers and pesticides, cattle, radios, and marketing. Most Ch'orti's were willing and accustomed to giving survey information, as the Guatemalan census bureau, local health centers, and development projects regularly take censuses. Many were reluctant until I explained my interests in documenting change so that their grandchildren would someday be able to read about what had gone before. Ironically, I, with my copies of photos from Wisdom's (1940) and Girard's (1949) ethnographies and folklore compilations by Fought (1972) and Dary (1986), became a source of knowledge about Ch'orti' history, which lent me some authority in explaining my project. All but twenty-seven households agreed to participate, and another ninety-seven households gave incomplete information. Rejections affected me personally more than they did the quality of my data, and involved accusations that I was after their children, a guerrilla, or would earn limitless wealth via my study. A few men in one community spoke of killing me upon discovering that their wives had cooperated with me without their consent.

The opportunity to explain my project and exchange informal conversation with hundreds of Ch'orti' households was just as valuable ethnographically as the survey information itself, and overall I found most Ch'orti's to be hospitable despite their poverty and justifiable suspicions. The census provided families with opportunities to ask me questions. Contrary to the image of indigenous peoples wishing to remain closed in their worldview, Ch'orti's are very curious about the outside world. I felt obliged to reciprocate their survey information by responding to their tireless questions, even if by providing them information I adulterated the information they would later give to me. Many asked more questions about the United States and the rest of the world than I asked them, including topics of prices and wages, geography, travel distances (times), weather, agriculture, market systems, migratory labor, politics, modern weaponry, diet, language, housing, other indigenous peoples, subways, and Columbus, to name but a few. The most precious gift I ever gave one host family was a $1 inflatable beach ball/globe, which the adults studied for hours and refused to let the children handle. Many asked to learn English, but my poor teaching proved too much for their patience.

The surveys laid the groundwork for tape-recorded personal interviews. By meeting every family in an aldea, I was able to select a sample of twenty friendly and forthcoming interviewees based on age, sex, wealth, and religion in each of the three aldeas. While six interviewees had to be replaced because of their suspicions, others were honored to be chosen, and some requested that I replay the entire interview on the recorder. Women, who are generally not asked for their opinions and are unaccustomed to talking to men outside their family, were especially reticent. I managed to interview seventeen women, eleven of whom were members of a women's cooperative in Pacrén who interviewed in each other's presence. I chose six interview topics according to common Ch'orti' concerns: 1) perceived differences between the remembered past and the present; 2) the problems and potential solutions in their community; 3) politics and politicians; 4) emigration; 5) organized religions; and 6) the long-term future. The topics were often discussed with little prompting from me, but not all interviews were trouble free. Some continued to suspect me of being a Protestant missionary, and virtually all interviewees required considerable explanation of what I meant by the distant future, which I usually conveyed by pointing to the ever-present toddler and saying "when they are parents." As a show of thanks, I presented each informant with an article of clothing, jewelry, or toiletries donated by my family and friends.[5] In large part, these interviews were the culmination of my twenty-two-month initial research project.

Besides this structured research plan, I, like other ethnographers, went on tangential investigations like a detective—following leads, uncovering motives, searching for clues, and taking advantage of fleeting opportunities. I undertook bibliographic research and archival research in the Central American Archives in Guatemala City and in Jocotán's and Olopas's churches and municipal offices. Learning about the brutality of Ch'orti' history sent chills down my spine, and explained much about Ch'orti' contemporary attitudes and values Ch'orti's have towards each other and towards outsiders like myself.

Since I ended my doctoral fieldwork in 1993, I have returned annually to the Ch'orti' region to continue my support of the Ch'orti' Maya Movement, compile more information, visit old friends and make new ones, and expand my geographical focus to the entire former Ch'orti'-speaking region of eastern Guatemala, western Honduras, and northwestern El Salvador.

5. Some colleagues and Ladinos insist that giving gifts for information sets a bad precedent, but clothing is the least I can do to reciprocate with the poorest of the poor.

CHAPTER TWO

History of the Jocotán Parish, 1524–1930

*[N]either commerce nor its profits should be at the cost of
the blood, health, and lives of the miserable, innocent Indians,
forced against the expressed and repeated provision of the law,
against the fatherly, benevolent intentions of the sovereign,
and against the interests of the State, the Kingdom, and
the Treasury, all of which hold the preservation of the
agricultural tribute-bearers in the highest importance.*

—Royal investigator Piloña, 1812 AGCA7876
"Diligencias instruidas sobre el contagio…"

I had set out to find a Ch'orti' culture and identity opposed to amoral, modern capitalist individualism. What I seemed to find was a destitute, divided group of campesinos ashamed of their indigenous heritage and desperate for any opportunity that came their way. My investigation broadened beyond the hypothesized divide between organized Christian religions and moral economies to the reasons behind the Ch'orti's' ethnic shame. Were these even "Ch'orti's" after all? While they themselves recognized the term, few seemed to use it as their principal means of self-identification. Some still used the term that Wisdom found most prevalent in the early 1930s, "lenguajero," which is ironically a local Spanish word for speakers of Ch'orti'. Rarely heard were the more stigmatized terms

"Indian" (*indio*), "indigenous person" (indígena), and "*natural.*" What had
prompted Ch'orti's, unlike the millions of Mayas in western Guatemala, to
slowly abandon their proud, distinctive identity? In the 1930s and 1940s
Wisdom and Girard recorded that already a social split was emerging
between Ch'orti's with an affinity to Ladino, nationalist society, and those
that were more withdrawn and faithful to traditions. A longer history
reveals how this process of ethnic abandonment was indeed nothing new.
In this chapter I will review this history by emphasizing the old colonial
Jocotán Parish, comprised of the contemporary townships of Jocotán,
San Juan Ermita, Camotán, La Unión, and northern Olopa, where roughly
twenty-two contiguous rural communities[1] (see map 2) continue to speak
Ch'orti' in the home and community and maintain the strongest sense of
Ch'orti' identity.

Today, the people of the old Jocotán Parish share collective memories
founded generations ago that inform daily practices through mannerisms, habits, settings, symbols, thoughts, and dispositions (see Watanabe
1992; Bourdieu 1977). The very distinction of Indian and non-Indian, with
all the derogatory connotations for the former and privileges for the latter, was established early upon the arrival of the Spanish and has changed
little since (Guzmán Böckler and Herbert 1970). Contemporary ethnic
demographics in eastern Guatemala, in which towns with a central plaza,
church, and town hall are populated by Creoles (American-born Spaniards) and the surrounding countryside by Indians, were established in
the 1500s, immediately upon Spanish settlement (Terga 1980:17; cf. Girón
Palacios 2001). Prevailing sentiments and attitudes among Ch'orti's such
as fatalism, inferiority, apathy, fear, suspicion, independence, resentment, and stoicism have precedents in both their history as a Mesoamerican people and as a colonized people, i.e., as "Indians." This does not
mean that they are trapped in a "heritage of conquest" (cf. Tax, ed. 1952)
or condemned to live in the past, but history is very relevant to Ch'orti'
and Ladino understandings, routines, spaces, and sentiments. Contemporary Ch'orti' culture is informed but not restricted by generations-old

1. The aldeas of Tuticopote Arriba, Tuticopote Abajo, Roblarcito, Agua Blanca,
   Rodeito, Tunucó Arriba, Tunucó Abajo, Ocumblá, Tatutú, Tontoles, La Arada,
   Pacrén, Oquen, Amatillo, Suchiquer, Pelillo Negro, Guareruche, Las Flores,
   Guarequiche, Matasano, Tierra Blanca, and Conacaste. One informant
   reported in 1998 that she found Ch'orti' speakers in the Chiquimula aldeas
   of Santa Barbara, La Puerta de la Montaña, San Miguel, San Antonio, and
   El Sauce. See appendix 4.

stories, names, and feelings about their physical landscape (cf. Rosaldo 1980), rhythms and values of subsistence life, house designs and eating habits, linguistic expressions, and ritualized behavior towards Ladinos.

"Ch'orti's" before the Spanish Invasion?

We have scant evidence that "the Ch'orti'" existed as "a nation" or ethnic group prior to the Spanish invasion, such that we can only speculate about the linkage between the Ch'orti' language, cultures, and political affiliation. The archaeological sites of Copán, Honduras, and Quiriguá, Guatemala—among many other sites in Guatemala, Honduras, and El Salvador—and the hieroglyphs documenting the competition between them, are testimony that what was the Ch'orti'-speaking area at Spanish contact (1524) was often divided politically but unified by Classic Maya culture (ca. AD 300 to ca. AD 900) and a Cholan or proto-Cholan language, the family to which Ch'orti' pertains. Hull (2003), in fact, argues that current poetic features used by Ch'orti' elder ritual specialists, such as parallel couplets, reflect the same poetic features used in hieroglyphic writing, which he is convinced was written by eastern Cholan speakers (cf. Houston, Robertson, and Stuart 2000; David Mora, pers. comm.). Soon after the Classic period, Nahuatl-speaking Pipils from central Mexico began invading the upper Motagua River valley and El Salvador, resulting in a cultural and linguistic fusion with Ch'orti's known as Alaguilac (Terga 1980:29–36; Girard 1977). Many place names in the region include Nahuatl as well as Ch'orti' words. In the Post-classic period (ca. AD 900 to 1524), Poqom Maya and Pipils, displaced by eastward-advancing K'iche', Kaqchikel, and Chontal polities, pressed the Ch'orti's from the west, while in the east Ch'orti'-speakers interspersed with Jicaque- and Lenca-speakers (Fox 1981; Girard 1949:1–30, 53; Walters and Feldman 1982). In the north, the Ch'orti' linguistic border was even more ill-defined as it blended with other Cholan Maya languages that extended as far north as the Mexican Caribbean coast (cf. Feldman 2000, 1975; Moral 1983; Quizar and Knowles-Berry 1988; Cambell and Kaufman 1985:192–94; Kaufman 1974:110; Wisdom 1940:1–7). In fact, of the three remaining Cholan languages—Ch'orti', Chontal, and Chol—Ch'orti' language and spiritual traditions are most similar to Chontal on the Tabasco-Veracruz coast hundreds of miles to the north (Moral 1983).

When the Spanish invaded in 1524, the Ch'orti'-speaking area ranged from northwestern El Salvador in the south to the Caribbean coast in the north, and the Departments of Chiquimula, Zacapa, and Izabal in the west to sixty kilometers into western Honduras in the east (Feldman 1983: 149–51; Wisdom 1961:18–23; Girard 1949:38–40, 44). The sensationalistic chronicler Fuentes y Guzmán ([1699] 1933), who wrote the first comprehensive Spanish history of Guatemala, described how the conquistador Pedro de Alvarado, after subduing the K'iche' in 1524, sent an armed contingent to conquer eastern Guatemala. Spaniards and their Mexican support troops were met by resistance from a confederation of Ch'orti', Alaguilac, and Pipil-speaking polities in eastern Guatemala and western Honduras, including Copán (near contemporary Esquipulas), Chiquimula, Zacapa, Esquipulas, Gracias a Dios, and Asunción Mita (Mitlán) (Orduna 1530; Walters and Feldman 1982:595–96; Fowler 1983:353; Fuentes y Guzmán [1699] 1933:204–9). They reportedly fought with a fierce and unified resistance, inflicting many casualties with surprise attacks of poison arrows and copper tipped, fire hardened spears. In 1529 the leader Copán Calel once again lead a confederation from Mitlán, Zacapa, Sensenti, Guijar, Ostúa, Esquipulas, and Chiquimula in revolt, but the Spanish and Mexican troops eventually overran what was thought to be Copán's unassailable fortress on a moat-surrounded mesa near Esquipulas (see Girard 1949). Copán Calel was eventually trapped in Citalá, El Salvador, after which he reportedly ruthlessly put down Ch'orti' resistance in his promise to the Spaniards to maintain the peace (Fuentes y Guzmán [1699] 1933:169–82, 204–9).

Fuentes y Guzmán ([1699] 1933:220–22) described the Jocotán Parish as a tropical paradise with great expanses of forest; fauna such as deer, pacas, rabbits, turkeys, partridges, doves, *guatusas*, tapirs, monkeys, *chacha* birds, macaws, parrots, *chiltote* birds, and *tutut* birds; and flora including oregano, *mataliste*, paprika, pepper, *achyomico*, *nacascolote*, cocoa, and gourds. Geological surveys note, however, that the steep, mountainous lands, reaching six thousand feet above sea level, have predominantly clay and chalky soils covered by a thin layer of topsoil, which is not optimal for intensive agriculture. Only in the narrow valley lands, with colluvial and alluvial soil deposits and where irrigation is possible, is sustained intensive agriculture possible (Proyecto 1991:7; Dary, Elías, and Reyna 1998:78). The irrigable lowlands produce four times more corn and beans per hectare (eight thousand pounds) than the dry mountainsides (less than two thousand pounds) (Dary, Elías, and Reyna 1998:84). The valleys are naturally arid due to a mountainous barrier blocking moist winds from the Caribbean, resulting in a low average humidity of 70%. This in turn makes irrigation especially important due to the sizzling average temperature of 82°F in the valleys during the growing season from March to November (Dary, Elías, and Reyna 1998:74, 79, 80).

Though the region supported intensive agriculture during the Classic period, it is commonly believed among archaeologists that Classic Maya sites like Copán were gradually abandoned due to overpopulation, over-use of land, and excessive demands for surplus by elites. Nevertheless, tens of thousands of people continued to inhabit the region (e.g., Sanders and Murdy 1982). When the Spanish arrived, all indications are that the population of the Ch'orti'-speaking region was high. If we accept Fuentes y Guzmán's ([1699] 1933:204–9) seemingly exaggerated number of thirty thousand troops fielded by legendary leader Copán Calel against the Spanish in 1530, their base population would have been at least between 120,000 and 150,000 (Veblen 1982:85–86; Gibson 1952 in Lovell 1982:108). As questionable as this number is, Pérez (1997:105) calculated the Guate-malan Ch'orti' population alone to be 120,000 at contact. Such a popula-tion density was not reached again until the twentieth century, and at the time would have likely caused deforestation, soil erosion, and conflict, as have been found for other pre-Columbian Maya areas (Sanders and Murdy 1982; Veblen 1982:98). Adding support to the population pressure hypothesis is that the land least suitable for agriculture, in the high, steep mountains, is littered with pre-Columbian artifacts, including obsidian, pottery, jade axes, and grinding stones. This high population, however, was in for a shock with the Spanish invasion.

The Colonial Period

When the Spanish conquerors first arrived, they pillaged precious metals, gems, and indigenous food stores. The Crown ceded the Spanish con-querors *encomiendas*, or grants of Indian labor and tribute, in exchange for a one-fifth (*quinto*) tax and the financing of the Catholic Church's evangelization of the Indians. Initially, the *encomenderos* hauled indige-nous men off to the sources of the metals, such as the gold fields near Tegucigalpa in central Honduras and northern Nicaragua, or the silver mines in the high Andes, where they were often literally worked to death (MacLeod 1973:46–61). The wars, dislocations, and introduction of Euro-pean diseases devastated the indigenous populations, and many died out completely. Smallpox, influenza, and pulmonary bubonic plague intro-duced via central Mexico may have decimated as much as one-third to one-half of Guatemalan Mayas even before the Spanish arrived (Veblen

1982:89; MacLeod 1973:7, 12, 19, 40–41, 403; cf. Fuentes y Guzmán [1699] 1933:210). The catastrophe in the Caribbean basin was such that New Laws were passed less than a generation later (1542) to protect the disappearing Indian labor supply. Encomiendas were to be rescinded after one to three generations, and the Crown was now to distribute Indian labor on a rotating basis in *repartimiento* drafts for the Crown and private entrepreneurs. Given the absence of major mines, in Central America the Spanish devoted more attention to marketing agricultural products, which nevertheless entailed living a parasitic existence off Indian labor and tribute (MacLeod 1973; Smith 1990).

The Ch'orti's must have suffered beyond description during this initial chaotic period of warfare, pillage, slavery, and dislocation. The conquistador Diego Díaz reported in 1535 that colonial order with tribute collections had still not been established (Torres Moss 1994:3–5; Brewer 2002), and Antonio Mosquera (1982:120–30) tells of starving Spaniards invading to raid Ch'orti' grain stores during a famine, but provides little documentary support. They were already suffering smallpox and malaria epidemics in the rebellion of 1529 (Brewer 2002:44), and the total indigenous population in the Chiquimula province—where the core of the Ch'orti' population resided—declined by 90% to twelve thousand by 1550 and thirty-three hundred by 1580 (Pérez 1997:106). In the northern Caribbean lowlands the Ch'orti's disappeared completely (MacLeod 1982:8, 10), although small populations of Ch'olti' or Manche Chol speakers—close linguistic relatives of Ch'orti's—held out in northern Guatemala and Belize until British-backed Miskito slave raiders drove them out in the early 1700s (Feldman 2000). Spaniards began to settle Chiquimula only in the second half of the 1500s (Torres 1994:13). They appropriated the fertile valleys around newly established towns, such as Jocotán, San Juan Ermita, and Camotán in the Jocotán Parish, where the remaining Ch'orti's, including those from El Salvador (to Camotán), were forcibly resettled (Morley 1920:603; Galindo 1945; Girard 1949:54).[2]

The Spaniards' primary interest in eastern Guatemala was the Motagua River (Río de Plata), the trade route connecting Santiago, Guatemala (today Antigua)—eventually the capital of the Viceroyality of Guatemala (covering Costa Rica to Chiapas, Mexico)—with a series of Caribbean ports that were

---

2. Girard also mentions neighboring San Jacinto as a forced resettlement, or *congregación*. Torres (1994:19) found no evidence that Jocotán and Camotán were originally founded as *congregaciónes*.

shifted due to periodic attacks by French, Dutch, and British pirates.[3] Supplies were sailed between the coast and the Ch'orti' town of Gualán on either the Motagua River or Río Dulce to the Ch'orti' town of Gualán. Between Gualán and Santiago, supplies were hauled up the Motagua Valley via barges and mule trains (Terga 1980:42, 61–64). Unfortunately for the Alaguilacs of the upper Motagua and Ch'orti's of the lower, more navigable reaches, including Gualán, San Pablo Zacapa, San Pedro Zacapa, Río Hondo, and Estanzuelas (Terga 1980:26), the trade route attracted Spanish settlers. They appropriated indigenous land for mule, horse, and cattle ranches that serviced the transportation industry, and exploited their labor in farming and hauling operations. Also unfortunate for the Ch'orti's, the Motagua Valley was noted for its prized cocoa, indigo, *achiote* (paprika), vanilla, fine woods, tobacco, gourds, cotton, coconuts, corn, beans, melons, plantains, pineapples, and other fruit (Terga 1980:43). Already by the 1570s, Ch'orti' population loss caused a labor crisis, and black slaves were introduced to tend cattle and work in sugar and indigo operations. Indigenous caciques, or chiefs, who served as intermediaries between the Spanish and Indians and had the privileges of riding horses, carrying arms, and receiving education, complained that they were no longer respected in their own communities. Between 1579 and 1589 most encomiendas were abolished, private ranches called haciendas and estancias became the predominant enterprises, and the repartimiento labor rotation system was introduced, taking an even greater toll on the Indians because they were forced to work at great distances from their home communities and fields (Terga 1980:45, 56, 69–70, 73).

As the Spanish colonies fell into an economic depression from 1580 to 1630, more Spaniards left the capital Santiago to establish small hacienda operations in eastern Guatemala and especially the Motagua Valley, creating constant tension with the remaining indigenous peoples, who lost land and crops to invading cattle (Terga 1980:75–76). Already by 1600, many indigenous people found the land invasions, the exploitation by merchants, and the excessive tributes to officials, priests, and community chests too much to endure. Some emigrated, others were forced into sharecropping (*arrendamiento*), in which they exchanged their labor for the temporary use

3. The principal ports included Trujillo, Honduras (1524), Caballos, Honduras (1536), San Antonio de las Bodegas del Golfo on the shores of Lake Izabal (1549), and Santo Tomás de Castilla on the Bay de Amatique (1604) (Terga 1980:42, 61–64).

of land, and most of all, many became indentured hacienda servants. As hacienda peons, the Spanish *hacendero* provided lodging, food, clothing, a small salary, the payment of Indian tribute obligations to the Crown, and de facto protection from church obligations in exchange for their labor, usually herding cattle and sheep (Terga 1980:90–92). Ultimately, the price was not just labor, but detachment from native communities, communal traditions, and native identities, despite their ongoing "Indian" status. Other Ch'orti's fled the Motagua to Jocotán and Camotán in the Province of Chiquimula (Brewer 2002:159–60), which may partially account for a twelve-fold population increase in the Jocotán Parish from 1680 to 1740 (see graph 1 and table 1 on following pages). Those remaining in their communities adapted to Spanish ways as best they could. Priests constantly complained. By 1653 some leaders in the Jocotán Parish had adopted Spanish surnames (Feldman 1982:148, #1092), and by the 1760s, all Indians of Gualán and most Indians in Chiquimula spoke Spanish (Terga 1980:89; Brewer 2002:135).

The Province of Chiquimula provides the eastern drainage to the Motagua, and its proximity to the trade route but marginality from the Spanish paternalistic bureaucracy meant dire consequences for the Ch'orti's. The first colonial record for the Jocotán Parish consists of tribute lists compiled in 1549–51 (Feldman 1983:157). Each of the three pueblos in the parish was originally an encomienda. Jocotán had one hundred tributaries, who were required to pay annually four servants to Antonio Salazar for his home in Santiago, Guatemala, and ten *xiquipiles* (eighty thousand beans) of cocoa and seventy-two turkeys to his children. The one hundred tributaries of Camotán were to give Hernán Pérez Penate three servants, thirty sedan chairs, ten *arrobas* (approximately 250 pounds) of honey, four arrobas (approximately one hundred pounds) of wax, thirty petates (reed mats), two *fanegas* (approximately three bushels) of corn, half a fanega ($^3/_4$ bushel) of beans, and four bundles of chiles. The forty tributaries of San Juan were to pay Antonio Salazar twenty pieces of cloth and twenty xiquipiles (160,000) of cocoa beans (Feldman 1983:157). The tributary lists were amended periodically and came to include lime, incense, baskets, cane sugar, rice, barley, wheat, anise, sesame, chickens, pigs, and, starting in the seventeenth century, coinage (Feldman 1985:103; Fuentes y Guzmán [1699] 1933:220–22; Cortés y Larraz [1768–70] 1958:275; Feldman 1989:248; Juarros [1808–18] 1936:30; Pohl and Feldman 1982:303–4). Though encomiendas were generally abolished within one to three generations after the New Laws, encomenderos continued to reap Ch'orti' tributes as late as the mid-1600s (Feldman 1982:146).

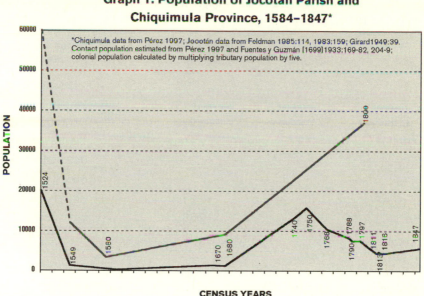

Graph 1: Population of Jocotán Parish and Chiquimula Province, 1584–1847*

*Chiquimula data from Pérez 1997; Joootán data from Feldman 1985:114, 1983:159; Girard1949:39. Contact population estimated from Pérez 1997 and Fuentes y Guzmán [1699]1933:169-82, 204-9; colonial population calculated by multiplying tributary population by five.

CENSUS YEARS

Tribute in cocoa beans is indicative of Ch'orti's population dynamics and treatment by the Spaniards. From Izabal in the north to El Salvador in the south, the hot, humid Ch'orti' area valleys were prime cocoa lands. Spanish entrepreneurs realized early on in the colonial period that cocoa was a key article of trade used by caciques to mobilize their labor population. They therefore demanded tribute in cocoa, often in excessive amounts, and struggled with the caciques over its production and distribution. By the end of the 1500s, however, diseases of the cocoa trees and falling Indian populations led the Spanish to shift cocoa production to Venezuela (MacLeod 1973). Nevertheless, cocoa production continued to increase in the Jocotán Parish, as production rose over three-fold from 1549 to 1652, despite declining Indian populations (see graph 1 this page and table 1 next page). In 1652 the Ch'orti's complained that their tribute was too high, especially considering that a drought made irrigation impossible. To meet tribute demands, they had to migrate to the Motagua towns of Zacapa, Gualán, San Pablo, Santa Lucía, and Chiquimula to earn coinage or corn, fowl, and achiote, which were acceptable substitutes for cocoa. As the population boomed in the 1700s, so did Spanish demands for cocoa. When a combination of epidemics and droughts, not to mention increased

Table 1: Recorded Ch'orti' Population and
Tribute in Jocotán Parish, 1549–1847

Year	Tributaries	Estimated Population (Tributaries X 5)	Tribute in Cocoa Beans
1549	240[4]	1,200	240,000
1652	216	1,080	792,000
1670	254	1,270	
1680	222	1,110	
1698			300,400
1734			3,006,600
1740	2,662	13,310	
1750	3,136	15,680	3,284 *tostones**
1768	2,076	10,380	
1788	1,613	8,065	
1790	1,480	7,400	
1797	1,495	7,475	
1811	860	4,300	
1813	929	4,645	
1816	849	4,245	
1821			252 *tostones*
1847	5,523		

**tostones* are silver coins

Data taken from Feldman 1985:114, 1983:159; Girard 1949:39. Unfortunately,
I have found no way of converting tostones into cocoa beans for 1750 and 1821.

exploitation, decimated the population again in the second half of the
1700s, cocoa tribute fell in tandem until the end of the colonial period in
1821 (Feldman 1983:157–58).

Besides tributes, Ch'orti's were forced to do repartimiento labor in
indigo sweatshops, which were notorious for their poor hygiene, insects,
and diseases. Indigo, a highly prized blue dye used for ink and clothing,

4. Veblen (1982:93–94) argues that this first tribute count by López de Cerrato
   (1549–51) was much too low because it relied on estimates by Indian caciques
   and did not take demographic disruption into consideration.

was the principal product of eastern and southern Guatemala and El Salvador from 1600 to the mid-1800s. Wisdom (1940:184–85) noted that Jocotán was once called "the Pearl of the East" for its booming indigo industry. The dye came from the leaves of a bush that took two to three years to mature, taking up valuable agricultural land, and was extracted by soaking the rotting leaves in vats that attracted flies, which brought disease (Rubio Sánchez 1976 in Dary, Elías, and Reyna 1998:66). So many Indians died in the indigo industry that the Crown intervened in 1738 to outlaw their labor in the sweatshops, but Chiquimula's Spaniards continued to use them regularly despite fines paid to the Crown (Rubio Sánchez 1976 2:17, 23; Archivo General de Centroamérica [AGCA] 1696–97; Dary, Elías, and Reyna 1998:67–69). Other areas of forced labor included regional iron and lead mines, the Motagua ports for loading and unloading cargo, textile sweatshops, and military and construction at the forts on the Caribbean.

As in other parts of Mesoamerica, Spanish-Ch'orti' contact was partly mitigated by Catholic clergy, but contrary to other Maya areas where sympathetic Franciscan, Dominican, and Mercedarian missionary friars ran the parishes, in eastern Guatemala the secular clergy (priests) were in control from the outset. The priesthood was a prized source of income for the Spanish, and the most powerful Spanish families monopolized the parish appointments of priests, such as the Paz family in Jocotán and Chiquimula from 1660 to 1750. They received tributes (*sinodos*), exercised forced commercial exchanges (*derramas*), charged baptismal, marital, and funeral fees, and collected the first fruits of harvest. Ninety-five percent of the parish incomes went directly into the priests' pockets. Consequently, the church had by far the richest tax base of any colonial institution, almost three times that of the Spanish administration. They appropriated brotherhoods' community chests, driving many to near bankruptcy (van Oss 1986:45, 109–15; Documentos 1978; MacLeod 1973:343–45).

Due to low numbers of priests in the Oriente and the Ch'orti's' resistance, the church had difficulty making inroads into the Indian population. Some priests learned the Ch'orti' language and thereby baptized countless Ch'orti's, but these were the exceptions (van Oss 1986:46, 59, 63–64, 69, 168). In 1555 there were still no Spanish clergy in the Oriente for Ch'orti' towns, and Ch'orti's were unreceptive anyway, sometimes openly refusing or hiding from the sacraments. The secular clergy in the Oriente had to tend to about twice as many parishioners apiece than the regular clergy in the Occidente in the 1570s. In 1586 priests complained that perpetually drunken Indians conjoined in prohibited sexual unions, undertook robberies, murders and other violent crimes, and that Ch'orti's generally did not pay them for their services (Brewer 2002:99–119). Not until the first quarter of the seventeenth century was Jocotán assigned a patron saint, Santiago Apostol (Saint James the Apostle) (Torres 1994:8–9, 12). Thus, Ch'orti's largely controlled their own ritual practices throughout the colonial period. In Copán, Ch'orti's were found to practice native "idolatry" literally behind the facade of Christianity, making sacrifices and burning incense behind church altarpieces (Fuentes y Guzmán [1699] 1933:210). In Jocotán, Ch'orti's in the 1700s repeatedly defied the priest's prohibition against burning candles in a local cave to a mysterious mulatto (Documentos 1978:35). In Chiquimula, they tried to withhold from priests the account books of the religious brotherhoods (*cofradías, guachivales*), where deposits and funeral, mass, burial, and other expenses were recorded (Cortés y Larraz [1768–70] 1950:269–72). Without the brotherhoods' donations of wax, wine, ornaments, communion wafers, etc., the churches would not have functioned at all (Dary, Elías, and Reyna 1998:47–49).

The exploitative pressures and epidemics took a heavy toll. The once thriving Ch'orti' town of Yupilingo (what is now northern Esquipulas) ceased to exist by 1688 due to the establishment of large haciendas there, including that of a particularly avaricious priest, Padre Escobar (Girard 1949:54; Documentos 1978:2).[5] In the neighboring Copán Valley, no Indians were registered on tribute lists by the 1700s, and land records mention only great extensions of pasturage and tobacco in Spanish and mestizo hands (Feldman 1983:150). As Indian populations declined, took refuge on haciendas, or fled to the forests, the remaining Indians were burdened with a disproportionate amount of the regions' tribute and

---

5. Torres, a sympathetic scholar of Jocotán, argues that the church was a benevolent patron of the Ch'orti's, who supposedly reciprocated by voluntarily helping the padres with church construction. This may have been true some of the time, but Torres himself admits that the church's incessant requests that the Crown relieve Ch'orti's of their tribute was motivated by its desire to divert resources to itself (Torres 1994:16–17). Torres himself presents evidence that in 1725 the Jocotán priest was ordered to stop misappropriating funds and apply them to church construction as planned (1994:35), and in the early 1800s a "diabolical" Ch'orti' uprising against Padre Manuel Calderón suspended a church reconstruction project (1994:54–55). Calderón's successor, Padre Bernardo Escobar, successfully petitioned the Crown to forcibly concentrate (reducción) hiding Ch'orti's into the town center to rebuild the church (1994:57–58).

labor obligations (Feldman 1985:114; cf. Terga 1980:52–53). Ladinos, who were defined as Spanish-speaking castes of mixed blacks, Spaniards, and Indians, also began to invade the region at the turn of the seventeenth century, subjecting Ch'orti's to further economic pressures. In 1681 the town of Jocotán consisted almost entirely of the straw homes of Ch'orti's (Torres 1994:27), but by 1740, 74 Ladinos resided there,[6] and three decades later they numbered 440 (Lutz 1988:24–26, 40–41), in blatant defiance of laws prohibiting non-Indians from entering Indian communities. As a matter of protection, the Ch'orti's of Jocotán in 1754 bought the title to 597 *caballerías* (255 square kilometers) of land and later gained legal title to 38 more (Dary, Elías, and Reyna 1998:52–53). By 1778, the 4,947 Spaniards and 11,124 Ladinos in the Province of Chiquimula were the highest numbers of any province in Guatemala (Lutz 1999:130; Horizont 2004:ix).

1750–1821, Overexploitation Again

Despite the great territory, population, and wealth commanded by the Spanish Crown, its power slowly waned. The huge quantities of silver mined in Bolivia and Mexico were spent on religious wars against Protestants in northern Europe and Muslims in the Mediterranean. Spain forever lost naval supremacy when its prized armada was destroyed by England in 1588, leaving shipping vulnerable to pirates. The flood of Spanish silver and gold in Europe resulted in price inflation, such that Spanish manufactures became more expensive on the international market, reducing demand. Reliance more on the sale of raw materials than manufacturing and commerce, combined with an ongoing feudalistic economy, disadvantaged Spain as more economically dynamic northern European countries expanded their colonies and laid the foundations for the Industrial Revolution. When the French Bourbons inherited the Spanish throne from the Austrian Hapsburgs in 1713, they tried to make the colonies more profitable by professionalizing the bureaucracy, liberalizing trade, extracting more wealth, and tightening control by appointing Spaniards born in Spain (*peninsulares*) to official posts. The Crown demanded that its colonies trade only with the mother country, but American-born Creoles, who felt increasingly left out of colonial bureaucracy, could get

---

6. The governor (corregidor) of Chiquimula recorded seventy-Wve Spanish, seventeen mestizos, and eleven mulatto confessants in Jocotán that year (Torres 1994:64–70).

better prices in contraband. The Crown's greater hand in managing the colonies sparked resentment, where "I obey, but do not comply" had been the attitude since the invasion (for Central America, see Woodward [1985:61–87]).

In the Jocotán Parish, the bureaucratic changes in the mid-1700s, including increased repartimiento labor drafts, corresponded with reports of poverty, disease, and natural disaster. Ch'orti's repeatedly petitioned to reduce labor and tribute, but their falling population is testimony that such tactics were inadequate (Feldman 1982:154–67). Archbishop Cortés y Larraz ([1768–70] 1958:269–72; Documentos 1978:30), who personally inspected all Guatemalan and Salvadoran parishes from 1768 to 1770, saw fit to mention the desperate plight of Ch'orti's. He described them as naked, living large distances from the town center, refusing to participate in church activities such as mass, schooling, and baptisms, and divorcing frequently. Ch'orti's were forced to undergo baptism and confirmation despite their claims that the practices made them mortally ill. Priests married them between the ages of twelve and fourteen to exact matrimonial fees and subject them to repartimiento labor (cf. Favre 1984:48–50). Ch'orti's complained that the *corregidor* (governor) captured them, made them serve without pay as soldiers against pirates in the Golfo Dulce, and for two years had robbed them of their maize, beans, and poultry stores, causing great famine, displacement, and death. Women were forced to weave cotton cloth all year in Chiquimula without time to weave for their own families. Men were drafted to carry cloth twenty *leguas* (roughly 110 kilometers) for wages below the legal requirement. When calamities inspired the priest to hire a Ch'orti' schoolteacher at one hundred pesos to replace indolent Spanish ones who earned two-hundred-peso salaries, the corregidor blocked the move as inappropriate. Ch'orti's also complained that Jocotán's police commissioner used the slightest infraction as a pretext to whip, jail, and force them to tend his cattle, horses, and sheep. Many men fled their communities, leaving their wives, children, and communities to fend for themselves. To make matters worse, in 1784 the Crown tried to revive the waning indigo industry by legalizing the use of Indians (Dary, Elías, and Reyna 1998:67–69). As evidence of the Ch'orti's' forced travel for repartimiento labor and tribute earnings, half of Ch'orti' marriages were exogamous by municipality and 10% involved spouses from as far as Rabinal, Guatemala, and Tejutla, El Salvador, both several days away on foot (Feldman 1983:161–63).

Life became even more desperate in the last two decades of colonialism. In 1798 drought and pestilence destroyed subsistence crops (AGCA ex. 4858).

In 1801–2, thousands were killed by a scourge of yellow fever, probably contracted during three- to four-day repartimiento expeditions to the docks of Gualán and Lake Izabal, where "the contagion" was known to abound (AGCA ex. 7876). Victims underwent days of fever, chills, vomiting, and pain afflicting the entire body before being relieved by "violent" death, while those who escaped the disease awaited death by starvation (AGCA ex. 7876).

When royal investigator Piloña was sent in 1802 to scrutinize the Indians' pleas for tribute exemption, the exploitation and suffering astonished him. He ordered that tribute be pardoned immediately, that the tribute lists be adjusted to account for the multitude of deaths, and that two-thirds of the community coffers be distributed to surviving Indian widows and orphans to buy food. The aid, he ordered, must be distributed in such a way as to prevent corruption by local officials, and "these poor, needy widows and orphans will pay back the community loans when they are able, and if they are never able to pay it back, it will be money well spent." As for repartimiento labor, he demanded,

> [T]he merchants should, whether it cost double or triple, look
> for Ladino or Black volunteers to load and unload their cargo
> by canoe, and other jobs of those places of death . . . or that
> navigation of the Motagua and Polochique rivers be facilitated,
> for neither commerce nor its profits should be at the cost
> of the blood, health, and lives of the miserable, innocent
> Indians, forced against the expressed and repeated provision
> of the law, against the fatherly, benevolent intentions of the
> sovereign, and against the interests of the State, the Kingdom,
> and the Treasury, all of which hold the preservation of the
> agricultural tribute-bearers in the highest importance
> (AGCA ex. 7876:26–27).

The regional administration responded by trying to extract tribute and labor not only from the walking dead but the resting dead as well. Government authorities disregarded the dramatic fall in population and demanded tribute commensurate with the number of preplague tributaries as well as the payment of a 3,241-peso debt incurred since the famine began—equivalent to almost a year's tribute. Adding to the debt was Jocotán's Indian governor's embezzlement of 2,000 pesos of tribute (AGCA ex. 4858). There were a number of suspicious deaths, robberies, and disputes at the time, including of Jocotán's governor, a sergeant, and

Table 2: Chronology of Disasters and
Ch'orti' Disputes in Jocotán Parish

1652–54	dispute over encomienda tribute amount;[*] drought in 1653[†]
1656	Indians ask pardon for tribute[*]
1681	hurricane, great fire, two-year pardon of tribute[§*†]
1691	Indians complain of corregidor abuses[*]
1694	bad harvest[†]
1701	tribute pardoned[*]
1703	crop failure, tribute pardoned[*]
1707	Indians behind in cacao tribute[*]
1709	drought, Indians behind in cacao tribute[*]
1712	crop failure, famine, Indians behind in tribute[†*]
1717	crop failure; Indians ask pardon for tribute; pirate invasion scare[†*]
1720	drought[†]
1721	Indians ask pardon for tribute[*]
1724	Indians granted tribute reallocation to rebuild church[§]
1725	Indians ask for funds to rebuild church; wander countryside trying to earn money for tribute[§*]
1727	Indians ask pardon for tribute[*]
1729	priest complains that Indians fleeing to mountains[*]
1733–34	earthquake; Indians ask that tribute be reallocated to rebuild church; complaints of nonpayment of repartimiento wages in Alotepeque mines[§]
1738	request that tribute be reallocated to rebuild church[*]
1739	request that tribute be reallocated to rebuild church[*]
1743	earthquake[†]
1746–51	drought, crop loss, famine, and epidemics; Indians request tribute pardon; insurrection over tribute in 1749; tribute pardoned in 1750[†*]
1765	earthquake[†]
1775	many native deaths[†]
1777	many native deaths; tribute pardoned[*†]
1786	priest complains that Indians not paying tithes[§]
1794	Indians rise up against schoolteacher[*]
1801–9	locusts, epidemics, drought, famine, thousands of deaths; five-year tribute pardon; Indians ask pardon from labor drafts, withdraw to the mountains; priest granted forced labor to rebuild church[*†§]
1812	tribute pardoned[*†]
1816	funds requested to rebuild church[*§]
1817	dispute over tributes[†*]
1818	complaint of tribute exaction abuses[*]
1819	smallpox epidemic, seven thousand dead[†]
1820	priest complains of harsh treatment towards Indians[*]

[†]Feldman 1983:160   [§]Documentos Históricos   [*]Feldman 1982:146–68

others (Feldman 1982:162–65). In 1819 an additional seven thousand died in a smallpox epidemic and the struggle over tribute continued to the end of the colonial period in 1821.[7]

Though some Catholic priests were sympathetic to the Ch'orti's' suffering, others saw to their own interests first. One sent some Ch'orti's to the capital to escape the plague, but others persistently demanded that the government force the Ch'orti's (*reducción*) to cut and carry *cedro* wood for the reconstruction of the parish church. One priest complained that the Indians had rebelled and destroyed the wood for the reconstruction project, and that despite the plague, more should be forced to work because he claimed that ten thousand Indian tributaries resided in Jocotán alone, a number grossly inflated even for the 1990s. Many were avoiding their duties to the church, he lamented, by taking refuge in the mountains and furtively receiving their religious sacraments in other parishes (AGCA ex. 49630).

The Postindependence Period

What could be worse than the last decades of the colonial period? Independence from Spain in 1821. Creoles no longer had to contend with the Crown's legal protections—weak as they were—for Indian communities. Immediately in 1821 Indian common lands, or *baldías*, were declared open for private ownership, never mind that Mayas practiced shifting cultivation on such land and used it for myriad other resources. In 1825 the Indian *cabildos*, or local elected governments, were officially replaced with politically appointed *ayuntamientos constitucionales*, in which local Ladinos could replace Mayas in leadership, but already two years before, Ch'orti' elders in Chiquimula were complaining that Ladinos in the ayuntamiento were appropriating their lands (Horizont 2004:xxiii–xxv).

When the Liberals wrested control from the Conservatives in 1829, they set a course for development based on the western European Enlightenment, which stressed rationalism, science, citizenship, and education over feudalism, Catholic fundamentalism, and Indian "superstitions" (Handy 1984:36–41; Woodward 1985:90–95; Jonas 1974:121). Northern Europeans were invited to settle northeastern Guatemala, but the few British who came

---

7. Tribute throughout Central America was abolished in 1811, then reimposed in 1814, and then abolished again in 1820, though many Indian communities disregarded tribute laws after 1811 (Carmack, Gasco, and Gossen 1996:213).

simply stripped the lands of their timber and left. Ever in search of funds to pay off the national debt, the state raised the head tax on Indians, seized their cofradía coffers, and sold their common woodlands (*tierras baldías*) to foreigners. They assaulted Maya culture by outlawing Maya dress and enforcing mandatory school attendance, and stipulated that all rural residents improve the roads three days per month. Many Mayas revolted (Woodward 1985:96–104; Handy 1984:44, 48–50; Jonas 1974:122–26; Weaver 1999). In 1837, riled by state attacks on the church and a state-enforced quarantine and vaccination campaign during a cholera epidemic, campesinos in eastern Guatemala united under mestizo Rafael Carrera in rebellion. This soon became a caste war as Creoles, Ladinos, and indigenous people indiscriminately massacred each other. The Ladino and indigenous insurgents took power in 1839, and the Central American confederation of nations was dissolved (Woodward 1985:98–112).

J. L. Stephens was a US agent who traveled through the Ch'orti' region during the war. He reported that large haciendas producing corn, plantains, cochineal (a red dye), cattle, and tobacco dominated the valleys. The Ch'orti's took refuge by farming the highest, most remote mountain slopes, still cloaked by tropical and pine forests (Stephens 1969:73–74, 77, 168–69). He described Camotán as a desolate village whose native leadership, marked by their silver-headed staffs of office, led Carrera troops to detain briefly his small entourage (Stephens 1969:79–80). In nearby Esquipulas, Ch'orti's sheltered their priest, who they respected "as a counselor, friend, and father," in the mountains for six months until Liberals recaptured the town from Carrera (Stephens 1969:168–69). Stephens (1969:168) depicts Carrera's troops as "mostly Indians, ignorant, intemperate, and fanatic, who could not understand my official character, could not read my passport, and in the excited state of the country, would suspect me as a stranger."

Though the Carrera regime allowed for a political and economic opening in the rest of Guatemala, rescinding Indian head and food taxes and returning Indian communal lands (Woodward 1985:112–48; Jonas 1974:127–30; Smith 1984:202–4; Carmack 1981:333; Weaver 1999), for Ch'orti's there was little respite. Corregidor Cerna of Chiquimula, who later succeeded Carrera to the presidency in 1866, continued subsidization of agro-export crops and the alienation of Indian lands and labor (Woodward 1993:333). In 1843 and 1844, for example, he asked to rent and sell Indian communal lands to non-Indians to raise money for a government building (Horizont 2004:xxviii).

In 1871 Liberals overthrew the Conservative government, and for the next seventy-three years, Liberal dictators brought Guatemala into the age of modern repressive capitalism. All communal lands currently being rented out to non-Indians were immediately given to the renters, and cofradía lands were given to Ladinos without payment (Horizont 2004:xxiii–xxv). Ultimately, communal lands generally were opened for sale to promote coffee cultivation. A series of forced labor laws drove "Indians" to work in coffee and on state infrastructure projects, and the army was professionalized and recruited Ladinos to enforce anti-Indian measures. Five US Protestant denominations were invited to instill a work ethic in the resistant Maya populations. They divided Guatemala into five regions to prevent competition (Burnett 1988:128; McCreery 1988; Woodward 1985:149–201; Handy 1984:60–83; Jonas 1974:131–48; Lovell 1988:37–42; Smith 1984:206–10). The Friends, or Quakers, agreed to evangelize eastern Guatemala, where they still enjoy a strong influence, especially among Ladinos.

In the Jocotán Parish, the primary industries at the end of the 1800s included coffee, tobacco, sugar, cattle, rice, corn and beans, maguey fiber, and tule plant for weaving mats (*El Oriental* in Dary, Elías, and Reyna 1998:70). Already in 1870, the last year of the Carrera era, Ladinos and Indians both were planting coffee throughout the Department of Chiquimula. Large-scale operations were not possible, however, because the Ch'orti's refused to work for the miserably low 1.5 reales per day offered by the Ladinos (Cambranes 1985:149–50). Competition over highland coffee lands that same year led Ladinos in southern Jocotán to secede and form the new highland township of Santa María Olopa, where the Ch'orti's lost their communal lands (Dary, Elías, and Reyna 1998:57). In mountainous northern Jocotán, Ch'orti's also fought a string of legal battles to protect the agricultural lands in Lampocoy, where they grew dry-season milpas, but Ladinos envied it for coffee. Eventually, Jocotán's officials ceded Lampocoy to the Department of Zacapa, with which it formed the new township of Estrada Cabrera (the current Guatemalan dictator), later to become La Unión. In other areas like San Jacinto, Ladinos simply invaded Ch'orti' lands and local and regional Ladino officials refused to enforce property laws (Horizont 2004:xxx–xxxv). When communal lands were put up for sale in 1885, Ladino officials immediately sold 456.5 manzanas (790 acres) in Jocotán and continued selling the land for the next two decades. Some of these were large extensions sold to Ladinos, while others were small parcels of one to two manzanas sold back to Ch'orti's (Dary, Elías, and

Reyna 1998:51, 62–63, 108). While lands were put up for sale, the Ch'orti' population was growing steadily. Pérez (1997:107–8) reports the Ch'orti' population in the Department of Chiquimula climbed from 36,937 in 1800 to 84,942
in 1900.

The 1930s were a watershed in the Ch'orti' area and Guatemala generally. The brutality of the Liberal Reform era came to a climax in the 1930s
and 1940s under the ruthless General Jorge Ubico, which happened to be
a time when the first ethnography on Ch'orti' life was being researched
by Charles Wisdom. Wisdom's ethnography was fortuitous because it
minutely described Ch'orti' life before the momentous changes to come,
after which their localistic moral confidence would be forever shaken. Lutz
and Lovell (1990:49), reflecting upon the great pressure put on eastern
Guatemala's indigenous peoples over the centuries, remarked that any
indigenous survival into the twentieth century was "against shattering
odds." As the twentieth century wore on, the Guatemalan state and society
would at times include Ch'orti's as nonethnic, nonstigmatized campesinos, but at others would slaughter them indiscriminately. Ch'orti' culture would change so dramatically that their ancestors in the 1930s, much
less in the 1530s, would scarcely recognize or identity with them today.

THREE

Las Ruinas

Many of us died unjustly.
—Ch'orti' campesino, Olopa

The Oriente does not exist.
—Priest who tried to raise awareness of
army massacres of Ch'orti's

uatemala in the second half of the twentieth century looks very
different from the Right and Left. For the Right, Guatemala faced the
problems of small, developing countries but with the added burden
of an indigenous population preferring to live in the Stone Age. The oligarchy, with a strong, patriotic army maintaining law and order, put the
country's economy on the path to tremendous growth by 1960–80.
Everything was on the right track when guerrilla terrorists, indoctrinated
in Cuba, began stirring up trouble and fooling gullible campesinos into
thinking that they were oppressed and should take up arms. Unfortunately, the army had no other choice but to exterminate these terrorist
traitors and their followers by whatever means necessary, although the
indios did a better job of killing each other in local disputes than the army
ever did. For the Left, Guatemala was an insufferable place for the poor,
the workers, grassroots development participants, centrist and leftist
political parties, academics, artists, and others. Elections were anything

but democratic as they were overturned, thwarted, and essentially restricted to the oligarchy and the army. Although the Guatemalan economy
was growing steadily, the rich were getting richer, and the poor, poorer.
Guatemala continued to have one of the lowest, most regressive tax structures in the hemisphere, making any sort of redistribution of wealth for the
benefit of the masses impossible. In fact, the poor masses were taxed to
support the economy of the rich. Any attempts at self-improvement
through development projects or campesino cooperatives—a strategy promoted by the US Agency for International Development (USAID) as an
alternative to campesino unions—were eventually persecuted by the army,
which was trained, advised, and equipped by the United States. An armed
revolution was the only option left.

The information I have collected for the Ch'orti' area during this
period reveals both of these narratives to be one sided. Many Ch'orti's
and the development project personnel supporting them felt persecuted,
but few joined the guerrillas. Some Ch'orti's joined the army voluntarily.
Most sought to avoid violence altogether. It is clear that they were eager
for political and economic change, as local conditions were deteriorating
rapidly (discussed in chapter 6), but attempts at self-improvement would
be severely repressed under the "real politik" ideology of the Cold War.

Slavery Again, "Indians" Again

The dictatorship of General Jorge Ubico (1931–44) militarized Guatemalan
society like never before. Ubico, the only presidential candidate in the
1931 "elections," saw no contradiction between European Fascism and US
"banana republic" political economics (Gleijeses 1989:30, 42). The United
States fully supported him, hoping he would be strong enough to protect
US banana, transportation, electrical, and other economic interests during the Great Depression (Gleijeses 1989:47). After an aborted Indian-
Communist uprising in El Salvador in 1932, in which thousands of Indians
were implicated and duly hunted and killed, Ubico fanned the flames of
fear in Guatemala, claiming Communist Indians were plotting to rise up
against their non-Indian masters and rape their women. Racist Creoles
and Ladinos naturally believed him. In reality, the Guatemalan Communist Party never had more than one hundred members, and the linkage
between the party and Mayas was ludicrous.

During Ubico's thirteen-year reign of terror, "Indians" were again
forced to work without pay. Rather than having the portion of the

population that benefited from roads, railroads, and other infrastructure pay for them in taxes or tolls, in good colonial fashion Ubico had the "Indians" construct them for free. His Vagrancy Law of 1934 compelled Indians with little or no land to work for the state and private elites for at least 100–150 days per year. His police force used the age-old tactic of capturing drunken workers in poor areas on Saturday night roundups (Gleijeses 1989:26–30). In the words of Petronilo, a Ch'orti' who survived the dictatorship, "Jorge Ubico did whatever he wanted with the people. When the rich asked for people, if they wanted to build a house, they asked for the poor, humble peasants like us to go and work for free... because we always render our sweat to the rich."

To enact such naked exploitation, Ubico needed both a modern, repressive "security" apparatus along with ideological or cultural control. In 1932 he deputized landowners, making the assassination of troublesome Indian workers fully legal (Gleijeses 1989:34). He appointed a US military officer as director of the Polytechnic Military Academy, where various other US officers were also integrated. He replaced town mayors, school superintendents, and the heads of the National Radio and Transportation Ministry and other state agencies with Ladino army officers. Indian soldiers were treated like animals, poorly fed, made to sleep on the ground, given miserable salaries, and provisioned with dirty, tattered uniforms. Virtually any transgression of military code was met with the death penalty. Throughout Guatemala *orejas* (ears, i.e. spies) were commissioned, and they along with police chiefs, commanders, customs guards, rural escort troops, and rural military commissioners (*comisionados*) constituted "little Ubicos" who terrorized the population such that even in the home politics were discussed only in a low voice. In eastern Guatemala especially, the rural escort troops routinely assassinated people to set examples. In other areas of Guatemala, however, Mayas supported Ubico as a hero. He visited the countryside frequently and used Maya caciques as intermediaries, many of whom did not realize that he was responsible for the exploitation and oppression they were suffering (Gleijeses 1989; Woodward 1985:203–18; Handy 1984:92–99; Jonas 1974:148–49; Adams 1990:141–42; Carmack 1995:197–98). (Nevertheless, some Indians of western Guatemala rejoiced when Ubico fell [Oakes 1951:71].)

Ch'orti' political memory begins with this "time of slavery." The Ladinos were fully in control of the military apparatus in the area, and they wielded it tyrannically. Ch'orti's were put to work on Ladino private projects as well as on state roads and railroads (see Grieb 1979:133). For elders subjected to the forced labor at the time, the suffering and resentment still smolders. Federico and his father explained that the Ubico "law" was harsh, and elderly Juan interpreted the law as "punishment of the poor, sad people." Eusebio, whose sugarcane was destroyed to protect state alcohol monopolies and who was subject to forced labor, minced no words:

> [T]he Ubico period was a criminal dictatorship. Ay no, in those
> times they borrowed to make those, those roads. That's right.
> Those were the times when they began to make the roads
> merely with picks. . . . Earning a piece of paper [not money].
> Ah yes, it was tough! That General Ubico was tremendously
> disgusting for all of that. He was a criminal . . . and bloody,
> an evil and bloody man.

Tereso recalled that the men were bound and forced to walk all the way to Ipala and Chiquimula, some thirty to forty miles one way, to work without so much as food and water. Nicolás remembered carrying a stack of tortillas, soon to become moldy, to last an entire week. In contrast, the Ladino crew boss was paid a princely sum of Q30 (about $30) monthly. The same crew boss, explained Sesario, bound them, viciously barked orders, and forced them to work for "the rich" for "not even a nickel." According to Tereso, during the building of the Chiquimula bridge, a cement pillar fell into a pit and crushed twenty-two men. They remain buried there today.

Reminiscent of the colonial period, Ch'orti's defended themselves by evasion. Tereso and Vicente mentioned that as the corporal patrolled the aldeas on horseback searching for labor recruits or offenders of the tobacco and sugarcane prohibitions, all campesinos whispered rather than talked. Dreams and songbirds gave notice of the arrival of the mounted police and other strangers, and coyote skin belts immunized their owners against peril and enabled them to turn invisible when pursued by state patrols. Fear of forced labor and army conscription was such that all avoided the towns save for market days (Wisdom 1940:24–25, 202–37; Girard 1949: 247–48, 297, 333). Many fled the country or to nonindigenous areas. Even for those born after Ubico, the elders' stories serve as reminders of the extremes to which the Ladinos will go if given the opportunity.

During the height of World War II, in 1943, university students, workers, and professionals organized mass protests against Ubico for being anti-democratic and more reflective of the Axis than the Allies, and he surprisingly stepped down. Much to his chagrin, neither the United States nor the Guatemalan elite defended him or asked him to retake the reigns. His handpicked replacement, General Ponce, brought two thousand Indians into Guatemala City to raise the specter of a race war, but to no avail. All were tired of the arrogant dictator (Gleijeses 1989:49, 56), and the protestors eventually overthrew Ponce. Their primary goals were democracy, modernization, integration of the Indians into national society, and support of campesino and labor organizations (Woodward 1985:230–32; Handy 1984:104). Presidential elections were held in 1944, and philosophy professor Juan José Arévalo, recently returned from exile, won. He immediately enfranchised indigenous people and literate women, pushed through the enactment of a labor code to protect workers' rights to organize and strike, and reformed health care, local democracy, and education (Handy 1984:106–9; Woodward 1985:233–34).

Some Ch'orti's celebrated the fall of Ubico and the abolition of the Vagrancy Law by storming Camotán and killing three Ladino "little Ubicos." During Arévalo, many took advantage of the region's first rural schools and united to demand local elections (Girard 1949:287). When I conducted my survey in 1993, I was skeptical when many in their fifties and sixties claimed literacy because Ch'orti' adult literacy was so low (18%, or 179 per 1000, in 1993), but some eventually explained to me that Arévalo's rural schools were embraced by many and teacher salaries were raised from the 10¢ per week they earned under Ubico.

When Colonel Jacobo Arbenz Guzmán was elected president in 1950, after literally eliminating his right-wing opponent before the elections, he strengthened local democracy. State-supported peasant leagues began to challenge the traditional authority of the Maya elders (Handy 1984:113–26). Unacceptable to the United States was Arbenz's enforcement of labor standards, such that the United Fruit Company (Chiquita Brands), of which Secretary of State John Foster Dulles and brother and CIA director Allan Dulles were major shareholders, was compelled to rehire and pay back wages to seven thousand workers fired for going on strike (Handy 1984:136–40). Worse yet was Arbenz's land reform. A prolonged study of the country's land use revealed that thirty-two landowners—including United Fruit Company—possessed 1.7 million acres but cultivated only 12% of it, while campesinos cultivated 80 to 95% of their meager land base. In 1950, 88% of farms were less than 17 acres (Comisión para el

Esclarecimiento Histórico [CEH] 1999 1:84).[1] Ethnically, the average Ladino landholding was 60.5 acres versus 7.6 for Mayas (Handy 1990:165). Arbenz sought to boost production by enabling land-poor but productive campesinos to buy on credit plantations in excess of 223 acres (Jonas 1974:156–58). About 134,000 families, the majority indigenous, including Ch'orti's, quickly claimed 16% of these lands, and half of these families received government credit for agricultural development (CEH 1999 1:102). In the whirlwind of activity, campesinos and plantation peons competed with each other and some expropriated lands illegally. Some Ladinos complain that Ch'orti's rashly expropriated their land without government approval, a reminder for them of the lengths to which Ch'orti's would go if given the chance. Most Ch'orti's, however, did not take part in the land reform for fear of a Ladino revenge.

This restraint proved prudent because the church, the plantation owners, and disgruntled army officers united behind the US State Department in accusing Arbenz of being a Communist. The CIA orchestrated an invasion of "liberation" forces into the Department of Chiquimula, which was bolstered by air raids on major Guatemalan cities and a mass misinformation campaign, making the "liberation army" seem larger and more popular than it really was. Arbenz appealed to the United Nations (UN), and the UN Security Council passed a resolution prohibiting foreign involvement in Guatemala. In a move that set a precedent for the next half century, the United States ignored the resolution and world opinion. The Guatemalan army was sharply divided as to whether to defend the country or not, compelling Arbenz to abdicate in June 1954. The United States flew the new dictator, a little-known colonel named Carlos Castillo Armas, into Guatemala City on Ambassador Peurifoy's private plane. The ambassador promptly gave him a black list of radicals—collaborators and beneficiaries of Arévalo's and Arbenz's reforms—to be neutralized, just as he had drawn up when he was ambassador to Greece (Handy 1984:127–51; cf. Wasserstrom 1976; Jonas 1974:156–69; Woodward 1985:238–41; Black 1984:16–18). Castillo named José Bernabé Linares, the hated chief of Ubico's secret police, as head of national security. Between July and November of 1954, the list of "Communists" grew

---

1. The Comisión para el Esclarecimiento Histórico (CEH) is the truth commission report stipulated by the Peace Accords of 1996 and supported by various European countries, the United States, Canada, Japan, the Guatemalan government, the United Nations, the American Association for the Advancement of Sciences, and the Robert F. Kennedy Center for Human Rights (CEH 1999 1:30).

to seventy-two thousand civilians. The Armas regime arrested between nine and fourteen thousand civilians and executed two to five thousand, particularly campesinos organized in unions in eastern Guatemala, including seven United Fruit Company union leaders (Cullather 2004:151; CEH 1999 1:108–9, 353, Anexo 1:278; May 2001:5–6). In October 1954, the army held a plebiscite and Castillo "won" 99.9% of the vote for president (CEH 1999 1:111).

The 1945 constitution was immediately annulled, including the voting rights of two-thirds of the country who were illiterate, and the Labor Code of 1947 was rescinded, making it illegal for agricultural workers to organize unless their employers had more than five hundred employees, 60% of whom had to be literate. Within a year after the coup union membership declined from one hundred thousand to twenty-seven thousand. Ninety-nine percent of the land redistributed under the reform was returned, prompting corn production to fall by 15%. With the help of US aid, Castillo claimed to carry out his own land reform, led by an agricultural oversight board on which not a single campesino was included. The land problem was "solved" not by returning lands to peasants, but by opening the Petén rainforest for settlement.

The state electric company established during the Arbenz administration was turned over to its only competitor, the US United Fruit Company–controlled Electric Bond and Share. Other small corporations supported by Arbenz to boost national industrialization were bought by major US corporations such as Goodyear Tires, General Mills, Coca-Cola Company, Pillsbury, and Purina. Petroleum exploration in northern Guatemala was deregulated, and eight of the largest US petroleum companies quickly bought rights for exploration. The church, an avid supporter of Castillo's "liberation," regained the rights it had lost under the Liberal reforms, and foreign missionaries were again invited to change Maya culture. Because the United States wanted Guatemala to exemplify the advantages of capitalism over Communism, it pumped $100 million in aid into Guatemala while giving the rest of Latin America only $80 million, and the World Bank began granting loans to Guatemala again (Cullather 2004:151; May 2001:79, 81; Handy 1984:185–91; Jonas 1974:169–71, 182). Castillo Armas was assassinated in 1957, and General Ydígoras Fuentes, who was notorious for being the enforcer of Ubico's Vagrancy Law and commanding his troops to rape Maya women and abduct their children, took over. He lost the subsequent election in 1958, but the army gave him the presidency anyway, after which he corruptly sold public lands to private investors without addressing the land distribution problem (Cullather 2004:66–67, 154; Handy 1984:171).

In the Jocotán Parish, the "liberation" meant that campesino leaders and collaborators with the Arbenz administration were assassinated or forced to flee from army sweeps of the aldeas. One of Castillo's officers was given a free hand to massacre Ch'orti' participants in the land reform, some of whom who had settled on his father's land. An elderly Ladino bragged how he and other Ladinos courageously fought in Castillo's "liberation" army to oust the "Communists." A decade later, he was a foundational member of the right-wing death squad The White Hand (La Mano Blanca), which was akin to a Ku Klux Klan brigade in the Guatemalan army. On the cultural or ideological front, foreign Catholic missionaries, including North American friars in Esquipulas and Italian and Belgian priests in the Jocotán Parish, entered the Ch'orti' area to convert Ch'orti's more fully to Catholicism.

Las Ruinas

In the 1950s and 1960s, as US foreign policy was dominated by Cold War "real politic," the US military establishment and university professors formulated the National Security Doctrine. This was a plan to replace unpredictable and unstable democratic institutions like political parties, elections, social organizations, and economic competition with tightened military control. Tens of thousands of Latin American military officers would be trained in the US School of the Americas in the Panama Canal Zone and later Fort Benning, Georgia, many of whom would later commit unspeakable human rights abuses in their own countries. With no conceivable Soviet invasion of Latin America, the "subversive" targets of "national security" were anyone who criticized military rule or might become a Communist revolutionary. According to the "US Overseas Internal Defense Policy" (OIDP) during the Kennedy administration (1961–63), all such "latent" subversion was to be eliminated by US-orchestrated intelligence forces before it formed (CEH 1999 1:118, 120), a preemptive strike on progressive civilians.

In 1960 discontented army officers, some of whom were loyal to the democratic governments of 1944–54, attempted a coup to regain Guatemalan sovereignty from the United States. The coup failed miserably, but the surviving coup leaders, still encouraged by Castro's overthrow of the US-backed Batista dictatorship in 1959 and the experience of democracy in 1944–54, reconstituted themselves. They received Cuban training in guerrilla warfare and in 1962 formed two guerrilla fronts in eastern Guatemala:

the November 13 Revolutionary Movement (MR-13) in Izabal and the Rebel Armed Forces (FAR) in Zacapa and Chiquimula. That same year, mass rebellions against Ydígoras's corrupt presidency were shockingly repressed. The Catholic Church supported the repression and the three major political parties (MLN [National Liberation Movement], PR [Revolutionary Party], and DC [Christian Democrats]), which had secretly made an "anticommunist" pact in 1960, remained suspiciously silent. Consequently, the revolutionary movement was soon joined by students, teachers, campesinos, urban workers, professionals, and the outlawed Guatemalan Workers' Party (PGT) (CEH 1999 1:123, 127; Handy 1984:230–31; Woodward 1985:242; Adams 1970:216). The repression and its support by the oligarchy, therefore, fulfilled the US National Security Doctrine prophecy that social critics would become subversive revolutionaries. During the run-up to the 1963 elections, in which it seemed that Juan José Arévalo would regain the presidency, the US-backed army overthrew Ydígoras and installed General Peralta Azurdia. Peralta promptly declared a state of siege under which all political activity was suspended and many leftist politicians were exiled, imprisoned, or executed (CEH 1999 1:131; Handy 1984:154–55; Jonas 1974:206; Black 1984:21; Woodward 1985:242–43).

Key to Guatemalan Dictators and Presidents
General Jorge Ubico: 1931–44
Dr. Juan José Arévalo: 1945–50
Colonel Jacobo Arbenz Guzmán: 1951–54
Colonel Carlos Castillo Armas: 1954–57
General José Miguel Ramón Ydígoras Fuentes: 1958–63
General Alfredo Enrique Peralta Azurdia: 1963–66
Julio César Méndez Montenegro: 1966–70
Colonel Carlos Manuel Arana Osorio: 1970–74
General Kjell Eugenio Laugerud García: 1974–78
General Fernando Romeo Lucas García: 1978–82
General José Efraín Ríos Montt: 1982–83
General Óscar Humberto Mejía Víctores: 1983–86
Marco Vinicio Cerezo Arévalo: 1986–91
Jorge Antonio Serrano Elías: 1991–93
Ramiro de León Carpio: 1993–96
Álvaro Enrique Arzú Irigoyen: 1996–2000
Alfonso Antonio Portillo Cabrera: 2000–2003
Óscar Berger Perdomo: 2004–

Peralta's state of siege from 1963 to 1966 resulted in the guerrillas gaining more strength and popularity. The autobiography of Julio César
Macías, whose nom de guerre was César Montes, offers a rare look into
guerrilla life at the time. They endured severe hardships like lack of food
and water in the mountains of eastern Guatemala and knew well the risks
of being captured, tortured, and executed in the cruelest ways imaginable. Various family members of Macías were tortured and killed by the
military even though they were not collaborators, including his brother
Jorge Victor, who died as a result of eighty bone fractures (Macías
1999:157). What motivated the guerrillas was a strong sense of destiny, the
idea that they were heroes, and that they were supported by many honorable Guatemalans, the international avant-garde, and Communist countries like Cuba. And without the backing of some eastern Guatemalan
campesinos, they would have been exterminated immediately. The life of
the guerrilla was seen by the international press to be sexy and adventur-
ous, and for some like Macías, it certainly was, even amidst the tortures
and executions of loved ones.

The United States, in the meantime, was equally convinced of its righteousness and was willing to use all means necessary to prevent "another
Cuba." It began a double-edged campaign against "Communism" in developing countries by both strengthening military aid and co-opting the poor
through grassroots development, which under the Kennedy administration
(1961–63) crystallized into the Alliance for Progress. To replace the campesino leagues or unions seeking land, labor protections, agricultural inputs,
and rural infrastructure, it established rural cooperatives, in which peasants pooled their resources, were trained by technicians from groups like
the Peace Corps, and created economies of scale for enhanced market
competition. USAID also funded infrastructure projects such as road and
school construction, serving both development and military functions. In
the 1960s USAID began promoting green revolution fertilizers and pesticides that increased production enormously but also made campesinos
economically dependent. These efforts were complemented by the Catholic Church's Catholic Action Network, which used European and American clergy to proselytize against Protestantism, indigenous spirituality, and
Marxism as well as promote cooperative development assistance. Already
in the 1960s, however, repression against the cooperatives motivated some
campesinos to reunite with the remnants of campesino leagues (May
2001:82, 87, 89, 94, 100–101; CEH 1999 1:137–38; Davis and Hodson 1983;
Carmack 1988; Warren 1989; Arias 1990; Earle 2001). Meanwhile, wages in the

Ch'orti' area remained the lowest in the country at Q.25 per day, accounting not only for their frequent attempts to organize but their seasonal migration to coffee plantations in Zacapa (Adams 1970:113, 129–32, 160–61, 388) and cotton and sugarcane plantations on the south coast.

On the military front, the US military establishment provided military assessors, training, vehicles, clothing, planes, helicopters, the most modern communications, and logistical support to the Guatemalan army (CEH 1999 1:142; Oficina de Derechos Humanos del Arzobispado de Guatemala [ODHAG] 1998 2:70). It also provided napalm bombs, from which shrapnel burns even after it is embedded in flesh and which were used against civilian populations where the guerrillas were active (Macías 1999:152). Reminiscent of the Ubico years and portending the Vietnam War, thousands of local military commissioners were deputized to serve as army intelligence and tyrannically accuse any disagreeable neighbors of subversion. The number of commissioners rose from three hundred during Ydígoras's reign to nine thousand under Peralta Azurdia. Soon, these military commissioners and spies, or orejas (ears), were working in tandem with thirty-five different death squads, fifteen of which were formed by the army in 1966 with collaboration from the MLN fascist party. In the Ch'orti' area, death squads had formed long before 1966 and were identified by the Ladino surnames: los Pachecos, los Portillos, and los Interianos (CEH 1999 1:143, 2a:163, 2b:181–82; Handy 1984:161–63; McClintock 1985 in Warren 1993:28).

In the Ch'orti' area, las ruinas of the 1960s were rooted in Ladino reactions to Arbenz's reforms.[2] After 1954, repression against Ch'orti' members of Arbenz's Local Agrarian Committees and campesino leagues, which organized for grassroots development and land reform, were harshly persecuted by the Ladino death squads, and according to one Camotán man, their bodies littered the streets. When in 1957 campesinos again began to secretly join the newly formed PR party—considered the legacy party of the Arbenz government—death squads ferociously persecuted them. The death squads, composed of fascist Ladino MLN military commissioners, followed a pattern of wearing campesino clothing during their actions (CEH 1999 2a:117). Ladinos not only repressed any campesino organization, but some expanded control over the best coffee, cattle, maize, and beans lands, as well as

2. I base this reconstruction on information from my informants, Diener (1978), May (2001:57), and the CEH (1999 IIa:52, 137–38, 141, 159–61, 181–82, 330, 351, 353, Anexo 1:277–82, Anexo 2:271–85).

extracting "ritual rents" by monopolizing sales of candles and incense used in Ch'orti' ceremonies (Diener 1978). For example, in 1960 Angel López Hernández of El Cumbre, Olopa, was denounced as a guerrilla and killed by military commissioners who sought to acquire his land (CEH 1999 2a:383). The neighboring aldeas of Amatillo, Olopa, and Carboneras, Esquipulas, were particularly sought by los Pachecos death squad for their flat, well-watered pasture lands, and eventually the communities were completely annihilated. Other Ch'orti's were denounced because they were late repaying a debt or simply did not show Ladinos the proper "respect" demanded of their racial status. The army characteristically followed up accusations with torture and murder.

The killings accelerated as the 1960s advanced. In 1962 Hilario Ramos of El Carrizal, Olopa, was kidnapped by local military commissioners, who turned him over to the army barracks in Olopa, where he was tortured for two months and executed (CEH 1999 2a:383). In 1963 Alfonso Pérez Ramírez of Piedra de Amolar, Olopa, was murdered by commissioners and the army, and Gabino López of the aldea Guayabillas, Jocotán, was executed by local military commissioners and his body left to be eaten by dogs (CEH 1999 Anexo 2:Caso 1025).

As early as 1964 FAR guerrillas began using the Ch'orti' area as a corridor between the Motagua Valley and Honduras. They had been trying to recruit Ch'orti's on the northern plantations, and twenty entered the Ch'orti' area itself to recruit (Diener 1978:110; see Adams 1970:216). They allied with the Ch'orti' agrarian movement and PR members, promising the Ch'orti's land and freedom. In the summer of 1965 the FAR killed two brothers—likely military informers—in a tract of pine forest twelve miles to the north of Olopa in the aldea of Guayabillas, Jocotán, which was the gateway between the main theater of guerrilla operations in the Motagua Valley and the Ch'orti' area (Macías 1999:221). In September 1965, the army responded by massacring five men (CEH 1999 Anexo 2:276), and nine days later they bombarded Guayabillas with napalm, captured fifty displaced campesinos, and massacred and burned them. The army set up an encampment in neighboring Tierra Blanca, and all campesinos of both aldeas fled (CEH 1999 Anexo 2:277).

About thirty miles south in the same year, some Ch'orti' activists organized under the cover of diminutive saints' images that were passed from aldea to aldea. When a Ch'orti' named Gregorio Ramos from the aldea Tuticopote Arriba, Olopa, killed a Ladino's cow for grazing in his bean field, he, along with the image of San Antonio del Fuego (St. Anthony of Fire) that he housed, became symbols of resistance. Some Ladinos described Ramos as nothing but a simple, illiterate, unarmed campesino. In November 1965, he and six other men were captured in the aldea El Carrizal, Olopa and executed by the army. Ramos's son Natividad and others continued the San Antonio cult and began assassinating oppressive Ladinos (CEH 1999 Anexo 2:Caso 1076; Diener 1978).

Nationally, 1966 proved to be a turning point in the conflict. Although the three major political parties had signed the anticommunist pact, they competed against each other in the 1966 elections. The MLN and the DC both ran army officers for president, while the PR fielded a civilian, Julio César Méndez Montenegro, who promised to reinstitute some of the reforms of 1944–54. Leftists, including guerrillas and their civilian bases, supported the PR, which won. Stunned, the army and MLN forced Méndez Montenegro into a compromise relinquishing the position of commander in chief of the armed forces (CEH 1999 1:134). Not realizing this, the guerrillas offered a unilateral cease-fire when Méndez Montenegro took the presidency, only to suffer an all-out army attack under Colonel Arana Osorio, "the Butcher of Zacapa," fully equipped and advised by the US Army (Handy 1984:160–62, 230–36; Jonas 1974:203–7; Black 1984:23–24, 76–78; McClintock 1985 in Warren 1993:28). The assault was greatly aided by key intelligence from the USAID Public Safety Division, which procured information about guerrilla hideouts and civilian supporters. CIA records document that thirty-three high-ranking guerrilla leaders and supporters were captured, tortured, and thrown from a plane over the ocean (CEH 1999 1:136; Macías 1999:115–19). Military commissioners and MLN death squads began mass killings of political undesirables in eastern Guatemala, especially members of the PR and campesino leagues seeking labor rights on plantations, resolution of land disputes, development projects like bridges, roads, schools, and drinking water, and an end to municipal forced labor and corruption (CEH 1999 1:137–38, 353; May 2001:151).

The Ch'orti' *municipios*, unlike the rest of Maya Guatemala, voted for the PR in the 1966 elections (Adams 1970:208), and consequently suffered severely. In Olopa, the army established a base in November 1966, after which it began assassinating upwards of three hundred campesinos, including Natividad Ramos, who were in any way connected with campesino organizations, the PR, the saint cults, or spoke Ch'orti' (CEH 1999 Anexo 2:271–87). Olopa's priest was persecuted by the army and forced to flee. His successor, an American-born priest (Padre Fernando), confiscated the image of San Antonio del Fuego and its whereabouts is unknown.[3]

Typically, death squads captured suspects, turned them over to the army for torture and execution, and with the information provided, reliable or not, they returned to the same area to capture more. For example, in June 1966 they killed two brothers in the aldea Cajón del Río, Camotán, and soon thereafter in neighboring Guayabo captured, interrogated, and killed two campesino PR members (CEH 1999 Anexo 2:283). In December 1966, two Ch'orti' PR members, one from Carboneras, Olopa, and the other from Piedra de Amolar, Olopa, were captured by los Pachecos, tortured, and killed (CEH 1999 2a:394). Eleven days later three more men were captured in Piedra de Amolar, tortured in front of the entire community, and killed, with their bodies left to be eaten by dogs (CEH 1999 Anexo 2:272, 2a:177). Three weeks later military commissioners captured four Ch'orti's in El Carrizal, Olopa, after which they were killed in military barracks (CEH 1999 Anexo 2:282). Eleven days later two more men and a boy from El Carrizal were captured by military commissioners, interrogated, and killed (CEH 1999 Anexo 2:282).

In one notorious case (CEH 1999 Anexo 1:277–82), Cajón del Río and other neighboring Camotán aldeas had been active in Local Agrarian Committees since Arbenz. When the army began operating out of Olopa in late 1966, the leader of the agrarian movement, Agustín Pérez, escaped capture, but his paperwork, with the names of agrarian movement participants, was discovered by the army. On the night of February 7, 1967, seven soldiers captured thirteen members, made them dig graves, shot them, and buried them. One fleeing campesino was also gunned down on the spot. Others managed to escape to Honduras where they remain today. The aldea of Cajón del Río ceased to exist, prompting its designation by famous author Eduardo Galeano (1980:184) as the community "without people."

The following history by a Ch'orti' octogenarian of Olopa evokes the sense of both terror and outrage over las ruinas, in particular the events leading to the priest's exile.

R: Aaaah, that one [Colonel Arana Osorio] combated the God of the Mountains [San Antonio] with airplanes. . . . Many of us died

---

3. I have been told of massacres in the following Olopa aldeas: Paternita, Cerrón, Piedra de Amolar, Cayur, Carrizal, Carboneras (Esquipulas), Tituque, Agua Blanca, Roblarcito, Tuticopote, La Prensa, Las Palmas, Nochán, and Amatillo.

unjustly. . . . Such that we hated ourselves. . . . And no. Only
for envy.

Brent: Envy by whom?

R: The townspeople . . . [we were] so-called guerrillas,
they said. We were with the guerrillas but we are nothing
[laughs]. . . . And so Arana fought the mountains with
helicopters. . . . There was a military commissioner that went
to accuse you. If he merely didn't like you, he accused you.
Once there was a boy lying here already dead. Horrible . . .
they only passed misinformation about the people. . . .
Envious, yeah, and the day arrived when they were killed
over there. . . . And buried. . . . Ah many strange men came here.
I took care since I have children. There are six of us. Only
my kids. And he believed I was having a meeting, a session.
But it was a lie, they were fooled . . .

Brent: And many were killed here, or just a few?

R: Oh God.

Brent: Many here in this same aldea?

R: Oh God, in this aldea there were a lot. A lot. By the army.
And there I was in the military compound. There were five
hundred. Asking, asking, asking, because one was tied up here
and dragged over there like pigs, hands tied. . . . The next day to
be killed. . . . One mayor was to be killed for being a guerrilla.
Ol' Juan de Dios Ramos. A political guerrilla. But he wasn't. He
was tied up, brought, and was to be killed over there. So, so the
colonel said, "Bring him over there and kill him, but first take
him to the padre to confess. Take him to the church to confess
to the padre, and bring the padre back to me alone." So, the
padre said, "If you want to kill a Christian," he said, "like these
people here, you'd better kill me first, I'll sacrifice myself. Kill
me first." Ah, they took off their berets and they didn't want to
kill him. So they went to ask it of others, "I don't want to, I don't
want to," and they let him go free and said "Get out of here,
they're not going to kill you" . . . that's what the colonel said.
"Let him go," while I was looking. And the poor man was set free
and he left without his hat or anything . . . once and for all. He
[the padre] went to Jocotán, to the mountains, and today he
lives in the Petén. That's where he is, he "liberates." But it was
the padre. Many are in the Petén. We became expatriated.

By the end of 1966 the FAR was driven from the Sierra de las Minas of Zacapa, on the other side of the Motagua, and some took refuge in the few remaining patches of Ch'orti' pine forests. They recruited a few campesinos and dug arms caches and trained on the weekends, returning by bus to their city jobs during the week. At least one aldea guerrilla "committee" was established at the end of 1967 but undertook only limited actions, such as killing some aldea army commissioners. Most Ch'orti's remained uninvolved politically according to one padre, who explained: "There's a lot of violence in Ch'orti' culture, but because of alcoholism and disputes over land, not because of political struggle. In fact, political power is very secondary for them." Regardless of their political involvement or sophistication, the killing continued. Some were the products of trigger-happy military commissioners, as in the case of a Ch'orti' killed while gathering firewood near Jocotán's cemetery (ODHAG 1998 3:52). The guerrillas were nearly extinguished by 1968, but the killings continued unabated and spread from Olopa and Camotán to Jocotán and Esquipulas (CEH 1999 Anexo 2:273–87). The last major incident in this wave of violence was the capture and disappearance of seven suspected guerrillas in Piedra de Amolar, Olopa, in September 1969 (CEH 1999 Anexo 2:284).

The number of deaths in eastern Guatemala in the 1960s is difficult to ascertain. The CEH (1999 1:73) estimates ten thousand, and the Catholic Church's investigation (ODHAG 1999 3:54) yielded an estimate of eight to twenty thousand. Jonas (1974) calculated that though there were never more than three to five hundred guerrillas, six thousand to ten thousand civilians were slaughtered, and May (2001:57) counts eight thousand from 1966 to 1970 alone. Guerrilla commander "César Montes" estimates six thousand dead in 1966–67 alone, while for the same period *Time* magazine speculated three thousand deaths, only eighty of whom were guerrillas and five hundred of whom were sympathizers (Macías 1999:151). One padre who lived in the area his entire life insisted on fifty thousand dead. Besides the dead, the Ch'orti' area lost hundreds of refugees who fled to northern Guatemala and Honduras, comprising the first mass displacements of the so-called civil war (CEH 1999 2a:215).

Political activity and repression subsided in 1969–71, but the army had by no means won over the population. When Colonel Carlos Arana Osorio, whose troops perpetrated most of the human rights abuses of the 1960s, "won" the presidency in 1970, he did so with only 4% of the popular vote, indicating Guatemalans' lack of faith in the political process. Demonstrations and protests soon began again with a miners' protest and a teachers' strike in the early 1970s, both of which garnered massive popular support.

The Guatemalan military government emphasized the stick of repression rather than the carrot of development programs. Most of the twelve thousand political victims from 1970 to 1977 were members of political parties in the capital and campesino activists in the Oriente, including Ch'orti's at the hands of MLN military commissioners (CEH 1999 1:73, 2a:331). The CEH documented three assassinations by Olopa military commissioners in 1971, and in 1972 it documented the capture of a PR member in Pacrén, Jocotán, whose dead body had its ear, tongue, testicles, and eyes excised (CEH 1999 Anexo 2:273–74, 282). In 1973 los Pachecos perpetrated another notorious massacre. As Diener (1978:107), the CEH (1999 Anexo 2:277), and my informants tell it, Ricardo Guevarra was a relatively prosperous campesino who started a Friends congregation in El Cerrón, Olopa (or neighboring El Tablón, according to Diener). Diener reports that Guevarra preached against the purchase of ritual items, thereby threatening Ladino business interests, but my informants emphasize that his neighbors and the townspeople were envious of his economic success and accused him of being a guerrilla (cf. Warren 1993:38, 48). He and several converts were abducted and later assassinated. One of my sources relates that after being abducted by the death squad, the Friends were taken into custody by the army and tortured for several weeks until it was realized that they were not guerrillas. They were butchered so badly, however, that the army would have lost face by releasing them. They were never found alive.

In 1974 guerrillas reentered the Ch'orti' area (Diener 1978:111). According to my informants, Ladino ranchers continued expanding their cattle lands into eastern Jocotán and southern Camotán, and rebels responded that year by burning an American's ranch in San José Las Lágrimas, Camotán, and a large landowner's truck in Nearar, Camotán. According to the CEH (1999 Anexo 2:285), guerrillas executed two orejas in El Carrizal, Olopa, in May 1974, and another man and boy in El Cerrón, Olopa, in November (1999 Anexo 2:274, 280, 282). The Valentín Ramos Front (whose relation to Gregorio and Natividad Ramos is unknown) then emerged in 1976, killing some military commissioners and informers, upon whom they left a blacklist of others to be killed (CEH 1999 Anexo 2:286–87). Many rumors and stories of Valentín Ramos persist to this day, in which he evades torture and death by turning himself into a plant or animal. The Guerrilla Army of the Poor (EGP), the largest national guerrilla contingent in the 1970s and 1980s, killed an auxiliary mayor in La Marimba, Camotán, in 1978 (CEH 1999 2b:481, Anexo 2:286).

Assassinations by military commissioners accelerated again, especially in the three contiguous aldeas of El Carrizal and Amatillo, Olopa, and Carboneras, Esquipulas, and the four contiguous aldeas of San José Las Lagrimas and Marimba, Camotán, and Naranjo and Colmenas, Jocotán (CEH 1999 Anexo 2:274–87). In Naranjo, military commissioners and the army massacred eight men in 1975. In another notorious case, two men from Tituque, Olopa, were owed Q.30 (about $.30) by a local Ladino landowner, but rather than pay up, the landowner accused them of being guerrillas, and they were executed (CEH 1999 Anexo 2:275). The commissioners also attacked strangers visiting from other parts of the country. For example, in Olopa on Christmas 1977, los Pachecos murdered four unidentified men and one local man (CEH 1999 Anexo 2:279). A Church catechist was also assassinated in 1977 (CEH 1999 Anexo 2:287).

With the combination of anticommunist hysteria, power hungry commissioners and orejas, death squads dressed as campesinos, campesinos envious of their neighbors, religious persecution, greedy Ladinos, and army persecution of government projects, it was difficult to sort out who was behind acts of violence (cf. Warren 1993:49). Some even doubt guerrilla activity in the area whatsoever. One Ladino claimed that the guerrillas killed no one in Olopa, and he suspected that death squads and the army were the sole perpetrators of all the killings. No one knows of a single battle between the guerrillas and the army, he added, and not a single soldier was ever killed. Once, when a close acquaintance of his was returning home with a rabbit after hunting, he was approached by a man in civilian clothes near the old barracks in Tituque. The man offered him money and guns if he would join the guerrillas, but the hunter refused. The man pressed him and then took his rabbit, and fifteen minutes later the hunter's sister saw the thief with the rabbit laughing among soldiers. He claims that on more than one occasion in the 1970s he saw the soldiers leave the barracks at night dressed in campesino clothing and return before dawn, followed by reports of assassinations and guerrilla activity in the area. He also recalled a case that Diener (1978:94) mentioned, in which three bodies dressed in camouflage were found shot and floating in Lake Tuticopote, Olopa. Many believe these were guerrillas, but he doubted whether guerrillas would foolishly dress so obviously. In Diener's version, residents of Tuticopote had been locked in a bitter land dispute with a powerful Ladino, after which three men were killed in the same aldea on two separate occasions. Two of the dead men in the lake were purportedly dressed in Ch'orti' white pajama-type clothing, but underneath they wore expensive clothing and had white skin, portending their probable links to death squads.

Many campesinos in Jocotán, perhaps out of self-defense or lack of direct contact, also refute the guerrillas' presence. One angrily insisted,

> [I]t was accusation only. They all died from accusations. If some commissioner thought one was a guerrilla, he merely said so. The state was seriously against us. So, the order was given that anyone who was a guerrilla was to be taken out, and *just* like that the security forces did so. And so the commissioners would say "that one there is a guerrilla," and it wasn't so! They didn't kill a single guerrilla.

One rural Ch'orti' informant living near the most violent aldeas recalled several innocent people who were killed but could report only a few cases in which known guerrillas or guerrilla sympathizers were killed. On at least two separate occasions suspected guerrilla sympathizers were trapped by the army in towns, tied to the bumpers of jeeps, and dragged to death from Jocotán to Olopa in one case and Jocotán to Zacapa in another. One guerrilla was pursued by the army through his aldea after he robbed a bus between Jocotán and San Juan, and he was captured and killed. Others were ambushed at their hideout on a forested peak and killed.

In Guatemala generally, the repression and military dictatorship, far from intimidating campesinos into submission, served as a catalyst for organized resistance. The Committee for Campesino Unity (CUC) formed in 1973 and slowly gained massive support throughout the country, and in 1977, one hundred thousand campesinos marched on the capital (May 2001:64). In 1978 the oligarchy was shocked at the massive protests against a 100% fare increase in public transportation, upon which the poor depended. Only 15% of the voting public participated in the rigged 1978 presidential elections, which General Fernando Romeo Lucas García won by default. The army responded to the discontent with increased repression, considering all campesino activists, catechists, union members, students, and malcontents of any sort legitimate targets of repression. Fascist death squads from eastern Guatemala now operated throughout the country, and they continued to disguise themselves as eastern Guatemalan campesinos. This sparked more campesino organization, and in

1980 untold thousands of CUC members held a strike on cotton and sug-arcane plantations despite army repression. In the 1982 elections, the two Social Democrat candidates, both moderates predicted to win, were assassinated on the days they registered their parties for the election. At the funeral of one of the leaders, Manuel Alberto Colom Argueta, two hundred thousand people defied the army by attending (Handy 1984: 176–83; CEH 1999 2a:117).

Due partly to the army's blockade of all avenues of reform, develop-ment, and democracy, throughout the 1970s the guerrillas made a slow recovery. To some extent they co-opted campesino organizations, unions, and other popular movements that now contemplated whether armed struggle was the only hope of change. The Sandinista guerrillas' success-ful overthrow of the US-backed Somoza dictatorship in Nicaragua in 1979 created the sense that a major opportunity was at hand, even if guerrillas did not yet have the popular support or arms to seize it. The US Congress had blocked military aid to Guatemala in 1977 due to the army's human rights abuses, but the Reagan administration (1981–88) was more deter-mined than ever to help the Central American armies crush the guerrilla movements rather than negotiate. Guatemala continued to receive mili-tary aid from the United States, including via the US-supported apartheid regimes of South Africa and Israel (Bodman-Smith 2002; Handy 1984: 172–74; Black 1984:161–62). Soon after Reagan took office, the neoconser-vative Evangelical Protestant general José Efraín Ríos Montt was brought to power in a military coup and immediately embraced by US ambas-sador Chapin (Black 1984:160). The army violence then began in earnest. During his eighteen months in power, any potential bases of guerrilla support, whether Catholic groups, human rights groups, social workers, artists, union members, students, professors, and most of all, Mayas, were methodically executed in the most hideous ways imaginable. Hun-dreds of Maya villages were ethnically cleansed, as tens of thousands of men, women, children, elderly, and sick were tortured and killed, and all their possessions, including crops, animals, and pets, stolen or destroyed. The CEH (1999 1:73) cites that of the 132,000 estimated dead from 1978 to 1996, the vast majority were in 1981–83.

Though the Guatemalan Right and neoconservative Evangelicals try to shield Ríos from blame, saying that he did not know of the massacres or could not control his own army, he himself justified the massacres: "Look, the problem of the war is not only a question of who's shooting. For everyone that shoots, there's ten working behind the scenes" (ODHAG

1998 2:5). One of his Evangelical spokesman elaborated (ODHAG 1998 2:5): "The guerrillas won a lot of collaborators among the Indians. Therefore, the Indians are subversives. Right? And how does one fight against subversion? Clearly, one must kill the Indians, because they're collaborating with subversion. And then they'll say, 'they're killing innocent people.' But they're not innocent: they have sold themselves to subversion." In religious terms, Mayas were evil, demonic, and met a righteous end. Meanwhile, rather than condemn the genocide, the Reagan administration did its best to cover it up, accusing Amnesty International, School of the Americas Watch, and the Washington Office on Latin America of exaggerating the human rights abuses (Black 1984:169). The US military establishment trained Guatemalan officers and financially supported the state throughout the war. US military, development, and food aid continued unabated throughout the violence, from a total of $124 million in the 1960s, to $225.2 million in the 1970s, $1,142.8 million in the genocidal 1980s, and $546.7 million from 1990 to 1996 (Bodman-Smith 2002).

The Ríos regime did indeed seem to be correct about mass Maya support for radical change, as hundreds of thousands, especially disenfranchised Mayas, were united in opposition to the regime, even if they did not necessarily support armed conflict (cf. Adams 1988:286–87). The question of whether this opposition was duped into supporting the guerrillas, forced to take sides because they were caught in the crossfire, or had a political affinity for the guerrillas is hotly debated. Only three to five thousand men and women composed the guerrillas at their maximum, and many of these were short on weapons and ammunition. The population was not really caught between two armies as much as it was caught between lightly armed guerrilla bands and a powerful army of forty thousand backed by the most powerful military apparatus on the planet. The guerrillas could not defend their base population, and it was "open season" for the army, whose ultimate desire was to control the population. Of every five army or Civilian Defense Patrol (PAC) massacres, only one was triggered by guerrilla presence in the area. The army forcibly enlisted only Mayas and conscripted entire Maya communities into PACs, which were forced to patrol—and often terrorize—their own communities (ODHAG 1998 2:7; cf. Carmack 1988:22–24).

Any treatment of the war without explicit mention of the barbarous atrocities committed by the army would be to whitewash Guatemalan history. The CEH and ODHAG truth commissions provide countless testimonies. The following are just a few examples taken from the ODHAG

Proyecto Interdiocesano de Recuperación de la Memoria Histórica (REMHI) report.

> They took the women 10–15 at a time, threw them into houses, and burned them, while they took their children by the feet and smashed their heads against the houseposts. (ODHAG 1998 2:5)

> They held them for two days [in the market] and the soldiers stuck red hot wires from their mouths to their stomachs. Others they kicked, regardless of whether they were toddlers or women, or if they were pregnant; they spared no one. (ODHAG 1998 2:12)

> To some they cut their throats with machetes, to others they split their heads, to others they cut up or skinned their faces (as when one whittles a stick), and that's how I found my parents. Ten lie dead in the house killed by firearms; first they shot them and then they cut their throats, to each one of them they cut their throats. Only the skin of the neck was left hanging. To our cousin's small daughter, they cut off her leg; it was thrown aside and her head was off in the distance. The young boy was going to flee but that's where they killed him; all that remained was his foot and head tossed aside. And my father was crouched in the middle of the house, and my grandmother was seated near the fire among the ashes, where they left her, her neck slashed, and our mom was seated nearby, covered in her shawl, in her bed where they put her. And to two cousins, they killed them, cutting their throats. And another little woman they also tossed away with her legs spread; there were others with their faces peeled away. They were unrecognizable as people, and the blood in the house was too much to withstand. (ODHAG 1998 2:16)

> After the rapes by the Civil Defense Patrols, they carried the children to their communities and laughed because they succeeded in wiping out the entire community of Río Negro. One said, "I killed 8, I 10, I 15." Another said, "20." And there listening were the children that they'd taken from our

community. And the children no longer went to school because they had to work because our community was destroyed. (ODHAG 1998 2:17)

A 15-year-old girl was abducted by the police, tortured and repeatedly raped for two weeks. In prison she was shown a man crucified alive, with his teeth extracted, worms in his wounds, hair removed, and face completely disfigured. One policeman came with a red-hot blade and cut off his penis, inciting the most terrible noise she had ever heard. He died. (ODHAG 1998 2:60–63)

Children were made to watch as their mothers and sisters were raped and killed, and then they too were killed. Pregnant women were cut open and had their babies extracted, which were played with like a soccer ball, after which they were hung from a tree. (ODHAG 1998 1:206)

The army told 12 women to each get a chicken. In the meantime, all males that did not participate in the PACs were killed by male relatives that did. The victims were then doused with gasoline and burned, while surviving women were made to cook for the rest. After the burning, the soldiers applauded and sat down to eat. (ODHAG 1998 1:207)

A mother and her 7-year-old daughter were raped repeatedly by a contingent of soldiers, resulting in thier deaths. (ODHAG 1998 1:211)

The women were killed by having sticks driven from their private parts up through their mouths. One woman was crucified with nails, including in the chest, and they burned her and her boy, who would not leave her side, to death. (ODHAG 1998 1:215)

Such brutality was made possible by army training in strict obedience and its sense of complete impunity (ODHAG 1998 2:55). The army trained its Maya recruits to believe that the guerrillas were the cause of the country's poverty, not the elites (ODHAG 1998 2:162), and Indian

children had to be torched, chopped, dismembered, and bashed to elim-
inate any possibility of communal reorganization and revenge: "Because
those little bastards are some day going to screw us" (ODHAG 1998
1:82–83). Women were systematically raped, tortured, and killed for information, for suspicion that they were guerrillas, for witnessing massacres,
for being the potential mothers of future guerrillas, for being heads of
households in the conflict zones, for pertaining to aldeas that were punished en masse, as rewards to soldiers, because of the soldiers' machismo,
and as a way of humiliating the male opposition (ODHAG 1998 1:216). The
soldiers were slowly hardened to cruelty and terror. First they watched
prisoners, then they participated in abductions, then they were told to hit
them, then observe the tortures, and then commit the tortures themselves, perhaps practicing first on delinquents, the homeless, or other
innocents (ODHAG 1998 1:34, 2:164–65). Those that refused were killed
themselves, or hung upside down and beaten in a punishment called
"Christ's Suffering" (ODHAG 1998 2:165, 169). Elite soldiers (*kaibiles*) were
hazed by being forced to capture dogs, cut their throats over a barrel,
drink the blood in paper cups, and eat dog stew afterwards (ODHAG 1998
2:170). When a soldier climbed the ranks, such as reaching the Presidential Guard, he could be expected to carry out thirty assassinations per
year (ODHAG 1998 2:190). The agents were always in danger of assassination by each other, either because they knew too much, were considered
too independent, or were simply disliked. Such "cleansing" was particularly common in the Oriente (CEH 1999 2a:120). One of my informants
related a possible such case in Olopa when the despotic chief of commissioners and his son were killed under suspicious circumstances after the
chief had had another military commissioner and his son killed.

The army, in line with US administrations, did whatever possible to
hide the truth. In 9% of the massacres investigated by the ODHAG (1998
2:9), the army hid its identity to cause confusion and blame the guerrillas.
The Presidential Guard savagely assassinated Mirna Mack, an anthropologist who uncovered the atrocities behind the massive displacements of
Mayas in western Guatemala, in 1990. Bishop Gerardi, who led the
ODHAG truth commission, had his head smashed two days after presenting its four-volume report.

Most accounts of the civil war characterize the late 1960s as a time of
Ladino class war in the Oriente, and the late 1970s and early 1980s as ethnic cleansing of Occidente Mayas. It is true that many Ladinos were
slaughtered in the 1960s, but it is also clear that in the Oriente Ch'orti's

suffered disproportionately. They continued to suffer throughout the 1970s and were targeted in the 1980s with greater ferocity than ever. It is also true that the violence was precipitated by different circumstances in each region, or even each township and aldea. In Alta Verapaz, there was strong discord between indigenous campesinos and plantation owners; in Huehuetenango, the presence of the guerrillas sparked an army response; in Baja Verapaz, the violence reflected longstanding ethnic tensions between Mayas and Ladinos; and in the Ixil area, the violence was directed at grassroots development projects (ODHAG 1998 1:243). In the Ch'orti' area, all of these factors were at work.

As mentioned, the EGP began operating in the Ch'orti' area at least as early as 1978, and earlier branches of the EGP such as the November 13 Front (F13N) may account for the light guerrilla activity in 1974 and 1975 (CEH 1999 2a:290, 2b:435). The guerrillas stepped up activities in the Oriente in 1981 (ODHAG 1998 3:193). In December they took hostages in Chiquimula (ODHAG 1998 3:194), and on Christmas they assassinated three orejas in Dos Quebradas, Camotán (CEH 1999 2a:280). In January 1982 they had military clashes in Zacapa, San Juan Ermita, Morales, and San Antonio La Paz (Progreso), and on June 21 they attacked the headquarters of the Guardia de Hacienda in Chiquimula (ODHAG 1998 3:194). In one infamous incident, the guerrillas ordered that an auxiliary mayor of Colmenas, Jocotán, unite his aldea so that the guerrillas could promise them land. After the man refused to do so, he and his son were found macheteed to death on Christmas, 1982 (CEH 1999 3:174, IIb:435).

One thirty-year-old informant recounted to Palma Ramos (cf. Menchú and Debray 1984:169) the following guerrilla activity in Tisipe, Camotán:

> They say there was a group of people that came from unknown parts and were hidden up in the mountains. They say they used to leave at night and threaten people in their homes. Luckily, they didn't visit mine. They wanted the people to unite or they would attack them, but if they did unite, the army would attack them. The people were always scared because there was no place to hide; they were caught in the crossfire. In 1982 it was especially bad. I arrived at my house from work and I had a fearful sensation. The guerrillas had gone as far as town and in front of everyone declared themselves against the government. They say that some joined them, and when this became known, the army had to respond. And so the army

came and investigated where the threat came from. And they
heard bombs and a battle. Who knows where these people came
from; we didn't know them. But they also caused a repression
even against people that didn't unite with them. From what
I know, no one died, but they carried off people and they didn't
return to their homes. Not all that fled were guilty, but they fled
from fear. When one is afraid, he walks as if he did something
wrong. And those that saw others walking with fear, the army
grabbed and took away, and who knows what threats they'd
made, you know? That's why the people are afraid to meet
because they said that they couldn't meet, because the army
would kill them. That was in 1981. (Palma Ramos 2001:153,
my translation)

Some of my informants reported guerrilla robberies and assassinations in
Olopa, including the killing of a young couple, leaving my informants
orphans.

In the last wave of violence (1981–83), the army used unrestricted force
against Ch'orti's organized for whatever purpose, killing men, women, and
children, the latter by smashing their heads. According to one Jocotán
testimony,

The army took a mother and her two daughters from the
kitchen, undressed them, and threw them on the ground. In
front of their family they were raped by all the soldiers, who
made fun of them. Then they passed over them, stepping on
them and sticking their bayonets in their private parts and
breasts. They killed the father in front of the mother and two
daughters, but the male children were left alive. They sprinkled
the house with gasoline and burned it. After the army left, the
three females were carried to the hospital because the girls were
bleeding a lot, and the mother was near death, but all died in
the Zacapa hospital. (CEH 1999 2b:54)

Even members of government development projects, commonly backed
by USAID, were targeted, confusing campesinos who thought that they
were complying with the state's wishes. The most persecuted social group
was the Catholic Church, especially catechists and priests (CEH 1999
3:150). The priests intervened on behalf of their catechists, and in some

cases liberated them, but the priests themselves were targeted (CEH 1999 Anexo 2:Caso 1209).

Homes were bombed and torched, and fleeing inhabitants were butchered without investigation. My informants mentioned fourteen aldeas where army sweeps, massacres, and assassinations took place. (Aldeas most often mentioned as sites of massacres include the contiguous communities: Dos Quebradas, Marimba, San Jose Las Lágrimas, and Nearar in Camotán; Tablón, Agua Blanca, Las Palmas, and Roblarcito in Olopa; and Tanshá, Colmenas, Tontoles, and Ocumblá in Jocotán, as well as Tierra Blanca and Orégano in northern Jocotán.) Worst hit was Tontoles, Jocotán, where in 1993 only thirty-five of two hundred households remained. The CEH (1999 Anexo 2:274–87) also documented several assassinations and massacres in the aldeas surrounding Nenonjá Mountain in Camotán, including La Marimba, Guayabo, and El Naranjo, after six tortured men saved themselves by reporting an EGP guerrilla encampment. In one massacre, twenty-five people, including fourteen whose identities were not verified, were tortured and killed (CEH 1999 Anexo 2:Caso 1007). In another documented case, military commissioners tortured babies to get their mothers to confess the whereabouts of their husbands (CEH 1999 Anexo 2:Caso 1210). Even in relatively untouched communities, repressive commissioners, orejas, and snipers suspiciously watched everyone's movements such that many were too afraid to walk to town. The brother of Jocotán's only Ch'orti' mayor until that time was killed by one such sniper. The Catholic-sponsored Ch'orti' colonies in the northern Petén rainforests also did not escape persecution, where the army completely uprooted the communities, killed many, and forced the rest, including legendary Belgian padre Hugo, to take refuge in Mexico (Dary, Elías, and Reyna 1998:210–11, 217).

As in the 1960s, many were displaced, and some Jocotán informants harbored terrified and hungry refugees fleeing from Olopa, some of whom died from injuries and others of whom continued north to the Petén and Izabal. Many of these refugees eventually settled in the city of Chiquimula, in the El Tesoro refugee camp in Honduras (eight hundred refugees), or among the five hundred clandestine refugees in Honduras (CEH 1999 3:150).

Ch'orti's continued to be captured for military service, some of whom were killed immediately, perhaps as practice for the other soldiers (CEH 1999 Anexo 2:Caso 1100). As in western Guatemala, civil patrols composed of lightly armed campesinos were established in all communities, which were divided into groups that combed the aldeas for guerrillas on a rotating basis every five nights. Although Chiquimula is a relatively small department and considered to have relatively little guerrilla activity, it was fourth among Guatemala's twenty-two departments in the number of PAC members, at 23,333 (CEH 1999 2a:234). One campesino told me that the patrols were ridiculous, as not a single guerrilla was ever encountered. When President Cerezo disbanded the PACs, he was considered a hero because the campesinos "could sleep again." The violence in the Ch'orti' area subsided in 1984, but the CEH (1999 Anexo 2:274–87) documents assassinations until 1994. Peace Corps volunteer Peter Joyce captured some of the tension in a mid-1980s report about Olopa's chief commissioner:

> The guy's a classic "finquero" [plantation owner]. He exploits
> peasants, and can be violent. Over the years he helped kill
> hundreds of peasants, especially in La Laguna de Cayur.
> He threatened to kill the people I've been working with a
> number of times, and at one time he told me personally that
> he'd do me in. He can be extremely friendly one minute, and
> threaten you the next.

Due to a confluence of factors in the early 1990s, including a failed coup, the attention to Guatemala surrounding the Columbian Quincentenary, the end of the Cold War, K'iche' Maya Rigoberta Menchú's Nobel Prize for Peace (despite a countercampaign by the state), and the leadership and pressure of the European Union and the US Clinton administration, the peace process began in earnest, and accords were signed at the end of 1996. The accords stipulated a truth commission report (CEH). The Clinton administration was helpful in providing information about US involvement in the war, whereas the Guatemalan government, army, and other "security" forces, as well as the Israeli, Argentine, Cuban, and Nicaraguan governments refused to cooperate (CEH 1999 1:49–50, 57). The commission investigated tens of thousands of human rights violations during the war, which resulted in numbers and conclusions very similar to the Catholic Church's report (REHMI). About two hundred thousand people were killed during the war, 83% of whom were Maya civilians and 93% of whom were killed by the Guatemalan army or its paramilitaries (CEH 1999 1:73). Mayas, it concluded, were collectively regarded as enemies of the state, especially from 1978 to 1983 (CEH 1999 4:29; cf. Stoll 2001:119–20, who argues that the truth commissions were one sided).

Heritage of las Ruinas

Guatemala's National Widow's Coalition (CONAVIGUA) organized a study of the psychological effects on family survivors of 1,093 extrajudicial executions. It found that victims suffer "crying fits, listlessness, insomnia, tremors, difficulty thinking, fear, headaches, and feelings of persecution," as well as alcoholism, fits of anger, jealousy, mistrust, and hallucinations (*Cerigua* 5/7/98:3–4). In folk etymology these constitute "nerves" or its subcategory "heat," which have been found in high percentages in Guatemala and El Salvador of the 1980s and 1990s, as well many other desperately impoverished and oppressed populations (Low 1994, 1989; Jenkins and Valiente 1994; Jenkins 1991; Scheper-Hughes 1992; Sluka 1989). "Nerves" are sometimes discernable in the Ch'orti' population, but more apparent are mistrust of outsiders, fear of any mention of the army and guerrillas, and the reproduction of dysfunctional family life. Among a population as plagued by tragedy as the Ch'orti's, the psychological scars attributable directly to las ruinas are difficult to discern, but in the words of Padre Milton, a lifelong resident in the area, "we are living the consequences of thirty years ago. Still we suffer that time, above all the years 1960 to 1970."

At a broader social level, some Ch'orti's point to las ruinas as the cause for the decline in communal religiosity. Jocotán's last of sixteen cofradías (Dary, Elías, and Reyna 1998:47–49) dissolved during the dictatorship of Ubico (Fought 1969:474), possibly due to the usurpation of traditional authority by the newly installed military commissioners (Dary, Elías, and Reyna 1998:265). Others point to "the revenge" or "the liberation" of 1954. One thirty-five-year-old Oquén man elaborated to Palma Ramos's research team:

> I am going to tell you something, something a little dangerous, you know? At times when one has lived, one knows what has happened. Before 1954, before the so-called "Liberation," there were more prayers and rituals. But during the Liberation this was all prohibited, because he who did those things, was made to disappear. Many people arrived investigating those things, and those who did the rituals were treated as sorcerers. Perhaps this is why they disappeared or hid themselves, out of fear.
> In other words, those values continue, but everyone fears what happened in 1954. Well, that's what happened and that's why

the people here are afraid. But over in the Occidente, as there
wasn't as much persecution, you know they didn't feel it as
much, because here in the Oriente the Liberation was present.
(Palma Ramos 2001:93, my translation)

When I undertook research in the early 1990s, reminders of las ruinas
haunted the landscape. *Xerb'aj* are the ghosts of the murdered and are not
content to reside in the next world but return to their places of death "to
play" and haunt the living. How else to explain the eerie sensation one
feels when passing the spot of a disturbing murder? Hundreds of political
deaths in the Ch'orti' area mean a landscape haunted with xerb'aj ghosts,
and xerb'aj encounters lead to fright, sickness, and death. Diener noted
that the mass graves in Olopa, such as the one in Tres Quebradas, are
locales "of spiritual distress and potential soul loss" (Diener 1978:110).

Besides spiritual distress, in the early 1990s army outposts were still
operating in Camotán and Olopa, and the police and customs guards
were known to prey on the campesinos. In fact, abuses by "security"
forces were and still are common background in Ch'orti' folklore (e.g.,
Pérez Martínez 1996:30–31). Bus travelers were subject to checks by soldiers armed with machine guns, and campesinos and Ladino landowners
continued violent confrontations. In 1991 a Ladino landowner murdered
an Olopa cooperative leader after a dispute, and in 1994 a Ladino shot my
Tuticopote informant in a property dispute, which resulted in no investigation or arrests by either the army or the police, despite my informants'
formal complaints. Political kidnappings and assassinations were periodically reported on the radio. During the 1993 Serrano coup Ch'orti' organizational leaders were prohibited from holding meetings and were very
apprehensive about a possible new wave of repression.

A few Olopa Ladinos were hostile towards me for living in the aldeas,
speaking Ch'orti', and conversing with Evangelicals, and attempted to intimidate me. Some Ch'orti's were also complicit in accusing strangers of subversion. For example, three army commissioners in Pelillo Negro accused me of
being a guerrilla because municipal authorities had failed to inform them of
my research project. I had initially thought the charges too ridiculous for
urgent consideration until I realized that Pedro and his family were terrified
that our entire homestead could come under attack. I immediately walked
to the army garrison in Camotán and pled my case with the lieutenant, who
promised to set things straight with the commissioners, but afterwards
twenty Pelillo households refused to participate in my survey.

Investigating las ruinas among Ch'orti's was difficult because they are fearful of army reprisals and uncertain about who was killing whom. Even in 1998, two years after the signing of the Peace Accords, campesinos in Guayabo, Camotán, and refugees in Carrizalón, Copán, were hostile when a Ch'orti' leader casually asked them to recount their experiences of las ruinas. My interview with Chilo, who I eventually learned was orphaned during las ruinas, is typical of Ch'orti' hesitation.

Brent: Do you remember those years?
      Chilo: I, I don't remember, I was only a kid during that time.
      Brent: Uh, during those years, perhaps, about twenty-five years ago or more? Maybe.
      Chilo: Well, I don't know.
      Brent: "R" told me that there were helicopters here, and airplanes, and everything.
      Chilo: Yeah, it's always been like that. Because since I was little, they always came, and during the harshest law, the helicopters always came. But only to fly by.
      Brent: How frightening.
      Chilo: Yeah, because we here don't know about things from other places, so one was startled to see such things.

Ch'orti' attitudes about las ruinas are far from uniform. Old men from Olopa are remarkably frank about the cruelty of military rule or "the law" (*e ley*), and some use military dictators as metonyms for the army. Some directly blame presidents Peralta Azurdia (1963–66), Méndez Montenegro (1966–70), Arana Osorio (1970–74), or Lucas García (1978–82) personally for las ruinas. One groaned that the presidents caused "a hundred tyrannies with the poor people." Just as Ch'orti's associate political parties with their symbols or acronyms (e.g., the Revolutionary Party equals "the map," and the National Alliance Party [PAN] equals "the bread"), some presidents' names lend themselves to Ch'orti' imagery. Castillo Armas, "castle arms," has a clear association with militarism, and the patronym "Méndez" is typically ignored, leaving just "Montenegro" or "black mountain." I have also heard "Ydígoras Fuentes" pronounced "*víboras fuentes*," or roughly "vipers-fountains." The following interview excerpt of an Olopa elder reveals the feelings of resentment towards the army.

C: Aaah, it was a massacre. The army entered to finish off all the fools, and yes they finished. And today those ruins never end.

   Brent: Oh no?

   C: Oh God. So in other words we haven't learned to conform; "the law" still does not keep us in line.

   Brent: So the, what, or why did the army come here, were there guerrillas here, or not?

   C: Aaah well, it was because the Ladinos [naming six of the most notorious in Olopa and Esquipulas] in town accused us of being guerrillas, and we didn't even know them. We didn't even know them. We didn't even know what a guerrilla was, you know? Maybe there were, but in other places. We here, OK maybe they killed perhaps. Over there is a guerrilla stronghold because they are like mariners. But we that—what we think in our lives and our journey, and our passing, how to live our lives, right? Thinking about eating and living. We think no evil thoughts.

Some poor, young Ch'orti' men in particular, on the other hand, respect the army for its power. With rising crime, many men, women, young, and old alike look to the army to establish law, order, and "respect." In the early 1990s, when a serious crime like murder was committed in the aldeas, if any authorities pursued the criminals, it was the army, not the police. When a husband and wife were murdered in Olopa in November 1992, for example, an army detachment rushed to the scene, apprehended the two suspects, beat one to death as they dragged him to town and incarcerated the other. During town festivals the army takes it as a matter of pride that they prevent drunkenness from turning to violence. When a man was macheteed by a drunk during the patron saint's festival in Olopa in 1993, the army and customs guards (Guardia de Hacienda) went on a controlled rampage and roughed up all men carrying machetes. On the other hand, one soldier lost his arm when he was attacked by a drunken campesino in the Camotán patron saint's festival of 1992. The army is also appreciated for its civic duties such as ensuring that all homes comply with sanitary laws or for protecting reforestation projects from poaching.

   Young men forcibly conscripted by the army have mixed feelings about the experience. Few willingly enlisted in the army, and before forced conscription ended in 1994, young men avoided traveling to the towns during times of the year like February when the army was known to kidnap recruits. Some Ladino professionals defended forced recruitment because the army experience supposedly "civilized" or "disciplined" the Indians and promoted their upward mobility. However, if serving in the army was such a positive experience, more Mayas would have enlisted willingly. Some Ch'orti' forced recruits managed to escape and return home, like one Pacrén man who was captured and escaped on four different occasions. Most Ch'orti's understood that Indians were used as cannon fodder, such as in the poignant case of a Pelillo Negro recruit who was shot in a guerrilla ambush, spent two years in a hospital, and was then arrested by the army for desertion.

Nevertheless, some young men have looked to the army for respect and adventure. One twenty-eight-year-old explained that he volunteered in the early 1980s because he was bored with day labor and had no money and little self-esteem. His friends ridiculed him for thinking about enlisting, but he explained, "'You know what?'—I used to say—'I *have* to carry my gun'—only like that did I say it—'I *have* to fire'—I said, that was all I said—'I *have* to carry my gun, I *have* to fire.'" Although from the start he was humiliated by the constant shouting of undecipherable orders, physical abuse, and a physical exam given by a female doctor, when he received his first uniform, "I felt very honorable, decent, and courageous, enthusiastic to serve in this fatherland Guatemala... I wanted my mother to be there to see me... or that my boss don V. was there... or my buddies who told me that I would fail there." He and his friend, later injured in a guerrilla ambush, fought for their lives in many battles in El Quiché and Huehuetenango and participated in scorched-earth tactics, burning all homes and potential food like sugarcane and banana trees. They suffered greatly from heat, hunger, thirst, fatigue, and fear of both guerrillas and army superiors. Today he is *raspado*, "scraped up" mentally and physically, especially when he drinks (as he did with me), but he is grateful that the army taught him to "respect," i.e. be responsible for his body and life. He no longer lies around sleeping but works hard, no longer bathes when he has a hangover or is sleepy (which is thought to cause mental illness from an overly "cold" state) and no longer exerts himself when he is recovering from affliction. Despite his positive assessment, he does not contradict national Maya leader Demetrio Cojtí's (1996:45) characterization that army conscription "generates traumas in young Indian veterans, producing symptoms of ethnic self-loathing and social maladaptation: alcoholism, unstable family life, rural delinquency, and becoming part of an urban lumpenproletariat." The informant has since left the Ch'orti' area to become a security guard in Guatemala City.

Another ex-recruit was unequivocally positive. While admitting that the army was hell for some, he described his army experience as a transition to maturity and self-responsibility:

> [L]isten, as far as I was concerned, I was very proud to be in
> the army. In other words, I looove the army, and until this
> day I will never forget it. When I was little like my brother here,
> I wanted to be there. I looked at the soldiers walking around
> as they do with clothes they have, and I had to have them.
> I looked at the guns, and I wanted one. . . . When I went I was,
> I was of another tradition, you know. Perhaps a little more
> unkempt, you might say. A little more closed minded, you
> know. . . . Perhaps I've changed myself a lot already, perhaps . . .
> more, more upright, more opinionated, more all of that.
> More energetic, you know. [The army] teaches to be obedient,
> perhaps to bath oneself well, to apply talcum powder and
> deodorant, to walk cleanly, orderly, or well polished, right?
> Or perhaps to comb oneself well.

Whatever one's personal experiences during the repression, although the violence has diminished at the national political level, at the local and interpersonal level Ch'orti's now turn violently upon each other to resolve their disputes rather than turning to elders. Nevertheless, Ch'orti's maintain a sense of centrality and many localized, unique traditions, which will be the subject of the next chapter.

FOUR

A Sense of Centrality

We're always the same.
—Lonjino, Ch'orti' of Olopa

One battles for the kids.
—Paulina, Ch'orti' of Olopa

It would seem that after such a long, brutal history, including various waves of religious persecution, that Ch'orti's would have abandoned their distinctive indigenous lifestyle and integrated with the Guatemalan nation for self-preservation. Exploited like burros, exterminated like vermin, legally and socially regarded as children, and engulfed in a sea of Ladinos, why would anyone want to be labeled "Ch'orti'" or anything different from Ladinos? From a domination/resistance paradigm, one would argue that Ch'orti's are resisting the dominant national culture and refusing to surrender. This makes sense to some degree, especially regarding what outsiders lament as some Ch'orti's' stubborn rejection of Western medicine, education, religions, and political control, but it is more the case that Ch'orti's have such limited options in the national political economy that the subsistence agriculture lifestyle remains one of the most viable, reassuring, and even satisfying strategies for survival. For Ch'orti's, the fact that some traditions seem to have been practiced roughly the same way since time immemorial lends credence to their rightness and righteousness. Even if one wanted to take up Ladino ways, give up self-subsistence, and move to town, the transition would require access to resources, contacts, and the knowledge to embody Ladino culture.

In this chapter I provide a summary of the Ch'orti' subsistence life-style to evoke why it has such inertia (for a more in-depth perspective, see Lopez and Metz [2002]). Long ago, Girard (1949:296ff) described an idyllic Ch'orti' culture and character with: exemplary ethics; natural, human, and social morals; a profound sense of community and reciprocity; charity, piety, and kindness to the weak; love of truth; respect of the foreign; neighborliness; a highly developed sense of justice; the inability to mistreat others or practice usury; honesty in borrowing; frugality; no covetousness of spouses or property; communalism; sociability; industriousness; pacifism; simplicity and purity of habits; frankness; tenderness towards animals, plants, and objects; respectfulness towards the elderly, dead, religious leaders, and other authorities; responsibility; respect for the government's maintenance of order; stoicism; and the same morality as the founders of Buddhism and Christianity, the "apex of civilized morality." If Ch'orti's lost their collective character—their "natural qualities"—he argued, then they would lose their purpose of opposing Western individualism (Girard 1949:409). From my experiences among Ch'orti's a half century later I know how Girard could draw such conclusions, but such one-sidedness is ultimately of service to no one.

Self-Subsistence

"Ch'orti's" are actually a diverse group of people with the full range of personalities one would expect in any population, and their microenvironments are diverse, ranging from lowland savanna and desert to highland cloud forest. Yet, they share cultures that distinguish them from the surrounding Ladino population, which to themselves and Ladinos warrants the application of an ethnic term like "People of the Country," "Indians," or "Ch'orti's." With a combination of resourcefulness, collective memory, and physical endurance, Ch'orti's continue to make do mostly with natural materials. Unlike the Occidente where many Mayas are merchants and commodity producers, the backbone of the Ch'orti' distinctive lifestyle is subsistence agriculture. Almost all Ch'orti's consider themselves subsistence farmers or "campesinos" and only secondarily wage laborers, craftspeople, and merchants. The tasks and responsibilities of self-subsistence inform most aspects of life, including ethics and values, social organization, worldview, and even humor and recreation, although due to dramatic changes to be discussed later it would now be misleading to call this lifestyle an integrated, functioning "system."

When Wisdom and Girard carried out their research in the 1930s and 1940s, Ch'orti's of the old Jocotán Parish were almost completely self-sufficient, exporting only sugar and tobacco and importing cloth, candles, metal implements, and salt from Ladinos (Girard 1949:3; Wisdom 1940:1–12, 19–20, 114). They were so confident of their cultural correctness that they defiantly criticized the more powerful Ladinos for being poor farmers, prostitutes, and gossips (Wisdom 1940:224–28). Tortillas and beans were supplemented with a cornucopia of greens, spices, cucumbers, onions, garlic, cilantro, radishes, *cidra*, pineapples, plantains, tomatoes, squash, sweet potatoes, chiles, coffee, oranges, jocote fruit (tropical plum), *zapote* fruit, avocados, chucte (an avocado-like fruit), *lima* citrus fruit, and mangos (Girard 1949:229, 240). Rather than buy medicine in pharmacies, they employed countless herbal remedies and spiritual cures (Girard 1949:338–43). Each aldea specialized in the production of particular crafts, including reed mats (pojp, petates), ceramics, rope, nets, baskets, pipes, soap, sombreros, chalk, guitars, mandolins, violins, and cotton thread (Girard 1949:253–54), which they exchanged in Jocotán's Sunday morning market.

Today, Ch'orti's maintain their subsistence economy and some sense of centrality despite tremendous pressures from without and within, and maize-and-beans agriculture largely structures their sense of time. Many still slash and burn weeds and brush for fertilizer, and men often plant with digging sticks local varieties of seeds selected from the previous harvests. The start of the growing season is ritually marked between San Marcos (St. Mark) Day on April 25 and the Day of the Cross on May 3 and ends in October (see Girard [1962] for possible ritual connections with ancient Mayas). In the highlands (about three thousand to fifty-five hundred feet above sea level), where it is more humid, cool, and fertile due to volcanic soil, two growing seasons are often attempted with a small-corn variety (*b'ikit nar*, *cuarenteño*), from May to August and then September to December. In the hotter, drier, less fertile lowlands (approximately one thousand to three thousand feet), only one growing season is usually attempted with larger and longer-maturing varieties of corn, from four to six months of maturation. Beans have a shorter growing season, about two to three months, and can be harvested twice per rainy season. Weeding, performed at least twice a growing season, is usually done with

2. *Young men planting, Pacrén, 1992.*

a curved machete used as a shovel and hook, rather than a hoe, when the soil is rocky (for more on Ch'orti' agriculture, see López and Metz [2002:73–111; Dary, Elías, and Reyna 1998:127–62]).

In many aldeas a few families grow sugarcane, which is ground with ox-drawn wooden presses (*trapiche*) of the kind Columbus introduced to the Americas (Mintz 1985:32–33). The juice is boiled in wooden vats and poured it into wooden molds to congeal as brown sugar cakes for sweetening coffee. Magueys and palm trees are cultivated principally in the lowlands, the latter for their highly desired leaves used for house construction. Various fruit trees listed by Wisdom and Girard—especially mangos, bananas, limes, coffee, and oranges—are still grown, and the pits and seeds are planted wherever possible. Chickens and turkeys, the only source of meat for most families, roam patios and house yards scavenging for insects, seeds, and leaves.

My hosts' resourcefulness never ceased to impress me. Homes are constructed without a single nail (see appendix 1). Walls are made either of wattle and daub, palm fronds, grass bundles, or sticks and fastened to tree trunk poles and beams. Roofs are constructed with palm fronds or grass. In most aldeas lay carpenters make beds, chairs, tables, violins, and

3. *Grinding sugarcane with ox-drawn wooden pillars, Pacrén.*

marimbas with local wood. Beds consist of handwoven reed mats either placed on the floor or on bed frames of crossed twine. Most understand the peculiar properties of different trees, knowing which termites prefer, which are most durable for furniture, and which grow well together. When Cresencio and his son cut down a palm, they used the fronds for house construction, the frond stalks for fences, the heart for food, the scraps for firewood, and planned to use the remaining trunk for a bridge that would last ten years. Various wild plants and animals are recognized as sources of food and medicine, including dozens of species of herbs and at least four types of mushrooms. Fish fry and freshwater shrimp are collected by diverting streams, and various birds and fowl are hunted with slingshots. If a flashlight or can of kerosene with a cloth wick is not available for illumination, one reverts to resinous pine for torches (*tajte'* in Ch'orti', *ocote* in Spanish/Nahuatl). If a soccer ball has a hole, it is repaired with sap.

For a people who rely on manual labor and local materials, work can be extremely arduous but personally fulfilling. Growing and processing one's own food on one's own land lends "work" a different connotation than "working" for wages to purchase such items. Men never cease to be pleased at their harvests and positively contrast their work to that of

Ladinos and gringos, who seem incapable of physical labor. They are proud of their strength and endurance and boastful of their ability to rapidly cover long, mountainous distances. When I was once invited to take part in a planting group, the young men raced back and forth competitively across steep slopes stabbing the ground with their digging sticks and dropping seeds in the holes so fast that I simply could not keep up. A month later they seemed pleased to tell me that some of the corn I planted did not sprout. On another occasion, men carried two 110-pound bags of cement apiece on their shoulders up and down steep mountain slopes. It was a major achievement for me to manage one bag at a time without taking a tumble. Pedro, who weighs about 150 pounds and stands at about 4'10", proudly threw what must have been a three-hundred-pound tree trunk on his back, which I, at 6'1" and 160 pounds, could barely budge, much less carry with a headstrap.

Work has a strong moral imperative and should receive its just rewards. When I asked Cresencio whether women inherited land, he responded that yes, "they work too."[1] On another occasion, he accused a group of young migratory laborers known to lounge, smoke, and play cards of bestowing more loyalty on the plantations than their communities. He explained that hard, devoted work when planting—ensuring that the rows are precisely two hand widths apart and the columns four hand widths wide—can mean the difference between a harvest of four thousand pounds of corn per manzana or only five hundred. Cresencio, Pedro, and other leaders are incensed when some campesinos reap the benefits of others' manual labor, even if the former offer to pay others to work in their place. Even outside development workers are occasionally criticized and distrusted for relaxing. Some like Paulo Antonio and Paulina opined that the poor are such because they are lazy, drink, and sell their land. Vicente echoed that the future is in one's own hands, as "he that has good plans, intelligence, does not die of hunger."

Especially valued is self-sufficiency and staying out of debt. Nowadays, poverty prevents most from complete self-sufficiency, but Ch'orti's are still jealous about managing their own affairs. Vicente remarked that he was proud to have never worked on a plantation. Others explained that they are ill at ease when in debt and could not believe that in the

---

1. Wisdom (1961:325–26) and Girard (1949:295) both reported that only men inherited land, but in all three aldeas where I lived, women received land as well as men.

United States living with mortgages, car payments, and credit cards is normal. Paulina and Tereso counseled, "he who wants rented money, no, because we go to rent from the bank, and the bank comes charging a greater amount. So, one has to continue even poorer!" When discussing economic independence, Pedro proudly said that they are really only dependent on townspeople for sugar and salt, whereas the townspeople could not survive without the campesinos. Ch'orti's, he boasted, need neither money nor the variety of foods gringos (like myself) and Ladinos seem to require, and he laughed when recalling the TV antennas in Guatemala City shanty towns that for him indicated a misplaced value on luxuries over necessities. Cresencio satisfyingly told me as he rested in his hammock one afternoon that as a farmer, he rarely works in the afternoons and feels sorry for those gringos (like myself) who race around and value every minute.

The basic social and work unit is the family. In the 1930s and 1940s, Wisdom (1940:226, 246–47) and Girard (1949:280ff) concurred that the extended family or lineage (*noj maxtak'*) led by elders referred to as "our fathers" (*katata'*) and "our mothers" (*katu'*) was the foundation of Ch'orti' society. Family members were ranked by age and gender; children were thoroughly admonished, counseled, and punished; special ritual language was used to initiate and end conversations between lineage members and compadres (fictive kin); and the men arranged themselves in single file by age when walking to town, with the women following behind (Girard fails to mention if or how women arranged themselves [1949: 296–98]). The home was the locus of pride (at least for men). Wisdom reflected that,

> [T]he average Indian seems strongly attached to his family, to its land and possessions, and to the neighborhood and region in which it has always lived. He feels himself an inalienable part of his family group and speaks proudly of the excellent maize it produces, its hospitality to friends and strangers, the fact that none of its members is lazy and unwilling to plant *milpas*, the fine houses in which it lives, and the superior climate and soil of its neighborhood. The average family head never tires of pointing out the superior qualities of his family establishment, referring to it as "my home" or "my ranch," even though he may own only three or four huts and perhaps a couple of acres of

rocky land. He considers most of the Ladinos and pueblo
Indians as unfortunate because they cannot or do not "make
milpa," and thus lead unnatural lives. His primary attachment
is to his family; his real home, the locale of greatest emotional
attachment, is the small area upon which are laid out his
family's houses, *milpas*, gardens, and orchards. (1940:258–59)

Girard (1949:296ff) also noted that on rare occasions when men sang, they
did so to praise their fields, women, children, and homes, expressing sorrow for less industrious Ladinos. Today, extended family structures have
disintegrated somewhat and many elders lament the loss of "respect," but
the family continues to take precedence over all other social units.

Every family member is productive starting at age six or seven, and
work routines are divided by gender. That men farm and women transform
the harvest into edible food seems as unquestionable as the sunrise.
Gender segregation is such that men and women are embarrassed to do
cross-gender tasks and segregate themselves at public events like religious
worship, project meetings, and fiestas. While agriculture is typically men's
work, women perform the relentless tasks of transforming corn into food
by hand-grinding it with stone manos and metates (*k'ab' cha'*), forming the
corn dough into tortillas with an artful slapping motion, and flipping them
bare-handed on fired ceramic griddles (*semet, comal*). They also perform
endless other tasks around the house, including daily sweeping, hauling
water, washing dishes, tending fowl, scrubbing clothes by hand in streams
over rocks, and making crafts. Ch'orti' aldeas make the same crafts with
local materials and handmade tools, such as polishing stones and chicken
bone reed-strippers, as in the early twentieth century, save for a few like
sombreros and sandals, which have been replaced with modern commodities. Men tend to take on the heavy tasks of cutting and carrying materials,
while women often complete the finer, more dexterous jobs of weaving
fibers, mats, and baskets. Even when socializing, women, except for elderly
matriarchs, always keep busy in craftwork, washing dishes, tending to
babies, or sewing. Kitchen houses, the primary female work domain, are
favorite social spaces for men and women alike. Women's seemingly incessant labor does not go unnoticed by some men. While some of my male
informants lamented that motorized corn grinders (which began to enter
aldeas in the early 2000s) and piped water would make women lazy, one
twenty-one-year-old man cited by Palma Ramos provides an equally popular opposing view:

4. *Mother makes petate (pojp) mat with daughter and
    niece, Pelillo Negro.*

It seems to me that the wife helps out more than the man.
I think so. Like I said, when we work in groups of up to 15 or
18 people, the woman has to work like mad. She has to get up
at 4:00 A.M. and make breakfast, and no one even helps her.
It's only her, and whether it's raining or not, she has to go and
bring water. And if she doesn't have water in the house, she
has to go and carry it [from the spring], all this before the men
start working. The woman, then, has to carry water in jugs,
one on her hip and another on her head. That's why the woman
is very valuable. She suffers more because she does more,
while the man sits around waiting for his breakfast. (2001:73,
my translation)

Husbands are particularly proud of their wives' stoicism when giving
birth at home without uttering a sound.

Prospective spouses are attractive according to several criteria, but
industriousness is key. Women and their parents desire husbands who
are good providers, are not alcoholics, and demonstrate their devotion

by giving premarital gifts of clothing. In fact, if a man is particularly industrious, strong, and has much land, he may be polygynous. Men want
a woman who will work hard—have the tortillas hot and timely—and
bear children. According to some friends, it is better to marry partners
within one's aldea—which 85% of Ch'orti's do—because one knows their
family's work habits. In the words of one man, "I know it's better if a girl
that we're watching knows how to work, gets up early, knows how to do
tasks like weaving mats. She is honorable in all senses, and we know it
because she lives nearby. But if you bring in a woman from afar, there's a
problem. We don't know whether she's obedient, if she gets up early, and
everything like that."

In the early 1930s, marriage was too important a contract between
extended families to be left to love. Many families strengthened their
alliances by marrying all their teenage sons and daughters to each other
(still practiced today by some), and grooms performed an extended
period of service for their new in-laws (Wisdom 1961:292; Girard 1949:279,
198). Today, while some parents do force their daughters to marry (Palma
Ramos 2001:137–38), their control over marriage has diminished along
with their economic ability to give marital gifts and inheritance. Commonly, prospective grooms and brides initiate courtship themselves by
exchanging glances and casual conversation, soon after which the groom
may give gifts of towels or clothes before having a relative ask her parents
for her hand (cf. Palma Ramos 2001:27–28, 54, 97), if he doesn't do it himself. The parents then privately raise the issue with the girl, and if she
accepts, the new couple may simply move to one of their parents' houses
without ceremony. Among more prosperous households, the groom's
family will give such gifts as bread, tools, and clothing, while the bride's
family will hold a celebration of feasting and dancing. The reception formally starts when the bride and groom's godparents ask them in the door-
way of the festival house whether they will respect each other and work
diligently. In one nineteen-year-old friend's experience, he exchanged
glances with his future bride in town, and never as much as spoke to her
or gave her gifts. Soon thereafter his desire carried him to her distant
aldea where he asked her parents for her hand. They questioned whether
he would be loyal, asked her whether she would accept him, and soon
wedding plans were arranged. Other couples may elope if they cannot
win their parents' blessing, but this can lead to violence, as happened
when several people from two families were macheteed after a man
"stole" a young woman from a relatively prosperous Ch'orti' family.

On the other hand, some Ch'orti's never find a partner. Some seem to prefer to live single with their parents, and others search without success. One bachelor in his thirties tearfully recounted privately how he courted a woman from another township only to discover that she was betrothed to another. Another man remorsefully recalled a longer courtship, in which he loved a woman so much that he risked spirit possession by traveling at night to visit her, but she ended it after seeing him speaking to another woman. Jealousy is in fact very strong once courtship has begun, and it can lead to divorce, as in the case of a young husband who would not even let his bride wash clothes alone at the stream. Obviously, some Ch'orti's are homosexuals and do not desire heterosexual unions. While homosexuality does not lead to the ideal reproductive situation, some Ch'orti' men regarded it with more titillation than stigma, and asked me sincerely why Ladinos find denigrating effeminate homosexuals so humorous. Some friends jokingly embraced each other from behind, and some teenage boys were said to practice sex on each other because girls are inaccessible. In my own case, my refusal to take a Ch'orti' bride and my undertaking feminine tasks like sweeping, cooking, and washing dishes put my heterosexuality into question, and two men even made sexual advances. No homosexual men seem to live alone together, but I suspected lesbian arrangements when in my survey I encountered women with different surnames living together without children. Both men and women were uncomfortable discussing lesbianism.

It is difficult to overemphasize the importance of children in Ch'orti' households. They are valued as workers as much as enhancing the household's quality of life, while in the long term they are seen as the parents' social security (for other Mayas, cf. Early 1982:135–37, 179–80; Sexton and Woods 1982:199; Carlson 1997:134–36). In the first half of the twentieth century, fertility, determined by women's actions and the moon, was so valued that a woman's sterility was cause for her husband to flog her (Girard 1949:187, 192–93, 201, 293). A man could only reach adult status, symbolized by colored stitching on his shirt, once he fathered children (Girard 1949:272–77). Today, babies are referred to as gifts from God (cf. Palma Ramos 2001:97–98) and remain such a moral imperative that some Ch'orti's find it telling that amoral Ladino and gringo couples have few or no children. Some friends critiqued an aldea development committee president who had been married for eight years for not having children. He obviously had no stake in the community's future.

Nearly everything is done for the children. Paulina summed it up well:

"One cannot battle for others, and for others you cannot battle either. One battles for the kids." When I asked twenty-eight-year-old Mariano whether he expected the future to be better or worse for his children, he interpreted my question as a commentary on the importance of children:

> [W]ell I like very much what you tell me because, OK, because at least one is working for their son, right? For the strength of the son one works, and the son acquires strength. It's the same as if you had a guisquil plant [vegetable pear; chayote in other regions]; you are watering it and it sprouts, you see. OK, and so we will see that if the father does not have luck, maybe the son has luck. Yes, it makes for a good thing, you know? He starts to work, you see, it has its rewards, that's what I think.

Parent-child relationships are more than just functional, of course. To meet Ch'orti' adults without their children, one might regard them as stoic, closed, and unaffectionate, but this image is reversed when one sees them kiss, cuddle, tease, and share with their children. Many proudly list the names of their children to visitors when asked. Reciprocally, adults lovingly recall the sacrifices their parents made for them. María Jesús remembered the discipline and skills her family taught her, which she has passed to her sons. She recalls her father instructing, "so there is always a pound [of corn] that you are fed, but you must always help me," while her mother taught her to work maguey fibers. About her grandparents she said, "my grandfather wasn't rich, but he said 'I want to teach you before I leave you,' he said. 'There is no money and I am dirty, but yes, I will always teach you how to pass your life,' he said." She proudly recounted how she raised her own children:

> I was pushing on, I was raising my kids who today are already big, one is twenty-three and another is eighteen. My little ones live and they are indeed full-grown. Yes, and already today I know it's different, more or less today we already have every-thing. In other words, every hour I am taking care of them and feeding them because they need it. Yes, and I tell them that my father never bought corn [i.e., he was self-sufficient].

When Cresencio's father was on his deathbed, his mother told him that she wanted to die with him, but his father insisted that she live on, care

5. *Fiddling for guests. Courtesy of Florian Klebs.*

for their children, and have the opportunity to see their grandchildren. Cresencio considered this "the insight of dying people." The spiritual attachment that parents have with their children was exemplified by Cresencio's son's motorcycle accident. Paco was hit by a car traveling at about forty miles per hour, and as he lay on the ground unconscious and not breathing, Cresencio and his wife happened upon the scene while traveling in the back of a pickup truck to town. When they realized it was their son, they fought through the crowd and the mother lifted his head on her lap while Cresencio fanned his face with his sombrero. Within minutes the son took a tremendous inhalation and began breathing again. All are certain that without their presence, the son would not have revived. As parents work for their children, children are generally loyal to their parents to the end. A poignant example is Carlos's brother, who was offered a scholarship to a university in Guatemala City, an unheard of opportunity for Ch'orti's, but he turned it down because it would have meant being away from his sick mother.

Ch'orti' pets are prized for their functionality and secondarily for their companionship. While hunting dogs are prized, given the virtual extermination of wildlife in the area, dogs are more appreciated for fierceness. Many men chuckle when their dogs attack other dogs, and one man proudly said that his female dog did not cry when giving birth and went out hunting the next day. Dogs are not coddled, and in the United States or Europe Ch'orti's would be accused of cruelty to animals. For example, the first task of a toddler, which brings much pride and amusement to other family members, is to beat with sticks starving household dogs that approach the kitchen or patio in search of food. Sometimes cats may be held and petted, but more often they are prized for their hunting of ever-pestilent mice and cockroaches. The price of kittens is about twice that of puppies, unless the puppies are considered hunting dogs.

In all, families continue to measure their success by standards of self-subsistence, gauging their self-worth by comparing their fields, homes, and food to those of their neighbors. Men are eager to show guests their fields and fruit trees, and women proudly offer their favorite treats if in season, including corn-on-the-cob, sweet corn gruel (*k'u'msa'*, *atol*), tamales, or fruit. Pedro, among many others, insisted that his mother made the best tortillas. Many women can hardly contain themselves when complemented on their hospitality and well-kept home, and they take special pride in throwing well-organized fiestas and providing timely food to their husband's or father's day-laborers. Visitors are customarily thanked for their visit and given fruit or other snacks to take home.

Beyond the Home—Barrios, Aldeas, Townships, Region

The Ch'orti' universe beyond the home begins with neighbors loosely related in barrios, agglomerations of barrios called "aldeas," and aldeas linked throughout the region by trade and cultures. In Wisdom's and Girard's day, aldeas were the principal unit beyond the family and were composed of at least twenty-five families with two to three hundred members occupying a territory of a two- to three-mile radius. They tended to be endogamous,[2] have common schools and ceremonial temples, and were distinguishable by their craft production (Wisdom 1940:218–19, 1961: 256ff; cf. Girard 1949:197, 645–56). Aldea solidarity was reproduced by communal work, finances, fiestas, and a "chief-priest" who bound the lineages through *compadrazgo* (godparentage). Representative elders (*principales*) from each aldea formed township (municipio) committees. Township boundaries were clearly marked and indicated by processions of patron saints, land titles, and standards. Lineages, aldeas, and townships informally managed a confusing array of land tenure systems—from private to communal, Indian-municipal, and nonethnic municipal lands. Girard witnessed Ch'orti's uniting across municipal boundaries in 1945 during the start of the Democratic Revolution to demand the right to elect township leaders (Girard 1949:280–97, 197; Wisdom 1961:259–60, 324–25).

Today, many aldeas have grown beyond one thousand people (see appendix 4), and no unifying clan structure can be said to exist. Personal and kin interaction is strongest at the level of the barrio, but aldeas continue to be synonymous with "community" more than any other social unit. They continue to be highly endogamous, and their members generally know everyone in their aldea, including those as large as Pelillo Negro with 260 households. Each aldea has its own lore about such place names like Cow's Head (Ujor e wakax) and Deer's Cave (Chen e masa'). One young man proudly recited his origin myth for Pacrén (meaning "crouched"), which actually is a popular regional story with strong Meso-american symbolism.

> Four angels went to the stream to fish but three of them killed the youngest and stole his fish. The angel was resuscitated by a *siguanaba* [female water demon] to hunt and fish for her. She took the form of his mother, the Virgin, but a vulture eventually warned him that his real mother was poor and sick in the sky and his host was a siguanaba. The angel didn't believe him at first, but he eventually placed a rock in his bed as a decoy. The siguanaba thought the lump in the bed was the angel, and shattered its teeth on the rock and fled screaming. The angel coaxed the vulture with meat to carry him back home to the

2. While Girard recognized aldeas to be composed of clans (*syan otot*, "many houses") with many lineages each (*piarob'*, "relatives"; *takarob'*, "helpers"), he considered the clans to be exogamous.

sky, but the vulture's headstrap pulled the skin off its head, which is why vultures are bald to this day. The angel then asked the hummingbird to carry him, but the hummingbird said it would be difficult. So the angel coaxed the hummingbird with nectar and honey, and the hummingbird indeed carried him, which is why hummingbirds are free to travel where they want and eat nectar, while vultures are condemned to eat rotten flesh. The angel found the Virgin naked and dying. He wanted to provide her with meat, so she said that he should recover his father's hunting tools, which were in the hands of his uncles. He lowered himself to the earth by a thread, but it broke, causing him to land crouched (*pacrén*) on his hands and feet, the impact of which can still be seen near the Pacrén school. Through trickery, he proceeded to get his father's machete from Uncle Deer, the drum from Uncle Monkey by shining the machete's reflection into his eyes, and the gourd canteen from Uncle Owl. With these objects he rose into the clouds and was able to make lightning (machete), thunder (drum), and rain (gourd). They say that all occurred right here in the aldea. (cf. Pérez Martínez 1996:46–48; Girard [1962] for ancient Maya symbolism)

Aldeas continue to be united by reciprocal work among kin and neighbors, although kinship tends to be irrelevant beyond first cousins, aunts, and uncles. Unlike Ladino employers, Ch'orti's always pay day laborers with both money and meals. They lead by example rather than giving orders, such that it is often difficult for the outsider to know who is in charge (see Smith 1987). During planting, day laborers are always given a lunch with meat, a survival from the traditional sacrifices of fowl to the Earth and rains at planting time. Because weeding is arduous, it is preferably done in groups of reciprocating campesinos, usually relatives or in-laws. Though sometimes young men compete, work is rarely hurried. Men gossip about women and feuds, and none bring a watch. Roughly every half hour small breaks are taken to drink and chat, and workers return to work on their own accord.

Women prefer to work together, even if the task does not require it. The process of making tortillas is grueling, starting with the husking and shucking of corn, the soaking in lime (chalk) water to soften the kernels, and then making the dough and toasting the tortillas. Company is sorely appreciated,

6. *Mother and daughters shucking corn, Tuticopote.*

and female visitors, especially kin and in-laws, often lend a hand. Group house construction and sugarcane processing are as much all night parties as they are tasks, with provision of food and drink by the owners and endless joking and gossip. Many people still do *lomos* or *cambiomanos*, in which owners of plots exchange days of labor with each other, and Pedro said that in Pelillo Negro some even continue to trade lands during agricultural seasons, depending on what crops they want to plant. Reciprocity can also be generalized to the extent that Cresencio let a penniless man pay off a debt by laboring in planting, inviting him to "come and eat chicken with us." Pedro permitted a man to plant beans free of charge in his field where he had corn. In Las Flores, another landowner invited the entire community to harvest mangos in his one-acre grove.

Food constitutes added symbolism regarding reciprocity, and López García (1993) concluded that food is the symbolic core of Ch'orti' culture. Sharing and eating the same food indicate alliance and ultimately shared humanity. The two categories of subhumans said to go to hell are sorcerers and those stingy with their food. Dary, Elías, and Reyna (1998:262) were instructed that one who does not share food, does not receive rain. One of the first questions I was often asked by new acquaintances was

whether I ate tortillas or not. Gringos, besides having an appetite for children, are presumably averse to eating tortillas. In Tuticopote I was constantly reminded that Jaime, a Peace Corps worker who served the area
for five years, was *buena gente*, "a good person," because he consumed
tortillas and beans. Formal oratory is an integral part of such reciprocity.
Parents give not just fowl, tortillas, beans, and coffee to their co-godpar-
ents (compadres) but ritual discourse in exchange for their lifelong concern for their children. One traditional saying used when greeting one's
co-godmother is "*t'ab'ay e k'inon, comadre*," or "our day/sun has arisen,
co-godmother."

A popular theme in Ch'orti' oral tradition is the value of sharing even
between the poorest and the wealthiest and most powerful (cf. Dary,
Elías, and Reyna 1998:255–56). As with the Earth Lord stories in western
Guatemala and Chiapas (Goldin and Rosenbaum 1993; Vogt 1969:308;
Laughlin 1977:149–51; Wagley 1949:58; Mondloch 1982:112–13; Gossen 1974:
294; Warren 1989:28, 80–82; Falla 1971), Ch'orti' stories emphasize that the
greedy, stingy, and haughty will be punished. A whole series of coyote (or
tiger) and rabbit (or tortoise, armadillo, etc.) stories tell how ravenous
predators are outsmarted by their prey and usually meet a brutal death.
The following story by Cresencio's son reflects how humility and generosity will ultimately prevail.

One of three brothers never worked and only fished, until a
duende [a supernatural, wealthy, exploitative Ladino, gringo,
or black trickster] asked him if he wanted to work on his ranch.
The lazy boy said, "Why would anyone want to work?" But when
the duende promised three bags of money for one day's work,
the boy consented. He walked the countryside generously
giving away the money, including to two girls whose mother
blessed him and his money. When he reached town only one
bag of money remained. The boy was filthy (*xuco*) from his
journey and asked a poor woman for a glass of water, but she
said, "Forget it, who would give a slimy man like you anything?
Filthy pig! Now get out of here!" So he went to a house of a king,
but the king responded the same, although he ordered his wife
to give him a half a glass of water anyway. Then the dirty boy
asked for a place to sleep, and the king insulted him again but
gave him a hammock among his cattle. While he was resting
he overheard the king saying "How am I going to pay for this

house, I owe so much!" Three times the boy asked the king what was troubling him, but all three times the king told him to shut up and sleep before he sent someone to kill him. Finally the dirty boy said he could pay for the house, and after much persuasion, the king finally agreed to consider it out of desperation. The dirty boy indeed paid for the house and still had over half a bag of money.

Now the king wanted to give him a chicken dinner and let him sleep in a nice bedroom on a nice mattress, but the dirty boy refused, his ego hurt by the king's previous insults. So the dirty boy slept among the cattle again, and in the morning the king took him down to an aldea where he told him to choose one of his five daughters for a wife. The eldest four said that no one in their right mind would want to marry such a filthy, stinking man. The youngest (*kume*) said that if it pleased her father, she would marry him. So she told the boy to buy her a gold chain for the wedding. Off he went but he spent almost all his money on it, which meant it was almost time for his soul to be given to the duende. So he returned to where he had encountered the duende, turned in the remaining money, and looked up to see the duende crucified because the money had earlier been blessed by the mother of the two daughters to whom he'd given money at the beginning of the story. So the filthy boy took three more bags of money from the duende's house and bought nice clothes, many cars, a nice house, and returned to marry the king's daughter. He pulled up to the king's house in his nice car and asked for a cow to slaughter, but the king did not recognize him and said, "Who would give a cow to just anyone who passes by?" The boy responded, "And after all I've done for you, you won't even give a cow for your son-in-law's wedding." "Ah yes," the king said, "you are the one, come, let's hold the wedding." Now all the daughters wanted to marry him, but the king castigated them for not wanting him before. The boy gave the gold chain to the youngest daughter; they married, and held a big ball. The other daughters were only given one plate of food, after which they locked themselves in a room and hanged themselves, which is how the king discovered them.

Palma Ramos (2001:162) recorded a similar story narrated by a healer, in which Jesus, sick with boils, passed from house to house in an aldea, but no one except a poor woman welcomed him. He warned her that the entire aldea would be destroyed by fire, and that she should flee without looking back when she heard a rumbling sound. She fled, but looked back, and she, her baby, and her dog were turned to stone along with the entire aldea, which is still visible near the aldea of Muyurcó.

Values of work and generosity are also seen in community leadership. Leaders are expected to work the most. In Pacrén, I repeatedly witnessed Cresencio and Augustín, the two leaders of a carpentry project, characteristically starting and finishing group tasks. Sefalino, a renowned entrepreneur, was tireless in his work and virtually ran over his laborers to get agricultural produce to the market on time. Cresencio contributed five times the money of other project members for the inauguration of a carpentry shop, and his sister Juliana distributed candy to all women and children except herself at the same event. Juliana, one of the most remarkable leaders I met, took it upon herself to embroider pieces for her entire cooperative when nuns threatened to call off the project due to low productivity. When at the funeral of a cholera victim attendants were hesitant to eat and drink as required by custom, Pedro stepped up and took the first plate so as not to offend the dead. Leaders also take experimental risks. When Romelio complained that it was impossible to organize people for projects in his aldea, Cresencio told him leaders lead by example, as when he planted trees and built terraces alone on his land to show the members of a soil conservation project that it is worth it. In 1997 at a workshop organized by the center-left FDNG (Frente Democrático Nueva Guatemala) political party and run by Guatemala's Civil Initiative for Democracy (INCIDE), twenty-five community leaders from Jocotán, Camotán, Olopa, and San José La Arada were instructed on practical democratic leadership. In one exercise the participants were asked how they determined a good leader. Their responses were striking in their unanimity: 1) for the work s/he does; 2) community trust; 3) ability; 4) honesty; 5) positive attitude; 6) sharing the same problems as his/her community; and 7) leadership in one's own family.

Leaders must also be gifted speakers. Cresencio and Juliana successfully encouraged a hesitant group of neighbors to sign up for literacy classes in their aldea by weighing the benefits against the costs and isolating the strongest dissenters. Juliana motivated women to participate in projects by frequently joking about her and other women's ignorance of such things as tools and door locks, reminding them that they are not alone. Never ashamed to speak Ch'orti' in town, Pedro often took a more direct approach, going into tirades that shamed the doubtful and hesitant. His leadership sometimes took the form of clever deception. For a long time I was confused about his contradictory stance on cholera prevention and medication. Privately, he was distressed with campesinos' refusal to take advice from health promoters, yet when the promoters held a community meeting he attacked them with the prevailing aldea doubts: the promoters' Spanish was unclear and required a Ch'orti' translation; their recipes for rehydration drink were too complicated; boiling and chlorinating water were costly and dangerous; prices of medicine were astronomical; and the health centers were burning corpses or throwing them in the river. I soon realized that he feigned these doubts so that the promoters could dispel them once and for all.

Though Ch'orti's face seemingly insurmountable divisive forces in their aldeas, including poverty, political violence, religious evangelization, and inequality, cooperation can amazingly override them at times. In Pelillo Negro and Las Flores, when drinking and violence reached tragic levels, a community-wide consensus was achieved to replace chicha-drinking with that of *sa'* (corn gruel) at celebrations. Many aldeas consciously do their best to bridge religious differences. Pedro of Pelillo Negro, though an Evangelical for years, regards evangelization of any kind to be beneficial and criticized his neighbors who ungratefully take advantage of the Catholic priests' economic assistance. Gabriel voiced his disappointment that Catholics, Evangelicals, and traditionalists always fight with each other. Cheo, a Catholic, concurred, elaborating that Evangelicals and Catholics worship the same god and are both hypocritical at times: one should not judge others by their group but by their actions. Don Pedro, a sixty-seven-year-old traditional ritual specialist since murdered, elaborated:

> [R]eligion, there doesn't have to be this hatred. One doesn't
> have to be angry when they see one another. No, better to do
> as a brother. If one is with the Evangelicals, let him study
> freely! And we in the Catholic religion, the same. . . . They're
> the saaame. And no hatred, there doesn't have to be fighting,
> of course. No, only to see. To only see, of course, that to
> each his/her own spirit. . . . My elders, the people of long ago,
> didn't have any religion.

The unification of aldeas for the sake of development is also impressive. It may be no coincidence that of the eleven Jocotán aldeas that organized themselves to receive DIGESA (Dirección General de Servicios Agrícolas) projects in 1993, all spoke Ch'orti' and were considered traditional (Guareruche, Las Flores, La Arada, Tesoro, Canapará, Guaroquiche, Pacrén, Matasano, Talquetzal, Los Vados, and Escorial). The ability to submerge intracommunity disputes for the benefit of the aldea was exemplified by the case of a Dutch-UN funded project in Pacrén. Two factions, upper Pacrén and lower Pacrén, had become sharply divided over the years but came together to receive project benefits. The rhetoric at the community meetings was that of unity, that they needed one group not two, that they needed to work together, that egotism must be repressed, that work should be free without some ordering others around, and that all should take Juliana's women's group as an example. The most compelling argument was provided by Moncho, who said that if for nothing else, they should unite for their children's future. In the end, the chasm between the two groups was too wide to be bridged permanently, but they maintained unity long enough—two years—to receive key benefits.

In Pelillo Negro, community organization during the cholera epidemic of 1992 was equally noteworthy. The community formed a committee of seven members to distribute rehydration mix and antibiotics to the sick. When the health center called community meetings, seemingly every adult man—some three hundred—arrived. The cholera committee called open meetings as well with strong attendance. At one, a multitude of young men listened and watched outside while inside the elders and middle-aged leaders argued over what form of water purification—chlorinating, boiling, or none—the community should unanimously adopt. The argument was heated but in a joking format, with each speech ending in a strained smile. Also impressive was Pelillo's subdivision into work groups and its fulfillment of a promise to use donated cement to build a latrine in each of its 260 households.

Allegiance to the township (municipio) is less important and a sense of pan-Ch'orti' unity across townships is weaker still if not nonexistent, but some institutions do unite Ch'orti's beyond their aldeas. As we will see below, various saints continue to serve as key symbols within and beyond townships despite the fact that no formal Ch'orti' religious organization (cofradía) in the Jocotán Parish has been operative since the 1930s (Fought 1969:474). Likewise, some town markets serve only the township, but others like those of Jocotán and Chiquimula are meeting places for the entire region. Within townships, public and private services and stores provide a common denominator where Ch'orti's across aldeas unite.

Ch'orti's are tacitly united across municipal boundaries by culture and ethos, which is especially obvious in language style. For example, polite conversation among Ch'orti's tends to have a unique rhythm consisting of a formal call and response banter in which the initiator introduces information and the respondent either repeats it word for word, repeats only the verb, or voices affirmatives "*b'an pues,*" "*b'anixto ya,*" "*jaxto verdad?,*" or "*ah vaya,*" "*sí pues,*" or "*eeeso.*" The repetitiveness was disconcerting to me at first, as people seemed to mindlessly repeat whatever I said as if they were paying no attention or disagreed with me. Another unique vocal style is a high-pitched song-call across valleys made between boys in which the callers may be so far away that they are barely visible. Greetings on the trail are also generalized and are practiced especially on Sunday when hundreds are leaving and returning to their aldea from the market. Some use "*yos'n*" (adios) and "*inko'*" (let's go) when passing, and others respond with "*ja',*" "*va pue,*" and "*koten pue*" (go then). When one visits another, the conversation is often initiated with "*kocha turet*" (how's it going?), and permission to leave is formally asked by saying "*k'ani inxin*" (I want to go) or "*inxi'x*" (I'm on my way), to which the response is "*bueno,*" "*vaya,*" "*koten,*" or "*kiki'*" (OK, go). I was once chatting in Ch'orti' with some friends in the back of a bus hours from the Ch'orti' area, and when by serendipity a Ch'orti' man from another aldea heard us, he forgot his embarrassment for speaking the language in public and enthusiastically joined in.

Not surprisingly, many Ch'orti's express a latent sense of ethnic solidarity. Many are very sensitive as to how I will present "the Ch'orti'" in this book. In all three of my host aldeas Ch'orti's sought to conceal feuds, murders, accusations of sorcery, and other events that lend a less than perfect image of themselves as "a people." When I raised the perennial complaint of lack of respect with Lonjino, he could not contain his irritation: "We, we respect people. In other words, a gringo arrives and we tell our stories, we are friends with him, he tells us his stories about the States and we tell about here again, and how we live, or how we eat, or how we drink. So, we're always the same."

Lest I overemphasize righteousness and order, the spices of life must also be included. Images of the mysterious Maya, the moral Maya, the exploited Maya, and the resistant Maya make Mayas seem asexual, humorless, and ultimately inhuman. Ritual humor and sexual symbolism have occasionally been reported, but with few exceptions (Nelson 1999; Paul 1974; Elmendorf 1976; Oakes 1951) little of sexual intimacy has been covered. Like Gillen (1952:202) among the neighboring Pokomams, I, too, was surprised to find Mayas so interested in sex. Perhaps Mayas have been desexualized out of respect—an honorable intention—but too much respect can dehumanize subjects.

Sex is a forbidden topic among parents and children. According to older women, despite the fact that adult couples and children sleep in the same room and often the same beds, teenage maidens know little to nothing about what to expect on their wedding nights (*noche buena*). Such taboos, of course, make sexuality all the more titillating. Male informants especially discussed, joked, and inquired about sex, some almost obsessively. On several occasions I was asked how many times gringos have sex per night. When a German man visited me, we were interviewed by a pair of brothers about gringo sex. This time the German had fresh numbers from a German magazine, which said that on average Germans had sex between two to three times per month, which disappointed the brothers who expected that much per night, as Ch'orti's purportedly have.

It is difficult to imagine how people in crowded aldeas could manage illicit relationships, but some do. Some men's marketing, migration to plantations, and pilgrimages offer opportunities both home and away. Some even clandestinely keep two households at once. One friend confided that extramarital sex involved lying to young women. So when I admitted to an attractive Ladina woman that I was still legally married, he said I had blown it. I should have said "no, I'm divorced, my wife and I are finished, and I only live for your love now." To lie to young women is the "sweetest" and easiest thing to do, and after all, no one is perfect, he argued. When I pleaded on behalf of the Ladina's feelings, he pensively replied, "yes, it is said that a woman's tears can bring tears to men," as if this were a kernel of ancient wisdom. Some men insinuated that they frequent brothels in Chiquimula, like the one run by two women years ago in Jocotán where drunks often violently competed for a $4 "turn." Men's visits to brothels would be a tragedy beyond reasons of infidelity and sexual objectification. Taking "turns" would strain the budgets of most families, and men seem little concerned about venereal diseases, although some contended that prostitutes are legally obligated to receive regular medical checkups.

Sex and the body are key sources of Ch'orti' humor, and humor is a much greater part of daily life than most ethnographies of Mayas reveal. Such humor involves pushing the limits of decency with references to bodily waste and puns equating penises with doves, bananas, machetes, and monkeys, of testicles with eggs, and vaginas with toads, monkeys, and mouths. I unwittingly prompted laughter when I would buy two eggs at a time, prompting suggestions that I must need them in the absence of my own. Old men instructed that the *tzujtzuk* bird is poorly mannered because it pokes fun at people, chirping, "*chinchin asuy*" and "*chakpwen asuy*," "your ass is rattling" and "your ass is pink." When Ladino health workers were making oblique references to excrement at a community gathering during the cholera epidemic, one man in the audience came directly to point, exclaiming "Shit!" in Ch'orti' (*ta'*) to an outburst of laughter.

As a man, the sexual jokes to which I was privy mainly involved men's objectification of young women (*ijch'oktak, patojas*). When a group of young men were hesitant to pull apart a tacky cement mold for a latrine project, the impatient mason barked, "What are you afraid of! Releasing a cement mold is like having sex with young women: if they don't like it from one side, you must work it from the other." Stories about gullible young women incite both humor and arousal. One tells of a young woman invited to a dance, and her mother warns her to protect her "monkey" (*mico*) because men would try to violate it. At the dance the young woman foolishly raises the issue to a man who asks her to dance, saying that she must protect her monkey. But the man responds that he has one too and challenges her to determine whose is stronger (his penis or her hymen), explaining that if hers is stronger she will have nothing to worry about. They went outside and the man entered her. The young woman returns home and innocently tells her furious mother everything but defends herself saying that her monkey would have won if not for its slipperiness (*gané el mico si no por el moco*). In another story, a poor, naked peon of the king tricks five of his daughters into "eating his meat" with their vaginas. Further male humor regarding the female body is seen in the popular story of the Devil and the fool. The Devil takes the form of a beautiful young woman and offers himself to the fool. As the fool is having sex from behind the Devil grows horns to scare the fool to death. The fool, however, only responds with glee, grabbing the horns for more leverage. In another story two fleas decide to seek warmth inside the "two caves" of a woman and complain to each other the next morning about the reasons for their miserable sleep.

It is little wonder that women are ill at ease among men, but women can be sexual jokers as well. The few times that I was privy to women's joking suggest that I was missing a lot. One woman made her newlywed son, grandson, and myself blush when she said the former is "working" (*war apatnob'*) to have children. At a fiesta some older women were surprised to hear that I was still single, and they joked about me finding a Ch'orti' woman because the nights are cold. When I reminded them of my presumed cannibalism, they cackled and invented many derivative jokes, which intensified my embarrassment, causing even more uproar.

Amusement with female promiscuity is intensified when it takes on an ethnic component, as seen in the Dance of the Huastecs during the Jocotán patron saint's festival in July. Although the dance is no longer performed as a narrative drama, it continues to include the *grasejo* monkeys, the black Indian king, the evil sorcerer, Cortés, and Malicia (Malinche, the Ladina mistress and translator for Cortés). The highlight for the largely campesino audience is Malicia's sexual offers to men (cf. Bricker 1973). One old man standing next to me giggled uncontrollably, "That little whore!" Once, I taught a poor, rural Ladino some words in Ch'orti', which he tried out on some young men, who only proceeded to ridicule him by acting as if he had said, "I want to have sex."

Ethnic ridicule is also a common theme of funny stories *(casos)*, for the performance of which some men are renowned. A few favorites pit campesinos against gringos and priests. One story tells of a gringo who challenges a campesino by saying that everything is bigger in the United States, but when the campesino presents a turtle as a flea, the gringo admits defeat. In another popular story, a priest rides up on his horse while a campesino is defecating. The man quickly covers his excrement with a hat and holds it down as if guarding an animal. The priest asks what it is, and the man replies that it is something very valuable but it would escape if he lifted his hat. The priest agrees to guard the hat and lend his horse to the man to bring back help. The campesino never returns, causing the priest to lose his patience, uncover the hat, and leap at its contents, dirtying his hands. As he sits reflecting, he scratches his head and smears it in his hair. In another story, a gringo is given an avocado, but does not understand how to eat it. The campesino explains that you peel off the outside and eat the inside. A little later the campesino notices the gringo gnawing on the pit.

Ch'orti's also playfully turn ethnic humor inward. One man laughingly recounted the story of his father and uncle who as young men went by train to a rally for revolutionary leader Juan José Arévalo in 1944. The uncle left the train to defecate along the way, and the train left without him, forcing him to undertake the three-day journey home on foot. Similarly, another recounted with hilarity that a poor campesino had to defecate in his sombrero and use his handkerchief to wipe when on a cattle truck that hauled workers to a distant plantation. When later in the conversation he asked me the distance by bus to the United States, he and his wife wondered how passengers managed their bodily necessities all that way. I explained about bathrooms on moving buses, and he quipped that it would be just like a campesino to arrive in the United States with shit all over himself.

The clever use of proverbs is another source for humor. Pedro's brother Raul, an expert in the verbal arts, provoked an eruption of laughter when he invented the following proverb in a Maya seminar about whether to celebrate October 11, 1992, as opposed to the twelfth (the Columbian Quincentenary): "The chicken does not celebrate the day before it's going to be killed." When it was suggested that a Ch'orti' group both march to the Copán archaeological ruins and perform a drama the next day to commemorate the preinvasion era, the motion was voted down as too involved after he quipped, "a man cannot sustain two women at the same time." On another occasion Pedro was in a heated argument with some rivals on a long, cramped ride in the back of a pickup truck, and to break the tension he remarked that two men whose legs were interlocked were "playing footsie" (*jugando la pierna*). His brother cracked, "when there's love, the sex doesn't matter," igniting an outburst of laughter.

Most exotic to me has been humor about pain and death. My pain was sometimes heartily enjoyed, as if I were a mere cartoon character. The times when I was struck in the head by a large exploding firework and hit in the face with a soccer ball come to mind. But all are potential clowns, including a man who tumbled down a steep ravine while playing soccer. The suffering of pets can be laughable as well, such as a whining dog that was held in the air by the collar, a dog whose ears were twisted for fun, and another that was made to yelp as a loop of thread was pulled tight around its ear by an old man. I once witnessed young men laughingly kick their dying, already putrid dog down a ravine. When one man jovially described in detail how he macheteed a family dog with rabies, the owner, after some silence, forced out a "thank you," prompting an outburst of laughter from the bystanders. When I expressed grief that a family cur I had befriended died from rabies, a group of women could barely cover their mouths in modesty as they tried to repress their giggles. Children raced enthusiastically to tell me when an orphaned kitten I had nursed back to health died unexpectedly. Many do express loss over the death of their animals, but indulging one's emotions in animals is absurd. Even human death is humorous. When others or I have been sick, friends joked that we might die. I once passed a group of men carrying their dying father, stricken with cholera, to town in a hammock. I gave them medicine and told them to hurry and get him an IV, at which point they burst out, "Yeah, because he might die!" (cf. Bowen 1954).

Here Be Dragons: Ladinos, Gringos, and Blacks

If Ch'orti's find ethnic humor particularly funny, it is because, like sexuality, ethnicity is a source of concern. Ch'orti' suspicions of ethnic others reflect and reinforce their localized lifestyles and worldviews, but as they are gradually having more contact with ethnic others, their perceptions and stereotypes are becoming more complex and sensitive. Like supernatural beings, outsiders like Ladinos, gringos, and blacks (*negros*) are "strange," potentially dangerous, and treated with caution. The Ch'orti' language has two words that translate as "strange" (*extraño*), *yantaka* and *intya'ch*. "Yantaka" refers to a strangeness that is unsettling, as when Carlos told me that he woke up feeling strange (*sakojpe'n yantaka*), meaning that he may have felt sick or had a nightmare. "Intya'ch" is more neutral, but is sometimes used to describe the current feeling of alienation (*intya'chix*, "life is already strange").

One conversation with a friend highlighted that the non-Ch'orti' world is yantaka. He asked whether there are people, like military experts, trained to look through forests. I said that I knew of none, but I did know of X-ray machines that can look through people's bodies. After some thought, he continued by offering that purportedly some "chemists" can walk into a mountain and come out the other side. "Maybe if there were a cave," I smirked, but he, offended, insisted, "No, they enter the rock and emerge on the other side." He had also heard that a large snakelike creature called a *siercón* lives in the mountains as well, and that some guerrillas in the Petén, when pursued by the army, jumped in a lake and emerged at the Canadian embassy. "Like magic?" I asked. "Exactly," he responded. He asked if it was possible, and I responded that I had heard of professional magicians but did not know the extent of their powers. He supposed it was a "study" (profession) like that of clowns. Spooked by clowns, he asked if it was true that they hurt people and found it humorous when I said that some clowns are women.[3] He then asked whether men walked across ropes or not, and I responded affirmatively, but pointed out that they are not always successful. I then contributed that some men can be tied up, submerged in water, and emerge untied minutes later. He was impressed and immediately categorized it as magic. This led him to discuss failed magic, like a fire-eating act in Zacapa that resulted in death. He asked if magic was a "study" or not, and I said it was, but I knew of no schools in Guatemala. This confirmed his suspicions that it is "subversive," like sorcery or making clandestine liquor (*aguardiente*).

On the few occasions I took Ch'orti's to Guatemala City, they were bedazzled by the mysterious wonderland. One was deeply impressed at my nonchalant operation of an elevator, which seemed like magic. Another was enchanted with the elite Zone 10 and recounted how his friend wondered what was hidden behind the walls lining the sidewalks. Much to his awe, I explained that the fortresses were homes protecting the wealth of the powerful. When one man and I went to a large shopping mall, he was captivated by the guitars for sale, their prices, and especially the pet store, with its frightening spiny fish, the coral snakes, and lizards. Though curious, he resisted entering any of the stores because he was certain we would be evicted if we looked but did not pay.

Suspicions of Ladinos are conditioned by both direct experience and a long legacy of ethnic relations. As will be elaborated in chapter 7, Ladinos have manipulated and tricked Ch'orti's in many ways. A skit in one Camotán aldea portrayed its history as one Ladino trick after another. I was warned by Ch'orti's to watch out for crafty Ladino vendors, such as those selling pork rinds (*chicharrones*) with trichinosis, just as Ladinos warned me about drunk, thieving, and unsanitary Ch'orti's. The preferred way of dealing with Ladinos continues to be avoidance, sometimes against one's immediate interests. On a few occasions, friends lied to unknown Ladino visitors, telling them that the person they had come to see was not home. In one aldea distant from Jocotán, two hydraulic

---

3. A cartoonish Mexican Catholic religious painting is popular in the Ch'orti' area and perhaps Guatemala generally, in which a nun, a nurse, a monk, and a beggar, among others, are walking to heaven, while an Arab magician, a clown, a gambler, a ballerina, and a wealthy man with women on each arm are walking towards the fires of hell.

engineers sent to dig community wells were treated with such suspicion that the project was nearly abandoned. In 1994 some campesinos refused to cooperate with national census takers due to rumors that children's names were being written for their eventual kidnap. The army was called in to enforce compliance.

Also demonstrative was the reaction to Ladino health workers during a cholera epidemic in 1992. The vast majority of parents are cautiously cooperative when the health clinics carry out vaccination campaigns and weigh children to determine malnutrition, but their nervousness is etched on their faces when their children cry. During the cholera epidemic, the nervousness, anxiety, and suspicion overrode trust in many cases. The propaganda campaign against cholera was suspected from the start, as many refused to believe that the vomiting and diarrhea were any different than the common worms, sorcery, or spirit possession. When the disease struck and people died at an alarming rate, rumors of the health care workers' evil intentions abounded. Some pointed out that the affliction came from outside their communities, insinuating that the townspeople were to blame. The recommendation to chlorinate their water was suspected as well, as all knew that chlorine is poisonous. Others spread rumors that the chlorination of springs would dry them permanently, and one even argued that boiling water is harmful to one's health. Many argued that the health center was charging what they considered to be unjust sums for their services, such as Q50 a day for inpatient care or Q.50 per pill, though the center staff insisted that they charged nothing. Another rumor had the center killing inpatients, stuffing cotton up their noses, and either dumping the cadavers in the rivers or burning them. Some, therefore, refused to seek medical attention or register family deaths, despite the threat of a Q100 ($18) municipal fine. Some victims even sealed their stricken loved ones' fates by hiding them from health care workers even as they passed their homes with IV fluid and antibiotics. Those who recovered were subject to further rumors that one should not eat beans, chicken, or greens within forty days. In the end, the health workers exhausted themselves as much in education and combating rumors than in actual medical treatment.

Although contact with gringos has been on the rise due to Christian proselytism, international development projects, and tourists en route to Copán—not to mention foreign anthropologists—they are more yantaka than Ladinos. Apprehension partly stems from their strange physical differences, such as having "cat's eyes" (*unak'ut e mis, ojos de gato*), light

7. *Burial of cholera victim, Suchiquer, Jocotán, 1992.*

skin, and enormity, standing a foot taller than the average Ch'orti'. Even snarling dogs have picked me out of Ch'orti' crowds. I overheard one man saying that gringos are light skinned because they eat white beans, instead of the traditional Ch'orti' black beans. When I first moved into Pacrén, a boy warned me about demons, and when I asked him what they looked like, he responded, "You." Some initially wondered whether I was a *kech'uj*—a tall, wiry, hairy, cannibalistic monster with backwards feet—and only my demonstration to an old woman that my feet were not backwards won me her cooperation in my census. Even when Ch'orti's knew me enough to suggest I marry a Ch'orti' woman, there were wild rumors and jokes in all three aldeas that I had a two-foot-long "machete," or penis, which may relate back to the *kech'uj* again, as its Nahuatl cousin, the *tzitzimitl* (pronounced *tisimite* in Oriente Spanish), is thought to drape its long penis over its shoulder (Carl and Mary Wolgemuth, pers. comm.). Not to leave white women off the hook, two men shared their desire to have sex with gringas but worried about the biting teeth in their vaginas.

The linkage of gringos to barbarity is widespread in Guatemala (e.g., Oakes 1951:264), and national rumors that gringos have been stealing children for adoption have done nothing to allay Ch'orti' suspicions. Unlike the rest of Guatemala, however, Ch'orti's assume that child abduction is for cannibalism rather than adoption. Even one of my best informants insisted that he heard on the radio that a gringo was apprehended on the Honduran border with a suitcase filled with human flesh. The roots of such suspicions likely lie in Ch'orti's' cultural emphasis on food. As sharing food is a defining characteristic of morality, sociability, and contentment, it is logical that creatures with anomalous physical features and behaviors, like kech'uj, one-eyed giants, gringos, and blacks are suspected not only of refusing to share with humans but eating them. Other anomalous beings also have "strange" eating habits. For example, *sínculos*, or "without anuses," are dreadful people condemned to receive their nourishment via aromas only. *Sipitillos* are diminutive humanlike creatures that sneak into people's kitchens at night and eat the ashes of their hearths. *Húngaros*—probably a reference to Gypsies who passed through the area at the turn of the twentieth century—eat only mucus, eye crust, and earwax. Cannibalism beliefs may also relate to the ancient Oriente indigenous custom of giving the flesh of children in sacrifice (García de Palacio 1985:38).

As if being cannibalistic and sexually monstrous were not enough, gringos are greedy for money and souls. Some Ch'orti's told me stories of a German or American archaeologist who illicitly robbed gold from Maya ruins, or gringos who offered little money for horses that campesinos later discovered were worth a fortune. Some, in fact, "know" that I am collecting a literal wealth of information and photos. One man apparently thought that I was a duende. I was new to his aldea and had met him on the trail, but he was reluctant to grant an interview as promised. After an interview fraught with suspicion, he refused to accept my gift of clothing and chuckled with his wife satisfactorily as if he had outwitted me by avoiding a spiritual debt. When US Evangelical doctors set up a one-day clinic in one of my home communities, the dentist called me over to verify whether a woman actually wanted her tooth pulled. Still learning Ch'orti', I spoke to her in Spanish. Yes, she wanted the tooth fragment pulled. Within ten minutes the dentist called me back because she refused to open her mouth. This time I asked in Ch'orti', and with a sudden burst of confidence she asked whether his extraction would rob her of her soul (*me'yn*, "shadow"), as other women had told her. Not surprisingly, surgery is out of the question for many Ch'orti's. Ladino acquaintances once convinced an aldea couple to permit doctors to take their daughter to the United States for a harelip operation, but the couple cried as if their daughter were being taken to hell. Another couple simply refused to have their son taken. Some elders feared that my photographs would rob them of their souls.

As mentioned in the introduction, all gringos are also suspected of being Evangelicals. Though foreign Evangelicals consider themselves spiritual saviors and are living legends to converts, many Catholics and traditionalists regard them as offensive and confrontational. Some Evangelicals have gone as far as to blast music into cathedrals to disrupt mass and yell that Catholics are going to hell during funerals. One Ch'orti' who witnessed an Evangelical worship session was certain they were praying to the Antichrist (Cristo del Infierno) because their heads were bowed to the ground.

Whites or gringos are assumed by some traditionalists to come from the primeval, sickening, and dangerous Four Corners of the universe, fears that periodic US wars do nothing to allay. In the early 1990s many had heard about the Panama invasion and the Persian Gulf War, by which they were both fascinated and terrified, some asking whether the United States would ever consider attacking Guatemala. Unwittingly, I explained that the United States already had. I added to a friend's terror when he asked about satellites racing across the night sky. My explanation led to his questions about whether they could watch us, and I confirmed the existence of US spy satellites. This gave him chills and he began to hear noises in his house yard. He already knew about the use of napalm against civilians only a few miles away, which he referred to as "burning bullets" but had not known they came from the United States. His uneasiness about gringos and their governments deepened when I could not resist expressing my anger at a US Supreme Court decision allowing the US government to kidnap or "forcibly extradite" suspected criminals from other countries, and at the Bush administration's undermining of the 1992 global environmental summit in Rio de Janeiro. Even more terrifying was my German friend's discussion of the Nazis and their employment in the US intelligence service after World War II.

Blacks played an important role in the history of the Oriente, including crafting the architectural artistry of the Esquipulas Basilica (Horst 1998b), but due to intermarriage, phenotypical "blacks" are rarely seen outside of the Department of Izabal and are thus more exotic still. Most tales about blacks refer to their cannibalism and sexuality, and often end in their gruesome deaths. In one, a man whose community was threatened by a cannibalistic black family enters their cave when their father is gone and machetes all the children, similar to another story in which a man captured by a giant eagle kills the brood in the nest. In the opening episode of another story, a campesino and two black men save a princess from a monster, but the blacks intend to rape her. The campesino bribes them with Q100 to spare her, and although they think he is foolish, they accept his money anyway. One man asked me whether blacks were all cannibals who emerged from local caves, because his brother, who had been attending pan-ethnic meetings in Guatemala, was now insistent that blacks were oppressed just like Mayas and had forcibly been brought to Guatemala for slavery.

God's Children

In a hostile world, traditionalist Ch'orti's still have the assuredness that they are God's chosen people. Fewer and fewer people, however, are traditionalists. Much of what Wisdom and Girard described about Ch'orti' spirituality in the 1930s, 1940s, and 1950s has long been in a process of abandonment. Gone is the Maya 260-day ritual calendar (Girard 1949:411), religious brotherhoods that organized the dance dramas of cosmogenic significance, such as Camotán's Dance of the Giants (Wisdom 1940:451–52; Girard 1949:351ff), and the times when only one priest served all eleven townships in the Department of Chiquimula (Girard 1949:401–2). Yet, while 60% of the 436 households in my survey identified themselves as Catholic and 10% Protestant, Ch'orti's regardless of religious affiliation tend to speak of natural forces as animate, especially the Sun, although many converts regard the traditional rituals as evil. Some Protestant leaders have confided that spreading the Gospel even among their own converts is an uphill process. The elders in particular still devoutly cling to the old ways by reciprocating with various unseen powers, to whom they "pay" (t'ojmar) food, incense, and especially candles for favors. They refer to their language as the b'ajxan ojroner, or "first language," and believe that cosmogenic events that formed the Earth and life in general took place in the region's aldeas. The Sun, the Moon, the Clouds and Rain, the Wind, and the Earth itself take special interest in Ch'orti' behavior.

Like other Mayas, for most Ch'orti's "God" is both the Christian god and the Sun, or "Our Father" (k'in, Katata'). Often elders will signal towards the Sun when they speak of God, and the intransitive verb e'ron means both "to shine" and "to be seen." Western Christian converts often speak of God bringing light into their lives, which only reinforces Ch'orti' traditional imagery. Valvino has faith in "the god passing at the moment," the Sun, because he guides them everyday, and if they failed to worship him, evil would befall them. Middle-aged Catarino explained, "It's always the same. . . . Is it not why God is with us? . . . If the people don't take care of him, he won't shine every day." In a prayer honoring the Black Christ of Esquipulas—the image most closely associated with God and the place to which pilgrimages have persisted at least since the image was sculpted in 1596 (Fuentes y Guzmán [1699] 1933:198)—a Ch'orti' prayer-sayer thanked him for bringing visibility (*claridad*) to the world and asked the Virgin (the moon, Katu') to shed light on his aldea. On March 12, some continue to make sacrifices to "the Lord above that shines here," as Valvino put it.

God takes many forms, but Ch'orti's, perhaps due to Christian indoctrination, perceive God as unitary. Even when speaking of God's helpers who bring the rains (*hombres trabajadores, ángeles, ajtakarsyaj*) and the Earth (Katu' Mundo, la Virgen), if asked explicitly, Ch'orti's will say there is only one God (*solo hay un Dios*). This expression, in fact, is sometimes used to emphasize the brotherhood between people of different religions and colors. Sometimes the rains are referred to as God, as in "God is not falling" (*ma'chi ak'axi e Katata'*; also *la bendición*, "the blessing"). In one conversation, Miguel mentioned that he had heard of rainmaking machines in Africa, and Mancho piously explained that Ch'orti's relied only on God. Other times God is equated with the clouds, as when forested peaks are referred to as "God's seat" (*ubanco e Katata'*). Ch'orti's' insistence on the unity of God was strikingly demonstrated at a Ch'orti' gathering with Mayas from western Guatemala. Three K'iche's explained their pantheon of heart of sky, heart of earth, heart of wind, etc., but when one Ch'orti' wondered aloud whether this was polytheism, the discussion grew tense with the Ch'orti's insisting on one God (see Girard [1962] for the ostensibly unitary nature of Ch'orti' and ancient Maya gods).

Ch'orti's need God as much as God needs them, as God gives food and natural resources to them in exchange for an annual cycle of offerings that sustain him/her/them. For traditionalists, reciprocal relations must be maintained at all costs, but "the new generation" finds these costs prohibitive. The following paraphrased story by Vicente emphasizes that God must be respected and appreciated.

Once, when the Earth was flat, there was a great flood over all the land, but a few saved themselves with canoes. After it had

begun to dry again, God sent the vulture down to show the
people where land was, but the vulture saw the fish rotting on
the shores and ate them rather than helping the people. From
then on God banished it to eating only rotten meat. So God
sent the hummingbird down three times but each time the
people responded that they did not need God's help. Finally,
their heads were cut off and they turned into monkeys and
raccoons, which is why these animals have hands resembling
those of people.

One of the most important traditional rituals in the annual cycle has
been the offering to the rains and Earth at the start of the growing season
(cf. Palma Ramos 2001:91; Girard 1962). In Quezaltepeque and Chiquimula,
adjacent to the old Jocotán Parish, communal and even regional rain ceremonies are still practiced (cf. Dary, Elías, and Reyna 1998:257–64; Ramírez
Vargas 1995; Girard 1962). In Quezaltepeque, five cofradía "slaves" are still
sent to Esquipulas to bring water from a sacred spring for controlling
the rains (cf. Girard 1962:164; Gillin 1952:204 for Pokomams of San Luis
Jilotepeque). Soon thereafter, the two padrinos of the St. Francis the
Conqueror cofradía lead visiting "assistants" from distant parts of the former Ch'orti'-speaking region, including men from the nearby barrio in
which San Francisco resides, up to a mountain top on the night of April 22
to call the rains. Women and small children stay behind to prepare tamales
in the brotherhood hall for the peregrine men's return. Offerings are taken,
and candles are lit in front of dozens of eastward crosses representing
previous padrinos, who serve for two years. A "table" of plantain leaves is
set with five burning candles (for the Four Corners and Center of the universe), tamales, cups of chocolate, tortillas filled with beans (*ticucus*),
liquor, cigarettes, sweet bread, chicken, coffee, and corn gruel, which, except for the corn gruel, are later consumed in the brotherhood. The corn
gruel is thrown into the source of the local river, where a male and a female
turkey are also sacrificed, the male by cutting its neck, and the female by
drowning in a deep pool with stone weights. According to my Olopa informants, if the spring dries, the gods have refused to accept the offering. It
has become increasingly difficult to find people to accept the position of
padrino because it entails sacrifices of time, money, and wearing the out-
moded traditional dress for the rest of their lives (Ramírez Vargas 1995:10).
    In the old Jocotán Parish—ironically the only area where Ch'orti' is
still spoken—a few underground padrinos still exist, but the cofradías

have long become bankrupt and the padrinos were persecuted for presumably praying for drought.[4] According to some elders, there was once a time when it was not male and female fowl that were sacrificed, but a boy "prince" and a girl "princess" who danced before being killed (cf. García de Palacio [1985:38] for Asunción Mita; Landa [1941:323] for Yucatán; and Eber [1995:24] for Chiapas). Today, if rain and fertility sacrifices of fowl are made at all, they are done in the field at night where female chickens' and turkeys' blood, candles, copal incense, and sweetened corn gruel (*chilate*) are buried in a hole in the center of a household's quadrangular field, a microcosm of the four-cornered universe. In place of field sacrifices, some families practice la limosna prayers and sacrifices at New Year's, at which ideally a fowl is sacrificed for people's consumption while an offering of blood is spilled on paths leading to the house plot. Often an eastward-facing, quadrangular table is adorned as an altar with a candle at each corner (and sometimes one in the center), an arch of poinsettia (*komte'*) flowers and leaves, and the offerings of blood or chilate. At the limosnas I witnessed, the Trinity and Virgin Mary are thanked for both the old and new year and beseeched for protection.

In some traditional aldeas like Tuticopote, on January 15th sacrifices are made of the image of the crucified Christ of Esquipulas, known by Ch'orti's as "El Señor", "El Milagroso" (The Miraculous One), and "El Doliente" (The Aggrieved One). Beyond local Ch'orti' society and throughout Mesoamerica and the Carribean, the image is known as "The Black Christ" (for a history, see Horst 1998a). Chickens, copal, and candles are offered, tamales and corn gruel consumed, fireworks lit, and rosaries and archaic prayers said by contracted prayer-sayers (*ajk'ajpesyaj, rezadores, delanteros*). The most devout observe the three- to four-day round-trip pilgrimage to Esquipulas, walking on mountain trails and sleeping on sidewalks, patios, and in public parks. Despite the arduous journey, it is customary upon arrival that penitents walk directly to the basilica and wait up to six hours in line to kiss the image's silver cross, rub curative

4. According to Fought (1969:472–76), religious organization in the parish has traditionally been more informal and less influenced by Catholicism than in towns like Quezaltepeque, which has been influenced by its location on the road to Esquipulas, the principal pilgrimage site in Central America. Even when Jocotán had a religious brotherhood, which dissolved in 1933, the padrinos, the most respected of the ritual specialists, bore little relation to *capitanes* and *mayordomos* who simply supervised rituals.

candles against it, and plead for reciprocal favors. With the paving of roads to Esquipulas over the past fifty years, it has become a mecca for millions coming as far as the United States, Mexico, the Caribbean, and Panama. The Central American Parliament is seated there, and in 1996 Pope John Paul preached in Esquipulas for the image's four hundredth anniversary, although no Ch'orti's attended. In fact, in 1993, Ch'orti's were outraged that the church intended to clean the image of its black soot, a result of millions of devotional candles burned at its feet.

Below The Miraculous One in saintly importance are a host of municipal patron and "walking" saints that are at once biblical figures and animate forces controlling rain, health, and prosperity. Walking or traveling saints are diminutive wooden images that once decorated the *retablos* of the town churches but are now passed by rotating attendants accompanied by drum and flute through a complex network of aldeas in the region. These are the same saint cults persecuted during las ruinas for supposedly serving as a cover for campesino organizing. In each aldea the visiting saint is carried from house to house for fifteen or thirty days, and prayers and festivities are offered daily. Saints are typically dressed in campesino clothing, and their wooden travel cases are adorned with photos of the sick, recently deceased, and forced army recruits (before forced recruitment was stopped in 1994), with written prayers "offering hearts" for miracles performed, and with flashy ornaments like tinsel, colored plastic wrap, and money. Saints, like the government, will not meet requests without money and the proper formalities, and even then, as Mancho warned, they will not reciprocate with just anyone (*ma'chi uyajk'u te kwalker*). The arrival of a saint to an aldea is a special occasion because, depending on demand from other aldeas, they might not return for up to six years. Those saints resident in the churches, like Jocotán's St. James the Conqueror (Santiaguito), are ultimately subject to the parish's control.[5]

---

5. San Antonio del Monte (Saint Anthony of the Wilds), the patron of Sonsonate, El Salvador, and still an image on house altars of healers (Girard 1949:247), is solicited on January 17 in some aldeas like Tuticopote with sacrifices of food, copal, and candles to protect domestic animals lost in the wild. San Miguel is considered the commanding officer of the angel helpers who bring the rains, and is venerated with prayers and offerings on September 29. Saint Anthony of Fire (San Antonio del Fuego), who protects crops from the dehydration of wind and sun, was confiscated during 1960s (cf. Diener 1978). Saint Anthony the Child (Niño San Antonio) protects children, and Saint Lucy the Healer (Santa Lucía La Curandera) of Zacapa is supplicated by female prayer-sayers.

8. *Santiago, being carried in Pacrén.*

Saint James the Conqueror (Santiaguito) is patron of Jocotán, protects petitioners and their cattle with his sword (lightning), and provides maguey. During the Jocotán patron saint's festival, thousands of campesinos offer candles and money to Santiaguito and de facto the church in exchange for favors. Saint James the Apostle (Santiago Apostol) is guardian of the rains, and like other patron saints of the region, is said to bring rain whenever he is taken out of the church. Both Santiaguito and Santiago Apostol are annually paraded through Jocotán on their name day, July 24. San Francisco Conquistador of Quezaltepeque also "walks" the aldeas and provides rain, as does Santo Tomás of Copán, Holy Burial (Santo Entierro) and San Manuel of Jocotán, and San Isidro (cf. Dary, Elías, and Reyna 1998:249). San Lucas of Camotán is the guardian of domestic animals, and Santa Elena of the same town assists women in protecting house fowl. San Manuel and Jueves Santo (Holy Thursday) provide campesinos with long squash and gourds, especially if on their saints' days they wear ropes around the waists. La Divina Pastorcita (Divine Shepherdess), once the matron saint of Olopa, is considered by some to be the Black Christ's mother. The images of San Marcos and San Lorenzo (Saint Mark and Saint Lawrence) were confiscated, but they are still recognized as commanding officers of legions of angels who compose the winds (cf. Dary, Elías, and Reyna 1998:249).

More distant but potent entities include the stars (*ek'*) and moon (Katu', "Our Mother"). Falling stars can destroy crops and even portend death. Federico instructed that the Milky Way is a snake (*chan*) and an unpropitious sign of dryness. Lunar lore, though interpreted differently, is employed for optimal planting and harvesting. Corn and beans are planted when the moon is still "young and tender" so that it does not "burn" the seeds, and coffee and bananas are preferably harvested at the same time to prevent withering. Maguey also must be cut when the moon is "growing" (like a gourd filling with water) so as not to dry and stunt the plants.

The ancestors are both remembered with tenderness and nostalgia, but also considered a potentially haunting threat. The spirit remains in the world nine days after death, during which the deceased is celebrated with prayers (*novena*) and feasting on meat. The deceased is then buried in the local cemetery with the head facing west, to orient them on their way to the netherworld—where life is similar to this one (thus it is dangerous to sleep with one's head towards the west because one's soul is attracted to that direction). The grave is decorated with a cross, a gourd (*murur, tecomate*) full of water, sandals, and a sombrero (for men) for the journey. Traditionally, the funerals of young children are occasions for dancing and feasting by the parents and godparents because their souls go directly to the *gloria* (cf. Girard 1949:205). The deceased miss their kin and the comforts of home, and thus return on the anniversaries of their deaths and during the Month of the Dead, or Tzik'in, which corresponds with November.[6] At *tzik'ins*, families offer feasts in spirit to the dead and in substance to their neighbors. Families decorate their house altars with either wild marigolds (*flor de muerte*) or poinsettias and a tablecloth of banana leaves, on which oranges, bananas, squash, tamales, bread, coffee, corn gruel, tortillas, and candles (representing each remembered ancestor) are offered. A prayer-sayer is contracted to recite rosaries and ask each ancestor, whose name is provided by the owner, to receive food. Some say that the presence of ancestors can be verified when the flowers flutter or "dance" during the ceremony. All visitors are invited to feast after the prayers, and in more traditional tzik'ins, people dance and drink all night to the music of the marimba, guitars, fiddles, and accordions. Total expenditures can reach $60, nearly a month's labor on the plantations.

---

6. Tzik'in is a day in the ancient Maya calendar represented by a bird. Ch'orti's talk about one's soul or life essence leaving as a bird when one dies.

9. *Don Pedro, prayer-sayer at Tzik'in altar.*

Ghosts, Ghouls, and Sorcerers

Just as Ch'orti's have perceived positive natural forces in a localized, animistic way, so too have they perceived natural threats. Contrary to touristic images of Mayas communing with nature, traditionalist Ch'orti's are apprehensive about the forces beyond their control. Gillen (1952:196–97) found that Oriente Mayas in the mid-twentieth century had an ethos of trepidation, finding comfort in traditional routines that accommodated natural forces and aimed for minimum risk, whereas Ladinos more confidently approached the world in terms of resources and opportunities to exploit. This certainly fit the Ch'orti' experience, as an array of threatening phenomena haunted the landscape. San Antonio del Monte, deer gods, monstrous owners of springs, angels, saints, wind gods, and horned serpents posed constant threats of sickness, misfortune, death, and natural disaster if one failed to appease them with sacrifices and prayers (Wisdom 1940:382–93, 430, 435–36; Girard 1949:332–35, 405). Children, with their weak souls, were particularly vulnerable to kidnap, exploitation, and consumption by dual-sexed, white or black duendes who owned the hills, valleys, cattle, and wildlife, and who provided sorcerers with power in exchange for land and their sons (Wisdom 1940:408; Girard 1949:329–32).

As one might imagine for a marginalized, self-subsistent people who have been oppressed by political economic powers they can scarcely fathom, supernatural powers are capricious and dangerous. Earthly and spiritual threats, in fact, do not form distinct dimensions for Ch'orti's, but are integrated in one. A frightening noise in the night could be the state "security" forces, Ladinos after one's land, feuding neighbors, evil winds, ghosts, sorcerers in animal form, or monsters. Still today, the wind, thunder, and the mountains, while necessary for human existence, strike with little notice (e.g., Pérez Martínez 1996:32–33; cf. Condori Mamani et al. 1996:44–45, 56–57, 64–65, 75–80 for indigenous groups generally). For every state of the heavens (varying from seven, to seventeen, fifty, or five hundred), are corresponding states of hell. Each is staffed hierarchically with a host of saints and angels holding the posts of white and black princes, kings, colonels, soldiers, helpers, and lawyers. Healers draw their benevolent powers from the states of heaven, while sorcerers make pacts with the disruptive forces of hell, the Four Corners, and nature—the Earth, mountains, water, wind, dead, rainbows, celestial bodies, and lightning—to send evil winds to sicken or drown people's souls (Girard 1949:209, 318–32; cf. Taussig 1980, 1987; Kane 1994; Gossen 1993; and Hill 1988 for other indigenous groups).

For traditionalists, all misfortune happens for a malevolent reason. When social relations are strained due to competition for resources and power, sorcery offers a provocative explanation. Spiritual harm can be caused by simple ill will or intentional magical harm by sorcerers. Wisdom (1961:378–89) and Girard (1949:318–32) reported widespread accusations of sorcery, such that Ch'orti's even asked the hated Ladino municipal authorities to punish suspects. Sorcerers go to cemeteries and burn candles (usually black) upside down along with chiles, lemons, and other objects, whose light represents the moon and stars (Palma Ramos 2001:134). The evil forces they evoke have such names as "The Criminals, Bloody Absent Ones, The Shot [by guns], The Evil Wind, Prince King Serpent-Recuperater-Encloser, Damned Shield King (*rey broquero infernal*), Saint Anthony Shield King (*el rey San Antonio broquero*), Damned Lanzers, Damned Child Lanzers, Damned Humans, Damned Ostinecos (*ostinecos infernales*), Damned Authorities, [and] Playing Children" (Palma Ramos 2001:156–57).

Some acquaintances provided examples of sorcery. One year a friend's crops had been growing faster than his envious neighbor's, but eventually withered while his neighbor's prospered. The same man once had a stomach ailment that kept him in bed for six weeks and nearly killed him, during which time his brothers overheard some of his enemies relishing his death. He was eventually cured after the "small animal" trying to enter his heart was banished by a healer. Once I came upon him with an ashen look on his face. He explained that he had just slipped and hurt his back near his enemy's house, a certain sign of ill will if not sorcery. When I was trying to interview a man whose wife repeatedly told me that he was not home, a friend informed me that the man was sick and that I should not repeat it to anyone or the sick man would be violently angry. I surmised that a sick man with a weak soul was vulnerable to sorcery, and he was impressed with my progress in understanding evil. In Tuticopote, nonparticipants presumably envied a broccoli project, and participants gossiped about suspicious happenings to their crops. Broccoli disappeared, and some glimpsed an animal-like creature that vanished in their broccoli patches when they approached. This was surely a sorcerer, as only they are capable of changing into animals at night, including into pigs, ducks, turkeys, cats, and especially black dogs. The most persuasive evidence were candles found buried in the fields and even in the house of one participant. They were certain of the sorcerer's identity but not the revenge they would take (cf. Nash 1973).

While humans are masters of the daylight hours, dangerous animals and monsters (*aparatos*) rule the night (cf. Palma Ramos 2001:50). Of all supernatural beings, Ch'orti's seem most preoccupied with xerb'aj, *ausentes*, or *fantasmas*—the ghosts of the murdered whose troubled souls haunt the living. Pedro taught that all humans have two souls. The *nawal*[7] is given by God and returns to the Holy Spirit after death, which many have difficulty distinguishing from the me'yn,[8] which is at once the shadow, intuition, heat, and essence seated in the heart (*uxne'r*). The other spirit is the diabolical xerb'aj that may haunt the living after death. Cresencio informed me that xerb'aj, like other frightening spiritual forces, are brought

---

7. Nawals are not associated with animals as in western Guatemala and Chiapas. Among Ch'orti's, only sorcerers take the form of animals (cf. Wisdom 1952:122). Pedro and others who use this concept may very well have borrowed it from western Guatemalans with whom they had occasional contact.

8. Otto Schumann informed me that Chols have nine souls, but they don't distinguish them by name either.

back from the Four Corners by the assistants (*auxiliares*) of the princes (*príncipes*) to "play" in the locations of their murders. People must avoid these locations because the mischievous xerb'aj may enter their bodies, give them "fright" (*b'ajk'ut, susto*), and make them "cold" and sick. One friend told me that when he was late returning home after dark, he passed a tree where a man had been murdered and heard laughing from no visible source, giving him goose bumps. The security of his machete was enough to prevent him from falling into fright.

The landscape is littered with xerb'aj due to the military massacres and Ch'orti' feuds, such that I often unwittingly passed haunted places. When I was sick with what I thought was pneumonia and intestinal parasites, Miguel and Cresencio suspected a xerb'aj possession because I had passed many murder sites while undertaking my census and interviews. When I saw a healer, he asked my symptoms, if they came and went, if I had a fever, and if I passed a place where I had heard voices in the night. Evil diseases vary, he explained. Fright or b'ajk'ut produces fever and a gradual loss of appetite; the afflicted only wants "good things to eat" like meat and some-times dreams of the afflicting murdered person. The sight of monsters kills much quicker, in a day or so, from high fever and vomiting.

Because the me'yn of the recent dead—murdered or not—may refuse to leave to the next world, all deaths are hazardous for survivors. It is said that if one does not visit kin while they are alive, the kin will visit after death. When I attended the funeral of a woman who died suddenly from cholera, the attendants tried to break the tension by joking with me about carrying the funerary bundle. Days later a friend reprimanded me for jok-ing about xerb'aj when, unbeknownst to me, he had been "seized" in the legs, arms, and stomach by the woman's spirit the night before. He had brushed the cadaver's head with his arm while carrying her funeral bun-dle. Bathing is always required immediately after a funeral.

Pedro's brother related two stories involving ghosts (*ánimas*) and b'a-jk'ut. One November, a local married man went to his lover's house carry-ing a gift of two pounds of cheese. He blacked out in the trail and saw a group of people (ghosts) eating tamales (the quintessential food offered to the dead during the Tzik'in) and chatting. He was awakened by a passerby asking why he was lying on the ground. With fright, he returned home and died eight days later. Another man, a merchant, was returning from Honduras late one night when he passed through a grassy knoll (a cemetery), lost consciousness, and saw a group of people cheerfully ask-ing each other what kind of tamales they had received. One said he had tamales of beef, another turkey, etc. The merchant regained consciousness, fled the spot, and somehow survived.

During the rainy season, when the streams become torrents, dampness pervades everything, and the spirit of insatiability (*xiximay*) begins to lurk because grain stores are low, ghosts and sickening angels bring diarrhea, fevers, and death. One healer from Tunucó explained to Palma Ramos (2001:132), "that's why one must fear the water currents, because a water current contains ghosts of the drowned, the murdered, and the shot. And it all depends on the water and the justice it brings. Like it's raining right now; when the angels from heaven come, there are thousands of maladies, so one must take care." Another informant related how a woman was possessed by the spirits of crying children from a well (Palma Ramos 2001:161).

Apparitions of terrifying animals and monsters also cause disaster, illness (soul loss), and death. *Chijchan*s, or "great serpents," cause earthquakes, erosion, landslides (*kib'itz'*), and flooding (see Fought 1972:83–85, 96–99). They emerge from the mountains and streams when it rains, and the traces of their movements are seen in arroyos and eroded shorelines. When one hears the rumbling of an earthquake or a loud thunderstorm, chijchans have probably left their shelters to search for mates. Cresencio related that in 1951 the movement of the chijchans caused a great earthquake, after which people began to buy fireworks to frighten them away. When the chijchans emerge and cause damage, it is the job of angels (ángeles, *ajpatna'r winikob'*) to chase them away by hurling jade axe heads (found occasionally in cultivated fields) at them, thus causing lighting. Some claim the chijchans inhabit certain lakes and springs, such as the one where turkeys are sacrificed in Quezaltepeque's rain-calling ceremony. Some also say that the chijchans rumble beneath the earth whenever a foreigner, like a Ladino, gringo, or guerrilla, penetrates the forests of the mountain peaks (Dary, Elías, and Reyna 1998:252).

Kech'uj or tisimite—the creatures with which I was initially associated—are hairy, tall, wiry, humanlike animals with reversed feet who own the springs, traits that can be traced to prehispanic times (Klein 2003). They abduct children and are known to hide behind waterfalls, in trees, and in high weeds surrounding springs. One man told a few stories of a kech'uj that once roamed the forests of the neighboring Pelillo Negro and La Puerta, Chiquimula, kidnapping children by entangling them in their long hair as they sped across the mountains. Another friend related that his father was once walking home from town when he saw a tall, lanky image coming towards him. With the blink of an eye the being was already well behind him, certainly a kech'uj. As forests have become depleted, fewer sightings of kech'ujs have been reported. Siguanabas are manifestations of the kech'uj in that they are also cannibalistic and associated with water, but they trick their victims by taking the appearance of another person, usually beautiful women, and victimize drunks in particular (cf. Klein 2003:46–48).

Duendes, *dueños de la montaña*, or owners of the wild—with whom I was also sometimes linked—tempt solitary travelers with money in exchange for their souls. Some say that one encounters a duende under an *amate* tree, where he attracts men to play cards and drink, after which he takes all their money. Some duendes are said to take the form of dwarfs with large sombreros (Wisdom 1940:408), like the Ladino diminutive *sombrerón*. For some Evangelical Protestants, duendes and other demonic creatures prove that Satan is indeed at work in the aldeas.

Cresencio's story of "The Duende and the Drunk" conveys the duendes' insidious persistence. A drunken campesino was thrown in jail one Sunday, and a Ladino appeared in his dream and asked if he wanted his freedom. The drunk knew he was a duende, so rejected his offer twice, but the third time he accepted his freedom in exchange for killing someone (*entregar inte' alma*). But upon leaving jail, the drunk did nothing and was promptly thrown in jail again. Again he made an agreement with the duende but failed to comply and was thrown in jail. The third time he was caught, the police chained him in front of the police station, but the duende made the man invisible and he simply walked away. The duende continued to harass him about killing someone, so he went to church and prayed to God for protection, but he heard the duende's voice saying he must comply. Years passed, until one day a giant vulture nearly grabbed him, and he realized that it was the duende. So he hacked a man to death, and was thrown in jail for five years. The duende offered his release if he would kill again, but the man was filled with remorse and opted to wait out his five-year term.

Seeing through the Opaqueness

According to the ancient K'iche' Maya narrative the Popol Vuj, the gods made the current race of humans so perfect that they felt obliged to cloud their vision and make them more subservient. Many of the forces and patterns governing life and death are now invisible or opaque, like breath on a mirror (Tedlock 1993). Unseen patterns and invisible forces have their signs, however, and spiritual specialists have special powers to read them. Some signs are popularly known. As in the other Cholan-speaking areas, to lose a tooth foretells losing a child, and the appearance of birds, butterflies, and moths can indicate the visit of a human visitor or spirit (Otto Schumann and Alfonso Lacadena, pers. comm.). A dog lying on its back, a cat cleaning itself, and the call of the robin (*chorcha*) also portend visitors. Black moths and owls mean death, as in other parts of the world. Seeing snakes can be good or bad luck, depending on which direction they cross one's path, while leg and abdominal cramps are understood as malignant snakes. Several animals, including swallows (cf. Palma Ramos 2001:67, 101), toads, and turtles, indicate rain, which is important for planting. Sculptures of the latter two, in fact, can be found in nearby Copán Ruins. Babies conceived during a full moon will be healthy. Those born during a full moon will be aggressive, while those born during a waxing moon will grow large. Those born during the rainy season will have special abilities to grow greens (Palma Ramos 2001:55).

Dreams offer many clues to future events and are routinely discussed upon waking. If their signs are yantaka, a diviner (*ajk'in*, *sajurín*, *sabio*, *xucurero*) might have to be consulted. Unlike the psychoanalytic approach, in which dreams are a window into one's childhood past, Ch'orti's interpret dreams as indicators of future events. Dreaming of black dogs is inauspicious according to Miguel, and Pedro related that nightmares generally portend the death of kin. Miguel instructed that if one dreams of a woman in red, one will die in nine days. He told of how one man dreamed that he was walking far away until he reached a cave where a woman in red invited him inside. He awoke terrified and died in nine days. Another man dreamed of a woman, though not dressed in red, and the next day he was thrown in jail for fifteen days. Pedro and Federico explained that women in red and dreams of snakes mean that one will be thrown in prison, have an accident, or have a confrontation with an enemy, and Federico added that a white dress portends illness. When I was sick and dreamed of a small skeleton peaking out from a pillar, some considered this a sure sign of a xerb'aj possession, or that my illness was b'ajk'ut. Not all dreams are inauspicious, however, and one man was optimistic after dreaming first about two Ladina women and then two daughters of a relatively prosperous Ch'orti' family. (I later asked his wife about her dreams, but she was too shy to respond.) Dreams can also involve one's me'yn or nawal dangerously leaving the body, always with the possibility of being killed or captured and leaving the body to die in bed.

In the old Jocotán Parish, each aldea tends to have its own cadre of specialists, including diviners, prayer-sayers, midwives, healers, and padrinos. Diviners are sometimes known as wise men or women (sabios), daykeepers (ajk'in, who in times past were able to read the Maya astrological calendar), and fortune-tellers (*sorteros*, from the Spanish *suerte*, or "luck") to whom the Black Christ has passed special powers. Besides interpreting troubling dreams, they diagnose illnesses and foretell such things as the compatibility of potential mates and the safety of distant journeys by reading patients' leg twitches while asking them questions, reading the movements of candle flames, and using taro or playing cards. According to one eighty-five-year-old diviner cited by Palma Ramos (2001:50), one can only divine with cards on Mondays, Tuesdays, and Saturdays because the cards deceive on the other days. Prayer-sayers (rezadores, ajk'ajpesyaj) include anyone who can recite archaic Catholic prayers at important ritual events. Though in the past prayer-sayers were generically referred to as padrinos, today "padrino" refers specifically to someone who can conjure the rains. Midwives (*comadronas*), who are always women, are specialized healers in their own right who proscribe certain activities, humoral and herbal medicine, and spiritual treatment. Besides caring for mothers and their fetuses, they are contracted to induce or prevent conception.

Healers (*ajnirom, licenciado, ajtz'akoner*) can be either male or female and are above all mediators or "lawyers" who plead that saints, princes, angels, and other invisible forces come to the aid of the patient rather than work against them. A force like electricity runs through the universe—through the Sun, the sky, the Earth—and can be harnessed to combat the evil winds that carry illness from the Four Corners. Simple healing ceremonies involve only prayer to adjust this energy, but in the more elaborate rituals healers offer candles, tobacco, incense, and household fowl to placate the angels. According to one eighty-four-year-old healer cited in Palma Ramos,

> There are instances when the ghosts of the infernal "missing ones" attack us on the trail; and they grab and tie us. What we do when they possess us is exorcise ourselves with tobacco and chickens. . . . We blow tobacco over the body to the chicken. Tobacco is good for all illnesses because it gathers up the ghosts. . . . We use red and black chickens, almost never white ones. We have to pray and everything in order to cure, but only in Ch'orti' because Spanish can't cure, only Ch'orti'. We also

pay the Lord to defend our lives. One molds copal incense into the form of a 25-cent coin and burns it. The copal is produced locally in the aldeas of El Guayabillo and Tierra Blanca, but you can buy it in town. (2001:49)

One healer explained that ten "coins" apiece must be paid to God, the baby Jesus, the Black Christ, the Holy Ghost, and San Antonio. Another healer advised that one can only heal Tuesdays, Wednesdays, Thursdays, and Fridays, but not Mondays, because it is the day of the spirits (ánimas) (Palma Ramos 2001:158–59).

During the two instances I was cured of spirit possession, which were manifest by fevers, upset stomachs, and prolonged weakness, I lay on my back as the healer chewed tobacco and blew over a live red chicken outstretched over my head, waist, and feet to absorb the spirits afflicting me. The healer went into a trance and at a dizzying pace pleaded with dozens of princes and saints (the exact patron of the xerb'aj is never known) from every state of heaven and hell to call back their helpers (auxiliares) to the Four Corners, for I was innocent (cf. Gillen 1952:204 for Pokomams; Oakes 1951:124 for Mams). I did feel better.

Ch'orti's follow general Latin American patterns in regards to balancing "heat" and "cold" in their foods, activities, settings, and corresponding cures (cf. Foster 1994). If one has a cold or flu, one should refrain from eating "cold" foods like bananas, avocados, and eggs, stay home during cold nights, and abstain from bathing at sunset. Corn and beans are "hot" and therefore counteract the symptoms of "cold" maladies. Pregnant women, whose heat is being lost to the fetus, should refrain from eating cold foods like onions, potatoes, avocados, greens, cabbage, and pork, while "hot" beef and chicken are desirable (Palma Ramos 2001:90). Those who are "hot," such as foreigners and sweating people, can give the evil eye to weaker, colder creatures likes babies and small animals, who can be protected if they wear red cloth or beads (see Girard 1949:194). Bodily secretions (except human waste) are manifestations of blood and thus heat, which can emit the evil eye and sicken.

Herbal remedies vary from aldea to aldea, but some are general. Palma Ramos (2001:20–23) recorded forty herbal remedies, and ethnobotanist Johanna Kufer (pers. comm.) recorded more than three hundred recognized plants. Many friends gave me *toxpe'* (*hojasalva, ruda*) for depression, oak bark for dry cough, and burned tortillas, beans, lemon, and coffee grounds (all bitter, *inch'aj*) for stomachaches. Other herbal remedies include: *ub'i'te'* (*pasote*), *waco*, *benadillo*, and *alcotón* (again for their bitterness) to rid one of parasites and alleviate sore kidneys; *tobardillo, chajte', curarina,* toxpe', *berbena, yerba buena,* and citrus fruits (except for limes, which are "cold") to alleviate flu symptoms; *sisarte'* for chills; and roots of young guayabo plants for body aches. *Pascinia* is said to be helpful for ridding one of evil winds (*mal aire*), sugar helps for rabies, toxpe' for fright (b'ajk'ut), mustard for calming spasms (*calambre*), and pine branches for "sweeping" away fatigue in front of crosses on pilgrimages. To repel xerb'aj, such as when food accidentally drops to the ground, one should reach for tobacco, chile pepper, or garlic. As in other Cholan-speaking areas (Otto Schumann, pers. comm.), the haunted place where one falls and is frightened can be dominated by consuming a bit of dirt or water from the spot, or in the case of children, by beating the ground with a stick to discipline the spirit.

Spiritual healing is not foolproof, as not all healers are equally adept, clients have varying strengths, and the spirits may not heed supplication. As Ch'orti's are prone to say of all constructive activities, one must "believe" or "obey" if the desired affect is to be achieved. Sometimes neither the sick nor the medicines "believe" or "obey" (*ma'chi uche creer, ma'chi uk'u'b'se*). One healer, who in the end refused to cure me, asked accusingly whether I believed in the force running through the universe, because otherwise the curing ceremony would be futile. Some townspeople contract Ch'orti' specialists, though most generally consider them sorcerers. According to one campesino, the Olopa townspeople blaspheme healers, yet they once contracted a padrino to bring rain. They purportedly threatened to kill him if the rain did not come, but it fell at the exact hour, frightening them. Because of sorcery accusations, some healers require a relatively high price for their services (up to Q40), while others insist that charging for services that come ultimately from God is a sin. Modern or "chemical" medicine complements spiritual and herbal healing in that it alleviates symptoms but does not resolve the cause of a malady. I once witnessed a client seek a healer who was not home, so the healer's wife simply gave him the "chemical" medicine her son had brought from the local health center.

For better or for worse, these beliefs and practices are in a state of flux due to crises caused by external pressures and opportunities, and internal contradictions. Localized culture is dissolving as "the new generation" has begun adopting and creating new cultures. The remainder of the book will elaborate on these pressures, opportunities, and contradictions, and what they mean for Ch'orti's' quality of life.

FIVE

The Dis-Integration of Subsistence Cultures

There used to be everything, everywhere there were trees.
—Cheo

Oh but today, as the population has grown, there are already people that want to do whatever they want.
—don Chico

When I initially set out to investigate the relationship between religion and the market economy, I presumed that Ch'orti' campesinos had a choice between self-subsistence and making money, including wage labor, marketing, and craft production. It did not take me long to realize that Ch'orti's have very limited options for income, and they must use any opportunity for survival, regardless of religion. It took me much longer to understand the structure behind this poverty and its social and psychological impacts. Ultimately, these impacts lead Ch'orti's to believe that they are, for better or worse, at the end of an epoch. While they reproduce longstanding traditions and create cultures distinct from the Ladino population, some of which contribute to survival in harsh circumstances, poverty above all undermines a sense of positive identity, especially when the poor are surrounded by a population that is fairing much better economically and politically. In this sense, extreme political and economic circumstances motivate Ch'orti's to question their subsistence lifestyle and explore alternative worldviews.

Too Little Land, Too Many People

Guatemala, like most world areas, has undergone a phenomenal demographic transformation over the past two centuries. The population doubled from roughly 600,000 at independence in 1821 to 1.2 million by 1880 (Lovell and Lutz 1997:120), and nearly tripled again to 3 million from 1880 to 1950. From 1950 to 2003, the population quadrupled to 12 million, despite massive emigration (Lutz and Lovell 1990:123) and mass political violence. Growing populations are linked to economic growth in industrializing countries, but for a country like Guatemala, in which so many inhabitants live off a land base that is in the hands of an oppressive few, population growth means mass malnutrition, disease, a low quality of life, and early death. Given that the elite are unwilling to sell the lands they value as status symbols, campesinos are quickly clearing the last stands of virgin forest in Guatemala (Bilsborrow and Stupp 1997:607). If campesinos and loggers continue to clear forests at the current rate of 1.2% of the national territory annually (seventy-four to one hundred thousand acres; *Cerigua* 6/12/97:4), forests will be only a memory by midway through the twenty-first century (Bilsborrow and Stupp 1997:595). This seems inevitable given that even if the 1980 birth rate of six children per woman miraculously falls to two by 2030, the population will still double to 24 million (Bilsborrow and Stupp 1997:589). One might hope that a growing economy could accommodate all of these people in jobs off the land, but the oligarchy and international companies favor mechanization over manual labor, exacerbating inequality, underemployment, and colonization of forests (Bilsborrow and Stupp 1997:595–96). Another solution is more emigration to the United States.

Few social scientists of Mesoamerica have taken population growth very seriously, if they have even recognized its problems at all, because they believe it to be strictly an effect of poverty, not a cause. From an orthodox Leftist perspective, attention to overpopulation and family planning overshadows the real and only cause of poverty: inequality. If resources were distributed equally in Guatemala, Central America, or the world, then overpopulation would not be a problem. From a modernization perspective, "overpopulation" is an outmoded term because development and industrialization can take a few acres of land on which fifteen campesinos cannot subsist, and create sustainable enterprises that can employ hundreds. Unfortunately, it is never as simple as this. Investors in development are rarely partners with their campesino-cum-proletarians, who are integrated as cheap labor at the bottom rungs of the global economy, where all minimum standards or worker and consumer protections, as ignored as they already are, are being made obsolete in "free" trade agreements. Others, including many Mayas themselves, hold a power-in-numbers logic, believing that family planning is a scheme to repress Maya power and even destroy their culture. The coercive family planning abuses of the past, though, do not obviate the fact that a poor and starving population is not a strong one. All of these arguments—Leftist, Modernist, and Mayanist—cruelly place politics ahead of human suffering.

Among the Ch'orti's, the rugged mountains that once offered refuge from overexploitation have slowly become a death trap. There are simply too many people trying to subsist by traditional methods on too little, increasingly infertile, land. According to the Guatemalan national censuses, the population in the old Jocotán Parish (Jocotán, Camotán, Olopa, San Juan, La Unión) grew arithmetically until the 1980s and has grown exponentially ever since (but see Adams [1996] and Early [1982:20–31] for problems with the 1940 and 1950 censuses, especially in regards to determining Indian ethnicity). This increase in rate is due to complete saturation of forests to the north by Ch'orti' emigrants and Ladino cattle ranchers, while chemical fertilizers increased agricultural productivity within the parish (see tables 3 and 5, and graphs 2 and 5 on the folowing pages). A cultural emphasis on fertility, the introduction of modern antibiotics, an absence of major epidemics, and no adequately funded, culturally sensitive family planning program have driven the population increase (Metz 2001b; Early 1982: 48, 50, 93–94, 161–62).

Some women long for the days when men could support eighteen children, but some young wives would like to space their births more broadly, and others anxiously express a difference between many children and too many children (Palma Ramos 2001:19; cf. Early 1982:140). Children are "too many" when families have little land, employment, and resources to produce crafts. Yet, there are few reliable and safe means of controlling the number and frequency of pregnancies. Modern contraception is culturally inaccessible, as Ch'orti's and family planning technicians have difficulty gaining confianza and understanding (see chapter 8). Some couples practice abstinence at key points in the menstrual cycle, but it obviously does not work for everyone, such as the couple I know

Table 3: Combined Population of Jocotán, Camotán, San Juan, La Unión, and Olopa*

1893	1921	1950	1964	1973	1979	1994	2003
24,952	43,617	48,030	61,945	64,150	66,941	91,438	130,562

*Data taken from the Guatemalan national censuses; 1950 and 1964 data based on Early's unpublished corrections to national censuses.

who practiced it but had fourteen births. Without careful recording, it is very difficult to know when an undernourished, overworked, and often breast-feeding woman is fertile or not (Early 1982:137). Breast-feeding, which lasts two to three years or until the next conception, is not considered a method for managing births but it probably contributes to birth spacing anyway. Some confided that menstruation normally resumes within two years after birth, but most periods between pregnancies are three to four years, and it is considered extraordinary that some women have blood strong enough to become pregnant every two years.

Graph 2: Population of Old JocotánParish, 1893–2003

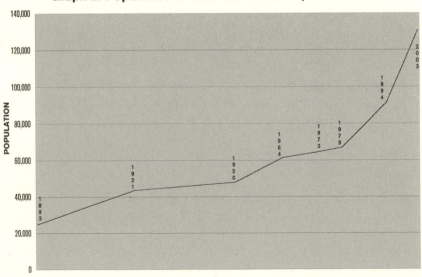

While Ch'orti's continue to have as many children "as God provides," averaging about seven to eight per woman,[1] the mortality rate has fallen due to the introduction of antibiotics and measures taken against malaria. The first pharmacies with modern medicine were established in the region in the early twentieth century, and the first health clinics were established during the Democratic Revolution. In the late 1960s malaria, a leading cause of death, was virtually eradicated by a joint USAID and Department of Health campaign (Maxwell 1974; Jocotán and Olopa municipal records; cf. Arias de Blois 1982:159; Early 1982:109–11; see appendix 3). Ch'orti's had also been contracting malaria in their labor migrations to the south coast in work on sugar and cotton plantations, and when the cotton industry collapsed in the 1980s, malaria virtually disappeared from local health records.

The effects of population pressure were already apparent in the 1930s and 1940s. No land lay fallow for more than four consecutive years, although Ch'orti's preferred to let it rest for seven to ten. Wisdom noted:

> The wild flora grows more luxuriantly in the lowlands than in the highlands; but, owing to the heavy population and the lack of uncultivated land, in neither section are there any great stretches of virgin forest. Except on the summits of the highest hills, where no one lives and where there are pine and cedar forests, and in spots too steep or too rocky for cultivation, such as the sides of cliffs and along the banks of some of the streams, there is no untouched land or vegetation. (1940:13–14)

The preharvest months of June to August were regularly haunted by Xiximay, the spirit of hunger (Girard 1949:333; Wisdom 1961:454). Highland forests were being and continue to be cleared for coffee production (Dary, Elías, and Reyna 1998:107).

---

1. Dary, Elías, and Reyna (1998:179) estimate five to six births per woman, and others have recorded seven per mother. There is no direct method of counting average births per woman because many parents do not officially register their births until they are certain the child will survive, sometimes not until they are three or four years old. Simply asking women how many births they have had does not take into consideration the births they will have in the future. Another way of estimating the birth rate is by taking the annual births per thousand people. A natural birth rate—i.e., without any family planning—is about fifty births per thousand, and the Ch'orti' birth rate is forty-nine (Metz 2001b).

The loss of forests has affected the climate. Intermittent droughts in the region have been recorded throughout the colonial period and may have caused the fall of Copán's surplus economy in the Classic period, but even recently the weather has been getting drier and the rainfall more unpredictable. The drought of 1915–16—the earliest event in Ch'orti' living memory—dried streams and springs, made farming impossible, and drove many campesinos to eat banana roots and seek water, charity, and wages throughout the region. Elder Ladinos recalled hundreds of begging Ch'orti's dying in the streets and on the trails, and Ch'orti's remember children and elderly as the first to die, almost as if they lived through it themselves. Fought (1969:474) marks this as the start of a long decline in the region's prosperity that eroded the Ch'orti' ritual system and sank Jocotán's last brotherhood in 1933.

The rainy season has gradually been starting later. In the 1600s, the rains seem have come in March, as evidenced by San Juan Ermita's plea in 1652 that its cocoa tributes be absolved because the river failed to rise in March for irrigation (Feldman 1983:157). By the early 1930s the onset of the rainy season came at the end of April (cf. Wisdom 1961:493ff.). Ch'orti's at the time, in fact, were in turmoil over drought-producing sorcery, as when the rains came late in 1932:

> A class of *padrinos*, called drought-makers (*ah hor q'in*), are considered bad and malicious and are extremely feared and hated. It is believed that they deliberately prevent the advent of the rainy season in May, produce droughts at various times during the year, and cause the crops to wither and die. Sorcerers sometimes do these things, but the drought-makers are said to do nothing else and are looked upon as being *padrinos* with antisocial tendencies. They live to themselves and, like the sorcerers, are given to queer and abnormal practices, such as visiting graves, wandering around at night, muttering to themselves, etc. Although many *padrinos*, especially the older and more eccentric ones, are known or suspected to be drought-makers, without exception they strongly deny it. In the rainmaking ceremony in April, God and the native deities are especially requested to permit no drought-makers to destroy the ceremony and thus stop the rains. They are often said to be hired by a number of families of one aldea to produce a drought in another, so that late in the year the families of the

> latter will have to buy maize from the former when the
> price is high. (Wisdom 1940:377–78)

By the 1940s, changing precipitation patterns had undercut the local production of honey, once a standard ritual offering (Girard 1949:241–42). By
mid-century some renowned *padrinos* were being hunted down and
killed for failing to bring the rains (cf. Hull 2003:54). By the early 1970s,
lack of rainfall had become so chronic that the image of Santiago, patron
of Jocotán, was paraded every year around Jocotán's park to bring rain,
instead of only during rare droughts (Maxwell 1974).

Since precipitation began to be officially recorded in 1970, the erratic
start of the rainy season and a slight overall decline in rainfall in April and
May can be seen (see graph 3 this page). The unpredictable onset of the
rainy season means that seeds planted too early are more likely to be eaten
by birds, "early" sprouts are more likely to dry up, and seeds planted in the
midst of the rainy season can rot (Dary, Elías, and Reyna 1998:130–31; see
Eber [1995:24] for planting on May 3 in Chenalhó, Chiapas, and among
ancient Mayas). The end of the rainy season is equally erratic, making
growing seasons and subsistence agriculture unpredictable and risky (see
graphs 4 and 5, p. 148). The effects seem to be fairly localized, as across the
border in Honduras and in nearby Quezaltepeque, deforestation is not as

Graph 3: Erratic Start of the Rainy Season

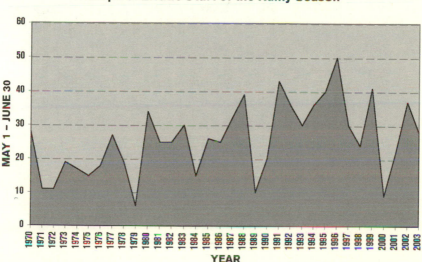

Graph 4: Erratic End of the Rainy Season

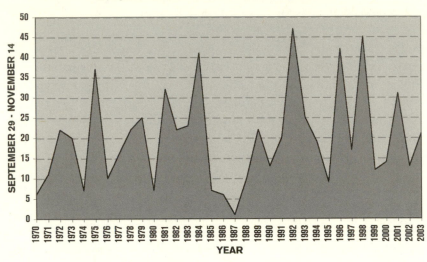

Graph 5: Erratic Length of Rainy Season, Camotán

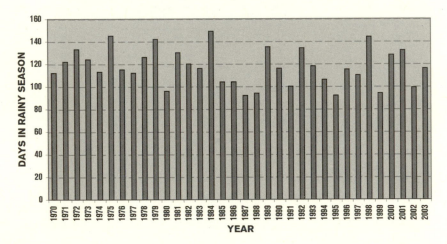

acute, rainfall is still fairly regular, longer-maturing varieties of corn can be grown, and no complaints are heard about dwindling rainfall.

Besides the direct effects of rainfall on agriculture, the clearing of forests and low moisture make life difficult in many ways. Without the capillary action of tree root systems, many springs and streams have dried permanently. In high aldeas like Rodeito, women must walk up to five hours hauling twenty gallons of water per day during the dry season (Dary, Elías, and Reyna 1998:94). Some women and children walk up to three hours per day looking for firewood (Dary, Elías, and Reyna 1998:111). Those constructing homes must go even farther afield to find beams and rafters. The destruction of tree canopies and root systems has also spelled greater erosion, as nothing protects soil on steep slopes from washing away during tropical downpours. Newly eroded gullies form each year, some as deep and wide as seventy feet from a single torrent. Hurricane Mitch in 1998 resulted in several landslides. Ch'orti's have increasingly turned to clearing steep slopes that were once considered nonarable, such as pockets of soil on rocky mountainsides, where ironically the rocks are valued for slowing erosion.

As more people occupy increasingly eroded land, productivity has declined and many are unable to grow enough food for themselves. Elderly Ch'orti's recount that their grandfathers shifted cultivation on anywhere from 14 to 73 acres, working about 1.73 acres (a manzana) every two to four years before slashing and burning a new forest plot. Today, as seen in table 4 (p. 151), the land has been so divided among descendents that the average household owns only about 3 acres, which rarely lie fallow (cf. Maxwell 1974; AVANSCO/PACCA 1992:4–5). According to Guatemala's national planning agency (SEGEPLAN), 3.5 acres is the minimum amount necessary for the average family's subsistence (Bilsborrow and Stupp 1997:590). Gauging from Ch'orti' economic patterns in 1992, 4.4 acres is desirable for household subsistence because only the 14% of households with this amount or more have no need to rent land or work for wages. The 46% of households that possess between 1.1 and 4.4 acres work their own land, both lease and rent, and work for and employ others. The over 40% of households owning less than 1.1 acre only supplement their meager production by working for and renting from those in the first two categories.[2]

2. Similar to my finding of 86% of households having less than 4.4 acres (2.6 manzanas), Dary, Elías, and Reyna (1998:127) recorded that 80% of "productive units" are smaller than 3 manzanas, 75% of which do not produce sufficiently for subsistence.

Elderly Ch'orti's recall that 1 manzana (1.73 acres) produced 45–50 *quintales* (about 100 pounds) of corn, which today is only possible on the virgin lands in northern Guatemala. Today, harvests have fallen to 6 to 16 quintales, depending on the quality of the land and the rains (see appendix 2). Chemical fertilizers boost production to 9–45 quintales, but their purchase involves a 30% annual interest loan (in 1996) from the government agricultural bank (BANDESA) and ultimately international investors, as well as potential losses and permanent indebtedness if the rains do not come.[3] For beans, the other major staple, production ranges from 6 to 16 quintales without fertilizer and from 8 to 30 quintales with fertilizer. Insect plagues have become so extreme that few in communities like Pacrén and Tisipe (Palma Ramos 2001:143) plant beans, and many households do not harvest enough to last the whole year, such that for months at a time the diet consists only of tortillas, salt (*tojb'en pa'* or "empty tortillas"), and greens when available.[4] Pelillo Negro was once renowned for its four-foot-tall bean bushes, but today plants are characteristically stunted and plagued with worms.

Based on the consumption of my host families, the average household of five with two adults, three children, fowl, one dog, and one cat consumes about 100 pounds of corn and 15 pounds of beans per week, totaling about 52 quintales of corn and 8 quintales of beans per year. To meet these needs, at least 4.8 manzanas (8.5 acres) with fertilizer or 8 manzanas (14 acres) without fertilizer would have to be put into production for corn, depending on the land and rain. For beans, at least 1 manzana would be needed regardless of fertilizer (however, these numbers do not count the loss of harvests due to rats, which Dary, Elías, and Reyna [1998:132] calculate to be as high as 40%). Some cultivate corn and beans on the same plot, while others intersperse corn with sorghum (maicillo). Sorghum was once eaten only as a snack (Girard 1949:233) but today is used for tortillas when corn is

---

3. Palma Ramos (2001:34) also found that in the aldea Pacrén, production varied between 8 quintals without fertilizer to 32–48 quintals with fertilizer. Dary, Elías, and Reyna (1998:160) recorded a broad difference in production among ten aldeas as well, from an average of 18 quintals in Suchiquer to an amazing 62 quintals in Muyurcó.

4. Schumann de Baudez (1983:222) considers only 5% of Jocotán and 8.7% of Camotán to be arable land, and found average production for corn and beans per manzana to be 8 and 3–4 quintals, respectively. She writes definitively that Ch'orti's could not produce enough food for themselves.

Table 4: Average Household Land Availability

	Average land owned per household	Ave. land rented per household	Ave. land available per household
Pacrén (n=104, excludes large Ladino holdings)	1.4*	.4	1.8
Pelillo Negro (n=236)	1.3	.6	2.0
Tuticopote Abajo (n=104, excludes large Ladino holdings)	1.1	.2	1.3
Averages across all households	**1.3**	**.5**	**1.8**
Averages by community totals	**1.3**	**.4**	**1.7**

*measurements in manzanas; 1 manzana=1.73 acres.

in short supply because it is more drought resistant than corn and beans. Nevertheless, even sorghum's productivity has declined from 24 quintales to 8 quintales per manzana in places like Pelillo Negro.[5] In any event, given that the average amount of land worked per household is less than 2 manzanas (3.5 acres, see table 4), most households do not provide enough food for subsistence, much less for sale.[6]

From a monetary perspective, many variables can influence agricultural profitability (see appendix 2). Most save the largest seeds from annual crops, but some consume them during hard times and must buy

5. Dary, Elías, and Reyna (1998:134) also recorded harvests of 8–10 quintals of sorghum per manzana without fertilizer. Palma Ramos (2001:67) mentions harvests of 15 quintals of sorghum in Oquén, but presumably this was production with fertilizers.
6. Dary, Elías, and Reyna provide varied results on the production of corn per household. They record that 70% of households produce less than 20 quintals of corn per year (1998:131), but only 3 of their 10-aldea sample do not provide enough food for subsistence—Canapará Arriba, El Rodeo, and Suchiquer (1998:157–58).

chemically treated and genetically engineered commercial seeds. Most
employ day laborers during planting, who are paid wages (roughly Q9.00
or $1.50 in 1997), breakfast, and lunch, which during planting involves the
added expense of meat. To weed, one can work one's own plot, use herbicides (in 1993 26.5% of households used herbicides and/or pesticides), or
hire day laborers if available. In harvesting, one has the option of employing others or carrying one's harvests oneself to home or the market. In
1992–93 the price of corn was Q.55 per pound, reaping profits for those
using only their own labor and seed at Q400–Q850 ($70–$150) per manzana. For those buying seeds, fertilizer, pesticides, and hired labor, profits
ranged from Q97–Q2,475 ($16–$412). The price of beans was Q1.40 per
pound, yielding profits of Q840–Q2,240 ($140–$375) per manzana without
inputs and Q214–Q3,294 ($107–$550) with inputs. Considering the variation in land, production, and prices from year to year, it is very difficult to
generalize about agricultural viability except to say that long-term planning is virtually impossible. Certainly, agriculture does not enable the
average Ch'orti' household to earn the $2,400 (~Q13,000) needed at the
time to cover the basic food costs in Guatemala (*La Nación* 12/31/96).

Across the border in Copán, Honduras, Schumann de Baudez (1983:
203–6) reported a similar situation. Ch'orti's began immigrating there as
early as 1913, near the time of the great drought, and population expanded
rapidly. Meanwhile, Ladinos monopolized the irrigable valley lands,
opened roads into the tropical forests where Ch'orti's had taken refuge,
and cut them down for pasturage. By the late 1970s, land was so scarce
that campesino corn and bean fields lay fallow only once every seven
years. The average family of six consumed only 29.4 quintales of corn per
year (.56 quintales per week), slightly more than half the amount required
by a Ch'orti' family of five in Guatemala, and because annual production
per manzana was only 7.3 quintales and no family owned more than 1.5
manzanas, no one produced enough to satisfy even this meager amount.
Most corn stores were depleted by April and May, well before the next
harvest in October. As in Jocotán and Olopa, bean and squash reserves
were quickly consumed, leaving many to rely on tortillas and salt for part
of the year. Most were compelled to work for meager wages on plantations to buy more corn, which Schumann argued was actually the original intent of the landlords.

Declining subsistence productivity has compelled Ch'orti's to explore
the market economy. Of 436 households in Pelillo Negro, Pacrén, and
Tuticopote Abajo, 339 engage in local marketing. Some have tried to grow

10. *Ladino middlemen with Ch'orti' crafts—nets, baskets, brooms, and hammocks.*

commodities like coffee, bananas, oranges, mangos, jocotes, sugarcane, broccoli, and okra, but most of these involve high expenses getting the products to the town markets and are subject to dramatic price fluctuations. Coffee and cattle are the most hopeful new commodities, but coffee prices have fluctuated wildly in the 1990s and Ladino middlemen take a substantial cut of the profits, while cattle require vast tracks of pasture and lead to erosion. Many have accelerated the production of crafts, but profits range from only $1 to $3 per week per person because Ladino middlemen control transport and therefore interregional marketing.

In most households, men supplement agriculture and local marketing with migrant labor on coffee and bean plantations, and some men have told me that they migrate as many as seven times per year. Unlike Occidente Mayas, there is no evidence that Ch'orti's seasonally migrated to coffee plantations during the Liberal capitalist expansion of 1871–1944, but some migrated in the first half of the century to United Fruit Company banana plantations in Izabal (cf. Gillen 1952:197–98 for Pokomams). By the late 1950s, some began to migrate regularly to coffee plantations in Zacapa and western Honduras, and in the 1960s some four thousand to

11. *Dinnertime, coffee plantation in Gualán, 1992.*

five thousand annually migrated primarily to cotton plantations on the south coast. While the cotton industry lasted, Ch'orti's, when they were actually paid, earned $6–$11 for two months' labor. The conditions were so unsanitary and rife with pesticides, flies, and dampness, that according to Cresencio, if the men returned at all they did so with fever and diarrhea (cf. Buysse and Alvarez 1974:22). All worked relentlessly, including the women who went along as cooks, such as Juliana, who worked from 3:00 AM to 11:00 PM. By 1992, 73% of all households in Pacrén and Pelillo Negro had at least one migrating member, principally to Oriente coffee plantations. On the coffee plantations one can make up to $2.75 per day, only about a third more than the rate (with food) in the Ch'orti' area, but coffee wages have not kept pace with inflation (cf. Maxwell 1974). The coffee workers talk disparagingly about the cold, damp, sleepless nights; the long, dangerous workdays carrying heavy loads in slippery mud; and pneumonia. Plantation food sits unprotected from flies, the water is contaminated, the housing consists of barns with wooden benches for beds, and the latrines are inadequate such that living quarters smell of urine. Work can still be found on Izabal banana plantations, but wages are only $4.00 per day, of which $1.70 is spent on food, while housing is substandard with poor sanitation. In 1998 banana workers tried to organize on Chiquita and Del Monte subsidiaries' plantations, but the organizers

Table 5: Migration, Old Jocotán Parish, 1949–1974

	Net Emigration
La Unión	-2,892
Jocotán	-4,326
Camotán	-3,057
Olopa	-2,131
San Juan	-1,377
Total	**-13,784**

were fired, some workers were shot by plantation guards, and troops arrived to "restore order" (*Cerigua* 4/2/98:1–2). Another alternative is the Petén bean plantations, many of which are owned by Ladino emigrants from Chiquimula and Zacapa.

Since the end of the nineteenth century (Girard 1949:38–40), thousands of Ch'orti's have been emigrating north to the Departments of Zacapa and Izabal and west to Honduras, despite the high physical and emotional costs of leaving one's community behind. Many were absorbed as squatters on expanding coffee plantations, but others remained semi-independent campesinos. Between 1950 and 1964, national censuses record that of all

Graph 6: Migration, Old Jocotán Parish, 1949–1974

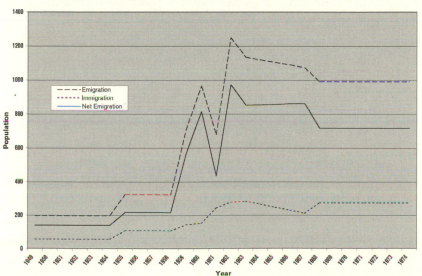

Guatemalan departments, Izabal had the highest annual population increase (5.3%) while Chiquimula had the lowest (1.8%, mainly Ch'orti's returning home), as over half of the latter's 32,247 emigrants went to Izabal (INE 1964). Meanwhile, Ladino cattle and coffee operations moved in behind the campesinos and began appropriating their land as Ch'orti's moved on until by around 1980 there was no more forest left in northern Guatemala or western Honduras to colonize (see graph 6, p. 155). This in turn motivated more use of chemical fertilizers, which 41% of Ch'orti' households were using by 1992–93.

Poverty and Health

Sickness and death cast a shadow on Ch'orti' life, inspiring an array of emotions from resentment, desperation, anxiety, apathy, and anguish to stoicism. My memories are haunted with visions of convulsions, vomiting, distended stomachs, worms, tumors, mothers' switching crying skinny babies between empty breasts, healers' urgent prayers over the bodies of the infirm, a girl's muttering for her mother who had been hacked to death before her eyes, funeral processions, wakes, stumbling dogs attacked by impatient vultures, rabid cows running wildly, and tearful blank stares. Worst of all was the incessant pleading for medicine by some who eventually died, such as a woman who likely had cancer, and a terribly malnourished man, both of whom out of generosity and hope of medical reciprocity shared their meager food supplies with me. The following are excerpts from my notes in Pelillo Negro:

> Last house is that of a very old man with swelling [protein deficiency] and the "itch." His house floor is incredibly rough and uneven, no comal [ceramic griddle], no wife, no children, holes in walls and roof, no blankets, only *costales* [burlap bags], yet he invited me to eat corn on the cob with him. I ate one wormy piece and he offered more but I couldn't possibly eat more of his food. A little girl and boy brought him a corn leaf of beans and he asked for water, which they brought later. It was a very touching scene and the little girl was so polite and delicate, and nearly as poor as him. . . . Asked me desperately for medicine for his itch, saying that he was freezing and crying every night, and from the poor looks of him I thought he could die any week now.

> We [two Ladina nurses trained to care for cholera victims and
> I] then waited outside and talked with the family, particularly
> with an elderly woman who looked dead already and wanted
> *suero* [rehydration drink], but didn't have cholera but *sampa'r*,
> or swelling. Her feet were puffed up like balloons, and shoes
> tied on with cloth, and she was clearly in pain and bowed down
> every few minutes in agony. Yoli explained to her that suero
> was the last thing she needed because it would only make the
> swelling worse. I explained in Ch'orti' about protein deficiency
> and how she needed to consume meat, eggs, fish, milk, or
> Incaparina [a high protein, vitamin powder] daily, but she
> wanted to know about pills and if the centro had them. I said
> I didn't know but that protein was the answer, to which she
> shot back "And if we can't afford it?"

The pills she was referring to are purgatives that draw moisture out of the body to reduce swelling caused by protein malnutrition, a basic treatment promoted by local pharmacists.

In some ways, Ch'orti's reflect the poor health of Guatemalans generally, as their main causes of death include a combination of malnutrition, respiratory infections, gastrointestinal infections (Robles 1997:379), violence, and accidents (see appendix 3). Actually, they are worse off than most Guatemalan campesinos. The Jocotán Health Center calculates the average life expectancy to be 45.88 years, twenty below the national average.[7] The population of the Ch'orti' area is 119 per square kilometer, versus the national average of 76.2, the fertility rate is four times the national average (20.2 per thousand versus 5.1, but I calculated 49), the infant mortality rate is 94.5 per thousand versus 84.1 nationally, and the general mortality is 37.2 per thousand versus 9 nationally (Dary, Elías, and Reyna 1998:224–27). With too many children and not enough food, some weaker children are underfed, consciously or not, so that the strong can live (cf. Palma Ramos 2001:47; Scheper-Hughes 1992).

Chronic, as opposed to punctuated, malnutrition seems to be a fairly recent phenomenon. Though Wisdom (1940:462) and Girard (1949:333) spoke of times of hunger, neither mentioned malnutrition. Today it is not uncommon to see ghostly elders and children with the signs of protein

---

7. When I sought an explanation why one of my best informants died in 1996, I was told, "she just died; after all, she was fifty-six years old."

12. *Malnourished children and nurses in Hospital Betania, Jocotán, 1996.*

and general malnutrition, including flaking, cracked skin, hair loss, swollen legs, dizziness, disorientation, listlessness, acute stomach pains, diarrhea, and distended stomachs. Protein malnutrition (sampa'r) relates directly to lack of beans and to periodic poultry epidemics (*el accidente*, "the accident," described by agricultural technicians as avian polio and smallpox) said to have begun in the 1930s, killing chickens, turkeys, and ducks alike. Some have begun to use vaccines for their fowl, but some claim that they are ineffective. The few fowl that families are able to maintain are used for eggs and savings to buy corn, beans, and medicine. Eggs are highly valued and sell for about 11¢ apiece, more expensive than in the United States. Ch'orti's used to depend on a variety of wild fish and game for protein, including monkey, tapir, wild boar, paca, rabbit, raccoon, agouti, opossum, turtle, armadillo, and iguana (cf. Wisdom 1940:14, 73), but due to habitat loss and overhunting, only occasional partridges, doves, and squirrels remain.[8]

8. Early (1982:130) reports that in Atitlán between 1810 and 1816, wild game was relatively abundant but the death rate was still very high.

As in Wisdom's and Girard's day, Xiximai, the spirit that prevents satiation, haunts the living during the months before harvest, when dozens of children are interned in the Catholic Hospital Betania of Jocotán for acute malnutrition. In July 2003, an average year, sixty children were interned the Hospital Betania and the Jocotán Health Center for critical malnutrition, certainly just a fraction of the malnourished children in the area. Much of the aid given by foreign agencies working the area, including the Catholic Church, Protestant World Vision, and other Protestant missions, is devoted simply to feeding the malnourished. One group of US Protestant missionary doctors who annually visit the Ch'orti' area treats all campesinos for malnutrition.

Early (1982:176–77) documented a pathological synergism between infant malnutrition and infectious disease in rural Guatemala. Mothers can provide sufficient breast milk to growing babies until the age of six months, but after this a food supplement is required. Among Guatemala's poor, this supplement is frequently deficient and the malnutrition slowly builds. The baby's immune system is weakened, causing greater susceptibility to infections and diarrhea, which in turn lead to greater malnutrition. Death usually results before the first year but may be prolonged to age four. In rare cases, like the one I witnessed in 2000, victims endure until the age of sixteen with an average size head on a stick figure, stunted body. This synergism helps explain why mortality records are often unclear as to the cause of death, and the high death rate is one reason why some parents do not register births and childhood deaths with municipalities until their children are older, if they do so at all (cf. Scheper-Hughes 1992).

Gastrointestinal infection, whether by hookworms, roundworms, giardia, amoebas, bacteria, or others, is generally accompanied by crippling stomach pains, diarrhea, and vomiting, and is caused by a variety of interrelated conditions. Considering that virtually every Ch'orti' is weakened by parasites, especially amoebas and giardia, the added stress of malnutrition and/or respiratory infections can lead to death. Until recently, few households have had latrines, and sanitation has traditionally been left to hungry but unreliable dogs and pigs. Trash, including countless batteries filled with dangerous chemicals, is discarded on the bare mountain slopes below homes. The greater the population, the greater the waste and less the vegetation to slow it from running directly into the springs and streams that constitute the water supply. Ch'orti's are fastidious, careful to avoid visible dirtiness and the touching of animals, but rarely are they concerned with water impurities. I once witnessed a man drinking out of a stream in which fifty yards upriver another man was bathing. Purification by boiling is expensive due to the scarcity of wood fuel, and chlorination—adding three drops of chlorine per gallon of water—is problematic because few have measuring devices and all fear chlorine poisoning. Herbal remedies are effective for worms in particular, and I have heard of sixteen roundworms extracted from a single child, but they sometimes suffocate children when they exit through the mouth and nose.

Cholera struck Jocotán in 1992. The Red Cross and town health specialists did all they could to prevent and prepare for the epidemic, but suspicious of their intentions, spiteful of their paternalism, and doubtful that cholera was different from other digestive afflictions, many campesinos refused to take the suggested precautions. The epidemic began in May, and by August, 109 deaths were officially attributed to cholera (see "Gastrointestinal" in appendix 3), though doctors admit that possibly hundreds more went unreported. The communities hit worst were those in which water sources were contaminated, causing dozens of deaths in quick succession. Though most who became infected with cholera survived, the disease was traumatic, as people woke up every day wondering about the disease's proximity and if family members were still uncontaminated. When cholera strikes, vomiting and diarrhea of up to a pint or more at a time occur as frequently as every fifteen minutes, such that soon only clear fluid is emitted. Within a few hours victims are so shriveled that they appear to have aged thirty years, and death often results the same day as the onset of symptoms. Some neighbors began vomiting in the evening and were dead by morning, and one twenty-three-year-old pregnant woman died within two and a half hours. Oral medicine and drinking fluids are no antidote because of the vomiting. This makes intravenous rehydration, given by visiting nurses or the town health centers, the only way of saving acute victims. Many sick Ch'orti's, however, hid from ambulatory nurses as they passed by their homes.

Respiratory illnesses are undoubtedly due in part to the practice of cooking with wood fuel (e.g., Engle, Hurtado, and Ruel 1997). Most Ch'orti's construct their kitchens with corn or cane stalks, sticks, and banana leaves, leaving gaps in the walls for ventilation, but when burning poor quality fuel like leaves, the smoke buildup can be suffocating, such that visitors like myself are forced by coughing and burning eyes to exit. When the weather is cooler, from October to January, illness and deaths due to respiratory illness climb dramatically (Keegan 1994), perhaps due to a combination of more time spent near the hearth, cold viruses, and labor on plantations where pesticides are applied. Aggravating this situation is a scarcity of housing materials, which has forced inhabitants to combine kitchens and dormitories. Homesteads used to consist of several houses, including dormitories, a kitchen, storehouses, and an altar house (Wisdom 1940:119–28), but today all these functions are often united under one roof, subjecting inhabitants to kitchen smoke night and day. Ch'orti's have little access to modern housing materials such as laminated metal and cement and rely on natural resources such as wooden poles, palm, thatch, canes, mud, bark, and vines (see appendix 1). Palm, the material of choice in the lowlands due to its pliability, lightness, surface coverage, and ventilation, has moved out of the price range of many, as it requires about $40 of palm to build a house. In higher elevation communities where thatch is the basic building material, even this has become a scarce commodity, leaving only sticks, banana leaves, corn stalks, and sheets of discarded plastic for construction.

The use of pesticides and herbicides influences respiratory health as well, and 26.5% of Ch'orti' households apply them on their plots. Four hundred campesinos die from pesticide poisoning annually in Guatemala, and 65% of the streams and rivers are polluted (*Cerigua* 6/12/97:4). Ch'orti's carry applicators on their backs with no special protection, and chemicals are sprayed without masks. Some admit that they have become very sick after inhaling the toxins and others have died by drinking from pesticide containers. According to the Jocotán Hospital Betania's records in 1991, one-third of all neurological afflictions (60 out of 178) occurred in the month of June, when campesinos most often use pesticides. Direct contact with pesticides and herbicides is also common on the plantations.

For many outside observers, Ch'orti' stoicism in the face of death is one of their most strikingly enigmatic characteristics. Girard (1949:297) cited the example of a father who returned home to find that his two youngest children had died in a house fire; without a word, he simply sat down and ate the provisions he was carrying. One Peace Corps volunteer told me of a Ch'orti' friend who, days after the murder of her husband, continued her daily chores as usual, muttering only "they took him." A teacher trained to treat cholera victims secretly asked me whether people in the United States cry when a family member dies. She had just witnessed the death of a young Ch'orti' woman, and her family showed no signs of remorse. In the home of a cholera victim, an elderly widow repeated that she was alone but expressed no grief. The nuns who manage the Hospital Betania relate harrowing stories of parents that left their starving children while they went off to the plantations. Sometimes their children die while they are away, but upon their return they refuse to believe that "their María" or "their José" has died. They search among the malnourished in the hospital until they are certain that they have found their child, and they attempt to carry him or her away. When finally convinced of their child's death, without shedding a tear, they simply turn around and walk home.

Some Ch'orti's also show incredible fortitude in their own suffering. In 2002 a Ladino friend's father had a urinary tract infection, and he was raced to the hospital in Chiquimula in insufferable pain. Serendipitously, a few days later Cresencio and his son discussed a Ch'orti' neighbor who had just died from a urinary blockage. Rather than seek medical attention, he tried to wait it out. He lasted eight days before his bladder burst, and the stench of his body was too much for many to withstand at his funeral.

Stoicism may in part be due to Ch'orti's' lifestyle of hard physical labor and malnutrition, but it is also cultural. Ch'orti's are concerned that the dead rightly leave this world for the next, which funerals are meant to ensure. Any crying or expressions of remorse can attract the soul to stay in the world of the living, and should thus be avoided (cf. Wagley 1957: 170). At the funeral of a thirty-six-year-old mother who died from cholera, the dispassionate look of the attendants made it impossible for me to determine her immediate family. Later I learned that they did not even attend the funeral so that the distraught spirit would not see them and be tempted to follow them home. Another family was terrified of a cassette recording I attempted to give them of my interview of their recently murdered relative.

Though the dead are feared, fond memories are cherished, as would be expected. I once gave a young man a photo I had taken of his best friend two years before, who I soon learned had died the year before. He slowly sat down and studied the photo for a half hour, chuckling to himself in happiness, remorse, and embarrassment as tears rolled down his cheeks.

Though anesthetized to pain and death more than most, Ch'orti's hurt. Each and every death weighs heavily, and the possibility of more suffering and death is unrelenting. Because malnutrition, parasites, and pulmonary illnesses are so chronic, family members regularly worry about each other's health, though they try to repress it. One young man could not eat and starved to death after he witnessed his mother's slow, writhing death when bandits shot her in the abdomen. One mother could not bear to see her starving boy die a slow, painful death, so she threw him down an old mineshaft. He survived with a broken leg and was brought to the hospital. Vomiting, diarrhea, or fever, especially among children, immediately alerts others to seek whatever medical attention is economically viable. Sometimes this leads to extreme desperation, such as Pedro's frenzy as we tried to save his brother from cholera, giving him sixteen different medicines between the two of us.

Only rarely do Ch'orti's respond to death with anger. When an elderly woman who had befriended me died, I went to offer my condolences the next day. Her daughter numbly said, "*se terminó*," "her life ended." As tears streamed down her face, I felt the need to say something. I told her that I thought her mother died of cancer, the same as don Donaldo, a gringo in town, but she interjected, "with no money, what could a poor campesino do?!" I sheepishly agreed, and added that the world will be a lonelier place now that her mother was gone, to which she angrily retorted, "and think how it must be for a member of the family!" The best condolence one can offer is to say the dead are no longer suffering.

The Social Repercussions of Poverty

One need be very careful when applying the concept "poverty" cross-culturally, as Western development planners have made industries of imposing overconsumptive standards on other populations. Ch'orti's, however, insist they are poor, sometimes as a show of humility, sometimes as a way of seeking a handout, but mainly because they are poor according to *their own* standards. Their faith in God, their neighbors, and themselves has been shaken by poverty. The elders still remember when, three generations ago, they produced and consumed a more diversified diet, including abundant squash, rice, potatoes, cocoa, beef, and peanuts. As the region, especially the Ladino population, has become more integrated into the global economy, they have become painfully aware of the growing rift in power and wealth between themselves and others. People can be quite content to consume beans, tortillas, and coffee three times a day, live in a thatch hut, and play handmade instruments for entertainment, until they find that Ladinos daily consume meat, eggs, bread, milk, cheese, vegetables, soda, noodles, candy, and luxuries they have never seen before, live in large cement houses, and watch satellite television from the United States.

Poverty can be measured by other objective means. Maxwell (1974) identified elopement as a good index of Ch'orti' poverty because it circumvents the costs of formal matrimonial gift giving and feasts, but risks breaking the all-important family ties. In the 1930s elopement was practiced only among the poorest (Wisdom 1940:299), while in the early 1970s it was increasingly prevalent. Today, formal marriages, including bride service, have become much less formal and expensive, such that many do not legally marry at all and many children have their mothers' surnames (cf. Schumann de Baudez 1983:204). Nevertheless, as mentioned in the previous chapter, the consent of the parents is still important for inheritance and security. One recently eloped young woman hanged herself when her family refused to have her back after it was clear that her husband was neither loyal nor a good provider. Another sign of poverty is the abandonment of many expensive rituals. Many families cannot afford to celebrate the tzik'in on an annual basis, because they do not have the resources to feed the rest of the community (cf. Palma Ramos 2001:62). An index of poverty relative to Guatemala is that the local orphanage (Aldea Infantil) is the only one in the nation filled to capacity with local children only.

Elders are both nostalgic and frustrated about how times have changed. They speak of the great forests that once "clothed" Mother Earth and sheltered the deer, wild boar, monkeys, and other animals, and others make a point to show me arroyos where streams once flowed. Some express sympathy for Our Mother Earth (Katu' Mundo, e Ixik), who is "tired" from overwork and "washed" of her strength by erosion. Eighty-four-year-old Sesario sighed, "Aaah, there was everything before." Vicenta was resentful, remarking that "the Earth is already almost cowardly when we work her." After concluding that his land no longer produces without fertilizer, Valvino snapped "and where are we supposed to find enough money to buy fertilizer?" In the tired words of eighty-four-year-old don Chico, "the same plot and the same plot, and the year ends and the next the same plot, because there is nowhere else to turn." Women are especially remorseful about their inability to feed the family. Inés, Juventina, Dorotea, Juliana, Macaria, and Selma agonizingly recalled their life histories—of being orphaned or widowed, of suffering hunger, of ceaseless production of crafts to buy food, and of fatigue, illness, and death on the plantations. Even don Francisco, a Ladino who employs Ch'orti's on his several dozen acres, admitted that life has become increasingly "difficult" for them because many have been forced into wage labor.

Most, like Cheo, acknowledge that deforestation is at the root of their problems.

> A long time ago the Earth gave corn, it gave everything, it used to rain, and whatever we planted gave fruit, and . . . if there was something we planted, it inevitably bore fruit. And the people didn't steal because everything was abundant. All the ravine that we see now was planted. There were bananas . . . there used to be everything, and the people had everything. They say that when everything was expensive, they turned to bananas to eat, and the people didn't steal because they had enough. And they say that all started to disappear when a great drought passed a long time ago. A great drought passed, and the rain didn't fall and corn became expensive, and there was nothing. Whoever had money survived. Whoever had money still ate. And whoever didn't have money or crops ate banana roots until they ran out. All began to be lost and the epoch continued as such, and each year less rain fell until only a little falls in our own time, such that now we see little rain fall and the prices of corn are rising. And a long time ago we also saw trees on all the land. There used to be trees, or as we say, "it helps you" and "the rain comes." "He brings the rain." There used to be everything, everywhere there were trees. There was everything before, or as we say, there was a lot of forest for house construction, but the people are cutting it down without planting more. And therefore the rain has stopped falling.

Sixty-seven-year-old Pedro, a ritual specialist murdered for sorcery in 1995, explained that the trees are the "seats" of the angels (the clouds), so that without the forests the angels have nowhere to rest. "The ancestors prayed before. Like my deceased grandfather used to say, 'he who goes and chops a tree, who gives a whack with a machete,' he said, 'Our Father knows it immediately,' he said, 'because he's injured there,' he said, 'as soon as he's hit.'" Santiago echoed, "it's that Our Father [rain] falls where there's forest, and where there are bare hillsides like today, there's nowhere for the clouds to rest. That's why our land is so poor, because there's no forest." According to a twenty-nine-year-old man interviewed by Palma Ramos's team in 1991,

It seems that when I was seven years old, it rained more
because there were more trees, and because the clouds that
emerged from the mountains came down to rest on the peaks.
Today, there are no trees and the clouds only come from the
north, and because there are no forests, those clouds pass us
by. Who knows on which mountains their rain falls! It falls
on other mountains because they have trees, their leaves in
turn are feeding the soil. On the contrary, here we're leaving
everything impoverished. Twenty years ago . . . we didn't use
chemical fertilizers, because there were plenty of forests that
maintained our lands' humidity, which is why today our fields
don't produce, because the rain has washed away the soil. So
the land is poor now that there's no natural fertilizers from the
leaves to replenish our land. (2001:52–53, my translation)

Why the forests were cut and the rainy season shortened is disputed.
God, the elders, or "the new generation of arrogant youth" are typically
blamed, although some municipal forests have been sold by mayors to
timber corporations. Rarely if ever is Guatemala's feudal sociopolitical
structure criticized. Many draw a correlation to population increase.
Macaria, for example, when discussing the frustrations of procuring
firewood, blamed the new generation for continuing to reproduce disrespectful children:

There's virtually nothing left; a long time ago there was still
firewood but families have abounded, it's not the same, they
wipe out each other. How many more children keep playing
around?! They chop the trees so that they can watch it all dry
up. Yes, there are many kids today. Long ago there were few
because we still saw bananas. We still had guisquil [chayote].
There was certainly enough and some left over then, but today
it's impossible. If there is a single tree, they cut it down. It's
really impossible.

One sixty-six-year-old man from the aldea Tunucó told Palma Ramos's
team,

Before, when I was growing up, there was enough land that it
didn't have to be divided, but the people abounded and when

13. *Deforestation and erosion, Jocotán.*

the fathers died, they had to divide up the inheritance. Today
the land is all divided, such that each one has only one
manzana. Nowadays we only plant corn, sorghum, and beans.
Nothing else grows. . . . When I was growing up, there were
beans galore, and all kinds. (2001:103, my translation)

Ch'orti's are far from united, however, about what, if anything, should be
done about overpopulation.

Elders also add that the new generation has been punished for refusing to reciprocate with God. Elderly Juan recounted the wisdom of his
friend: "It's not the land that is tired, he says. We became tired from our
own sins." He added that people, in their laziness, simply forgot how to
perform the rituals. If one wants crops from the Earth, one must pay her
with sacrifices. Don Chico elaborated,

[A]s the gods are no longer paid, then the rains no longer
fall . . . because here a license was asked of the Earth, so it
gave too and there were harvests, and whoever worked
without a license was unable because it would have been

as if we wanted everything for free, including tortillas for
free . . . it's not free because God doesn't want it that way
and therefore has left us. One needs to ask of the Earth, too,
because the Virgin provides food.

He went so far as to say that they were Catholics before, but today he's not
so sure "because there is no longer our agreement with God. There is none.
We pass without God, alone." In a sense, the elders may have indeed had
more respect for the forests, because in the 1940s, the forested peaks were
off-limits to farming despite their esteemed fertility because spooks were
thought to reside there (Girard 1949:47–48).

Certainly, elders chiding the youth for disrespect is not unique to
Ch'orti' society. Considering that ancestors have a godlike status in communities throughout the Maya area, it is not surprising to hear people
lament the immorality of the new generation (cf. Oakes 1951:268; Eber
1995:210). But changing traditions have been documented as early as
the 1930s and 1940s, when Ch'orti' religion was said to be disintegrating
into disjointed customs, superstitions, and folklore (Girard 1949:265–66;
Wisdom 1961:52–56). According to Girard (1949:409), "still some old-timers
long for the good ol' days, when the people were more respectful of tradition, more religious and consequently more hard-working, and of better
moral character," when the Indian collectivist mentality still opposed
Western individualism (cf. Oakes 1951:268). Girard himself lamented that
"mestizoization" was dissolving Ch'orti' religion into isolated customs,
superstitions, and folklore, and communities into secular, isolated, competing individuals.

The new generation, on the other hand, feel they inherited poverty
from their elders. Benjamín parodied the elders: "Our Father gets a bit
angry, they say, he doesn't want to give us rain, so they think, and that he
doesn't want to give us trees, they say, which is why all the trees have been
lost. *We* are seeing that the rain doesn't fall for lack of trees. They believe
all of that, but still think that it's because there's no more respect, they
say." Federico, an educated leader, also accused the older generation of
failing to realize the importance of trees. Having witnessed the replacement of forest by savanna and erosion that takes place after burning one's
fields for planting, he concludes that infertility and ultimately dependence on plantation wages are due to poor traditional ecological practices. The flexibility of the new generation can be clearly seen at planting
time. Though most elders still slash and burn and plant between April 25

and May 3, many in the new generation clear their fields by weeding, use the detritus as barriers against erosion, and gauge when the rains have come to stay before planting.

Why the old rituals are no longer unanimously practiced is disputed. Some like Genario explain that the true old people have already died out, and the new generation has failed to learn the customs. Mercedes simply argues that the padrinos, the bringers of rain, are now "against" the temporal order (*contra tiempo*). Pedro elaborates that the customs and padrinos were no longer effective in providing rain or fertility, and the people logically abandoned them. When rainfall began to diminish, the padrinos lost their authority and their lives as they were accused of praying for drought. The same can be said of anyone else who practices traditional rituals. Agricultural rituals are no longer practiced publicly because traditionalists fear that if their enemies discover the location of their sacrifices, they could work a reverse ritual at the spot causing barrenness instead of fertility.

The "new generation," however, misunderstands all traditional spirituality as sorcery, a perspective that traditionalists blame on Catholicism and Protestantism. Vicente argued that since the "second Pope" (Vatican II?) began using the "new Bible" and burning the images of the saints, las ruinas have been with them: it no longer rains in April and the prices have risen. In Pelillo Negro, where roughly one-sixth of the population is Evangelical, Evangelicals and non-Evangelicals alike credit Protestantism for undermining the customs.

Many say they just do not have the means to reciprocate with God. In the paraphrased words of don Chico, "if we are dying from hunger, to reserve animals, candles, and copal for sacrifice is unthinkable." The angels have left for more fertile and forested places like Honduras and the United States as local offerings of turkeys, chickens, copal, candles, and sa' have become unaffordable (cf. Diener 1978). Many, like Pedro and Gerarda, now perform the rituals without them. Prayer ceremonies are too expensive, according to Juliana, because prayer-sayers now charge too much money (about $4) for services that the church has trained campesino catechists to do free. Macaria lamented that the festivals people enjoyed so much in the old days, like the tzik'in, are celebrated less because harvests are so depleted and prices so high. The July 24 patron saint's festival in Jocotán, once attended by Ch'orti's throughout the region, is now mainly a Ladino event because late rains have delayed harvests until the middle of August and wages from coffee-picking season are not earned until September. Saturnino, Petronilo, and Valvino all regarded the pilgrimage to Esquipulas on January 15 as too dangerous and expensive.

Going hand in hand with infertility, drought, and the abandonment of the rituals is discourse on "the loss of respect." Disrespect is said to abound in envy, aggression, greed, and alcoholism as opposed to the supposedly traditional humility, generosity, and self-control. Wisdom and Girard noticed that Ch'orti' kinship and social solidarity were disintegrating in the 1930s and 1940s. Agriculture was no longer a social obligation and individualism was replacing communal cooperation. Though it was customary never to charge interest on loans, aldeas near the towns began to expect the repayment of a level gourd bowl of coins with a heaping gourd bowl of coins (Girard 1949:265–66; Wisdom 1961:52–56), and Wisdom (1961:58) documented that a few wealthier Ch'orti's were known to charge 50% interest monthly. Today, eighty-four-year-old Sesario remarked, "the new people no longer respect, because they do whatever they want, but it was different before." Petronilo added that respectful prayer has been supplanted by envy and anger, by sorcery, murder, and barrenness. Don Chico: "Oh but today, as the population has grown, there are already people that want to do whatever they want."

In Copán, Schumann de Baudez (1983:204–6) painted a bleak portrait of how poverty had created fertile grounds for antisocial sentiments and behaviors. She found few households that would even open their doors to speak to her, and extended families were not unified because mothers were resentful of daughters-in-law for bringing more mouths to feed. Even within the family, "the most minor bit of property is ferociously defended" (1983:205), and when visitors come, the owners talk about all the disasters that have happened to them since their last visit. When visitors ask to buy eggs or some other food, the response is always negative, even for family members. In April and May, when corn stores are depleted, envy leads to hatred and violence.

Young and old tend to disagree when respect for the old ways was lost. Some say it happened with the Democratic Revolution of the 1940s and 1950s. Lyons's (2001) findings in Ecuador that the discourse of respect emanated from the hacienda economy, when the social hierarchy was brutally enforced, is suggestive for the Ch'orti' case as well. Could it be that the Ubico dictatorship and those preceding it pervaded Ch'orti' culture, such that Ch'orti' communities were as authoritarian as the national oligarchy? Generally, scholars have argued for a more egalitarian community structure, and therefore higher solidarity, when Mayas are under repression, but this may depend on the degree of solidarity before the repression begins (Carmack 1988).

Ch'orti's are not of one mind on the linkage of respect to the repression. According to elderly Vicente and his wife, life was tough during the Ubico era, but all were "quiet" in fear of being discovered by the mounted police. A "strong law" was enforced, and no one yelled obscenities at women, no one played loud music, no one was drunk, no one danced with women or bragged, and the people still had shame. "Everybody was well mannered. And from then on, with the government of Dr. Juan José Arévalo, the youth of so much arrogance and so many luxuries emerged." With President Arbenz, they claim, people began to demand tractors, cars, buses, and airplanes, disregarding the law and threatening to ransack stores. More popular, however, is the opinion of a thirty-five-year-old who acknowledged less crime during Ubico, but only because the state was killing everyone. Fifty-year-old Benjamín recalled disrespect already in the 1950s when his brother was an alcoholic at eighteen, abused his wife, spent the family inheritance, and died young of malnutrition and intestinal parasites. Then in the 1960s his mother and other brother, one of the first in his aldea to win a teaching position, were shot to death by thieves. For another man, whose parents were robbed and killed by "lazy," "vicious" guerrillas, the political violence of the 1960s spawned the absence of "law" and respect.

Vicente, from another aldea, emphasized that a dramatic change was seen when people began to enter homes to murder, which before was unthinkable. Twenty-eight-year-old Mariano accused his parents' generation of not teaching him Ch'orti' and being poor role models in the 1960s and 1970s. His childhood was "sad" because he had no father to teach him to work.

> *Mariano*: Suddenly when my mom found herself with a
> man who was somewhat sinister! Not sinister, but a matter of
> experience; that is, he didn't have experience, we might say,
> experience with patience. But he had experience but distorted!
> > *Brent*: So he wasn't well "educated."
> *Mariano*: Yeah! It's that he told me to do something, as
> if you were to tell me "Get up and get that bag!" And if you
> didn't get up, "Do it now!" That's how he said it. Now do you
> understand? And it's good, you see. The things they teach are
> good, serious things, but he never said to me "Look, son, look."

No! My stepfather no! With him it was "Do this but now! And if you don't, you won't eat!"

In another case, an informant's mother complained that her daughter-in-law talked to other men and never worked, but only gossiped and played the radio. The son and his bride responded by angrily moving to her parents' home in another community.

Youth are showing less and less concern for their ties with cousins, uncles, aunts, and even grandparents. Much of the ritual language that once dictated conversation between kin and fictive kin, elders and youth, has fallen into disuse. Elders are quick to recount that standard address in the old days was precipitated by "to the sacrament" (*al sacramento*) or "María," followed by a series of formal phrases leading the host to offer the guest a seat, food, and drink. This was later replaced by "good morning," "good afternoon," and "good evening" (*buenos días, buenos tardes, buenas noches*) but even these formalities are being abandoned. Vicenta explained that the people do not speak Ch'orti' like before and are "already different" (*intya'chix*). Máximo complained that though the youth are more "advanced" and "developed" today, they are not "educated" in manners, and their adoption of Spanish over Ch'orti' offends God. Ninety-one-year-old Juan also complained that the insertion of Spanish words into Ch'orti' means that the old times are over.

For many, like Raul, Tancho, Federico, Vicente, and Felipe, lack of formal respect correlates with the erosion of reciprocal obligations. They find revealing that people used to exchange services (*sutk'ab'*, "lending a hand") and food rather than more alienating coin. In the words of Petronilo, "in previous years everyone wanted to give to each other. I give you a little, I receive a little. But nowadays no."

As the value of every conceivable resource has increased and inequality has deepened, envy has become a prevalent concern, especially for those who have more than others. For Benjamín, envy and gossip are the most serious problems in his aldea, as "there's always 'what are they saying over there?'" Similar to "the image of limited good" described by Foster (1965) in Tzintzuntzán, in which campesinos feel that others' gains are their losses, Ch'orti's are very competitive and deeply resentful of their neighbors' economic advantages. Cresencio provided the example of the 1993 national election campaign. A congressional candidate invited campesino voters to a cow and pig roast at which gifts were to be distributed. Though told to wait in line, the "crowd of vultures," fearing there would not be enough for all, raided the food truck and trampled each other when plastic balls were tossed out. Cresencio and his daughters, who had waited patiently in line, ate nothing. I witnessed such mob behavior at a festival in Olopa, resulting in the minor injury of children. Obviously, such unrestrained greed is nurtured by Ladinos who treat campesinos as animals, simply throwing things to them instead of insisting on an orderly line.

Besides events when goods are actually limited, envy is also rooted in Ch'orti' concerns for reciprocity, equality, and humility. Gringos like myself are presumed to be the sources of limitless wealth, and I was often accused of unfairly giving to some and not others. Many suspected me of paying massive sums of money to my hosts or procuring work in the United States. During my census and interviews in Pelillo Negro, I discovered that some had refused to participate because they were certain that I would be taking Pedro to the United States, as Fought had done with his main informant, Isidro González, thirty years before. Others had heard that I was paying him Q80 for each Ch'orti' word he taught me, or that I had bought him a car. Similar rumors surfaced in Tuticopote, with accusations that I was paying Miguel to teach me Ch'orti', that I was to marry one of Carmen's daughters, and that I was the one who introduced a broccoli project to some in the community and not others. Such accusations prompted my friends to insist that I only do my census and interviews in the morning before envious drunks were likely to retaliate in the afternoons.

Disrespect and envy are manifest in thievery, in which "real Mayas" do not engage according to some scholars. They might beg, but they do not steal. Whether all campesinos in the Ch'orti' area are Maya or not, today some seem to have taken on the attitudes of the Ladinos who were stealing their land and killing them during las ruinas. The theft of cattle and horses is a constant threat. Houses, harboring such goods as chickens, turkeys, corn stores, and tools, are small fortresses surrounded by thorny *pinuela* and maguey plants and/or barbed wire, and guarded by various dogs and at least one family member at all times. Development-minded Paco has been subject to the thievery and poisoning of his fish pond, rabbits, and chickens. According to Miguel and others, few parents punish their children for stealing today. As if to confirm this, that night all the ripe limes from his sister's tree were stolen. Doña Tonia, a storeowner for some thirty years in Jocotán, told me that campesino stealing became a problem only in the 1980s.

An Age of Violence

Violence has long been a part of the Ch'orti' landscape. In the 1930s and 1940s, Ch'orti's had to fear each other as much as anyone else. Wisdom (1961:145, 296–97, 489–90) noted that men never traveled without machetes, which they used on each other during drinking sprees at town festivals and weekly markets, when animosity over land disputes and marital infidelity tended to surface. For Girard (1949:299–304), Ch'orti' violence was due to "civilization," which presented a "sociological problem" by dissolving the Indian communal ethic and their respect for each other. Purportedly for "ladinoized" Indians living near the towns, neighborliness had deteriorated to envy and meddling in others' affairs, and unfortunately for Girard himself, clan solidarity had devolved into distrust of all outsiders, and wage labor was spurned.

Las ruinas and poverty certainly have contributed to what many Ch'orti's claim is an increasingly violent age. While some campesinos and priests are certain that Ch'orti' violence has diminished since the arrival of the Belgian Mission in the 1960s, others, like priests themselves, claim that las ruinas have exacerbated violence.

> *Padre*: Listen, I know that Indian violence has not been turned against the Ladino, nor the mestizo.
>
> *Brent*: Against themselves.
>
> *Padre*: Exactly. In other words, it's been turned against themselves. Now, the mestizo, the Ladino, deserves much of the blame in this respect, because I believe that alone the Indian is not violent. Alone. But the former has induced the latter to be violent.... Yes, so the Indian has also internalized, has made these things his own, and hasn't valued himself, because they [the Ladinos] are taking and stealing a lot of land. And this has caused a lot of serious problems, but it's a violence that hasn't been directed towards the Ladino nor the mestizo, but against themselves.

Another priest, who saw El Salvador turn violent with the onset of civil war, acknowledges that poverty is a prime motivator of disputes but argues that political violence immunized many from the suffering of others. Violence has become an increasingly conceivable option for resolving problems. Army recruitment has added to such a culture, and ex-recruits seem to be involved in a disproportionate number of violent acts (see Green 1994: 233–34). Since at least the start of las ruinas, the use of firearms has been on the rise. I know of several feuds in which entire campesino families arm themselves with guns by whatever means, and pistol-wielding hit men are paid between $60 and $200 for assassinations. Tragically, homicide has emerged as a major cause of death, accounting for fifty-seven deaths (19%) in Jocotán in 1996–97. With a population of roughly twenty-nine thousand, this homicide rate of one per one thousand matches Guatemala's high rate, exceeds Latin America's rate by a factor of four (*Cerigua* 7/29/99), and is about eleven times that of the United States (US Department of Health and Human Services 1997). Even visiting Mayas from western Guatemala are ill at ease with the way Ch'orti' men carry their machetes with them everywhere.

Some aldeas seem especially prone to violence when land and women are involved. Properties are poorly marked and often untitled, and inheritance can be lopsided in favor of the oldest and youngest siblings, leaving some with unlivable amounts of land. As the state legal system is highly corrupt, individuals tend to take land disputes into their own hands, especially in April and May when men mark their property by clearing and planting it. In some communities, people are injured or killed on a monthly basis due to feuds over land and women. Feuds that may have started over a minor incident may last for decades when murders are involved, and an attack may quickly draw in kin from other aldeas who rush to the scene with machetes or guns. In the words of a man whose father was killed by a rival faction, "perhaps one's father dies and he wants to even the score; that's when the problem begins to grow and will never resolve itself." Because of the constant threat, some go to great lengths to circumvent the homes of their enemies. I am now accustomed on my arrival each year to ask hesitantly whether anyone has been killed (cf. Stoll [2001:114, 119–20] who defends the state by citing Maya-Maya violence, a distinction between the state and large landowners, and the state's role as independent mediator in land disputes).

One friend, Diego, gave his version of a feud in which he is involved. His cousin married one of José's daughters and slaughtered a pig for the occasion. José's daughters interpreted such a lavish outlay as intentionally trying to show up the bride's family. Diego foresaw trouble and did not attend. Later, José's daughters exchanged words with Diego's sister at a spring, and the sister scratched one of their faces. José's family demanded $3.50 in damages or they would go to the municipality, so Diego reluctantly paid. Then some of José's sons-in-law spread rumors that Diego was the culprit in a murder, and when Diego was returning from town one day, five of the murdered man's male relatives confronted him, and Diego asked why they were so angry. Diego insisted that he attended an Evangelical celebration the night of the murder, and they both exchanged biblical passages that peace is better than violence. They left on good terms and became friends. In yet another incident, four of José's sons-in-law confronted Diego and his two cousins on the trail and the former group began swinging machetes. Diego swung back, badly cutting one of them in the hand, and pleaded that he is a man of peace, but if they wanted to keep fighting he was ready. The injured man took a few more futile swings but just spattered him with blood. They all departed saying they wanted no more fighting, but all still carry machetes for protection. He said every family is involved in at least one such feud.

Random acts of violence are less common but on the rise. Countless campesinos still warn me to either stay home or be careful walking in the late afternoon and evening, especially on Sundays, because of drunks. Whenever we passed drunks in the trail, we were very cautious and attempted to pass them as quickly as possible. Some elders and women rarely go to town for fear of drunks. Ladinos often tell stories of drunk campesinos who attack pistol-carrying Ladino horseback riders, as if the Ch'orti's disbelieved that the pistols could do them harm. I myself was threatened four times by drunks on the trail wielding machetes, each time they blocked my path, grabbed my arm and chatted with me aggressively. One of them caught me on the trail at night, cursed a star, and screamed that he was ready to kill somebody. In 1997 I was confronted by two drunk young men with machetes who demanded money. Luckily I had a few quetzals, and thankfully they sent me on my way. Some drunks have worse reputations than others, and campesinos will avoid their neighborhoods in the afternoon if at all possible.

Gabriel, Cheo, Demetrio, and Fidel independently claimed that disputes have always existed, but people used to be more patient and able to hold their liquor. For Catarino, "today there are no longer any 'legal' people, only screwed up people, because when they get drunk, they want to attack us." Drinking chicha has long been a festive activity and was once generally confined to the towns on Sundays, but today it is a daily practice for over a third of men in some aldeas (cf. Eber 1995). A few claimed that alcoholism begins in childhood, as babies in some aldeas are weaned on chicha, which I witnessed myself. Fiestas are now rarely held, precisely because of the likelihood of drunken violence, such as a fistfight that verged on a machete contest at a wedding I attended. Beyond spontaneous violence, drinking is a customary means for preparing oneself to attack, the liquid giving courage to overcome one's inhibitions, defy the authorities, and attack a potentially armed person. While drunks are feared, alcoholics now fear others, such that discussions of respect are often introduced by the phrase "today one can no longer get drunk and pass out in the trail without getting killed."

Most disturbing is that women are now being attacked and even raped, which most, especially women, say was unthinkable before. Women do not have the protection of the machete as men do, because metal tools are thought to be masculine. Though they have more stamina than I, women defer to men when heavy tools are to be used. They are always vigilant about rape and rarely travel far without an escort. Even at home, or perhaps especially at home, they may be subject to rape and abuse from drunken husbands and fathers. One ex-recruit known for his unpredictable violent streak raped and mutilated a sixty-year-old woman one Sunday afternoon in 1994.

A Ch'orti' culture of violence is evident in the way violence is often justified, even by bystanders. One man, who had participated in the murder of an old man, justified a drunk's machete attack on another's motorcycle because riding a moto in the aldeas is an ostentatious provocation. The local army commissioner who went to arrest the attacker nearly lost his hand when the drunkard delivered another machete blow (after which the commissioner's kin nearly hacked the drunk to death). When one well-educated Ch'orti' merchant couple, known for winning their court disputes, reabducted their daughter from an aspiring husband, they were nearly macheteed to death by the bachelor and his kin. Most of my friends supported the attack, saying that the merchant couple received their just desserts. When one couple was killed on a Sunday afternoon, a friend blamed the murdered husband for being drunk and not carrying his machete.

Lack of respect for oneself and lack of respect for others like oneself are two sides of the same coin. In the words of one alcoholic ex-soldier,

> I passed sooo many trials and by the grace of God I am still healthy, you see, I am somewhat, somewhat scraped up, look, somewhat tired but by my own labor. Because at times, how do you say, we like what is called chicha, you know? You

understand? We like it and sometimes one gets very drunk and
irritated, and already I feel somewhat scraped up, paaaained,
tiiiired. That's why... why? Because one doesn't take care
of himself, let's say one doesn't respect his life. Now you
understand me, don't you? In other words, one doesn't have
his reward, one doesn't respect his own life. One doesn't
respect the life he doesn't have.

I thought his aldea had hit bottom in 1993 when it had eight chicha vendors, but the number rose to fourteen, and violence is said to be more
rampant than ever.

The story of forty-two-year-old Chilo of Tuticopote encapsulates many
of the interrelated problems of the new era. He was orphaned during las
ruinas and raised in poverty. He eventually acquired a small piece of land
and sold chicha out of his home. When I interviewed him, he complained
about the loss of respect for traditions: "It's no longer the same, because
now they only want to walk boastfully, doing things, problems. Already they
don't want to respect an elder... alright, and if we wanted to dance? We
danced. Nobody had a machete in his belt." A few years later his wife, a mid-
wife, was murdered for witchcraft because she delivered a stillborn child.
He tried to get the police to arrest the perpetrators, who were a secret to no
one, but he gave up. Within the year, locals say he drank himself to death,
orphaning his five daughters just as he had been orphaned.

Visions of the End

In 1993 several elderly Ch'orti' men recounted to me a prophecy: God has
given up on the current race of humans and will destroy them to create a
new race that obeys him better. This is a popular Protestant Evangelical
theme throughout Latin America, but it also falls in line with Mayan ways of
thinking about multiple, improving creations. In fact, Ch'orti' Catholics,
Evangelical Protestants, and nonaffiliated elders alike recounted the prophecy. Vicente, a Catholic, explained that "'the ruins' are with us because we
don't want to give to nor even respect our neighbor." In 1993 he warned that
six months before the year 2000 all the repentant should appear before the
Black Christ in Esquipulas to seek forgiveness because the world would be
engulfed by a twenty-four-inch carpet of fire. A great flood would ensue,
and God would turn all people into fish for consumption by a new race.
Juan, also Catholic, had deliberated at length with his friends but was

uncertain how many people would be saved or whether it would pass in the year 2000 or after. Petronilo, once a Protestant, forewarned that we do not know when God's patience will end or whether God will even grant us another ten years of rain. Pedro, a prayer-sayer, left some room for hope, warning that only with a return to the old customs and the authority of the padrinos would time correct itself (*o'sta*). Palma Ramos's (2001:107) research team recorded similar expositions, such as that of this sixty-six-year-old: "Yes, there's plague, but it comes from above, from the heavens as a punishment from God, because there's little time left before the next creation (*renovación de la familia*), and not a single one of us will remain."

Don Chico, a Catholic, said he was unsure about the end, but voiced these doubts:

> [W]ho knows how. . . because according to the word left by God, who knows which world the Scriptures address, which day the world will be lost, because the world must be lost in a fire, it is said, and so all the sinners will be judged, so no more people will remain on Earth. No more, they say. But I, I don't know how, but the people, the elders as well, those that already died used to prophesy that the Earth will be consumed, you know. It will be wasted, they said. And so no people will remain, nothing, the place will only remain by itself, in other words. So God always gives a sign, he always assigns two people among the sinners, a woman and a man. And with them the world, the people, will multiply again. But I don't know either when the world will be lost.

He added that many say that God will come down to judge sinners a little after the year 2000, and that a worldwide sickness, which seems to have started already, must come to pass. Either way, he laughed, he would not hide because death will always find him, which indeed it did two weeks after the interview.

Cipriano, once a Protestant, was more certain:

> So, eh, it's bad, but we used to know long ago, the old-timers used to tell that a time must come when a people must only kill each other, they say. And maybe it's the time that's passing right now, perhaps. The people are doing much evil; we're doing nothing good.

Brent: So it will get worse still?

Cipriano: Worse still, it's a matter of twenty years now, maybe, and I think that perhaps it will look a little worse!

Brent: Well, a healer in Olopa told me that perhaps the epoch will end as well, it will change, but he said by God, that God wants to finish this epoch—

Cipriano: —And it's God who will do it, will complete it! God said, "I leave and come so I must waste the Earth, the surface of this Earth," he says. Indeed. He has to waste the surface of the Earth. Because God cannot accept what he sees, sooo much evil. And as he's Our Father, he must come and waste the evil men. Because before the year 2000 there must come to pass something that will not be pretty! . . . All that because of sin. If we only did right, God wouldn't waste the land, but since we're only doing evil, he must come and destroy it. "I'll come again," God says. "I must return to waste the land, but you will know," he says, "because the leaves of the *pinyaj* are a sign of God. When you see," he says, "the arrival of the pinyaj here, all will start to dry, all will start to fall. You will know that the time has come." It's a fruit like that, and it will be certain when the pinyaj sprouts, beautifully green! But when it comes the strong Sun will dry everything. It will dry. And that's how God will assemble the people, as they will use the pinyaj for shade. But the truth is that God must consume, must waste us from the surface of the Earth. He must come in the year 2000, but only a little time remains. Just a little.

Protestant Catalino provided other particulars:

The Bible says that "you will see the trees will lose their leaves, all will dry up, so that you know that the drought is near. That's when the Son of God will come. So you must be watchful. Famine, sickness, so many things must come to pass. The people must kill each other. The same family must kill its father, and the same parents must kill their son, so that you know the time is drawing near . . ." We are ending time because a day will arrive when hunger increases. This still isn't the famine because none of us has passed the great pestilence. It is said, "the sickness must come." OK, because they say that the warning must fall again, the sky must revolve too. The sun will not shine, nor will the moon. Only darkness once and for all, there will be no day.... Um, everything will finish.... The people don't believe; they say it's a lie, but that which is written must come to pass.... They say it's a lie. They say that by doing the old rituals they can save themselves and thereby prevent the judgment.... But God must always come because his word is written, it lays written by God and will not be prevented. The Gospel was not written so that God wouldn't come; they are fighting it, but one must repent. One must repent and leave all evil, leave sin, all that, and change one's liiife.

Felipe, also a Protestant, echoed the warnings of Catalino:

It will be more difficult because the Scriptures are saying "there's a time to come when there's hunger.... There's a time when hunger will come so that what the people said will be realized. They will go to another place. But, the famine will be everywhere. Wherever there are people, there will always be hunger.... There will be nowhere to find favor." In other words, from this we know that the epoch in which we stand has already changed quite a bit.... The Scriptures say "the people must kill each other..." It's already certain because the Scriptures said so. Because, because Christ must come to Earth. He must come. "They who come and obey me by the Gospel must prepare the place." And so, the Earth must be burned, as they say in Spanish, it must burn, but it's the evil. It's the evil. The land must be burned and nothing will remain. All the animals, everything.

Though the new generation is generally unconvinced about the end of the epoch, some are nonetheless pessimistic. Fifty-year-old Jesús said that the world will not end around the year 2000, but mourned that the ancestors at least had hope for rains and abundant harvests. Those days seem to be gone forever. Benjamín, ordinarily optimistic about education and agricultural development, was no less resigned that population will continue to increase and many will have to migrate to the plantations or emigrate permanently. Eighteen-year-old Tancho displayed the same mixed emotions. Already in the ninth grade, he dreamed of leaving the land and finding employment by way of education. But in regards to the future, he dejectedly said "more, more poor, there's no more room, because the people have multiplied so much, each year they multiply. And as far as the land is concerned, it is being spent. Each year it is being spent, and all the trees and savannas are being cleared for the fields, and in the end, perhaps in twenty years, the fields will remain *cleared* and none of us will be able to cut firewood." He swore that he would have fewer children if and when he married.

SIX

Excluded from "Nuestra Patria Guatemala," Our Fatherland

I once and for all was never anything, I was, I was a private.
—former Ch'orti' soldier

Who creates money?
Chi uche e tumin?
—campesino

On the face of it, it seems like a good idea that Ch'orti's question their traditions and abandon the notion that they are God's chosen people. Any ethnic group that believes it is God's chosen should be "brought back to earth" with the rest of us. After all, is it not better to "melt" into Guatemala's national "pot" than be stigmatized as different? One cohesive, predominant national culture is certainly better than people practicing many cultures misunderstanding each other and coming into conflict. Is it not romantic or nostalgic to lament that Ch'orti's are losing their ethnic distinctiveness? Should we not, as many policy makers alike feel, let "evolution" take its course with these "primitive" people? Although strongly trained in cultural relativism, I was challenged by these questions throughout my fieldwork by Ladinos, gringos, and even some Ch'orti's.

A desire to preserve indigenous cultures—as if this were even possible—for the sake of exoticism, romance, or science is obviously mistaken, and reflects more the anomie and disenchantment with modern(ist) cultures than an understanding of contemporary indigenous peoples. On the other hand, a politics that promotes the safeguarding of indigenous cultural production from enforced cultural homogenization and hegemony is not ipso facto romantic and nostalgic, especially if people are forcibly homogenized culturally but socially excluded due to their "race." If indigenous people are not invited as equal participants into national societies, then for their own wellbeing it is optimal that they bolster their own proud cultures and identities. If inclusion and "evolution" mean working part-time for subhuman wages in the cellar of the global economy with virtually no way of securing a basic education, minimal level of health, or security in old age, then to maintain a distinctive way of life is not so romantic or exotic. If losing faith in one's indigenous traditions, identity, and distinctive cultural production combined with national exclusion leads to a negative identity, then rejecting evolutionary, modernist myths and holding one's unique history and traditions dear is necessary for reconstituting pride and motivation.

From Dark to Light

It is impossible to understand Guatemala without taking the structural racism in which most are trapped into consideration (Nelson 1999; Casaús 1998:10, 64; Guzmán Böckler 1975). Scholars of Guatemala and Latin America generally, including me, have overemphasized identity and culture when explaining discrimination, as if indigenous peoples were discriminated against for their cultures only, not their bodies. Race supposedly has nothing to do with Guatemalan inequality, such that if indigenous peoples abandon their distinctive cultural practices, especially their language, dress, subsistence farming, and religions, they can fluidly become Ladino or mestizo and vice versa. In fact, some Mayas do this on a daily basis when they go to work as Ladinos and return home as Mayas. While such descriptions of pragmatism and plasticity are accurate on one level, on another level they overlook the five-centuries-old dichotomy of "European"-looking people and "Indian"-looking people. In Latin America, Europeans have had phenomenal success in propagating the linkage between light skin, blond hair, and blue eyes to beauty, intelligence, and overall superiority in the popular imagination. It is no surprise that in Guatemala the twenty-two families that comprise the oligarchy—mainly colonial elites who control agriculture, industry, and commerce—refer to themselves predominantly as Creoles (American-born Europeans), not mestizos, and four trace their ancestry directly to Spanish Andalusians (Casaús 1998:60–61). Owning the prestigious private universities (Francisco Marroquín and Del Valle) and media, they have a heavy hand in molding national ideology. They also dominate the most powerful business lobby, the Committee of the Agricultural, Commerce, Industrial, and Financial Associations of Guatemala (CACIF) (Casaús 1998:42–44). Nevertheless, the oligarchy's racial purity (i.e., "whiteness") is questioned, especially in international circles, which makes their loathing of Indian contamination all the deeper (Casaús 1998:72). "Creole" agricultural oligarchs in particular are highly protective of their daughters' virginity, so that they do not have children with someone stained by "Indian blood," while, as in other parts of Latin America with a strong Spanish colonial heritage, believing it their sons' right (*derecho de la pernada*) to practice sex on indigenous servants (Casaús 1998:84).

While "whiteness" continues to constitute social capital in Guatemala and the world in general, having "Indian" phenotypic features or "stains," which themselves are arbitrarily marked (low stature, dark skin, protruding lips, straight dark hair, etc.), indicates a propensity towards superstitions, traditionalism, conformism, drunkenness, submissiveness, introversion, physical endurance, laziness, low intellect, and social immaturity. Someone with such features might eventually pass as a Ladino, but they will never pass as a Creole, like three out of four of Guatemala's past presidents (León Carpio, Arzú, Berger). The imagined traits of laziness and physical endurance are an especially useful fiction for justifying colonialist exploitation (Casaús 1998:19, 22, 26, 67–71, 106–8).

Ladinos, or mestizos, are neither "Indian" nor "white," but often affiliate themselves with whites. "Ladino" was originally applied to all in the Spanish empire who spoke Spanish but were not of pure Spanish-Christian heritage. In Spain, Spanish-speaking Jews, for example, were Ladinos, and by the 1700s in eastern Guatemala mulattos, Indians, mestizos, and eventually even poor Spanish Creole campesinos (as opposed to Spaniards born in the Iberian Peninsula) became Ladinos (Dary 1994:1, 10). Still today, "Ladino" refers to those, including nationalized Mayas, practicing Guatemalan national culture but who are racially not purely white/Creole. Some "whites" in the Oriente, then, reject the term Ladino because it implies that they are "stained" with Indian or black "blood." In eastern Guatemala especially, Ladinos are subconsciously categorized on a spectrum running from whites (Creoles), mestizos, Indians, *sambos* (black/Indian), to blacks. Mixed-bloods of any variety face subtle racial discrimination even when denying the parts of themselves with indigenous or black heritage (Casaús 1998, 2001). Neither white nor Maya, they occupy an identity that Guzmán Böckler (1975) calls *ningunidad* or "nothingness," trying to approach whiteness socially and culturally while distancing themselves from Indianness (Casaús 1998:117–18; Guzmán Böckler 1975).[1]

Indigenous peoples become "nothings" when they deny their indigenous heritage while still suffering the Indian "racial stain." While mestizos aspire to be Creole, indigenous "nothings" aspire to be mestizos. Only recently, when indigenous movements have gained symbolic, political, and economic capital in the global arena, has this directionality reversed to some extent, with more mestizos and indigenous peoples embracing their indigenous heritage (see Hale 1996). These movements, in fact, have formed partly in reaction to political violence with strong racial overtones, including the systematic torture and massacre of indigenous-looking men, women, children, and elders during civil wars (e.g., ODHAG 1998 2:1–32, 159–227; Bastos and Camus 1996; cf. Chapin 1989 for El Salvador). Among Ch'orti's for example, regardless of whether they practiced distinctive language, dress, or religion, they were persecuted with acute cruelty because of their "race."

The stability and inescapability of discrimination based on physical features belies the fallacy that people have the liberty to unilaterally invent just any history, identity, or tradition. No doubt, people remember the past in partial, distorted, and biased ways, but they do not imagine just any past, but a past that informs and even frames their memory and imagination. People are both products and producers of the past.

Disentangling "Race" and Culture

Understanding racism, or racialism, requires a disentanglement of terms, because "races" are cultural constructs. "Races" are conceived differently in different societies, and even within Western societies races are defined differently and arbitrarily by the racialists who use them. The human

---

1. Sometimes Ladino mestizos distinguish themselves from Creoles. In the November 2003 national election, the principal division was between the mestizo/Ladino military and the white oligarchy, with the latter winning handily.

body varies in innumerable ways from one person to the next, but Western racialists chose to focus on nose shapes, hair colors and textures, skin tones, and tooth shapes. Each of these features vary along a continuum, not in naturally exclusive types. Moreover, the features do not coincide, such that nose "types" do not coincide with certain skin "types," hair "types," etc., much less genetics. The straight black hair, tooth shape, and brown skin associated with "the Amerindian race" are not found in all "Amerindian" people and are found to varying degrees or clines in "non-Amerindian" populations, including Europeans. Fixing race to a geographical region or continent creates more confusion. Africans, for example, might be placed in a black or negroid race, yet Africa has more genetic diversity than all the other continents combined. Solving this contradiction by dividing Africans into more numerous races begs the question of how many races are needed. Since people have been moving and intermarrying since time immemorial, how would a "pure" race be identified? If we count twenty-five years as one generation and go back five hundred years when intercontinental mixing accelerated due to European colonization, each of us would have 2^{19} or 4,194,304 ancestors (i.e., 2 parents = 2^1; 4 grandparents = 2^2; 8 great-grandparents = 2^3, etc.). Obviously, no one knows the "races" of all their ancestors. Though "race" is a cultural means of identification, it has objective consequences. When social conservatives denounce affirmative action policies meant to redress racism (cf. Morales cited by Warren 1998:42), they deny racism but not races, and are therefore wrong on both fronts.

More subtle than naked racism is equating a particular culture or "character" with a "people." Since the founding of anthropology as a profession in the late nineteenth century, the discipline has generally avoided any explanation of culture in terms of race, yet tribal societies and cultures in particular have been approached as if they were static systems, lending to the misleading notion that their cultures are primordial or timeless (Hervik 1999). Outside of anthropology, race, peoples, tradition, culture, and identity are often mistakenly used interchangeably, especially when applied to nonwhite populations or people of color. Some of my white students have used people of color and people of culture interchangeably, as if "they" have eccentric cultures and "we" have rationality or common sense. Even some people of color equate their "race" with culture and personality, as if identities, ethos, and traditions were innate. Under assumptions of functionality or primordial cultures, there is an expectation that indigenous or tribal peoples in particular should not change; otherwise, they are inauthentic. Such fixity, of course, is impossible, especially for severely exploited and oppressed people (Turner 1993; Handler and Linnekin 1984; Stavenhagen 2001:373).

If race is pseudoscientific, what term best connotes a group of people with a shared identity based on a longstanding social and cultural unity? "Society" and "population" imply people in the present, such that using the phrase "indigenous society" to refer to generations of people would insinuate the primordialist notion that the people of today, like "the Maya," are essentially the same people of a thousand years ago. In the absence of a good term, many activists and scholars employ the word "peoples." Though "peoples" can be mistaken as race or an unchanging society, if used with caution it can serve to convey a group united by distinctive physical and traditional heritage across multiple generations (cf. International Labor Organization [ILO] 2003; Bodley 2000).

Indices of Guatemalan Racism

There have been two popular misconceptions about Guatemalan inequality in recent decades. One is that it is based principally in socioeconomic class. Many nations have undergone at least a partial transformation from a caste or ethnically based society to a class based society, but inequality in Guatemala is still strongly ethnic and racist. The second misconception is that the Guatemalan state has done its best to integrate Mayas into the nation and therefore exert cultural hegemony over them. Actually, the Creole-dominated governments have generally shown little concern for the Mayas except when they are less than submissive. Exceptions can always be found, of course, and one government is never the same as another, but the pattern is undeniable. Guatemalan elites have done much more to exclude Mayas from Guatemala than include them (Casaús 1998:34–35). According to some elites with whom I have spoken or whom I have heard speak, Mayas do not want to be modernized or included in anything beyond their local communities. They are happy eating tortillas and going without shoes. Those who demand improvements are contaminated by communist troublemakers. Such a position, of course, is very cost effective for elites who pay only minimal taxes for developing the country and wish to have a pool of ignorant, desperate, and cheap laborers. For Evangelical military elites like Ríos Montt, Mayas represent the forces of idolatry and evil (Casaús 1998:37). Given Mayas' less than submissive attitudes in recent decades, the army has devoted itself to disciplining Mayas more by force than by culturally hegemonic means (cf. Schirmer 1999).

The numbers reveal that, except perhaps for the Arévalo/Arbenz period, Guatemalan governments have always been neoliberal in their lack of social investment (Portes 2001:232). After the CIA-orchestrated overthrow, Guatemala became a major agro-exporter of coffee, cotton, sugar, and cattle, particularly for the US market. From 1950 to 1964 the acreage devoted to coffee increased by 85%, cattle ranches displaced as many as 120,000 Maya colonists in Izabal and the Petén, and cotton producers applied the most lethal types and amounts of pesticides in the world, to which its workers were directly exposed (Handy 1984:149ff; Jonas 1974:169ff; Black 1984; Woodward 1985:241–43). While the army was receiving a windfall in US aid, it began to reap profits in emerging capitalist sectors—agrarian, financial, commercial, and industrial. US aid and gross national product grew in tandem with repression and corruption (Handy 1984:149ff; Jonas 1974:169ff; Black 1984; Woodward 1985:241–43). Remarkably, during the period of sustained economic growth from 1960 to 1980, taxation and state spending on social programs were the lowest in Central America (CEH 1999 1:86).

The unequal land distribution recorded during the Democratic Revolution remained largely the same throughout the period, which is particularly serious in a country with a burgeoning campesino population. Although the percentage of Guatemalan landholdings of nine hundred hectares or more was reduced from 41% in 1950 to 22% in 1979, landholdings above forty-five hectares remained basically the same, from 72% in 1950 to 65% in 1979. Throughout this period, the owners of these large extensions composed only 2%–2.5% of the landowning population. Meanwhile, the percentage of the population holding 1.7 acres or less rose from 21% to 31%. In 1964, 44% of landowners possessed only 3.4% of the land, and by 1979 60% owned only 3.7% (CEH 1999 1:84; Bilsborrow and Stupp 1997:591; Early 1982:65). Today, Guatemala has the most unequal land distribution in Latin America, with two-thirds of the land in the hands of only 2.6% of the population, while 54% of farms (with less than 3.4 acres) occupy only 4% of the arable land (CEH 1999 1:77). One might equate the erosion of the campesino lifestyle with modernization and development, but agriculture employs 70% of the economically active population outside the capital, and average agricultural salaries in 1995 did not even cover 50% of the minimum cost of living (CEH 1999 1:78).

During the worst years of the war, Guatemala's economy became heavily dependent on loans from the International Monetary Fund, the

World Bank, and USAID. These lending agencies, in turn, have demanded that the state cut already meager social programs and promote the campesino adoption of nontraditional agro-export crops for the US market, entailing high risks, low profits, dangerous pesticides, dependency, and international trade barriers (AVANSCO/PACCA 1992). The few remaining programs of the Democratic Revolution, such as Social Security, the Labor Code, and free hospital care, have been most severely undermined *after* the Peace Accords of 1996 (*Cerigua* 10/23/97:1). Despite uncharacteristic demands by the global financial elite that Guatemala raise its taxes to pay for needed infrastructure and social investment, the oligarchy, still largely synonymous with "the state," has successfully kept taxes at the lowest percentage of gross domestic product (GDP) in the hemisphere at 9%, much lower than the average 29% of developing countries worldwide and even the pitiful 13% of Latin America as a whole. Unlike other developing countries, in which 65% of state revenue comes from taxes on income and property, i.e., on wealth, 75% of all Guatemalan taxes come from sales tax (IVA) on basic consumer items (*Cerigua* 5/14/98:4). Much of this sales tax, when collected, is shouldered by the 80% of Guatemalans living in poverty, who even if they were earning the minimum wage of $75 per month, would not meet the basic living costs of the average family at $200 per month (*La Nación* 12/31/96). Although only 21% of the national population and 13% of the nation's poor live in the capital, government budgets have characteristically favored it (for statistics, see *Cerigua* 12/4/97:2).

Low taxes on wealth means no redistribution of wealth from those whose opulence is such that their identities are based on conspicuous consumption to those without enough to eat. Such lack of social investment is reflected clearly when Guatemala's indices of poverty are compared with its Central American neighbors. The life expectancy in Guatemala in the late 1990s was 59.3 years, while the next lowest was Honduras with 67.5 years. Costa Rica's was 76.8 (CEH 1999 1:85). Guatemala spent only 5% of its GDP on health care, compared to 9.2% in Costa Rica, even though 9.2% of Guatemala's health expenditure was paid by foreign aid compared to only .8% in Costa Rica (Ramesh Govindaraj and Murray 1997:163). Only 25% of the general population was serviced by the Ministry of Health, and health expenditures per capita were double in the more affluent Guatemala City compared to the rest of the country (Robles 1997:378–79). Despite official denials, parasitic diseases like cholera have killed countless thousands of campesinos in the 1990s due a combination of high population density and poor sanitation (*Cerigua* 5/8/97:4). Guatemala spent only 1.8% of its income on education, again the worst in Central America, and three times less than Costa Rica. Guatemalan adult illiteracy was 44.9% compared to the next lowest, Honduras, at 29%, and in sharp contrast to Costa Rica's 6.9% (CEH 1999 1:85). Though adult illiteracy steadily dropped from 52.3% in 1985 to 33.3% in 1999, it continued at over 60% in the neglected indigenous areas (*Cerigua* 7/29/99:4). Illiteracy partially explains why voter turnouts are so low, such as 21% of the electorate in the 1994 legislative elections, 47% in the 1995 general elections (*Cerigua* 11/13/97:3), and 18% in the 1999 national referendum for constitutional reforms based on the Peace Accords.

Not surprisingly, according to the state planning agency (SEGEPLAN), the gap between rich and poor has widened since the 1980s, when the richest 10% received 41% of the national revenue and the poorest 10% received only 2.4%. In recent years, the richest 10% has received 44%, and the poorest 10% below 2% (*Cerigua* 1/15/98:3; CEH 1999 1:77). Consequently, as many as one and a half million Guatemalans are working legally and one million illegally—one-fifth of the total population—at any one time outside the country, predominantly in the United States (CEH 1999 1:79). The CEH (1999 1:79) concluded, "the concentration of economic and political power, the racist and discriminatory character of the society towards the majority of the population that is indigenous, and the economic and social exclusion of the large poor sectors—Mayas and Ladinos—is expressed in the illiteracy, isolation, and exclusion of local communities from the nation."

"People of the Town," "People of the Country"

Writing about racism and ethnocentrism in eastern Guatemala, just as writing about Ch'orti' internal problems, is not easy because I am being critical of the cultures of those who have collaborated with me. However, giving a sanitized account in which negatives are glossed over would be paternalistic and disrespectful to Ch'orti's and Ladinos who suffer at each other's hands (see Linnekin 1991; Foley 1995). Ladinos have often been unfairly essentialized as amoral, without traditions or "culture," without a sense of community, and responsible for all Maya problems. In Guatemala's national imagination, Ladinos of the Oriente are thought to be hotheaded, pistol-wielding cowboys, as if the hotter the climate, the hotter the temper, but they are far from homogeneous. Some get by on as little as $70 per month farming or street vending, while others own large plantations, small industries, and trucking operations. My Ladino friends in eastern Guatemala are some of the most generous people I know, and I certainly do not want to paint non-Mayas with a broad, negative brush. Since the start of the Maya Movement in the early 1990s, there are also signs that Creoles and Ladinos in eastern Guatemala are beginning to respect Mayas more.

That said, discrimination against campesinos, especially "Indian"-looking ones, in the Ch'orti' area is manifest socially, economically, and politically, and results in the rejection of indigeneity. The structure behind the discrimination is complex and sometimes seems nonethnic and nonracial, as reflected in the terminology used. "Ladino" in eastern Guatemala is synonymous with "mestizo," or having mixed Spanish, indigenous, and/or African heritage. As most aspire to be "pure" Creole or white (and indeed some clearly are), the term is considered offensive. To call someone "black" (negro) or "Indian" (indio) constitutes the worst racial slur, and even the polite terms *moreno* (brown) or indígena (indigenous person) are considered derogatory. Many prefer to distinguish themselves from the "Indians," or politely, "the people of the aldeas" (*gente de las aldeas*) by calling themselves either "people of the town" (*gente del pueblo*) or "the civilized people" (*los civilizados*).

Phenotypically, Ladinos in the Oriente range from those with seemingly unmixed European ancestry, mestizos of all varieties, seeming unmixed indigenous people, Ladinos Pardos (black Ladinos), and Chinese. Many dark-skinned Ladinos could easily pass for Ch'orti's with a change of clothes and mannerisms, while a few Creole- and African-looking campesinos speak Ch'orti'. Black features are more stigmatizing than "Indian" ones, and it is a grave offense to recognize publicly another's dark skin, "frizzy" (*crespo*) hair, full lips, and broad nose, except when joking among friends. In fact, verbal sparring and joking offer the clearest evidence of such racism. Because many "people of the town" exhibit physical features that they themselves consider Indian and black, they are in a sense tormented and torment each other by their own ideology. When Ch'orti's called Ladinos "sambos" (blacks/Indians) in the early 1930s (Wisdom 1961: 266), they were no doubt playing on Ladino insecurities about racial purity. As seen in Ch'orti' ethnic humor in chapter 4, Ch'orti's have also internalized the racial hierarchy to the point that they poke fun of themselves.

What is often more distinguishable about Ladinos than physical features is culture. In places like Ocotepeque, Honduras, where many self-proclaimed Ch'orti's are phenotypically mestizo or even Creole, it is impossible to tell by sight who is Ch'orti' and who is not. Ladinos tend to have clothing, cars, hats, and shoes indicative of global and often Mexican or US influence. Rather than sombreros, professionals wear baseball hats, and youth wear shorts and no shirts. Rather than sandals or rubber boots, many wear cowboy boots or sneakers. Women may have short hair, instead of a long ponytail, and may wear pants, T-shirts, and miniskirts. What unites Ladinos is relative integration into national and global cultures and societies. Most successfully strive for modern amenities like cars, a cement house with a television, VCRs, stereos, computers, washing machines, and microwaves, and many watch pirated satellite television and videos from the United States, Mexico, Spain, and other countries. Most townspeople own small businesses buying and selling to the Ch'orti' population, work as professionals, or are among the hoards of schoolteachers, many unemployed, in the region. Some youth especially eye migration to the United States and increasingly drug trafficking as a means to wealth. Nearly every family has at least one relative working in Guatemala City, the Petén, or the United States. At any one moment hundreds of thousands of Oriente Ladinos are working in the United States, especially New Jersey and Los Angeles.

Because many townspeople are proud of their towns, class-conscious, and aspire to modern tastes, tragically, they feel inferior, powerless, and frustrated at times when comparing themselves to North Americans and Europeans. On several occasions I was told that Latin Americans speak inferior Spanish, and one professional ruefully believed that they generally have lower IQs than Europeans. Others joked that drunkenness is Guatemala's national pastime. Some have expressed disdain towards me for my relative wealth and privilege, even though many townspeople are far wealthier than me. Some argue (correctly) that they should have the same right to enter the United States as I do Guatemala, and some are savvy enough to know that US politics has much to do with their disadvantage. One drunk once barged into my room and wanted to fight because he was "angry seeing my computer." Another young woman shopkeeper initiated a conversation with me by saying that she was just as good as I was because she was a US citizen who had spent twelve years there. Occasionally kids will shout derogatory epithets at me, thinking I do not understand. One proud, college-educated woman was nearly driven to tears when I showed her a chart illustrating that Guatemalan growers, like her ambitious brother-in-law, earn only 1¢ on every dollar of cantaloupe sold to the United States, while US import companies reap 79¢. Her husband rhetorically asked what percentage the brother-in-law's campesino workers were earning, but she was not about to show concern for campesinos.

Ladino youth are increasingly brazen and lack the politeness of their grandparents, who, similar to Ch'orti's, exchange "buenos días," "vaya pues," or "adios" with anyone they pass in the street, including strangers like me. Many youth have little idea about local history or life in the aldeas, and over the past two generations the information and economic gap between Ladinos and Ch'orti's has widened considerably. Many migrants are impressed by US and especially Mexican music and fashions and seem taken by the individualistic lifestyle in which identities are constructed with commercial products. Others return to Guatemala even after twenty-five years, having never felt at home in the more private US lifestyle. Whether they stay or return, these risk-taking, entrepreneurial migrants are influenced by US ideology emphasizing that success comes strictly from hard work and intelligence, not unequal opportunities and privileges. One merchant quipped, "he who is poor is poor because he wants to be poor," as there are plenty of opportunities for everyone (Dary, Elias, and Reyna 1998).

Aspiring to the First World, townspeople's attitudes towards Ch'orti's range from sympathy to paternalism to derision. Some count the campesinos as a part of their world. Many poor Ladinos consider a meal incomplete without tortillas, employ humoral body classifications, and hire Ch'orti' healers. Some poor, little educated townspeople have lifestyles and localized, enchanted outlooks overlapping considerably with Ch'orti's (Dary 1986). Some asked whether there are dinosaurs in the United States, and one hat vendor continually insisted that I look for a buyer for his perpetual energy–producing machine. Some give handouts to needy campesinos and express real concern for their welfare, especially for children. Teachers, nurses, and religious workers devote their lives to jobs that assist Ch'orti's, become their compadres, and have taken Ch'orti' language classes. One elderly Creole storeowner who moved to the capital related that what she misses most is the constant flow of respectful Ch'orti' patrons. One rural Creole family donated some of its best agricultural land for a community soccer field in Pacrén, something desired for decades, and took classes in the Ch'orti' language.

For others, the thought of their children sharing schooling and health facilities with Ch'orti's, many of whom live in huts without electricity, running water, cement floors, or shoes, is disgusting, and they prefer to spend more money to send their children to city schools and visit private doctors. Many find it inconceivable that I have lived in Ch'orti' aldeas and learned the language because they consider the indios to be slovenly, thieving, drunken beasts (*muy pícaros*). Admittedly, after all their warnings, I grew increasingly nervous about moving to the aldeas or loaning money to Ch'orti's at the outset of my fieldwork. A more prevailing sentiment is that Ch'orti's, who speak a more rustic Spanish than the townspeople, are simply harmless pigs in regards to intelligence and cleanliness. One woman complained that they ate all parts of an animal and showed no remorse at children's funerals. A mayor of Olopa once referred to a Ch'orti' with protein malnutrition as a *cochino*, a "little pig," for failing to care for himself. Some show no sign of remorse when they pressure destitute Ch'orti's to buy their goods or when Ch'orti' dogs are killed in town due to periodic poisonings by the local governments. I have seen some Ladino campesinos take advantage of their Ch'orti' neighbors by capturing the fish that the latter have spent hours congregating in manmade pools in streams, buying their way out of work on community projects, and overcharging Ch'orti's for musical performances. Some show frustration that development aid is wasted on the aldeas. Despite all the church has done in the towns, many have pressured the church for more town projects. Many Ladinos were outraged when Rigoberta Menchú, in their minds a guerrilla and a hoax cultivated by romantic, ignorant foreigners, won the Nobel Prize for Peace (cf. Nelson 1999 for Guatemala City). To take a Ch'orti' seriously, as I do, is often considered laughable except as an exercise in collecting folklore, and the idea of a multicultural nation is considered a ludicrous and romantic, but dangerous, foreign imposition.

Whether paternalistic or spiteful, townspeople often impolitely ignore indigenous campesinos, like parents who talk to others about their children while they are present. Countless times Ladinos interrupted me while I was talking to Ch'orti's, as if they were invisible, and once when I asked not to be interrupted, the Ladino angrily told my Ch'orti' interlocutor that I cared nothing about Ch'orti's but was interested only in my career. Several townspeople, even development workers, suggested that I covertly tape-record or take pictures of Ch'orti's if they refused to consent to an interview. Once, while a group of Ch'orti' friends and I sat in the back of a pickup truck in the rain waiting for the driver, he invited only me under a shelter to drink beer with him and was offended when I refused. One Ch'orti' also heard a Ladino say in his presence that it is not a shame if an Indian dies of hunger. When one Ch'orti' health technician and I visited a store, the owner's son—an accountant for a multinational corporation—happened to be there, and curious about Ch'orti' life, he asked me instead of my friend about it. The owner and son could not get beyond their preconceptions anyway, saying the campesinos are filthy and have too many children. My Ch'orti' friend humbly responded that they are simply uneducated. But the accountant insisted on an innate distinction between civilizados and indígenas, and defended both violence and corruption by Guatemala's capitalist elite in social Darwinist terms: survival of the fittest. As a Creole-Ladina couple remarked to me in Copán about Ch'orti' poverty, "we all have to evolve."

The Creole/Ladino cosmogony of Ch'orti' origins is enlightening in its contradictions. Most know shamefully little about the ancient Maya and tend to explain "the conquest" in racist terms, although youth are beginning to learn more sensitive histories in school (cf. Casaús 1998: 89–94). Because many romanticize and even appropriate the ancient Maya past, they have considerable difficulty believing that Ch'orti' ancestors have anything to do with it. Three Ladino businessmen were fascinated at my explanation of the overlap of Ch'orti' cosmology with that of ancient Mayas, but they ultimately brushed it aside, saying Ch'orti's are too stupid (brutos) to be descended from the makers of pyramids and inventors of alphabets. The ancient Mayas must have come from Egypt or outer space, they speculated. In 1997 I unfortunately sat on a three-hour bus trip across the aisle from an Evangelical Creole who was quite vocal about cosmogony. He had placed a note on a seat to reserve it, but in good Guatemala City bus etiquette, someone sat on it. The culprit, who had Maya features, was then subject—as was everyone else within five seats of him—to a lecture on how Indians originated in Malaysia (Mal Asia, with the double entendre "Evil Asia"), as did the Jews, who everyone knows are the Devil's children who lied about the Holocaust. In fact, it has been proven that Hitler himself was a Jew. People might doubt him if they wish, but he has "experience," having once traveled to Mexico with the national opera. Besides, he knows that Jesus is God, which is the cornerstone of all knowledge, so therefore he knows everything. I whispered to the Maya-looking culprit, "I praise God that I'm not sitting next to the preacher," but he ironically responded, "the pastor knows a lot!"

Sadly, even townspeople who serve the Ch'orti' population exhibit disrespect. I once housed four Ladinos employed by the Red Cross to urge campesinos to build latrines during the cholera epidemic. They were disgusted with our aldea homestead and irritated that we had no eggs for breakfast. Their radio blared with little regard for the aldea's tranquility, and they rudely yelled into house plots, harshly condemning inhabitants for not digging latrines. On another occasion, one of my Ch'orti' hosts invited his Ladino compadres (who, as outsiders, are considered by most Ch'orti's to be more prestigious and potentially more useful cogodparents) to a lunch in honor of their godchild who had recently graduated from a technical school. They shattered the serenity of the afternoon by arriving on motorcycles, laughing and shouting, appropriating the hammocks, and tearing into the lunch like starving lions at a fresh kill. When the fury seemed to have subsided, the obese woman asked "more rice?" After some tense whispering in Ch'orti', the hosts nervously told her, like deer that had been feeding crumbs to a jaguar, "there is no more." To her credit, she did her best to brush it off, saying it was no problem, and resumed her attack on the remaining food. When Ch'orti's visit Ladinos, it is a different story. Many townspeople do not invite Ch'orti's to eat in their homes, but even in the aldeas, Ladino and Creole campesinos break with aldea tradition by typically offering neither Ch'orti' visitors nor workers coffee or food even when they themselves are eating. Some also fly in the face of tradition by charging daily interest on loans.

Exemplary of paternalism was the Ch'orti' Regional Folklore Festival of 1992, founded by Jocotán teachers in 1986 to celebrate the Oriente's cultural heritage. As some townspeople told me, the festival was meant to boost Ch'orti' ethnic pride, but until recently most Ch'orti's have viewed the festival as an event by and for townspeople. In 1992 the festival began with a teachers' dinner, including the few token Ch'orti' bilingual teachers who were required to pay the Q10 entrance fee whether they went or not. This was followed by inauguration ceremonies in which Ladino children were paraded around Jocotán's park in traditional Ch'orti' outfits. The next day, costumed dancers from the neighboring townships, Jocotán's Huastec (conquest) dancers, and the Jorchán serpent (in which men zigzag in a spotted serpent costume based on Girard's speculations about ancient Ch'orti' rain dances) paraded through town and danced briefly in the park. Trailing the dancers were the token Ch'orti' "Queens of Maguey"— nervous teenage Ch'orti' girls clothed in their finest traditional dresses and coached on their posture and "formation" by Ladina teachers. Some of the Ladino organizers also wear traditional Ch'orti' dress and street shoes, which unintentionally lends them an air of clownishness for Ch'orti' spectators. Last, Rafael Girard's grandson arrived from the capital to extol Ch'orti' and Jocoteco virtues.

The climax of the festival was a variety show featuring the queen contest, in which the "queens" were instructed to dance and recite a few memorized lines in front of a crowd of three hundred or so Ladinos. Few Ch'orti's could afford the Q8 entrance fee. Except for the queens themselves, all performers and the variety show audience were Ladinos. Some found the queens quaint or funny, and they laughed and paternalistically gasped during the anxious moments when the queens performed their dances and recited their lines. A few Ch'orti' friends (whose entrance I paid) and I were torn with feelings of pride at their performance and embarrassment at their humiliation. Sunday morning was the closure of the festival, and one Ladino in Ch'orti' costume railed against the townspeople for not appreciating "our national patrimony" while urging Ch'orti's to continue teaching their language and culture to their children. There was no applause or even recognition that he had finished. Miguel from Olopa ended the ceremony in Ch'orti' by wryly thanking them for their support even though they did not pay for the Ch'orti' participants' food, transportation, and lodging as they did for the Ladino performers. In a hopeful sign of the future, the variety show is still a private, expensive event, but the schoolteachers have taken the queens contest and a Ch'orti' variety show to the public park free of charge.

Cresencio and I had an illuminating experience with one of the founders of the Folklore Festival, a venerable Creole and aficionado of Rafael Girard. Cresencio greeted him, but when he recognized me as "the anthropologist," he launched into one of his pro-Maya/anti-Spanish treatises, portraying the Spanish as evil gold seekers and religious zealots. Echoing Girard, he pontificated that three hundred years before Christ the Maya were more advanced than the Europeans, emphasizing their beautiful writing system and sculpture. Cresencio was silent as he lamented the collapse of Maya "civilization," even claiming that Pacrén and Tunucó, the former of which is Cresencio's aldea, were less Ch'orti' than other areas. As we passed by stores, others courteously greeted the respected the elderly Creole and his son, and one woman offered tamarind drink to all but Cresencio, who shrunk back embarrassed. When I gave him mine, the conversation died instantly.

Another twist on the "our Indians" theme was when an organizer for a hemisphere-wide indigenous symposium visited Jocotán to recruit a delegation of Ch'orti's. He asked a Ladina where he could invite Ch'orti' leaders for the event, and she made herself organizer. She eventually invited seven Ladinos and six Ch'orti's to accompany her to the international event, where all fourteen wore Ch'orti' outfits and profited from basketry sales. Another prominent Ladino half-seriously said that we could make a killing if I led tourists to him dressed as a Ch'orti' "chief."

Immersed in social structures dating back for generations, many townspeople do not realize their paternalism. There is a fine line between helping and patronizing, and I myself unknowingly crossed it many times by sharing my knowledge and opinions with Ch'orti's. When town nurses and teachers visited the aldeas for cholera education, they typically addressed the crowd with "good morning," to which the men responded in kind like third graders. The call and response continued: "There is a sickness that has come to the township, can you tell me what it's called?" "Cholera!" "Yes, cholera, and we're here to tell you how to protect yourselves." The speakers went on to say that cholera comes from poop (*popó*), and that they should bury it like cats instead of leaving it uncovered on the ground, at which point many chuckled and a few turned to me to share the laugh. As the epidemic wore on, the "advice" became increasingly accusatory and aggressive, with the nurses calling on men in the audience to respond to their questions and labeling them "dirty." Then came the threat that army escorts were going to visit every home to ensure they had dug holes for their popó. At her first day of adult education, a young Ladina teacher castigated the Ch'orti' class for arriving late though most did not own a watch, and asked whether they wanted to learn or not, demanding a show of hands. Most were understandably hesitant after her tirade, so she pressured each to answer one by one.

While relations between Ladinos and Ch'orti's are usually cordial on the surface, Ch'orti's are easily reminded that some Ladinos have a more sinister side, as was demonstrated by the Ubico era and las ruinas, in which the Ladinos ruthlessly leveraged their connections with the state. Three Ch'orti' informants in Olopa defined a "good" mayor as one who does not shout and frighten the people, nor call in the army for every accusation created by their enemies. Many elderly Ch'orti's are certain that Ladinos would like nothing better than to turn back the clock to the "time of slavery." One recounted,

[A]nd so Arévalo entered. So it was better during his term because they worked for money. Yes, yes. And so it continues, the people are paid. So sometimes they [the Ladinos] still want the people to work for free, but the people here already know

how to write and read and they already know how to talk.
So they have to pay them. They must. And so, when someone
says that he doesn't want to work for free, then they also kill.
They still kill, which is why there is so much violence, yes, and
they don't like it when someone talks back when they order
them about.

Another elder claimed that the Ladinos desire a return of the Ubico dictatorship: "One more time, that's why, that's why, it's that there was a party
that took out Ubico, it was the Revolutionary Party, and they do not like
it . . . it favors the campesinos."

Plantations are places where indeed Ladinos rule by force. All have
their own gun-toting paramilitary guards known to kill workers. When in
December 1992 I visited a plantation in Gualán, Zacapa, where many
Ch'orti's pick coffee, I was unaware of how isolated it was from the nearest town. When I arrived after a two-and-a-half-hour ride in the back of a
pickup truck in the rain, I was alarmed to discover that there were no
rides back to town until the following day. I had come to ask permission
to visit the plantation, and the suspicious administrators were not sure
what to do with me until they spoke with the owner, who, as luck would
have it, was on his way from the capital that very moment. The administrators, some with guns clearly visible, were uneasy because the owner
was hot tempered and strict about keeping visitors off plantation
grounds. One administrator continually threatened that the owner would
rough me up and send me back to town on foot in the rain without a
flashlight. The tension was high for all of us when the owner sped up in
his Bronco with two bodyguards, marched up to me nose to nose, gun
flashing in his belt, looked me straight in the eye, and asked what I was
doing. I explained my predicament, and that I was interested in Ch'orti'
"culture and folklore" only. Eventually, he settled down and saw me as an
opportunity to practice his English and discuss his college days in the
United States, feeding me in the administration mess hall and letting me
stay in an administration dormitory for the night with two armed guards.

Economic Marginality

Ch'orti' economic marginality is both cause and consequence of their
treatment by Ladinos and Creoles. Guatemala has long been at the
margins of larger markets and empires. By the end of the Classic period

(AD 900), Nahuatl-speaking Pipils from central Mexico had begun colonizing southern and eastern Guatemalan in various waves of settlement. Guatemalan kingdoms and chiefdoms provided key raw materials, like prized cocoa beans, quetzal feathers, and jaguar skins, for trade with the larger empires of central Mexico during the Postclassic period (AD 1200–1517). During the colonial period, Guatemala eventually became the seat of a colonial jurisdiction (*audiencia*) that stretched from Chiapas to Costa Rica, but it was overshadowed by Mexico and Peru, which themselves were at the periphery of the Spanish Empire. The empire itself soon became the periphery of the emerging northern European industrial economies. As a peripheral country, then, Guatemala has offered raw materials—cacao, indigo and cochineal dyes, coffee, bananas, cotton, cattle, sugarcane, cardamom, timber, winter vegetables, textiles, and, increasingly, cheap labor—to more powerful countries in exchange for industrial products. While as a nation Guatemala has sold cheap and bought dear, its elite have benefited enormously as the monopolizers of agro-exports, internal industries and services, and merchants.

If postmodern capitalism prioritizes wealth and luxuries over concern for one's fellow human beings and life in general, many Guatemalans, from the richest of the rich to the poorest of the poor, are archcapitalists. Although Guatemalans do not have the same power to harm others and the environment as US citizens have and do, many are prime opportunists. The same people in whom I would trust my life, who are the most generous I have ever met, often cannot resist temptation when the opportunity to earn a lot of money arises, regardless of whether it is at others' expense or not. I know of two cases in which gringos bought land for the sake of communities but had to title it in the name of a Guatemalan—their most trusted friends—and the Guatemalans appropriated all or part of the property at their communities' expense. Prostitution, a clear example of renting humans, is rampant in Ladino cities. Ladinos, Creoles, and even some Ch'orti's routinely lie to me about prices of all sorts of goods and services. Bus personnel habitually lie about departure times of their own buses and those of their competitors to win customers. It certainly is no sin to cheat a gringo, and one would be a fool not to.

Ch'orti's do their best to maneuver at the margins of this economy. Though some can be as amorally opportunistic as other Guatemalans, their social and therefore cultural marginality is such that the functioning of the market is mysterious to them, limiting their maneuverability. Taussig (1980) and Scott (1976) argued that economies based on self-subsistence or "use value" are fundamentally different from capitalism in that the latter aims at unlimited individual accumulation while the former emphasizes distributing surplus or working only until one's needs are met. Taussig explained that for peasants recently introduced to capitalism, the ideas of money growing as capital and people working for limitless accumulation seem unnatural and evil. Limitless accumulation for the sake of redistribution and power has never been alien to Mayas, but Ch'orti's have indeed found money to be mystical and unnatural. Earlier in the century, they never undertook monetary transactions or even touched money except after dark, so that the coins, which among other things repelled evil (Wisdom 1961:57), would not lose their magical powers (Girard 1949:234). Just as they saved animal skulls and bones to attract game, they left pennies in boxes to attract money (Girard 1949:243). Nor did they trust the new quetzal bills when they were first introduced in the 1920s but preferred to deal in the time-tested peso coins, which had yet to fully replace cocoa beans, salt, and corn as standards of exchange (Girard 1949:299–304).

Today, traditional Ch'orti's continue to regard money as something inexplicable and mysterious. When they appease the spirit world with copal incense, they "pay" in the form of coins (*bambas*). As mentioned in chapter 4, the entire ritual-agricultural cycle is referred to as "paying" (from transitive verb *utoyi* and antipassive *atojma*). Some told me that money used against the will of God, such as that of a healer who charges patients for services or a prostitute who has sex for money rather than love, "burns" (*uputo'n*) and is "heavy" (*imb'ar*). The whimsical nature of money's value and the forms it takes, as well as the power it has to make people commit immoral acts such as murder and theft, lend it an aura of enchantment. Elderly Sesario recounted how in the old days only specific types of money worked in particular towns: silver (*plata*) in Esquipulas; pennies (*centavitos*) in Chiquimula; royals (*realitos*) in Olopa and Jocotán; silver in Honduras, etc. While I was chatting with Pedro's brother, he suddenly asked, "Who makes the money?" "Why don't they make more?" and "Why is it that money in different countries has different values?" In my difficulty answering these questions in Ch'orti', I realized that the workings of money and capital are a mystery to me and other US citizens as well, except that we tend to accept them uncritically.

Many express a remorseful sense of powerlessness to money and prices. When asked about whether life was better or worse in the old days, many framed their answers in terms of the efficacy of money. Macaria commented, "we grew up sad because it was impossible. They walked around earning money, you know, by working for Ladinos." Most agree that wages were much lower in the past, but life was better because the prices were lower still. Vicenta explained that they simply had more in the past, more coffee, more sugar, and more maguey with which to buy food. She added that people no longer celebrate weddings because the money is no longer adequate. Another Vicenta quipped, "twenty-five cents now is worth nothing, it's better we die, our food no longer abounds." Wages and prices have favorably affected some, like those in Olopa who own cattle or work for expanding local Ladino enterprises, but they too gauge their tenuous quality of life by the elusive forces of money.

The Spanish term *carestía*, connoting both costliness and scarcity, is used to characterize the current era. Why the carestía began is a matter for speculation, but many simply explain it as a change in epoch. In the words of Catarino,

> [T]oday everything is expensive. The times are new today.…
> A new time, because the old time ended. Today there are only
> expensive things, we carry money but it's not worth anything;
> we spend it rapidly because all is expensive. And in times past
> when it was cheap, it abounded … the times past.

The reification of prices is exemplified by Silverio, who referred to prices during Arévalo and Arbenz times as "well-behaved" (*educados*). Vicente agreed, saying that the carestía began with Castillo Armas, who raised corn prices from 3¢ to 15¢ per pound (for Andean peasants, see Condori Mamani et al. 1996:95–96). Younger men like Raul and Paulo Antonio feel that the carestía began in the 1980s, during the dictatorship of Ríos Montt or the presidency of Cerezo. Valvino explained "each government has its own law," and President Kjell Laugerud ordered that one pound of corn reach Q.50 and a pound of beans Q1.50. The Revolutionary Party—the now defunct party once linked to the Democratic Revolution—is the party of low costs (*la barateza*), he added. Another elder, don Chico, turned the tables and asked *me*, "when will the carestía end?"

Price fluctuations have been extreme, making money all the more capricious for starving Ch'orti's. In July 1996, when rains were late and corn prices jumped from Q.80 to Q1.80 per pound and bean prices from Q1.50 to over Q3.00 due to speculation on rising fuel costs, several dozen severely malnourished children overwhelmed Jocotán's Hospital Betania, which had to send many more away on an outpatient basis. Day laborers were requesting to be paid in corn and campesinos were flooding the market with crafts, but their selling prices not only fell behind inflation but some goods like hammocks were even cheaper ($3) than the ones I bought in 1990, as the town merchants were exploiting their vulnerability.

Lack of information and access to markets as well as intimidation has much to do with economic subordination. Many townspeople have long lived a parasitic existence off campesinos by buying cheap and selling dear. In the 1930s and 1940s, communities nearest the towns served as seasonal labor reserves for the townspeople (Wisdom 1940:24–25, 202–16, 220–22, 229–37), who paid them 10¢ per day when they were not working gratuitously under Ubico's Vagrancy Law (Girard 1949:234). Ch'orti's who produced luxury foods like milk, cheese, and eggs sold them in town in exchange for basic necessities like salt and candles (Girard 1949:229, 265–66). Though Ladinos grew milpas just as Ch'orti's did, they flaunted their presumed superiority through European dress, aggressive bartering, ostentatious homes, and use of beasts of burden and machinery (Wisdom 1940:245, 28–29). They even monopolized the sale of Ch'orti' men's clothing by selling white cotton cloth at prices that undercut home weaving in the aldeas (cf. Girard 1949:272–77).

Today, the very existence of dozens of town stores, only a few of which would be adequate to supply the townspeople themselves, is testimony to this. On market days, exhausted campesinos haul products on their backs over miles of mountainous terrain, or pay a Ladino pickup driver, to earn just enough to buy staples, soap, and salt. Many must sell in order to buy the same day, and even if they can wait to buy provisions another week, the thought of carrying their products, which if fruit or vegetables are perishable, back up the mountains in the afternoon sun is too much to bear. Some Ladinos, therefore, wait like vultures until desperate Ch'orti' vendors come around door to door in the afternoon when their prices can easily be haggled down by as much as 75%. I watched one exhausted man, who had walked roughly twelve miles with a seventy-five-pound load of firewood, unsuccessfully try to sell it to a number of storeowners for anything over 80¢. The Ladinos sell the wood for about twice that amount.

Similar to money, modern technology is mysterious, powerful, and threatening, and Ch'orti's have little access to it. The gap between themselves and the world of computers, international finance, and multinational corporations widens daily. Until recently, dozens of campesinos could be seen in the towns jostling just to get a glimpse at a television through a window. When the first radio was brought to the region by a rich Camotán plantation owner in the 1930s, his profits almost outdid his distillery business, which itself was known for its exorbitantly priced moonshine. Still today, even the most basic of technology for survival, like pumped water, is lacking in some aldeas. Until very recently the vast majority of aldeas had no roads connecting them to town, and even today many existing roads are navigable only in the dry season by the Ladino's four-wheel drive trucks. Until 1999, electricity was out of the question for all but a few aldeas close to major roads, and even those campesinos who have electricity today find it difficult to pay for installation and minimal bills of $4 per month. The few known professions like carpentry and construction would be profitable if only basic tools were affordable.

Many Ladinos and Creoles simply cheat campesinos out of their money and labor. During the cholera epidemic, one health center hired and trained about a dozen schoolteachers as nurses, while a Ch'orti' man who was trained as a health technician volunteered long hours without remuneration. In a joint USAID-state road project, the Ch'orti' road crew was paid by the state only a percentage of the wages due, and this three months after work had begun. Plantation labor recruiters are notorious for lying about the wages and conditions on plantations, and some merchants have reputations for fixing their scales to shortchange campesinos. As for those Ladinos living in the countryside, some have frankly admitted that they make a living by cheap Ch'orti' labor.

Due to their desperate situation, Ch'orti's find it easier to compete with each other than with Ladinos, and they rarely unite in cooperatives. The few attempted cooperatives have dissolved due to repression (cf. Dary, Elías, and Reyna 1998:193, 217), internal disputes, corruption, and the inability to compete with desperate individuals who undersell in an oversaturated market. Even a coffee cooperative backed by the church in 1997 ran into threats from town middlemen. Low market prices and extreme seasonal fluctuations are the result. In Jocotán, during the rainy season when food and wages are scarce, the number of aldea craft venders in the Sunday market increases from a few dozen to hundreds, enabling predatory merchants to buy at pitifully low prices. According to one woman, reed mats (tule, pojp) are worth about $1.00 all year—equivalent to a day's supply of corn for a small family—except between June and August, when they fall to about $.60, and she does not understand why (Palma Ramos 2001:75; Dary, Elías, and Reyna 1998:182). Another man noted that net bags are worth the least from June to September: "When we're the poorest, the rich screw us the most" (Palma Ramos 2001:114). Although the materials used to make crafts

14. *Ch'orti' pottery vendors, Jocotán market, 1993.*

are generally natural or minimally cultivated, the labor that Ch'orti's put into the crafts should make them expensive, but they are not. Twelve palm brooms can be made per person per day for a total price of only $1.60. Each woman can make at most one net bag per day, at a price between $.70 and $1.00 (Dary, Elías, and Reyna 1998:174). One large basket requires a day's worth of labor and is worth only $1.00. Ch'orti' pottery, which requires the arduous work of hauling the clay, drying the formed pots, firing them with a lot of precious firewood, and hauling them to market, are worth only about $.70 for a small one, $1.00 for a medium, and $2.00 for a large (Dary, Elías, and Reyna 1998:135–36, 174, 180, 188–90).

While low prices are due partly to the poverty of the campesino buyers themselves, Ladino merchants sell these crafts to distant corners of Central America in their large trucks for as much as ten times their original prices (cf. Dary, Elías, and Reyna 1998:165–66, 281). These merchants are known for their aggressive haggling, to which Ch'orti's tend to bend. Cresencio raged that a neighbor had refused to sell him a chicken for $5, but soon thereafter succumbed to a Ladino's offer for the same price. For those able to find work in the towns, the salaries are only about $50 per month (cf. Dary, Elías, and Reyna 1998:218).

Foreigners in One's Own Land

Ch'orti's, as indigenous people, epitomize marginality from the nation-state. In the 1930s and 1940s, few traveled outside the department or even had a concept of "Guatemala" as a nation (Wisdom 1940:24–25, 202–37; Girard 1949: 247–48, 297, 333; cf. Gillen 1952:197–98 for the neighboring Pokomam). Today, the especially immobile, illiterate women have little knowledge of the nation and know "Guatemala" only as the capital. In a cogent display of national apathy, during the inauguration of a church-sponsored aldea school in 1997, no Ch'orti' except an obvious ex-soldier paid any attention to the national anthem. In a world where knowledge is power, money, and survival, many have no idea where other Latin American countries are and regard points of interest like the United States, Belgium, and Jerusalem as towns speaking languages similar to western Guatemalan Mayas (*cobanes*). All distant points or "corners" merge in the traditional Ch'orti' cosmos, and Europe and Argentina are imagined to be near the United States, a little farther beyond (*más delantito*) the capital. Not one of a group of young men recognized a world map in a classroom in which we were standing.

I mention these examples not to humiliate or exoticize Ch'orti's, but to convey the tragedy of their marginality. Some have told tragic stories of becoming lost in Guatemala, spending all their plantation wages trying to catch the right bus home. Many are considering migrating to the United States and are desperate for knowledge about the journey. One man from Pelillo did in fact make it to the United States only to run out of money and return home half-starved. Another group of teenagers from Tuticopote were nabbed at the Guatemalan-Mexican border, had all their possessions and money seized, and returned home four days later by hitching rides. They had no idea about the extension of Guatemala, Mexico, or the United States. One nineteen-year-old Ch'orti' took me by surprise by showing up on my US doorstep in late 2003, after paying three coyotes (smugglers) a total of $5,000 to ride in the backs of semitrucks, in boats, and on boxcars to cross Guatemala, Mexico, and Texas. He had borrowed the money from relatives and Ladino patrons, and was migrating to earn enough money to go to college back in Guatemala.

Ch'orti's fare no better regarding national politics and world events, as they have little access to media. Newspapers, which numbered only 2.1 per 100 Guatemalan inhabitants in 1995 (*Crónica* 7/95:11–14), are bought for toilet paper rather than sources of information. Most do not own radios (only

42% of Ch'orti' households owned a radio in 1993), and radio news consists strictly of sound bites from Ladino perspectives. Consequently, some thought that President Serrano (1991–93) was a US citizen, and others were ignorant of his coup and ouster in 1993 until three weeks after they occurred. In 1993 one man was shocked to hear that the USSR had dissolved in 1991, because he had still been hearing old military propaganda that the guerrillas were Soviet puppets. One educated man whose social circles included Ladinos and Evangelical missionaries regarded all student protestors and political assassination victims as criminals, terrorists, and troublemakers. Few knew of K'iche' Maya Rigoberta Menchú's Nobel Prize for Peace in 1992, and among those that did, many swallowed the army's line that she was a phony. Her only redeeming feature was that she made the Ladinos angry. The state, in fact, ran a campaign against her when it became clear that she was being seriously considered, and desperately promoted a wealthy Ladina philanthropist, Molina Stahl, for the prize.

The Challenge of Education

Decent education would go a long way towards preparing Ch'orti's for outside opportunities, but only 17% of school-age children (7–18) attended school on any basis in 1993, compared to 47% for the entire nation in 1999 (*Cerigua* 7/29/99:4). Consequently, only 17% of school-age children were described by their parents as literate (156/906). Only 18% (179/1000) of adults claimed literacy, and of these, only 14% (25/179) were women. In 1997 the percentage of children attending school rose to 30%, but almost all were registered for elementary school (Dary, Elías, and Reyna 1998:230). For those students who complete elementary school in their aldeas, getting a secondary education is against the odds. Junior highs are located only in the towns, requiring money for travel or for renting a room, which is prohibitive for most. Public high schools are even more distant and found only in department capitals, which for Ch'orti's means either earning the money to rent a room or going to a private high school in town for about $100 per year. More popularly, many take classes in the Maestro en Casa (Home Teacher) radio program, which, with little student-teacher interaction, presents virtually insurmountable challenges in subjects like mathematics and English.[2]

---

2. In 2005 Jocotán's new mayor, a native of Pacrén, was in the process of acquiring televisions for distance learning in aldea schools.

Government underfunding of education can also be seen in teacher employment. Throughout the 1990s, despite the availability of thousands of unemployed teachers, many communities had neither schools nor teachers. If they did, they were funded by nongovernmental organizations, like the Catholic Fe y Alegría (Faith and Happiness) program, which still accounts for almost half of the elementary school education in the area. For those teachers who do acquire jobs, which can involve bribing officials with body or money, the working conditions are harsh. In 1993 some teachers walked as many as five hours per day back and forth to class or had to live in the run-down schools themselves, all for less than $125 per month. Adult literacy teachers faired even worse, earning less than $25 per month to teach up to sixty-three native Ch'orti' speakers at a time. Today, although schoolteacher salaries have doubled to $250 per month and dirt roads have made aldeas more accessible, the cost of riding in Ladino pickup trucks deeply cuts into salaries. Paco's wife was only netting $6 per month in 2002 before she finally quit.

Understandably, many teachers do not teach a full five-day week and strategically hold frequent town meetings to cancel classes. Countless times I witnessed children dress up and eagerly trot to school, only to return dejected because the teachers did not arrive. When the teachers do teach, the material may not be relevant or may be racist, such as presenting Dictator Justo Rufino Barrios, who abolished Indian communal lands, as a national hero. Only after the Peace Accords have textbooks begun to include Mayas and sensitivity to Maya cultures.

The presence of teachers in the aldeas, even if irregular, does have a cultural impact. They only speak Spanish, and can lend new ideas and moral support. Those aldeas without teachers feel forgotten. Many teachers I met were idealistic and critical politically, which is not surprising given their low pay and mission to educate the poor. During the peace process teachers were trained to instruct in human rights, and they have often been the first to protest unpopular government policies. They are more aware than most of the injustices of the global political economy. The only Ladinos to participate in Ch'orti' language classes were teachers, and despite the paternalism of the Folklore Festival, the teachers sincerely organize it more to promote Ch'orti's than themselves.

Some Ch'orti' parents are hostile to teachers and schools nonetheless. Some have burned provisional schools, and some resident teachers have been threatened with rape. Morning classes conflict with child labor, as children become productive members of the family at seven or

15. *Graduation celebration, Pelillo Negro, 1992.*

eight years of age. Two girls I met were unable to attend school because
they cared for their blind mother. Many traditional parents are also wary
of sending their girls to school where they are not segregated from boys.
With the overcrowding, the quality of education is also wanting. Most
Ladino elites send their children to private high schools outside the area,
as educational resources like books are scarce, such that some high
school students sought me as a source of books for their reports. Fewer
still are opportunities for university education. One Peace Corps volunteer arranged full-ride college scholarships for female Ch'orti'-speaking
high school graduates, but we found only two in the entire region in 1994.
Jacinto, who has fourteen acres and eight children, knew that his land
would not be enough for all, so he encouraged them to study. His oldest
graduated from high school and was given a scholarship of $1000 per year
to study medicine in Cuba. This amount was insufficient to cover minimum costs, so Jacinto took two jobs, including night watchman of a hard-
ware store, but he simply did not earn enough, and the son returned after
two and a half years of a six-year program.

Many of the new generation stake their future on education. One
remarkable twenty-five-year-old said he is resisting marriage until he
becomes an accountant. One father moved his family to town so that his

two boys, one now a mayor and the other a US migrant, could become better educated. High school graduation is a major event, with several hundred attending to see a few dozen students, mainly children from campesino families, graduate.

According to my three-community survey, households with at least one literate member or at least two years of total schooling have significantly more land, cattle, modern home improvements and homestead structures, legally married couples, and participation in development projects. Marking their relative prosperity and national integration, their ownership of radios (66%) is much higher than the general population (42%), while households with less than one year of education use modern health services significantly less than the general population (25% versus 30%). Modest math literacy no doubt explains part of the success of these more educated Ch'orti's, for inability to work with numbers puts one at a severe disadvantage in the world of money. Few have the arithmetic skills to effectively manage their household finances or calculate their costs and income. One family was incapable of calculating how much they spent and earned on coffee production and asked me to help. They were making much less than expected. I met another man on the trail who asked me to calculate how many manzanas his ninety *tareas* composed and how much it was worth, because he was receiving many offers to buy them.

State Health Services

Since their establishment during the Democratic Revolution, the rural health centers have been critical for drawing Ch'orti's into national society. Though Ladino nurses and doctors are paid minimally for their services, the ardor and care with which they work is moving. Their vaccination campaigns are incessant and require arduous walking. I have known some to walk twenty miles a day over steep terrain to do everything in their power to seek out and save cholera victims. Many Ch'orti' have responded positively to health centers, and the vast majority takes their children to be vaccinated.

However, the health centers can be part of the problem, rather than the solution. Their staff, while sometimes saintly in their care towards Ch'orti's, other times treat them as errant, dirty children. Many Ch'orti's find the visits to the health facilities too fraught with misunderstanding and humiliation and the costs (usually less than a dollar) too expensive to endure, instead preferring herbal and spiritual curing. When the health

center and many Ladinos blamed the cholera outbreak on Ch'orti' dirtiness, some Ch'orti's privately lashed back, insisting that many homes in
town are filthier than aldea ones and that the towns have inadequate sanitary facilities for aldea visitors.

The state has done relatively little to provide basic sanitary services in
the aldeas. According to the 1994 census, only 55% of the population in the
Ch'orti' area had access to potable water and 10% to electricity. Only about
12% of Ch'orti' homes had pit toilets in the mid-1990s (Dary, Elías, and
Reyna 1998:228–29), partly because Ch'orti's simply prefer not to use them
and partly because resources for building them have not been available.

Mental health care for Ch'orti's is unheard of. One night in 1999 I
nearly stumbled over an emaciated Ch'orti' woman naked from the waist
up, mumbling and shivering. A nearby foreign development worker took
her into her house and gave her dry clothes, and we asked her who she
was and where she was from. Eerily, she said she was from a distant aldea
and had been left in town two days before. We weren't sure whether she
had been traumatized by abuse or had other psychological problems. I
thought it strange that the woman continually spoke like a prayer-giver,
and sometimes seemed to refer to herself as a saint. We eventually took
her to the nuns in the Hospital Betania and asked their advice. They
related that no help is available for poor souls like her, as the closest mental institution is in the capital, which treats them with drugs and sends
them back home. Underfunded as the local hospital is, they have no
training or means to care for the mentally ill, and when they tried with
one woman, she spent her days baptizing all the inpatients. As we chatted, the woman quietly slipped away out of the hospital yard and back
into the margins.

Law Enforcement

The police and customs guards see their role as protecting the towns from
the Ch'orti's, and never the Ch'orti's from the townspeople or each other.
They switch posts every few months and have no loyalty to the communities they "serve." On election day, May 9, 1993, when drinking was prohibited, the Jocotán police chief got drunk and demanded a liter of beer at a
local cantina and refused to pay for it. In 1995 I asked police in Jocotán about
the major problems in the aldeas and how many murders were committed
there, and they replied that they had no idea nor cared because policing the
aldeas was not their job. They in fact refuse to pursue criminals beyond

the outskirts of town. One Sunday afternoon in 1993 a campesino couple was hacked to death just four hundred meters from the police post. Though the police were contacted immediately, they casually walked to the scene and ordered some kids to dump the body parts in the local cemetery—leaving them exposed to dogs and vultures—until the survivors came to claim them the next day. They then threw an innocent drunk in jail, all while a surviving twelve-year-old daughter remained unattended in the police station in a state of shock. In 2002 another Ch'orti' acquaintance's father was murdered by five aldea men, but the police refused to act until the son received a court order in distant Chiquimula, which came a year later. With the order in hand, the police agreed to search for the criminals in the aldeas, but only if the son paid $12.50 for gas for the fourteen-mile round trip. When in June 1997 the mayor's principal enemy was killed by hired Ch'orti' guns (ex-soldiers) whom everyone recognized, the police and the army did not make an arrest until one month later. The mayor was never brought to justice. The Customs Guard (Guardia de Hacienda) is more effective because they are notorious for the fines they collect from chicha vendors. Homemade alcohol is illegal in Guatemala, no doubt to protect the virtual one-family monopoly on alcohol production in the country.

When campesino offenders are apprehended, judges often fine and/ or jail both them and their victims with little investigation. Exemplary of such arbitrary "justice" was when a man, his wife, and their daughter were nearly killed in a machete attack during a feud over a marriage. The judge took stock of the victims' liquid resources, two cows worth Q3,000, and made their bail exactly that. When the family asked the police for protection in the face of more threats, the police advised them to sell their land and move away.

Ch'orti's know that the wheels of "justice" creak forward a bit when greased with bribes, but few (except young women, perhaps) have the means to offer attractive ones. Those in Tuticopote who were targets of broccoli and sprinkler theft were unwilling to go to the police or Customs Guard because they had no money and feared that the conflict would only escalate if they did. Sometimes mayors are sought to resolve disputes, but only if bribery or other self-interests move them to action. Most Ch'orti's logically prefer to take the law into their own hands, but as an imprisoned Pacrén man discovered after killing a Ladino's cows for eating his corn, one need be cautious about to whom one administers justice. Women, especially, blame the lack of police enforcement for loss of respect. According to Macaria, young men get drunk and kill because "the government has no law."

Ladinos also are known to take the law into their own hands. The Oriente's infamous reputation for a wild west culture and *caudillos* (mob bosses) is not a total exaggeration, as the region's right-wing death squads attest. Many carry guns and most will not visit the aldeas without them. One friend from Guatemala City recounted how he was contracted for a development project in the Oriente after the 1976 earthquake and surprised to be supplied with an armed guard. Paramilitary violence is endemic in Oriente politics, and national representatives have up to a dozen bodyguards. Before one representative (*diputado*) was chased from the country after two assassination attempts in 1993, it was said that so many were out to kill him in his hometown of Esquipulas that even his ten to twelve bodyguards were inadequate.

Judicial inadequacy is hardly confined to the Oriente. In 1998 throughout Guatemala, fifteen homicides were committed per day, but only 11% resulted in arrests (*Cerigua* 3/5/98:3), which helps explain why lynching has become so rampant. From all accounts, violent crime was much worse under the supposed "law and order" FRG (Frente Republicano de Guatemala) party of Ríos Montt (2000–2003). Attacks against young women and human rights activists have grown dramatically since 2000, with 520 murders of the former and 122 attacks against the latter in 2004 alone (Amnesty International 2005; Plataforma de Solidaridad 2005). Yet, sadly, some campesinos have swallowed the right-wing Ladino line that lack of law enforcement is due to "human rights," which presumably are designed to allow criminals to get off on technicalities, not to protect campesinos from ongoing abuses and corruption.

Locally Elected Officials

Locally elected officials are likewise notorious for corruption, and the Peace Accords' promise of "democracy" is still a long way from fruition at this level. In the 1998 mayoral elections, including in the Ch'orti' area, the ruling PAN party (Partido de Avazada Nacional) used the National Peace Fund (FONAPAZ) for campaign finances and bribing voters (cf. *Cerigua* 4/23/98:4). Likewise, when Ríos Montt was initially prohibited from registering as a presidential candidate in 2003 because he had once been a dictator, his FRG party paid thousands of members, including Ladinos from the Ch'orti' area, to travel to Guatemala City and disrupt civil affairs. In local politics, it is a cliché that candidates promise everything, like roads, bridges, water systems, and schools, but do nothing once they are in office except embezzle the 11% of the national budget given directly to the townships.[3] The vast majority of Ch'orti's do not vote at all, pleading that they do not understand politics or trust politicians. Chilo summed up the general attitude: "The best one should do is listen to what they say, and say nothing." The Ladinos, while envious of the mayors' access to so much money, bemoan corruption as well. All privately express a general cynicism that working for the common good is either foolish or ultimately a guise for self-aggrandizement. All candidates run on an "anticorruption" ticket only to pilfer once they are in office. With the embezzled money they traditionally buy large tracts of land and houses or hotels in Guatemala City or other countries, to which they often move after their term in office is finished.

Despite being in the vast majority in some townships (like Jocotán and Olopa), campesinos, with few guns and little money, have rarely gained power democratically. Palma Ramos (2001:7) reports that five Ch'orti' mayors were elected between 1944 and 1966, but I could find evidence of only one, in Olopa. In any event, only one Ch'orti' mayor, in Jocotán in 1970, has been elected since (and the recent Jocotán mayor from the aldea of Pacrén does not speak Ch'orti' or identify himself as a Ch'orti'). For many, the idea of uniting as an ethnic group under an identity of which most are ashamed is out of the question. Ch'orti's do not tend to run as candidates anyway, as they have little money, sponsorships, or organizational skills. The Ch'orti' mayor in the 1970s was condemned by Ch'orti's for his lack of experience and lack of attention to his Ch'orti' "friends." When he ran for mayor twenty years later, his greatest weakness was that he had no money to bribe voters, which Ch'orti's have come to demand. He received only one hundred of about three thousand votes.

Factors influencing Ch'orti's voting are varied. Little ideological difference usually exists between candidates, and everyone knows that their campaign speakers are hired rather than committed volunteers. One Ch'orti' acquaintance was paid by various candidates to speak at rallies, farcically announcing in Ch'orti' that each was the only true, honest candidate who would provide chicha for everyone. At one candidate's speech I heard in 2003, a repeated message was "not another famine," as he did not realize that "the 2001 famine" is actually chronic and based in structures that no one mayor could possibly correct in a four-year term.

---

3. When it was 8% in 1993 and Jocotán had eight candidates for mayor, Ladinos sarcastically called it the "eight for eight" campaign.

16. *Voting day, Jocotán, 1993.*

Some candidates, like one 1993 Olopa candidate for mayor known for his hot temper towards his workers, take the alternative route of equating wealth with respectability and knowledge. He lost miserably, but others have won with this strategy.

The 1993 elections were exemplary of flawed democracy. Ch'orti's were lured by the PR's image as the legacy party of the Democratic Revolution and some admitted that they liked the PR only because the Ladinos despised it so much. When the PR's leader was shot in an assassination attempt, some wondered whether local Ladinos were behind it. The PR leader ran an intimidation campaign of his own. He interrupted the Ch'orti' Folklore Festival with a speech over a booming sound system, and when a twelve-year-old boy was sent to ask politely that he wait until the end of the ceremony, he grabbed the boy's hair and slapped him in the face. A few weeks after the election, one of his bodyguards put six bullets into a high school protester in the capital. Many Ch'orti's were swayed less by the PR's ideology than by its open, shameless bribes, which seem to be the only conceivable benefit of elections and range from bananas, to chicha, plastic balls, picks, shovels, lanterns, guitars, laminated metal, and even feasts with bands. The PR spent the most by far on election gifts and drove voters to town on voting day, as some campesinos are inclined to renege on voting after accepting gifts. After the elections, Jocotán's PR mayor did indeed bring many campesinos into the municipal office, but within the first year he was also rumored to have embezzled Q500,000.

This prompted some townspeople to found a critical newspaper, the *Ch'orti' Sun*, which periodically reported on the mayor's latest embezzlements. Tellingly, they called him an "illiterate Indian" because of his aldea birth and mestizo features, and were angered that he presumably favored aldea development over town projects. The tension came to a head on the symbolic Day of the Race (Columbus Day) in 1995, when Ladinos stormed the municipal building with pistols and held it for two weeks before federal mediators installed an interim government. Some of the Ladinos connected to PAN (National Alliance Party), the national party in power, procured the diversion of national development funds (Fondo de Inversión Social) away from the mayor's control to the church's. The mayor, however, was back in office again by early 1996, and soon thereafter suffered an assassination attempt as his home was sprayed with bullets (*Prensa Libre* 3/20/96:25). In response, he hired two Ch'orti' ex-soldiers to kill the editor of the *Ch'orti' Sun*, as he had also done to a campesino who had demanded that he fulfill a campaign promise to employ him. Campesinos in one community sent over forty letters to the president because the mayor threatened assassination if they did not sign receipts for work they had done but had not been paid for. It was also rumored that a campesino was hanged under the mayor's orders for trying to block a project in which hired masons and the mayor were embezzling funds.

The Olopa mayor who won in the same elections and was known for his sincerity stole only Q100,000, purportedly an accounting error, which he was forced to return to the municipality in a rare case of an effective government audit. He proceeded to undertake many aldea development projects, including building chapels, procuring teachers, repairing schools, leveling land for soccer fields, and building bridges, but he lost to a more corrupt and ineffective mayor in the next election. To the Ch'orti's' credit, he has since been reelected twice and is considered one of the most committed, least corrupt, and effective mayors to date.

Campesinos are justifiably fearful about political involvement. Some men and women note that danger is the reason why most women (88% in 1993) do not even have *cédula* cards for voting. The Ch'orti' mayor in the early 1970s was plagued with threats and assassination attempts, prompting

the state to provide armed protection. Some friends only cautiously participate in politics and shy away from leadership positions partly due to fear.
Many are intimidated from voting for leftist parties. One Olopa man
explained his community's thinking on leftist parties in 1999: "Do you know
the party of Alvaro Colom [presidential candidate for the leftist Alianza
Nueva Nación (ANN) party]? Yes, it fights for the poor Indians. There is the
URNG [the ex-guerrillas'] party, but it's no good because the Ladinos don't
want us to vote for it. They don't want it. They'll kill us for being guerrillas.
Uh huh, therefore it's better to vote for another party. It's that the Ladinos
have a lot of money and aid, and we in the aldeas only have God."

Some campesinos, in fact, insist that they are indeed learning about
Guatemalan "democracy" and are not as politically gullible as before. For
example, many leaders revealed secretly that they receive gifts from various political parties but do not obediently vote for them. As one man told
me, "one can receive [gifts], but when they arrive [to vote] in secret,
nobody knows [for whom they vote]." In the words of middle-aged
Lonjino of Olopa,

> [A]nd so it is by the power of the people . . . so that a campesino
> cannot be kicked around by a mayor because a campesino
> is more powerful. He's an Indian of the wilds, but an honest
> Indian, not a liar like they are. Right? In other words, a mayor
> is going to win but by a stupid Indian . . . and so the people
> will vote, and if once in office the mayor doesn't do what
> he promised, the same people can go and complain to
> the department to replace him with another. . . . Today as
> yesterday there are ignorant people, but today there are
> more clever people, between foolish and clever. Today one
> is no longer tricked. . . . Few are tricked anymore, because
> the tricks have become obvious over time, and he who
> uses tricks never returns.

A Sense of Inferiority: Better to Be Ladino?

Given all the ways in which the Ladinos and Creoles take advantage of
Ch'orti's, it seems that the very definition of Ch'orti'-ness should include
victimization. Many Ch'orti's, in fact, have come to believe that to be
Ch'orti' is to be a victim, and to be Ladino is to have opportunities.

Ch'orti's have faced discrimination and marginality for centuries, and the modern era has proven especially corrosive to Ch'orti' distinctive cultures and identity. In the 1930s, Creole/Ladino discrimination and exploitation was already prompting some Ch'orti's to doubt their culture (Wisdom 1940:224–28). What makes for a strong or weak identity for Ch'orti's is an interplay of security and opportunities. Ch'orti's have long found security in subsistence agriculture, but this is waning rapidly. Meanwhile, all the opportunities lie in the global economy, which the Creoles and Ladinos, by definition, have long dominated. Since the 1930s, Ladinos have enjoyed tremendous increases in social, intellectual, political, and economic capital. Local townspeople have become well integrated in the global political economy, with motor transport, electricity, stereos, refrigeration, telephones, satellite TV, and migration to and from the United States. Ch'orti' campesinos are attracted to these marvels, but find themselves shut out of the market by lack of knowledge and contacts. Opportunities are blocked by a national society that denigrates Maya campesino cultures, compelling humiliated Ch'orti's to compete for outside economic, educational, and political handouts. Ch'orti's' competitiveness and lack of respect for each other hinder their own unification and ethnic confidence. In contrast to Occidente Mayas, Ch'orti's have long lost control of the modern, politically connected town centers. Many individual Ch'orti' families are doing their best to overcome inequalities by rejecting their indigenous identities.

Various scholars of Guatemala have noticed that when indigenous percentages of local populations fall below a critical threshold, the abandonment of their distinctive culture and identity is almost impossible to halt (Adams 1996:55; MacLeod 1982:8; Early 1982:165). The percentages of Ch'orti' "Indians" in the Departments of Chiquimula and Zacapa have slowly declined according to national censuses (see table 6).

Indices of ethnic abandonment abound. As the population has grown, the proportion of Ch'orti' speakers has fallen. Wisdom and Girard documented that Ch'orti' was spoken throughout Jocotán, Camotán, Olopa, La Unión, Copán, and Quezaltepeque in the 1930s and 1940s, and the Summer Institute of Linguistics counted fifty-two thousand Guatemalan Ch'orti' speakers in 1973 (Lovell 1988:27). Today, no more than twenty thousand people speak Ch'orti' (see appendix 4), there are no speakers in Quezaltepeque, only a few aldeas of Olopa and Camotán have speakers, and the small number of speakers in Copán are emigrants from Jocotán (Moral 1988:398). The Ladino population has been rising due to attrition in the Ch'orti' ranks and

Table 6: Decline of Ch'orti' Percentage of
Eastern Guatemalan Population

	CHIQUIMULA			ZACAPA		
	Indigenous		Non-indigenous	Indigenous		Non-indigenous
1950*	75,114	67%	37,727	12,173	16%	63,211
1964*	76,265	48%	82,363	12,853	13%	82,956
1973*	110,083	60%	72,116	13,096	12%	98,189
1981	59,862	35%	109,001			
1994	68,154	30%	158,127	6,899	4%	147,724

Data taken from the national census, Instituto Nacional de Estadística
* The years 1950, 1964, and 1973 were adjusted by Early (1982:31).

natural growth, such that ethnic distinction has become vague, particularly among non-Ch'orti'-speaking campesinos who compose the majority in all municipios except Jocotán. In most communities of Jocotán virtually everyone speaks Ch'orti', and many women and children rarely use Spanish, but in about half the Ch'orti'-speaking communities listed in appendix 4 only the older generation or a few extended families still practice it. The reason for parents' refusal to teach their children Ch'orti' is commonly explained in terms of Ladino ridicule. Some of my informants, I was slow to realize, avoided me in town because I naively addressed them in Ch'orti'. I once began chatting in Ch'orti' to a man well respected in his aldea, only to have Ladino children silence him through ridicule. Even their parents joined in the laughter. Some speakers lied to me about being unable to speak it. Palma Ramos's research team elicited the following statements from two men about language in 1991.

> We prefer to speak in Ch'orti'; we all speak it, but only here in the aldeas. When we go down to town, no, because we're ashamed, because they only speak Spanish there and don't understand us. We're ashamed to speak Ch'orti'. I personally am ashamed to speak Ch'orti' because not everyone likes to hear it. I've heard people criticize us; they treat us rudely, asking "why do you speak like that?" Due to this pain and shame, we don't speak Ch'orti'.

The youth of today speak Spanish; the dialect [Ch'orti'] is
already disappearing because some are ashamed to speak
it in front of the Ladinos, because they say that the Ladinos
are going to make fun of them. But the Ch'orti' language
lives on, and the old folks still speak it. (2001:31, 59, my
translation)

Language is but one of many factors indicating indigenous cultures
and identities (Vaughn 2002). Distinctive clothing has also been slowly
abandoned. During Wisdom's day, women wore *huipil* blouses and skirts,
and men wore white cotton pajama-like clothing. Since at least the 1950s
(Oakley 1966), the women's clothing has changed completely, and only in
a few aldeas do women wear a distinctive flamenco-like dress, while very
few men wear the white cotton garb. Change in clothing styles is partly
due to the cheaper Western clothing available in the local markets, but
also because the old costume is the target of Ladino ridicule (cf. Palma
Ramos 2001:18). Many, like Pedro, his wife, Cipriano, Félix, Petronilo,
Maura, and Macaria, remarked that the past was very "sad" and "poor"
because men could only afford the white canvas clothing with palm hats,
and women only wrapped themselves in lengths of cloth. Soldiers used to
refer to them as "white mongrels" and on the coastal plantations others
made fun of them by calling them "white horses" (cf. Palma Ramos
2001:31, 98–99).

Ch'orti's also express their sense of inferiority more directly. For
example, many believe light skin is the most beautiful. One twenty-nine-
year-old man told Palma Ramos's (2001:97) research team that when a
child is born under a full moon, his skin color will be more "perfect" and
light. Some male Ch'orti' friends doubted whether a gringa could ever
find them—dark skinned and short—attractive. Three sets of Ch'orti' parents suggested that I, with my light skin, would contribute *buena raza* or
"good blood" to the family line by marrying their daughters. In sharply
ethnically segregated Olopa, some campesinos, not knowing about the
US linguist who married a Ch'orti' man and the Belgian priest who married a Ch'orti' bride, doubted whether it was even legal for an Indian to
marry a gringo.

Many have a habit of saying that they, or more often their neighbors,
know nothing, are stupid, and could never possess the intellectual and
speaking abilities of the Ladinos. Cresencio's father used to refer to
Ladinos as *mojratujoro'b'*, "greater are their heads," while elderly Felipe

said that Protestant Bible translators' heads are different from his stupid one. When I asked one elder why some campesinos are so poor, he replied without hesitation that they sell their land and cannot manage their affairs, while townspeople are intelligent merchants (*negociantes*) who do not drink. Vicente, who had earlier been hesitant about having his picture taken because he and his wife "looked like pigs" eating tortillas next to a fire, argued with his wife about manners. She insisted that he should not have traded profanity with an ex-soldier, to which he retorted that he is just an old fool not expected to speak well, but soldiers are supposed to be "educated." The army's indoctrination was also evident in my interview with an ex-soldier. When I asked him why, if his tour of duty was so positive, he did not make a career of it as an officer, he replied: "Because, well, it's that to become a lieutenant one at least has to have an eighth- or ninth-grade education. And one has to have aggressiveness and *xeca*. 'Xeca' means that one has experience, ready for anything, and the ability to make commands at a moment's notice, you know? Now do you understand me? On the contrary, one, I, I once and for all was never anything, I was, I was a private."

At a UN human rights seminar attended primarily by young Ch'orti's, the Ch'orti' facilitator asked that I come to the front of the class. He asked me whether it was true that I am equal, not superior, to Ch'orti's, and all waited in suspense for my response. After joking that I am uglier, I said of course we are all equal. The facilitator ran with this, telling the astonished and applauding audience that the color of my skin and my height made no difference in my worth, and that the Ch'orti' language is important even to gringos.

Dr. Julián López of Spain led a research project in which Spanish and Ch'orti' fourteen- and fifteen-year-olds wrote essays about their imagination of the other and then exchanged them. The Ch'orti' schoolchildren unfailingly contrasted themselves with their positive imaginations of Spanish schoolchildren, who they presumed to be very happy, healthy, well dressed, religious, white, tall, blond, hardworking, studious, intelligent, wealthy, understanding, loving, creative, obedient, respectful, beautiful, attractive, smiling, punctual, caring, friendly, generous, always victorious in soccer, and with beautiful two-story houses, instructive parents who do not strike them, much time for play, many friends, yellow motorcycles with new tires, all the necessary school supplies, expensive pants costing Q200 (about $35), and living arrangements "much prettier than here in Jocotán." The following essay is typical.

The Life of a Spanish Child

I believe that in Spain the children study a lot for their future
so that they have a good life. They are very happy; they respect
from the youngest to the oldest, and help each other. They are
very clean personally, like in the hygiene of the food they eat,
and they also like to play all sorts of games, and I believe they
practice soccer, volleyball, and basketball. I believe that they
work in the fields with their fathers, but their fathers are
wealthy. Their houses are very pretty, all so that the child can
be in good spirits to continue with his studies so that he will
not be needy later in life. I believe that they all have a good time
playing and joking, they are all good friends in the high school
where they study. They are confident in everything, so that the
child doesn't become discouraged in his studies, and they don't
scold them, hit them, or mistreat them. You [Spaniards] know
that children are the people's future because they grow up and
serve the people and so take care of problems and make peace.
I believe that the child has rights, too, when they go to high
school and study with uniforms. And where they study is clean.
They are collaborators and help the needy. I believe that in
Spain the children go to mass with their parents and they obey
in every way so that the father feels happy that his child obeys
everything he commands.

Ch'orti' women are the most affected by feelings of marginality,
shame, and embarrassment. Their mobility and experience in the outside
world is especially limited, as their duties confine them to the home
except when washing clothes, hauling water, gathering kindling, or occasionally going to the market. They often play a secondary and supportive
role for men, eating after the men have eaten, cooking for ritual occasions
organized mostly by men, and customarily walking behind men in the
trail. Many couples are candid that the wife is in charge, even of the
finances, and jokes about henpecked husbands are not uncommon, but
women embarrass easily outside the home. In Ch'orti'-speaking aldeas,
Spanish is rarely heard, providing women with few chances to learn it
well. Juliana lamented that women are embarrassed to wear their pleated
dresses in town, since they are decades behind the latest town fashions. I
painfully recall inviting some aldea women to a registration for a movement organization in town, only to have young, educated, town-dwelling

17. *Ch'orti' gender-segregated schoolchildren, Pacrén, 1993.*

Ch'orti's intimidate them with the latest haughty fashions and virtually
ignore them.

    Rather than encourage women's participation in public events, men, if
anything, dissuade them unless perhaps they are young and pretty. At one
development project meeting, one of the coordinators asked to hear the
opinions of the women. Every time one woman began to speak, a ridiculing
man interrupted her. When they organized an aldea-wide committee the
same day, I asked whether any women would serve on it, but the men
snorted that the women are illiterate and would not be interested anyway.
Even in general meetings, such as those addressing cholera, women constituted less than 5% of the audience despite being responsible for families'
health. Just as lack of esteem can inspire Ch'orti's to disrespect their neighbors, entrepreneurial women must deal with the ridicule and envy of other
women, who accuse them of being whores. Some men discouraged me
from interviewing women, saying that they would not respond to my questions and knew nothing about religion, politics, and development anyway,
and some women concurred. Although the low numbers of women who
vote is due in part to fear, lack of confidence also plays a major role.

In Girard's day (1949:299ff, 191, 237), women purportedly endured corporal punishment and special restrictions when pregnant or menstruating. Today the discrimination tends to be less violent. I once witnessed a toddler walk into the path of his three-year-old sister swinging in a hammock, and he was accidentally knocked to the ground in tears. A teenage sister harshly scolded her and permitted the toddler to strike her twice in the face. Their father had earlier criticized his wife for their two sons' deaths, citing an obscure belief that women endow sons with their spirit and men endow daughters with theirs. When one male friend was about to migrate to the plantations, I said that his wife and children would miss him. He retorted, "Why? I'll be bringing home money for them, won't I?" He later accidentally divulged that he was supporting another family. When I was about to present some jewelry to a friend's wife and sister-in-law, he insinuated that they would look ridiculous and that the children would destroy it. I gave them the jewelry anyway, and his thirty-five-year-old sister-in-law was so moved with her first set of earrings that she had difficulty holding back the tears. Another complained that he wanted a new wife because his does not rise at 3:00 AM to make tortillas, although most other women do not rise until 4:00 AM. Some drunks told me that women do nothing but wait for their husbands to bring food. A few claimed that if women have access to motorized corn grinders, they would become lazy.

With such negative self-images, it would seem that the Ch'orti's are overdue for a cultural and identity overhaul. Much has been written about the plasticity, imagination, and multiplicity of identities, but identity is historically overdetermined, limiting maneuverability and imagination (cf. Nelson 1999:5; Mauzé 1997:12–15). In other words, identities must be negotiated with other culture-bearing individuals. Identity—the sense of who one is and belongs with—is nurtured by interaction in culture-producing social circles, and as these are multiple for each individual, identities and allegiances can be multiple and even conflicting. As social circles are fluid, there is nothing permanent or primordial about identity, even when it comes to physical characteristics like sex, facial features, or height. Nonetheless, identities are stronger when these features, traditions, and social statuses coincide. In the Ch'orti' case, they can attempt, against all odds, to gain the cultural capital to be accepted as Ladinos, but they can never escape the Indian "stain" and become Creoles.

SEVEN

New Opportunities, Identities, and Challenges in the Global Market

Work, well, it's where we are. If we work it will bear fruit.
—Pedro of Las Flores

He that has good plans, intelligence, does not die of hunger.
—Vicente

I prefer to suffer here.
—Vicenta

And I know that there's a change that we're seeing today.
—Juliana

The Ch'orti' predicament may seem hopeless, especially considering that the subsistence lifestyle, the Ch'orti' safety net for centuries, is no longer a viable option and ethnic shame thwarts initiative. Many Ch'orti's some of the time accept their fate, place responsibility on God, and resign themselves to being an inferior people. Some simply die rather than try something other than subsistence agriculture. I could have entitled this book "The Fatalistic Ch'orti'," and it would not have been an exaggeration. It would, however, have been one-sided. While some are complacent some of the time, others experiment, lead, resist, and investigate much of the time. The push and pull between passivity and engagement with new opportunities inheres in each individual Ch'orti' as it does with anyone, but for Ch'orti's the challenges are much greater due to their extreme marginality and poverty. When Ch'orti's do seek to take advantage of modern technology, new markets, churches, state programs, and international development projects, sometimes they find that because these institutions are integrated in a world of extreme class, racist, ethnic, and gender inequality, embracing them can reinforce problems rather than provide solutions.

Fatalism versus Will

The fatalistic Indian is a long-standing trope in Mesoamerica. Despite contemporary politics that condemns it as imperialistic, fatalism is undeniably present among indigenous Mesoamericans; however, it is not universally felt, often serves more as a post hoc explanation, and does not prevent people from actively and creatively pursuing their own interests. When scholars and politicians simplify indigenous peoples as fatalistic all of the time, they are typically lobbying for top-down cultural engineering, with the Left seeking a more revolutionary Indian and the Right seeking a more consumeristic Indian.

Some scholars have noted how indigenous fatalism, submissiveness, reticence, humility, and stoicism can easily be mistaken for complacency (e.g., Oakes 1951:32–33). Of Santa Eulalia Kanjobal Mayas, La Farge (1947:6) wrote, "as enemies they are quiet, underhanded, meek, and interminably patient. They hate the Ladinos with a great and consuming hatred and almost never show it." He added that largely due to the conquest they are "melancholy in the extreme," never mix play with work, and "occasional bouts of drunkenness do them good." Gillen (1952:206–8) described the Pokomams of San Luis Jilotepeque as relatively calm and expressionless only on the surface due to socialization in the rigid caste system. Of the Pokomams of Chinautla, Reina (1966:26) wrote, "on most public occasions when Ladinos are present, the Indians tend to be very reserved," and they seem to feign misunderstanding of non-Indians' questions as a "defense mechanism." Watanabe (1992:57) argues that "the cruelties of racism, both great and small, . . . reinforce Maya withdrawal into the stoic inscrutability of their own communities." He (1995:30–31) explains a cycle of suspicion, in which Ladino oppression stimulates Maya stoicism and secretiveness, which in turn provoke Ladino suspicion and further oppression.

While harboring such resentment and demonstrating their resolve, traditionalist Ch'orti's especially do occasionally express what can only be referred to as fatalism or destiny. Many told me to go ahead and travel in the afternoons despite the threat of machete-wielding drunks, because God determines the time of one's death. According to don Chico, "one's sign is passed to them at birth by God, as whatever death awaits one, so they must die." Paulo Antonio recalled the time he was confronted by an angry drunk only to have the drunk's machete fall mysteriously from his hand, which surely meant that his time had not come. God also provides us with differential skills and professions. Mancho explained that God gives us a spirit that determines our weaknesses and our strengths, like the ability to lift heavy loads. Two elders instructed that Indians were created poor, as the first Indian man, Adán Cristo, was a pathetically diminutive doll made by Christ, who himself was poor and naked on the cross. Elderly Pedro explained destiny to me this way:

> God ordained you in your study. You are traveling, and with
> it you pass your life. And there are others destined to work
> with machetes, and there are others to whom marketing comes,
> and there are others to whom comes work on the plantations.
> But their destiny was established by God, they say, it was left
> by him. Destiny. To each person a destiny. And to each person
> a language, as they used to say, but they used to say "whoever
> goes to the coast [plantations] such is their destiny to return
> home poor, and although they go to the coast, there's no way
> for them to find money because it was ordained by God that
> they are laborers, and as laborers they are addressed . . ."
> Those are the words of my dead ancestors.

When I asked Chilo what steps must be taken to improve his aldea's situation, he responded:

> [B]ut how can one make himself wealthier if he can do no
> more? . . . Where, where can one go to sell something in order
> to become rich? It's too much! . . . Because he who was born to
> have it, must have it, and he who was born to be poor, poor he
> must die. . . . If one has been born poor, so he must be. Because
> by searching for good, one encounters bad. So, it's better to
> remain as God can help one. Yes, because I'm one that roamed

and I am a vagrant as much as any other, but by God's light
I came home again and here I am. I'm no longer moving
about evading death.

Later he added, "it's never the same as it is in one's own little home, even
if it's sad... and in other places—like you walking around here, right?—
they don't trust you... better that one remain in his sadness and not look
for riches."

Though some like Gerarda, Joaquina, and Catarino claim to refuse to
emigrate because they are needed at home to help their relatives, others,
like Miguel, revealed that the underlying rationale is one's soul (me'yn) must
be able to return to where God placed it in the world. Mercedes explained
that it is better to die in one's place of origin because that is where God will
pass to reclaim the spirit. Vicenta remarked, "some of my relatives told me
that there is good land, good harvests on the coast, but I won't go, it's not my
birthright. No. I prefer to suffer here." Likewise, Federico opined, "I don't
think I'll travel because it's better if we live in our—where we were born and
where we must die." Don Chico said that he never migrated to the plantations: "I'm lazy. I don't work. I don't work because as far as I'm concerned my
birth is in this aldea."

It is tempting to apply Gramsci's concept of hegemony and Foucault's
of power/knowledge to traditionalist Ch'orti' beliefs in destiny, because it
would seem that Ch'orti's are subordinated to such a degree that they cannot fathom an alternative to their subordination and therefore do not challenge it. Such a take would be misleading, however, because Ch'orti' beliefs
in destiny actually pertain to Mesoamerican traditions distinct from and
alternative to Guatemalan national culture (Foucault 1994; cf. Dirks 1994;
Watanabe 2001). Ch'orti' notions of destiny demonstrate that they are far
from fully integrated into Creole and Ladino national cultures. The reproduction of their distinctive cultures, in fact, is partly a defensive reaction to
Ladino domination and can produce meaning, comfort, and contentment
that alleviates the weight of oppression.

That Ch'orti's are not complacent can be seen in their political involvement despite the tremendous dangers, emigration out of the social safety
net provided by family and neighbors, and experimentation in the market.
Cresencio and his sister Juliana, for example, practice spiritual and herbal
curing, follow traditional Ch'orti'-Catholic religion, and speak Ch'orti' as
their first language, yet value education, lead many development projects,
and are typically the first to experiment with outside information. In some

situations they lament the loss of the old ways, and in others chastise their neighbors for shunning experimentation. Cresencio's son Paco, more firmly planted in the modernist world, has completed junior high school, been trained as a health technician, acquired a professional job in town, and has been the greatest promoter of development in his community. He even refuses to carry a machete and shows sympathy for his domestic live-stock. In Ladino terms, he is becoming more "civilized."

Ch'orti' will or resolve is manifest in their value of being their own bosses. For Lonjino, it is undesirable to work for others, as it takes one away from home and subjects one to others' commands. One plantation admin-istrator complained to me that the campesinos of Jocotán and Camotán "are more difficult" (*cuesta más*) than the supposedly more humble and obedient Indians of western Guatemala. Dary, Elías, and Reyna (1998:213) were told that labor contractors for cotton plantations prefer not to hire Ch'orti's because they "don't know how to work," such as in the case of a group that filed a complaint with the labor inspector and forced a planta-tion to pay them back wages. One aldea Ladino corroborated that Ch'orti's cannot be tricked anymore by labor recruiters and will not work for the pit-tances of the past. One pushy gringo acquaintance who was paying campe-sinos to build a house bemoaned that it is difficult adapting to their snail's pace, which good pay did not seem to alter, and the looks on their faces reflected their resentment towards him. Dozens of aldea children have dropped out of Jocotán's Fe y Alegría boarding school because the teachers regiment the entire day. When women in Pacrén felt that the promoters of a development project were scolding them, they boycotted meetings. I once lost my temper when a young Ch'orti' arrived two hours late for our bus trip to Guatemala City, delaying our arrival to the dangerous night hours. He refused to converse with me the entire trip.

Sources of Development

Although until recently the Oriente has received much less aid than the Occidente due in part to accessibility (cf. Nelson 1999:158 fn 28) and simplis-tic notions about indigeneity, development projects, fleeting as they are, have encouraged Ch'orti's with new opportunities and offered new identi-ties. Many Ch'orti's remember the euphoria nurtured by development pro-jects begun in the Democratic Revolution, including the introduction of new agricultural technologies, health centers, and rural education. Others point to the wave of Catholic projects in the 1960s, critical for drawing campesinos out of a culture of suspicion and refuge. A few fondly recall that the Friends began development projects even earlier, evangelizing and teaching literacy in Jocotán aldeas like Pelillo Negro in the 1930s and initiating agricultural projects in 1961.

In the 1960s, US Friends Homer and Evelyn Sharpless introduced soil conservation, natural fertilizer, and modern apiculture to Ch'orti's, techniques still used by some today. Recognizing the deteriorating environmental and demographic conditions, they procured a loan in 1968 to move thirty-three Ch'orti' families from Jocotán to virgin jungle in El Florido, Izabal, near Río Dulce. Remarkably, the colony quickly paid off the loan with agricultural profits and began to employ Ch'orti's from Jocotán seasonally. The Canfields replaced the Sharplesses in the late 1960s and early 1970s and sponsored additional agricultural projects in Jocotán, El Florido, and Chiquimula.

Perhaps more important than the Friends' technological and financial development has been these powerful foreigners' attention to the Ch'orti' and their language. Ch'orti's from Pelillo Negro, Matasano, and Guareruche still warmly remember the stewardship of now legendary Misinéz, who walked the aldeas and translated Bible chapters from 1940 to 1960. Her protégés, the McNichols, spent much of the fifteen years after 1956 in Ch'orti' aldeas, where they translated Genesis and the life of Jesus into Ch'orti'. The Lubeck family arrived from Texas in 1973 and, funded principally by the Wycliffe Bible Institute and Summer Institute of Linguistics, began to translate the Bible into Ch'orti'. They raised their family in Guareruche, Jocotán, for five years, learned the language, organized aldea worship groups with Ch'orti' liturgy, and founded the Ch'orti' Church (Iglesia Chortí) in Jocotán, where services were once given in Ch'orti' and attended by as many as one hundred campesino families. They along with Diane Cowie published the first Ch'orti' textbook (Lubeck 1989), and in 1996 they and their Ch'orti' assistants published the first Ch'orti' New Testament (Wycliffe Bible Translators 1996), for sale for less than $3 per copy. The commemoration of the Bible attracted nearly two thousand Ch'orti' attendants to Jocotán's park. Their mission now is to promote Ch'orti' literacy and continue proselytizing, and they have recently founded a church in Pelillo Negro. All these activities have lessened the Ch'orti's' sense of marginality and instilled them with pride in their language.

Converts to Protestantism often show a marked change in attitude. They seem more self-assured and willing to discuss the intricacies of religion, including whether certain actions are sins or not and what their ramifications would be. Alcoholism and profanity are strikingly absent among them. Benjamín explained that his father, a Catholic, raised them to be religious, but cursed them if they did not recite the rosary correctly. Evangelicals, on the other hand, would never do this, he claimed, and they reject those who pretend to be Evangelicals but continue to disrespect their neighbors. The forty-two Protestant households in my survey were more likely to have literate adults (52% versus 36%, significant at the .05 level), use health clinics (93% versus 74%, .01 level), engage in local marketing (98% versus 77%, .01 level), and legally marry (62% versus 32%, .001 level). Evangelical church services certainly motivate Ch'orti' confidence, as they are dynamic, participatory, and encourage parishioners to stand and tell how God intervenes in their daily lives. In contrast, Catholic masses and celebrations are more liturgical and hierarchical, emphasizing repeated recitation and actions led by the priest and other functionaries. Masses seem more like rituals of penitence, whereas Evangelical services are more akin to celebrations.

Other Evangelical Protestant groups, like the Assembly of God founded in the late 1970s, use markedly different tactics than agricultural development and proselytizing in the Ch'orti' language. They rely largely on modern technology like movie projections, electronic music, and expensive sound equipment to dazzle the campesinos with great effect. Occasionally, professional Evangelical bands appropriate the airwaves in the local parks on Saturday nights, attempting to drown out the Catholic mass. Evangelicals and Catholics have comically tried to outshout each other in the park over bullhorns and speaker systems, with Evangelicals charging Catholics of idolatry for worshiping saints' images and the Pope, and Catholics calling Evangelicals gross materialists for trying to buy converts with modern technology.

While Bible translation can instill ethnic pride, some Evangelicals have directly attacked Ch'orti' traditions and undermined their sense of a proud, independent identity by accusing them of sorcery. Evangelicals often regard traditionalists as Satan worshipers, which, when taken to heart by Ch'orti's, can result in murder, whereas Catholics more often see traditionalists as merely backwards and misguided. One US missionary assured me that Mayas secretly sicken Christians and sacrifice them to the Devil. When I mentioned the Maya revitalization organization Majawil Q'ij to another missionary, he interrupted, "oh, you mean the group that is trying to bring back Mayan paganism?" Politically, many also hold a blatantly conservative, pro-US ideology. For example, some seethed at Rigoberta Menchú's Nobel Prize in 1992, relegated all human rights activism to a fashionable ploy to protect criminals and guerrillas from their deserved death penalties, and insisted that Evangelical dictator Ríos Montt has been unfairly vilified by the Left.

As a show of good will and democracy, the local Academy of Maya Languages Ch'orti' branch invited a Ch'orti' Evangelical to a seminar to present on sociology, his major in college. He impressed the audience with a confused recitation of unfamiliar terms like "gens," "clans," "tribes," "matriarchy," "patrilineal," "geography," and "biology," and then quickly launched into a condemnation of his hosts and the movement generally for presumably supporting the guerrillas and violent resistance, despite the fact that they had spent much time in the same seminar denouncing both. He characterized his audience as stupid, uneducated, and unsanitary in their attempts to recover lost traditions, singled out the visiting K'iche' leaders for their inferior language, and criticized the Academy of Maya Languages for rejecting the Summer Institute of Linguistics' orthography. He recovered their sympathy by attacking the United States, and by a thinly veiled extension, me, for defying God by reaching for the moon and for failing to recognize that "Maya civilization" "collapsed" because it was pagan. Whenever someone challenged him on a point, he snapped back, "it's already been proven" (*comprobado*), and continued. He ended his presentation in standard fire and brimstone form saying that the Ch'orti's could be saved if they followed him, his literacy program, and read the Ch'orti' Bible.

The Catholic Belgian Mission in the Jocotán Parish has transformed the Ch'orti' landscape even more profoundly than the Protestants. Catholic Action Network, a Latin American evangelization campaign meant in part to stem the growth of Protestantism, took on counterrevolutionary goals in Guatemala in the 1950s. Around this time Italian priests arrived to the Jocotán Parish and American Benedictine monks to Esquipulas. Within a few years the Italians were replaced by the Belgian Mission in the Jocotán Parish. The Belgians, including priests and nuns, began a series of development projects, the reason for which may have been competition with the Arbenz reforms, Evangelical incursions, or the realization, as one padre argued, that Ch'orti's are extremely poor and religion cannot be detached from living conditions. One of their first projects demonstrated their tenacity. In 1962 they successfully organized all able-bodied campesinos of the aldea Pajcó, Camotán, to spend four hundred days each digging and dynamiting a canal to divert the Camotán River into an irrigation system (cf. Dary, Elías, and Reyna 1998:101–2). Afterwards the mission steadily funded and organized the construction of roads and oratories in the aldeas, and today it pays campesinos in donated food to maintain the roads during the rainy season. Through its Appropriate Technology program campesinos have been given the know-how and technology to carry out their own sustainable projects such as creating irrigation tanks and potable water. In the towns it paved roads and built a gymnasium in San Juan Ermita, a high school in Camotán, a print shop, and the immense Payequi multipurpose center in Jocotán. The Hospital Betania and Dispensary in Jocotán, the only inpatient hospital in the parish, provides subsidized medical services. The mission also organized Ch'orti' colonies in the Petén in the early 1970s, which were subsequently persecuted by the army for presumably supporting the guerrillas. Another project has included the Spanish-funded Inko' Xanikon (Let's Walk Together) small producer cooperative, with a $200,000 warehouse and processing plant for coffee and fruit jellies. Though now largely in disuse, the co-op was once successful enough that some Ladino merchants threatened its managers.

The mission also has promoted education through various media. It built a boarding school in Jocotán for about two hundred aldea children of all grades, which the Jesuit Fe y Alegría foundation runs, and twenty more aldea schools in the late 1990s. It founded the Radio Ch'orti' for the parish in the late 1960s, from which Home Teacher (Maestro en Casa) programs are broadcast for grades one through nine. The radio station has also been used to broadcast masses, papal addresses, and rosaries along with Appropriate Technology lessons, programs on the Ch'orti' language, music, and folklore, the Popol Vuh, biblical readings, medical education programs, a bulletin board service, discussions of human rights, women's issues, and Alcoholics Anonymous. The radio's bulletin board service remains the principal means of communication between aldeas regarding funeral announcements, the arrival of plantation recruiters, lost and found animals, and other local news.[1] The nuns also teach embroidery, sex education, health care, and

---

1. Unfortunately, just as the Maya Movement was starting to take off in the Ch'orti' area, the church turned over management of the Radio Ch'orti' to Ladinos, who "modernized" it by canceling all Maya-related programming and broadcasts in Ch'orti' and replaced Ch'orti' traditional music with Mexican rancheras. Ch'orti's have tried to establish their own radio station, as the Peace Accords stipulate that the state must make frequencies available for indigenous projects, but the state has auctioned off frequencies at prices too high for both Ch'orti's and neighboring Pokomams (Cerigua 12/4/97:4).

songs and prayers to women, enabling women to eclipse in part traditional prayer-sayers. The pride and courage the nuns instill in the women is moving, and I have even observed them scold Ch'orti' men for urging the women to dance with them because the men know the dangers women face from protective fathers and jealous husbands. Familiar with nearly all one hundred aldeas in the parish and employer of dozens of campesinos, the mission is by far the most influential development organization in the area. Both town and aldea appreciation for the Belgian padres was celebrated at Padre Juan Boxi's twenty-fifth anniversary in the parish in 1995, at which an estimated twenty to twenty-five thousand people filled Jocotán's soccer stadium.

Besides economic development per se, no organization has contributed more to Ch'orti's' political awakening, fellowship, and positive identity than the Catholic Church. Many elderly Ch'orti's recount that they hid behind closed doors until the church began working in their communities during las ruinas. According to Alejandro, who has visited aldeas for the Belgian Mission for over three decades, before the mission arrived Ch'orti's cowered in their homes whenever strangers arrived, but today they generally welcome visitors. Most demonstrative of the priests' fellowship with the campesinos was their courage during the war. When the army was massacring and bombing campesinos, the priests pleaded their innocence over the radio, resulting in their own persecution and assassinations of catechists and cooperative members. The devotion of one Belgian padre was such that he married a campesina, formed a Ch'orti' colony and cooperative in the aldea Sakpuy, San Andrés, Petén, and was forced along with his parishioners to flee to Mexico during an army attack. Another Belgian padre was reportedly sequestered by the army in 1981 and expelled from the country. Yet another was caught in guerrilla-police crossfire in San Juan on New Year's Day, 1982, when guerrillas attacked a police outpost. As one of the guerrillas lay dying on the ground he asked for the blessing of the padre, to whom a disdainful Ladino blurted, "he's calling for his commander."

More recently, one priest, clearly influenced by liberation theology, carefully summarized the church's focus on the poor this way:

> [T]he Christian project, of Christ, is always in solidarity with
> everyone—right?—It does not love only the poor, no. But it
> prefers the poor, they are weaker, and it's logical—right?—that
> one is always ultimately going to support those who are the

poorest. But this is not to say them alone, but everyone, yes everyone, but especially he who is most in need. But the church is for everyone. Christ didn't only have disciples among the poorest; he also made disciples who had "posture," who were rich, but the Lord came for everyone—right?—but with preference for the most needy because they are the ones who require the most attention.

Former Bishop Toruña of Zacapa, who became a key player in the negotiation of the Peace Accords, went farther in his periodic sermons in Jocotán in the early 1990s. To a congregation of hundreds of Ch'orti's, he expressed sadness that their language and culture were being abandoned. He emphasized that in their poverty, humility, and exploitation, Ch'orti's are what the church is all about, and the New Evangelization program is meant to respect their customs. At the patron saint's festival in 1993, he preached against forced army recruitment, explaining that we all have human rights to food, clothing, medicine, survival, and equality. He placed a campesino boy on a chair in front of the packed congregation and said he has the same rights as the president, a colonel, and the bishop himself. And women are no different. The congregation was electrified, as if hearing something truly revolutionary. The church has recently attempted to invent traditions by organizing communal marriage ceremonies and communal tzik'ins, which have traditionally been household observances (cf. Warren 1998:183–86).

Some priests also credit themselves for diminishing the Ch'orti' culture of drinking and violence. One opined,

> I believe that the violence has diminished. This is my impression, you know? I believe that the violence has diminished. In Jocotán it was daily bread to have injuries. Daily bread, aaay! And in San Juan Ermita as well. I believe that the church's pastoral mission has influenced this. The church has played an important role in stopping the violence, to calm it a bit in this zone, also in Jocotán.

Some Ch'orti's have credited the church for the virtual disappearance of the monsters of the past, such as the chijchan serpents, which have been conquered by the Black Christ. Certainly, the greater feeling of security promoted by the church has contributed to the deanimation of the environment.

As with the Protestants, Catholic services come at a price. While the church has introduced cooperatives, development projects, and above all political consciousness-raising in Maya communities (e.g., Warren 1989; Brintnall 1979; Watanabe 1992; Carmack 1995; Earle 2001), the consequence has in some cases contributed to Mayas' tacit support for the guerrillas and the placement of all in grave danger (cf. Stoll 1993; Earle 2001).

Maya traditionalists throughout Guatemala have seen Catholic Action Network as a threat to their autonomy, and some Ch'orti's have regarded the Belgian Mission no differently. Among traditionalist Ch'orti's, even those employed by the church, the Belgian Mission has long been seen as such a threat. Just as some Ladinos and Creoles view the church as representative of the guerrillas, some Ch'orti's believe the church represents the towns and non-Ch'orti' world. Some accuse the new generation of padres of subverting traditions like the tzik'ins, drinking, dancing, and the saint cults. Two priests, one lamentably and one defiantly, recounted that the church indeed tried to appropriate the saint cults in the 1960s, including by destroying the saints' images, because they presumably motivated drinking and fighting. Rumors abound that disappearances of traveling saints, such as San Marcos, San Lorenzo (guardian of the winds), and San Antonio del Fuego, were due to a plot by priests or Evangelicals to burn or throw them in the river. Some recounted that when an Olopa padre tried to stop Santiago's (Saint James's) movements in Olopa, the saint became miraculously heavy and could not be budged. In Olopa and Esquipulas, I was told that a new mobile aldea saint, La Divina Pastorcita (the Divine Shepherdess), was once the matron saint of Olopa but was "banished" by the priest and replaced by a newer "Ladino" image. Much to the dismay of clergy in Esquipulas, no renovations of the Black Christ can be as much as suggested without campesino outcries of conspiracy. Some also accuse Catholic Action Network and charismatic Catholics in the Opus Dei movement of undermining the cofradías (Ch'orti' religious brotherhoods) (cf. Palma Ramos 2001:8).

I witnessed religious manipulation on a few occasions. One padre, perhaps thinking I was an observing Evangelical, berated a group of about two hundred Ch'orti's who were ritually passing Saint James from one aldea to another in the Jocotán church. They ceremoniously dressed him in the receiving aldea's saint's clothes, petitioned him, and offered coins and candles. The padre scolded that the idol is not animate and quipped that "an ignorant Catholic is food for the Protestants" (*Católico ignorate, comida de Protestante*). They paused to listen to him out of respect but continued as soon as he left. I witnessed another padre during Mass lambaste the communities of Tuticopote, Agua Blanca, Roblarcito, and Tituque—known for their traditionalism, Ch'orti' language, and alcoholism—for lack of "education." When I asked him later what the church meant by evangelization, he explained that it is not just spreading the word of God but altering the people's whole way of life, though not by "conquering" or tricking them, because they are too smart for that. Besides development projects, rural oratories, and Bible reading groups, the church continues time-tested missionary methods used since the invasion: colorful spectacles like saint's processions but now with the aid of bullhorns, electric generators, lights, tinsel, and other ornamentation. Some Catholic auxiliaries also throw wads of cotton used to wipe the wounds of the crucified Christ image on Good Friday to crowds of campesinos, who scramble to collect them. Many merchants within and outside the church have realized the business potential for such fetishism, as a visit to the trinket mecca of Esquipulas will attest.

The 1992 Columbus Quincentenary revealed where the church stands on history. Despite criticism from educated Ch'orti's in the emerging Maya Movement, the Jocotán Parish commemorated the "500 Years of Evangelization" with a procession of St. James the Apostle in a boat to the Calvary shrine overlooking the town, with new cement crosses at the entrances to town, and with one-act skits by schoolchildren dramatizing the church's conversion and protection of bare-chested, feathered Indians. So few campesinos attended the procession that the padre had difficulty finding enough carriers for the boat. He led the procession by reading passages from the pastoral letter "The New Evangelization," which states that all cultures should be integrated into the church rather than attacked by it. I noticed one of my Ch'orti' friends who had earlier condemned the Spanish invasion, but church employment outweighed his politics. Later in the week a padre was invited to a local Maya Movement meeting to present the church's position on the Quincentenary, where he was met with a hostile reception. He admitted abuses by the friars but emphasized that the church respected Maya cultures and defended them from exploitation.

The church's stance on family planning also undermines its goals of Ch'orti' development. Some Creole and Ladino Catholics are adamant that the church has nothing to do with population increase, or that population is not a problem at all. Indeed, in the Ch'orti' area, Catholic households are not significantly larger than Protestant families or those "without religion." Nonetheless, the church hierarchy is complicit in repressing knowledge about family planning. According to an interview I had with members of the Guatemalan Demographic Institute, Guatemalan politicians, though recognizing population as a problem, are loath to alienate the church, and by extension Catholic voters, by addressing family planning. I have heard the padres themselves in Mass rail against state-proposed legalization of abortion and sterilization programs. One priest spelled out the church's position very clearly:

> What is noble, what is great of a man and woman is to
> consummate their relationship and have a family. That's
> what is noble, while birth control comes from just an
> economic question, in order to have more to consume.
> So in this sense the birth control specialization is incorrect,
> because it is done in terms of egoism. . . . It's not human . . . .
> In other words, it's not certain that there's no land, it's not
> certain, because there are great extensions of it, but the
> problem is in the distribution of land. The problem is that
> the poor don't have land. . . . What is better, a cassette player
> or a child?

Another priest admitted that Ch'orti' lands are overpopulated, but when I worried aloud what they would do in twenty years, he gruffly responded that they will do what they have always done: emigrate to the Petén.

The Guatemalan state was actually the first to introduce campesino development projects under the Arévalo and Arbenz administrations in the 1940s and 1950s. A few old-timers fondly remember their promotion of *maguey castellano*, a species whose fiber for nets, bags, hammocks, and rope was easier to process than *maguey criollo*. During the counter-revolution of the 1960s and 1970s, the state, with funding from the US Alliance for Progress, introduced projects like cooperatives that were eventually repressed by the army. In the mid-1980s when the state attempted to regain the support of the rural population after the genocide, the first civilian government in decades founded new development agencies. The most important in the Ch'orti' area were DIGESA, promoting agricultural self-development and sustainability, DIGESEPE, aiding in livestock care, BANDESA, the agricultural development bank, and DIGEBOS, promoting the conservation of forests, soils, and water. Dozens of aldeas took advantage of DIGESA's programs to conserve soil with stone and live retaining walls, replace inefficient open hearths with adobe stoves, and experiment with organic fruits and vegetables, the seeds of which were provided free of charge. All of these programs were cut in the 1990s as the Cold War ended, US funding declined, and the quasi-democratic state was pressured to make cuts in social spending to pay off previous military governments' debts.

In the mid-1990s more state development funding (11% of all national revenues) began to be channeled directly to municipal governments as well as aldea Development Committees (Comites de Desarrollo) and the Social Investment Fund (FIS). During the Arzú administration (1996–2000), Vice President Luis Flores, who had done his dental internship in the Ch'orti' area and been moved by its poverty, channeled millions of quetzals to the area. For the first time, the most remote communities took precedence in modern infrastructure projects. Pelillo Negro, for example, was awarded a potable water project, a bridge, a Fe y Alegría school, a community cellular telephone, a sewing project, a *madre de cacao* reforestation project (by the Central American and Panamanian Nutrition Institute), cement basins for springs, and road construction projects. The euphoria among Ch'orti's and Ladinos alike overcame perennial problems, such as intra-Ch'orti' envy, sabotage, poor communication, refusal by some to work, and murders. In Pelillo Negro, friends and enemies alike united their funds and labor for the construction of electrical lines. Some households received zinc-laminated metal from FONAPAZ, the two-billion-dollar peace fund provided by foreign donors. On the other hand, a communal truck project was abandoned due to the residents' disagreement over who would drive, and some have been denied access to potable water and the Fe y Alegría school for refusing to work. The Ch'orti' intermediary with the townspeople was gunned down in January 2005. The townspeople, for their part, received the biggest prize of all. Since the early 1960s they had been lobbying for a paved road to run through the region to Copán Ruins, across the border in Honduras, and finally the multimillion-quetzal project was funded and completed in 2000.

International projects, whether by nongovernmental organizations or bilateral assistance between countries, are difficult to distinguish from state programs because their staff are often interchangeable, and many state projects are funded and partially organized by international donors. Therefore, many international projects have similar benefits and problems as state projects. USAID is a clear example. It is one of the longest running development organizations in Guatemala, and it works closely with government agencies in project implementation. Rural Roads (Caminos Rurales) and the Peace Corps, for example, are administered by Guatemalan government agencies, and many of the supplies in the local health centers are donated by USAID. As US development programs were formed under the Alliance for Progress during the height of the Cold War, whose overarching goal has been security, they have coincided nicely with the concerns of the Guatemalan oligarchy, which include the pacification of destitute populations with aid as long as the oligarchy itself is not footing the bill or economically threatened.

Rural Roads is a program with both market and military functions. Under the philosophy that greater market access through roads will lead to development, the roads theoretically offer aid, optimism, and pacification of the poor. Because roads allow the army to move quickly to trouble spots, they also enhance military security. It is no mystery, then, why Guatemala, with US funding, went through a flurry of rural road-building activity during the height of the civil war in the 1980s. Under the liberal market philosophy of the 1990s, in which market integration was supposed to solve everyone's problems, road construction continued to be a major project activity. While rural roads are appreciated by Ch'orti' campesinos, many of whom now ride with produce and fertilizer back and forth to town in pickup trucks, and while various road-building projects have paid campesinos relatively good wages (roughly $3.50 per day), they have also bifurcated Ch'orti' communities into those that can afford to pay for rides (the majority), and those that cannot. Ladinos, who until recently have owned virtually all the vehicles, have profited the most financially, although the cost of gas and repairs and the introduction of cheaper used pickups have compressed profit margins and opened the market for Ch'orti' drivers.

The Peace Corps has also had a significant impact on the region. Whether their projects are ultimately sustained or not, Ch'orti's appreciate them for their effort and their camaraderie. Several volunteers in Olopa, including Jaime, Pedro, and doña Carolina, are legendary for their long stays and accomplishments in the township despite enduring sickness, Ladino threats, and fatigue. Doña Carolina moved there permanently in 1989, running a sustainable farm, teaching English in the local schools without a salary, buying a town dormitory for aldea school girls, and establishing Amigos de Guatemala, which provides scholarships to pay the school expenses of poor students. When she died in February 2003, she received the highest praise attainable by having the town park named after her, where her ashes were buried and several tearful poems were read in her honor. In Jocotán, some Peace Corps volunteers, like Phil, Linda, and Beatrice, are fondly remembered for using their own money to buy land for

18. *Tearful goodbyes for Peace Corps volunteers, Pacrén, 1992.*

reforestation and carpentry projects, starting scholarship programs, and connecting a group of female basket weavers with Pueblo to People, which paid them $5.50 apiece versus about $.35 in the local market and sold the baskets in the United States and Europe (until demand fell in 1997).

Some USAID-linked projects promote the expansion of private US companies. Alimentos Conhelados S.A. (ALCOSA), for example, accompanied by the Chiquimula governor recruited campesinos to grow nontraditional export crops like carrots, chiles, lima beans, broccoli, okra, cantaloupe, cauliflower, and brussels sprouts for the US market. At the inauguration of one broccoli project, funded by campesinos at the company's urging, the project director gloated,

> It gives me much admiration and satisfaction that here we're making that great step from the farmer who consumes all of his product with only a little to sell, to the farmer that is sending products *to the United States*. It's a great climb we've made to represent this farmer. I want to make it loud and clear that you should be very proud of this assistance.

19. *"The great step of sending your product to the United States . . . ,"*
Tituque, Olopa.

The company representatives, however, never clarified that the growers
were obligated to buy fertilizer, pesticide, and other materials from the
company, which would be deducted from their profits, and the company
is the sole authority over what broccoli is rejected from contamination by
insects or overexposure to pesticides (cf. Dary, Elias, and Reyna 1998:103
for okra). They promised several hundred dollars per grower, but in the
end the campesinos earned only $36–$236 per manzana for three and a

half months of intensive labor. Mass monocrop production led to a sudden florescence of plagues, and all nontraditional agriculture for export in the Ch'orti' mountains has been abandoned.

Another aid program that had a significant impact on the Ch'orti' area in the 1990s was the multimillion-dollar Rural Development Project for Small Producers in Zacapa and Chiquimula (PROZACHI), founded in 1990 primarily by the Dutch government and the UN International Fund for Agricultural Development (FIDA). PROZACHI, which employed hundreds of staff throughout the region from 1990 to 1998, inaugurated several projects to augment campesino production, including new technology, credit, new processing and marketing techniques, and improvements in communication and transportation. Examples include training and support for jocote (tropical plum) orchards, experimentation with traditional crops, the provisioning of milking goats, fish ponds, vaccinations for fowl and farm animals, construction of multipurpose buildings, and construction of roads. PROZACHI's professionalism and attempts to unify entire aldeas were impressive, if not always effective. Its roads and multiuse centers have transformed the landscape and introduced many new agricultural concepts to Ch'orti's, particularly women, but ultimately it failed to bring Ch'orti's out of poverty. According to its director, if he were to do the project again, he would deemphasize subsistence agriculture and emphasize entrepreneurialism.

The US Protestant World Vision organization has run an adopt-a-child program in the region since the 1980s, in which First World donors send a contribution regularly to pay for the food and medicine of a Third World child. It has supplied selected aldeas with free laminated metal for roofs, organized knowledge banks for herbal medicines and organic pesticides and fertilizers, provided basic education, and organized and subsidized a campesino store, among many other grassroots projects. Like most other organizations, they give equal if not greater attention to women.

Among several other international nongovernmental organizations, CARE has given food for health centers' malnutrition programs, instruction in soil renovation, and construction materials. One of the most successful projects for instilling pride and responsibility is CARE's communal banks for women, founded on the principals of the Grameen Bank in Bangladesh, in which women are trained in basic accounting and simply provided with a small start-up loan of about $30. The Spanish Cooperation for Development has been a major funder of medical and development programs since the signing of the Peace Accords, and even set up an

office in Jocotán's municipal palace. In 2004–5, Spain's Movement for
Peace, Disarmament, and Liberty (MPDL) initiated a major women's educational and grassroots development project in Olopa. These European
development programs tend to be more focused on grassroots development and show more of a concern for social justice than USAID's global
market/security-oriented emphasis.

The Challenges of Development

Development projects, whether administered by the state or international organizations, face almost insurmountable challenges. Few of the
dozens of development workers I have met have had faith that their projects would have sustained benefits. Most project benefits indeed end
within a few years if not months after the organizational staff has left the
area, as Ch'orti's have insufficient training, organizational abilities, funding, and sense of community to continue (e.g., Palma Ramos 2001:78).
One frustrated director of a high-profile project remarked over beers one
night that it would probably be better if the campesinos were kicked off
the miserable land and sent to work in the cities.

One of the most fundamentally difficult challenges of projects is fitting
project goals to local needs and understandings, because donors have their
own agendas, politics, and philosophies that often conflict with aldea reality. Besides political considerations, such as with USAID, bilateral and mul-
tilateral country to country aid is rife with economic interests, calling into
question whether "aid" is the correct term for this activity. Large international infrastructure projects, funded with taxpayer money, are awarded to
construction companies, engineering firms, and equipment manufacturers
that are closely tied with the ruling elite in the donor countries.[2] Donor

2. From 1982 to 1990, for example, the international "donor" countries
    transferred (i.e., invested) $927 billion in loans, assistance, and private
    spending in the developing world but their businesses received $1,345
    billion in return by selling their own equipment and materials and collecting
    interest (George 1992 in Bodley 1997:369). Emblematic of such behind the
    scenes dealing was the US government's awarding of a no-bid contract to
    Halliburton and Bechtel to rebuild Iraq, both of which were directly linked
    to the right-wing group New American Century that called for an invasion
    of Iraq in 1998. Halliburton, which had most of its assets in offshore
    accounts to avoid paying US taxes, was then found to be overcharging
    the US government for fuel in the Persian Gulf.

agencies tied to national governments also facilitate the production of goods that complement rather than compete with "donor" markets. USAID, for example, discourages the production of grains produced in the United States like wheat and corn (AVANSCO/PACCA 1992:3), and given the opportunity under the Central American Free Trade Agreement (CAFTA), US negotiators have pushed through policies that allow subsidies to US agroindustry but not for campesino agriculture. It is little wonder why campesino and worker groups are not invited to the table when such "free" trade agreements are negotiated.

Other aspects of projects are simply ill-conceived, underfunded, or exhibit serious cross-cultural misunderstanding, all of which tend to be interrelated. One example is the transportation projects mentioned previously. Transportation could be a tremendous benefit to Ch'orti' craft producers, as roads provide not only access to markets but wages to Ch'orti' construction workers. Roads, however, mean greater dependence on Ladinos entrepreneurs if transportation projects do not include the purchase of vehicles and the training of aldea drivers. Townspeople can afford four-wheel drive vehicles with large business proceeds, state contacts, drug money, and migration to the United States. Ladino transportation undercuts the employment of destitute Ch'orti' porters, as the former currently (in 2003) charge about $2.25 to transport a Ch'orti' and his load (about one hundred pounds over ten miles), while a porter charges the same for the load alone.

Many projects attempt to avoid nurturing a Ch'orti' handout culture and foster sustainability by giving aid in the form of loans rather than grants, but these are risky for the most destitute of the population. PROZACHI, for example, gave loans with interest rates of 21%–30%, matching state loan rates, but this was prohibitively high for many Ch'orti's, if they even realized the implications of such rates. Many simply did not pay back the loans. Other projects provide raw materials of dubious value. Free food characteristically comes in the form of milk, oatmeal, cooking oil, and Incaparina protein powder, all of which Ch'orti's find distasteful and prefer to sell to Ladinos.

The lack of consideration for family planning in development projects exemplifies the disconnect between local needs and broader politics. Regional, national, and global redistribution of wealth would go a long way toward redressing poverty, as leftists argue, but so would the greater ability of poor families to plan their births. According to the United Nations Population Fund's 1997 annual report, the world need for family planning is $17 billion per year (about what is spent weekly in armaments) but only about half that funding is received (*Cerigua* 7/31/97:4). The United States continually refuses to pay its share of the fund because a minor fraction goes towards abortion education. President Bush's first act as president in 2001 was to cut US funding to international family planning agencies, undoubtedly contributing to the world's population of unwanted and unsupported children.

While Latin American countries have taken great strides in family planning since the 1960s, Guatemala has the highest birth rate in the hemisphere as of 1999 (5.0 births per woman) and lags far behind especially in the indigenous countryside, with an average of 6.2 children per woman versus 3.8 in the cities (Santiso-Gálvez and Bertrand 2004:57; CEH 1999 1:78; Robles 1997:375, 380; *Cerigua* 6/3/99:2, 8/26/99). Four factors have thwarted family planning in Guatemala: 1) leftist opposition emanating from the national university (San Carlos) from 1960 through the 1970s; 2) the cultural challenges presented by large indigenous populations; 3) the violence of the 1980s; and 4) the Catholic Church's strong-armed meddling in national politics (Santiso-Gálvez and Bertrand 2004:58–59; Metz 2001b). The national university refused to train their medical students in family planning because it was supposedly a US plot to distract from social and economic reforms. The Catholic Church has gone as far as to block collaboration between the largest provider of family planning, the nongovernmental family association APROFAM, and the Ministry of Health, and slander IUDs for being abortifacients (Santiso-Gálvez and Bertrand 2004:59, 62). In 1999 the Arzú administration cut state subsidies of all family planning technologies, insufficient as they were, because they contravene the constitution, which, betraying the church's meddling, guarantees human life since conception. Couples should have the right "to decide for themselves the method of birth control" (*Cerigua* 6/3/99:2), which translates as the right to practice abstinence. As a result, state health services still only account for 24% of family planning while APROFAM, underfunded and run mostly with US donations, provides 37% (Santiso-Gálvez and Bertrand 2004:63).

In the Ch'orti' area, no major development project offers family planning, meaning that projects try impossibly to keep up with population growth rather than giving Ch'orti's the means to prevent it. APROFAM has long operated in the area, but it has not met the challenge of family planning among Ch'orti's. Lately, APROFAM has been selling contraceptives at a discounted rate, but there was little cross-cultural explanation to Ch'orti's about them. Early (1982:141) pointed out long ago that "new models of family planning need to be developed for peasant systems, and the use of paraprofessionals with whom the peasantry can identify is a necessary ingredient," but one local Ladino APRPOFAM promoter I interviewed in 1993 was so frustrated by Ch'orti' culture that he called them the most superstitious and least intelligent of all Guatemalan Mayas. Some Ch'orti's told me that everyone is interested in family planning, but few know much about it. Suspicious of Ladino motives, few took advantage of the free contraceptives and education of health centers and APROFAM. Nick (1975 in Early 1982:141) found the same in the Maya community of Santiago Atitlán, where 36% of women mentioned embarrassment and 32% fear as reasons for rejecting modern contraceptives, supporting Rogers's (1973 in Early 1982:141) assertion that the expertise and the trust gained by promoters are keys to family planning. Ch'orti's really have no reason to trust outsiders who promote fewer children.

Ch'orti's certainly do not make family planning education easy. Some seem to believe that each woman has a preordained number of children in her womb, such that any family planning—"natural" or "modern"—goes against God's designs. When one mother of seventeen discovered that I had been married for two and a half years without fathering a child, she accused me of sinning, of killing the seed (*la crianza*). She and her family argued that because we gringos sin, we are not blessed with many children, and even suggested that free contraceptives are a trick designed to exterminate Indians. To family plan, then, would be to kill unborn children (cf. Ward, Bertrand, and Puac 1992:61–62). Many men are also unwilling to relinquish control of their wives' fertility. One, distressed that his eighth child was on the way, was frustrated that birth control pills could not simply be given to women immediately before or after sex. He wanted to withhold the pills while he was away at the plantation, so that if his wife had extramarital affairs, it would be revealed by her pregnancy. It is no wonder that, as one health worker confided, some campesina women take the pill behind their husbands' backs. Men also see condoms as silly, unmanly, and desensitizing.

Such problems are reflected throughout Guatemala, where 64% have access to contraceptives, but only 38% use them, the lowest rate in Central America, which contributes to the fact that in 1997 two women per day died of pregnancy related causes (*Cerigua* 7/31/97:4, 8/26/99). The most invasive measure, female sterilization, was the most common method of birth control, and only 15% of sexually active women between the ages of fifteen and nineteen used contraceptives. Fifty percent of the adult female population had no family planning orientation, yet 58% desired no more children (*Cerigua* 8/26/99).

Cultural misunderstandings and ethnic cleavages account for other development failures as well. Like me when I began my fieldwork, many project directors assume that Ch'orti's are communitarian and will work together harmoniously. When they usually do not, few directors—who attempt to adhere to project schedules and deadlines—have the patience to comprehend Ch'orti' divisions, rumors, insecurities, and work habits. Cursory attempts to unify opposing aldea factions often result in the disintegration of projects. Democratically elected committees are sometimes formed to legitimate local leadership, but Ch'orti's insist on consensus over majority rule, and leadership is legitimated in actions, not votes, through strength of personality, motivation, speaking abilities, self-sacrifice, and reliability. Gabriel humbly placed responsibility on the Ch'orti's, saying "hope lies in the projects, but we have a hard time understanding them."

Women present additional challenges. Before the leaders of one women's group were elected, project coordinators failed to inform the women that leaders would have to travel to distant towns to sell their products. Those married women who were elected soon found themselves in disputes with their husbands, who did not approve of them traveling. When some women and I suggested a revote to the coordinators, they, already angry that the women were behind in the project, brushed the issue aside, saying that there could only be one vote. Coordinators sometimes do not understand that many Ch'orti' women speak only rudimentary Spanish, which undermines whatever confidence they have at meetings. Some coordinators who grew increasingly desperate at their lack of progress asked me to attend all meetings as a linguistic and cultural translator.

Some coordinators' treatment of Ch'orti's unwittingly deepens the feeling that they are unworthy of respect. They often arrive late to meetings if at all and fail to comply with promises. In Tuticopote, for example, campesinos were invited to see a film on tomato production but in the end were never given seeds. In other instances seeds arrived late, like corn in Pacrén that arrived six weeks after the planting season. While campesinos expect others to greet them on the trail, they complain that many coordinators rudely pass them without acknowledging their presence. Even national representatives of the Academy of Maya Languages twice failed to arrive at Ch'orti' seminars, and some Ch'orti's had walked four hours to hear them. Timeliness is very difficult to maintain in mountains where the transportation and communication systems are poor, but Ch'orti's are sensitive to being disrespected.

Coordinators may also be unwittingly paternalistic. At various project inaugurations I attended, they awarded campesinos with prizes for hard work and organized games among adults to convey a point. These are generally well received, especially when coordinators themselves participate, but often they are followed by "I told you so" lectures, pep talks reminiscent of grade school coaches, or flowery, meaningless speeches.

Given the failure rate of projects, projects benefit their employees as much or more than the target population. Some employ dozens of Guatemalan workers at good wages and spend hundreds of thousands of dollars on infrastructure, boosting local economies. One large project was notorious among townspeople and campesinos alike for its promoters' tendency to spend more time in their offices and on their motorcycles than in the aldeas (though some were extremely devoted), and the director quipped that the organization had played the role of matchmaker for many couples. In this sense, projects are worthwhile for staff and infrastructure regardless of whether Ch'orti's are directly assisted or not.

On the other hand, the Ladino and Creole benefits from projects can reinforce a structure of ethnic discrimination. Some Ladinos and Creoles have made a living of taking advantage of development assistance. Many prey on the misguided food aid that Ch'orti's find unpalatable at bargain prices and either consume it or resell it. Others simply cut corners on their project employment. Many use project vehicles as their own personal means of transportation.

"The most infamous episode in the history of Jocotán," according to one local doctor, occurred when aid began pouring in during the famine of 2001. Rain did not fall at all in some aldeas during the critical agricultural months of June to August, and international coffee prices were so low that plantations were not hiring Ch'orti's at the start of the picking season in September. Many Ch'orti's had no corn nor money to buy it, although those in the higher elevations harvested a little due to more rain and the temperate climate. In the hardest hit families, the children and elders went hungry. The famine of 1996, when corn and bean prices tripled in the preharvest month of July, was worse, but in 2001, the mayors of Jocotán, Olopa, and Camotán notified the press that the area was under a "yellow alert." Two out of three of these mayors were from the PAN opposition party, and the FRG mayor of Camotán was reprimanded by his own party for publicizing a social crisis. The Guatemalan press, more influenced by the oligarchy and its PAN party than the army's FRG party, used the famine to attack the FRG. Soon thereafter the international press arrived from China, Japan, the United States (CNN, Univision, the *New York Times*), and various European countries and filled the local Betania hospital searching for starving children. A group of Cuban medical doctors working in western Guatemala arrived and began bringing starving children back to the town health facilities, overwhelming them. The Hospital Betania, which is designed to house up to about 20 children, was flooded with 90, and the local state-run health center received 173 over a four-month period. As with the cholera epidemic of 1992, many Ch'orti' parents tried to hide their children because they did not trust the prying outsiders.

The oligarchy and other social sectors demonstrated their concern by organizing food drives and donations, which arrived in Jocotán haphazardly. Companies donated truckloads of bananas from the Atlantic coast, the government brought fertilizer and chemically treated, inedible corn and bean seeds, and private donors gave clothing and medicine. At one point, twenty semitrucks were lined up at the entrance of Jocotán. Much of the assistance was simply dumped on the side of the road, in the health facilities, or in Jocotán's park, far from the remote aldeas that needed assistance. Some Ladino families, like vultures on a dying animal, seized the opportunity. Many of the donated items immediately began appearing for sale in their stores. As if in some García Márquez novel, several Ladino families placed their children on the side of the road entering town to plead with truck drivers for food and provisions. The truck drivers literally tossed their supplies out to save them.

After weeks of chaos, the health centers managed to take stock of the donations and gave twelve pounds of food, including rice, corn, beans, cooking oil, and dried milk, as well as some articles of used clothing, to several hundred families. Much of the milk was simply appropriated by Ladinos because they knew that Ch'orti's generally do not like it. The only long-term structural input was the construction of emergency centers for every three to four aldeas, which are provisioned with medicine, IV fluid, beds, and radios to call the town health center. The Spanish Cooperation now also has a medical mission in Jocotán, and Doctors without Borders and Doctors of the World began projects in the area.

Ch'orti' Agency

The Ch'orti's themselves, of course, have much to do with their own development. Many have taken advantage of new resources and opportunities in the market economy to complement subsistence agriculture. In fact, the most opportunistic have moved to town and become Ladinos. My census data in 1992–93 demonstrates a clear bifurcation between Ch'orti's with more economic resources who take advantage of projects and new opportunities, and poor, marginal Ch'orti's who do not, either because they are unwilling or unable. The census measured twenty-three variables pertaining to: a) land ownership and rental; b) migration; c) family size; d) female members who have a state identification card (cédula); e) literacy and school attendance; f) legal marriage versus informal unions; g) the practice of a profession or trade; h) project participation; i) religious affiliation; j) the use of modern household infrastructure like latrines, zinc roofs, and adobe stoves; k) ownership of a kitchen house separate from the dormitory; l) the use of health clinics; m) the marketing of crafts; n) the use of agrochemicals; o) the ownership of a radio; p) the ownership of cattle; and q) the use of male traditional dress. The data reflect a strong correlation (chi-square at .001 level, or 1 in 1,000) of households with greater wealth (land, radios, cattle, number of household structures, legal marriages, larger number of family members) and participation in education, development projects, and agrochemical use. Moreover, the poor are much less likely to exhibit closely correlated signs of national integration, including literacy, women with cédulas, the practice of a profession (other than agriculture), owning a radio, participation in development projects, the use of health clinics, and project innovations like fuel-conserving adobe stoves (versus three stones supporting a griddle), latrines, and zinc roofs. Some remote communities have never been reached by development projects or state services, and some simply distrust them.[3]

Those households with a practicing professional, like a chicha vendor, carpenter, mason, or merchant, are few (15%) but form a class apart.

---

3. Interestingly, traditional dress, religious affiliation (Protestant, Catholic, or "no religion"), and seasonal plantation labor were nonfactors, although households with migrants (73% of Jocotán's respondents) are much less likely to own cattle and use chemical fertilizers, refuting the notion that migrant wages are used to buy fertilizer (cf. Palma Ramos 2001:106, 117).

20. *Scraping maguey to extract fiber, Tuticopote.*

Though they own land and farm, they invest little in fertilizers and pesticides. Most are young entrepreneurial men, including twelve from Pacrén
who have risked their neighbors' envy to buy and resell merchandise in
Guatemala and western Honduras. While their earnings are minimal for
the travel and time spent, they have become successful enough to own
cement houses, bicycles, and gravity-powered sprinkler systems to irrigate their crops in the dry season. A few of them have been the first to
migrate to the United States, with some going several times and returning
with cars. One family in Tuticopote was remarkable in its entrepreneurialism. The father once made maguey bags for Q.25 apiece until his wife
suggested that they raise chickens to sell eggs. This strategy, along with

their *chichería*, has enabled them to buy fertilizer for beans, corn, coffee, and bananas, which they irrigate with a gravity-powered sprinkler system in the dry season. He proudly claims to produce enough corn and beans to support his family year-round and buys only salt, sugar, soap, clothes, bread, and cheese.

The contrast between developing aldeas like Pacrén and nondeveloping ones like neighboring Tunucó was stark in the early 1990s. Pacrén's landscape was crossed by horizontal terraces, rows of maguey and *izote*, and reforestation to prevent erosion, while barren Tunucó had maguey rows running vertically. Many of the Pacrén homes shined with zinc roofs, while virtually all the Tunucó homes had palm and thatch roofs. In reforestation-minded Pacrén, the first deer in decades were spotted (and killed) in 1996, whereas no large patches of forest remained in Tunucó. When radish seeds were donated to some men of Pacrén for the first time, one succinctly expressed his group's attitude, "one must try new things."

Some families have been able to accomplish phenomenal development with newfound assistance, knowledge, and confidence in the market. Doña Carmen's family in Tuticopote is exemplary. Coffee cultivation was introduced to the area in the 1940s, but has been used primarily for local consumption (89% of all households owned coffee trees in Tuticopote Abajo in 1993). With a 10% interest loan from BANDESA and instruction from DIGESA, doña Carmen's family planted a manzana (1.73 acres) of coffee seedlings and built a drying patio and hand-crank coffee-huller in the mid-1980s.[4] By 1993 their annual net earnings reached Q6,000 ($1,200), and they planted more. By 1996, when international prices skyrocketed after a Brazilian frost, and local prices reached Q15.00 per pound (about $2.70) for dried coffee, their earnings rose as high as Q20,000 ($4,000) per manzana. Doña Carmen's family, selling two to three thousand pounds of coffee annually, paid off its original loan and continued to plant more land in coffee, as one grandson decided to forego all corn and bean agriculture for it. The intensive process of processing coffee for the market, which involves picking each bean by hand, grating the exterior flesh from the bean with hand-crank hullers, washing the coffee in cement vats, drying it

---

4. Dary, Elías, and Reyna (1998:154) report that the productivity of coffee trees varies between fourteen thousand pounds per hectare with new trees, which only some can afford, to five thousand pounds with old trees. Unfortunately, no one realizes that the quality of old tree coffee is very high and worth about three times more than the new trees.

on cement patios, and carrying tons of it over muddy mountain trails to town, is no problem for Carmen's large family, and they even hire day-laborers. Her family has also worked exhaustively at cultivating bananas, hauling as many as thirty loads of three hundred bananas each month by bus to Chiquimula, earning a net total of Q300 a month. In 1998 their profits climbed when they purchased a used pickup truck. They also sell singed banana leaves for tamales to townspeople for roughly $10 per two hundred (in 1993). They have become one of the most prosperous Ch'orti' home-steads in the region, possessing horses, a barn, several homes, guitars, and a marimba. By 1998 virtually the entire aldea was planting coffee. Epitomiz-ing the optimism of the coffee boom, Carmen's family asked me the peren-nial question, "how much money do you make?" Usually my hesitant answer involves a quick explanation of the expensive cost of living in the United States, but this time they said it does not seem like very much at all. By 1999, however, the coffee boom ended when Brazil recovered from a damaging frost years earlier and Vietnam fully entered the international market, but government guarantees and the abundance of cheap labor ensures that coffee continues to be marginally profitable. For the poorest Ch'orti's on the edge of existence, however, experimenting in such a volatile market instead of planting corn and beans is not possible (Dary, Elías, and Reyna 1998:155).

Another area of opportunity and risk is the use of agrochemical fertil-izers and pesticides. In 1993, 39% used agrochemical fertilizers and 27% herbicides and pesticides (however Dary, Elías, and Reyna [1998:131] recorded that only 20% could afford fertilizers in the mid-1990s). Macaria, Dorotea, and others mentioned that without chemical fertilizer, corn and beans agriculture would be a losing proposition. Sefalino calculated that with two applications of fertilizer for a total price of Q450 (about $80), one reaps four thousand pounds of corn (worth about $500) per manzana in Tuticopote, but without it, harvests scarcely reach eighteen hundred pounds (worth about $220).[5] Some who use fertilizers regularly, like onion growers for example, are already complaining that more and more fertilizer is required every season to maintain productivity (Dary, Elías, and Reyna 1998:98). Herbicides are used in place of manual labor for weeding. Most rarely use herbicides because they fear contamination and

---

5. Similarly, Dary, Elías, and Reyna (1998:132) documented sixteen hundred
   to twenty-five hundred pounds with fertilizer, and eight hundred to sixteen
   hundred without.

high costs, have plenty of family labor for weeding, or prefer to pay their neighbors, but some like Cresencio claim they are indispensable because drunkenness has purportedly thinned the labor pool. With herbicides, he can weed eight tareas (.9 acres) per day for less cost than eight laborers doing the same work in the same amount of time. He is also sufficiently concerned about the dangers of herbicides to request from me a safety mask from the United States, but for everyone else the costs of a $40 applicator and the herbicides themselves are so high that they feel they cannot afford the luxury of a mask (costing about $35–$45).

Cresencio and his son Paco's properties are outstanding for applied development knowledge. Cresencio bought two hectares of cattle land in the late 1980s that had only two trees and three palms. Today it has dozens of trees and palms, and the few tareas (.3 acres) that he left fallow have reverted to brush forest, despite the pleas of many would-be renters to clear it. He and his neighbor selectively trim the live fence-post trees surrounding his terrain for firewood, and around his homestead his wife and daughters irrigate gardens of tomatoes, onions, cabbage, sweet potato, cilantro, cashew fruit, and radishes amidst stands of large trees, including mangos. His wife expertly raises turkeys and chickens, usually selling or slaughtering them when they have reached the growth peak, when they no longer produce eggs, or during Christmas holidays when the prices double in town. Paco has utilized the best of development knowledge to build a home with a laminated metal roof, plastic tables and chairs, a gas stove, rabbits, a fish pond stocked with fingerlings and snails, canals taking away the water waste, and a cement wash basin. He and his wife have planned to have only two children, and he has investigated the possibilities of migrating to the United States. Thanks to his initiative and leadership at an aldea meeting, he managed to convince 40% of Pacrén's households to pay Q26.50 (about $5.00) for the installation of electricity in 1998. Cresencio had calculated that the monthly bill should be Q8.00–Q10.00 (about $1.45–$1.80), which is less than he pays in kerosene for his wick burner, though other campesinos have been unable to keep up with the bills of the privatized electric service.

A conversation with Félix and his son poignantly expresses the optimism occasionally felt by the new generation. While people use to "soil their pants" in fear of passing airplanes,

> *Félix*: Suddenly the people changed; now it is only new people, because the people of before are few. The people of before

ended already. Now the majority of people are newer. They're already more changed in all aspects of life. Yes. That's why we and the others think that this time is better...

    Son: There was a lot of difference. Now the people are, now... they have awoken a lot, you know. Before the people were more, like more humble; they didn't have anything of their own. But now the people have more knowledge.

    Brent: And why did the people change? Do you know?

    Son: Look, the truth is that other people have created new things for the people, like that health promoter, like that... orienting the people, and the people have lived more.

Dorotea of Pacrén emphasized that "a long time ago there was absolutely nothing. Today we've seen everything already." Benjamín echoed that they have learned more (*más k'anseyaj*) today—that burning is bad for the land, for example, while Paulina pointed to schooling: "It's that they were times in which the people were only ignorant, and now no, now there are already people who have been awakened." Others like Minche and Juventina expressed that today is better simply because wages are higher and there is enough food.

    Cresencio's sister, Juliana, led a profound transformation in Pacren's women's attitudes due to her leadership in development. After her husband and brother died from illnesses on the cotton plantations, she began to attend DIGESA training sessions with Cresencio's encouragement, despite being terrified at the prospect of being surrounded by men speaking Spanish. She soon began to teach other women, and, along with a series of three female Peace Corps volunteers, attracted dozens of women to agricultural and basket-weaving projects. Nuns began to teach the women to pray and embroider, and their Spanish improved. Despite jealous accusations by other women that they were whores, they persisted and their numbers burgeoned to thirty-seven wives, widows, and single women. When Protestant World Vision arrived in Pacrén, they were undeterred by allegations that it was a Protestant trick, and many joined. Juliana's group was the only one I know that rented land in common and rotated labor on each other's plots. Their arduous work in building terraces was admired by all, who recognized that her group and the women of Pacrén generally are better organized than the men. They are usually consulted on decisions involving the entire community. When Pedro visited me in Pacrén, I showed him photos of the women building the carpentry shop, and he

21. *Women at carpentry shop project, Pacrén.*

giggled until he saw the furniture and baskets they were making. When he discovered that they were earning nearly $6 per basket from Pueblo to People, he wondered how he could procure such projects for Pelillo Negro. In 2004 an adult education center was inaugurated by Jocotán's mayor in honor of Juliana, at which Chiquimula's female governor spoke.

Dary, Elías, and Reyna (1998:199–200) are correct in saying that no projects reverse Ch'orti' women's low self-esteem, but only perhaps in the long run, because in the short run, women's self-esteem while participating in projects rises dramatically. During the florescence of women's projects in Pacrén in the early 1990s, women carried themselves with humility and frequent embarrassment, but they showed fierce determination in the face of ridicule and inexperience to take advantage of opportunities. They competed for the attention of the male Peace Corps volunteer who trained them to make furniture, and gender segregation began to dissolve. Some married women had to contend with drunk husbands who reaped the benefits of their labor, but the women knew they were no longer dependent on men. They also led the way in family planning, and the APROFAM representative in Jocotán referred to them as the exception to the Ch'orti's' rejection of family planning. They were also passing their independence on to the next generation, as Pacrén was the

only one of thirty-three Jocotán aldeas where girls outnumbered boys in
school (24/17 in the first grade).

In Macaria's words,

> [W]e grew up sad because it was impossible. Before they went
> earning, you know, in day labor for the Ladinos. . . . Today it's
> very different because we're doing our tasks, as this sister
> [Juliana] with whom we're working is getting and giving to
> us. In that, we are always receiving our strength. We are
> happy to see that we are still working with her, and they're
> acquiring fertilizer for the land, we're acquiring dishes,
> and we're empowered. We are realizing that it doesn't
> abound but it's better than when we grew up.

When I asked Jesús to discuss her life, she enthusiastically responded,

> I'm always happy today to work with my sister Juliana. We,
> when we go and I do work, today we are realizing that it's *happy,*
> *content*, when she says "I want to have a meeting with you."
> We always do tasks seriously, we come and she tells us to work
> hard, and our happiness is profound. *Content*, and we always
> work. . . . Yes, like very thankful that she is always busy among
> us. Long ago I knew nothing . . . and before I never felt happy
> because everyday I sat like that, spending time with my family,
> but a happy day arrived.

By the mid-1990s women of other aldeas began to be targeted by projects, and they expressed the same sense of liberation and confidence.
One cogent example occurred during a ride in a pickup to Pelillo in 1996.
The pickup was packed with about ten men and one woman. The men
argued heatedly about development projects and occasionally picked on
a drunk to defuse the tension. The drunk adeptly redirected the attention
to the woman and me with his own jokes. She, however, with the courage
to go to town on her own, resolutely outwitted the drunk quip for quip,
winning all of our admiration.

Juliana summed up the changes in women's attitudes:

> There's a change in the work that we're seeing, which we
> [women] didn't see in the past. We understood absolutely

nothing about [agricultural] work before. We used to see that only the men used machetes and picks, only men worked. In contrast, we women discovered that it wasn't our work before, but today as the men work, so we work as well, if still not with the pick. We do indeed work the same as the men. Maybe we don't work as much as the men, but more or less we're learning to work too. And I know that there's a change that we're seeing today. . . . Today the women are more awake because now they are not afraid. When they see a gringo coming they don't say "Uy! Here's comes a gringo, maybe he wants to take our children," but before it was so because they didn't understand, that's the way it was, they didn't go out either, they didn't understand meetings, they were only embarrassed. They couldn't respond to men, either, because they were only embarrassed. It was strictly embarrassment. But not any longer. When I call a meeting with them I ask them "why are we having the meeting? To erase all the embarrassment," I say, "we cannot live our entire lives in shame," I say. "The meetings are to throw out all the shame," I say, "to forget the embarrassment we held before," I say. . . . If, if we have a meeting with the men, we no longer say "it's too much with the men," but we're thinking that we'll have a balanced meeting, as a man is treated so are the women, we no longer think of being embarrassed. Rather, embarrassment we are almost forgetting completely.

"Sometimes Our Own Worst Enemies"

The enthusiasm for development projects and modern technology often does not overcome their incessant problems, in part due to Ch'orti's' own interpretations, routines, and sentiments. One major problem is Ch'orti' fear and suspicion. As explained earlier, the idea that ethnic outsiders are cannibals makes perfect sense given Ch'orti's' history and their emphasis on sharing, especially food. The first Peace Corps volunteers and Protestant World Vision coordinators in Pacrén, for example, were thought to be secretly plotting to capture and consume Ch'orti' children. Why else would these suspicious outsiders want to give them food (cf. Palma Ramos 2001:118–19, 121, 124–25)? Some of these rumors are intentionally propagated by those who do not participate in the projects but seek to undermine them nonetheless (Palma Ramos 2001:45). While the cannibalism beliefs may be slowly abandoned, other rumors abound. Some believed that the small flies propagated by the government to attack flesh-boring worms in cattle are really plagues that will eat their crops (Palma Ramos 2001:68). In 2003 PROCH'ORTI' project staff who were using survey equipment to measure aldea land for titling were shot at several times because it was thought that they were trying to expropriate land. PROZACHI technicians were also chased on their motorcycles by machete-wielding men on foot who distrusted their projects. Some no doubt also see development projects in a political light, as the army persecuted all types of projects in the 1960s and 1970s (cf. Palma Ramos 2001:81).

Also problematic is Ch'orti' noncompliance with project demands. Organizations like Protestant World Vision, CARE, and the Catholic Church have delivered countless tons of food and resources to Ch'orti's in recent decades, but they now blame each other for cultivating a pervasive Ch'orti' handout culture, especially in heavily targeted aldeas close to towns. Some Ch'orti's like Petronilo and Cipriano concur. The former remarked, "it's like I told you, the people are tired of working; we want our money for free." Jocotán Health Center and the Catholic Hospital Betania have placed nominal fees on routine services such as stool analyses (Q.25, about 4¢) and medicine (Q.50, about 9¢), but this has only prompted some campesinos to reject their services completely because any fees are unjust. Some projects have offered loans or aid in exchange for labor, but many campesinos refuse to work or repay the loans, resulting in project abandonment. State loan programs have hardly been favorable, with their high interest rates (about 30%). Campesinos for their part often see millions of project quetzals spent on buildings and salaries, while they are asked to repay loans with high interest rates. Consequently, perhaps more Ch'orti's defaulted on PROZACHI loans than paid them off, and some told me that they never intended to repay them in the first place. As one forty-year-old man told Palma Ramos's (2001:106) research team, "as you know, what is acquired by loan is barren, because by this system we have debts. Some guy from the institution told us that there was aid, but we learned that it wasn't that easy." Even low-interest and interest-free loans, such as those offered by the Belgian Mission in the early 1990s, are often left outstanding. CARE initiated a communal bank project, loaning women small amounts with which to experiment and invest, but in some aldeas a few women never considered repaying and were dropped from the project. One Ch'orti' representative for Protestant World Vision was jobless and landless but infamous for embezzling project resources. He was the first Ch'orti' to own a two-story cement house and a motorcycle. When individual World Vision donors drove all the way from the United States to meet their "adopted" children and drop off a van-load of supplies, for example, he convinced them to leave the supplies with him, which he proceeded to sell. Eventually, he moved to a distant town to become a Ladino.

A culture of expecting something for nothing often leads to project breakdown. The demise of one aid agency, Adespro, is illustrative. The three Ch'orti's composing the local board of directors could not account for Q8,000 of a Q19,000 loan, and the project was abandoned. One of the three later stopped a padre's bulldozer at gunpoint during a communal road construction project because the padre had purportedly agreed to the man's bribe of Q3,000 for the road to pass through his land, but for reasons of engineering the padre bypassed his property. Even Maya organizations (discussed in the next chapter) that explicitly preach against egoism and for ethnic unity have suffered embezzlement and accusations of nepotism.

Cipriano, who had just miraculously survived from being hacked in the head in a machete attack, offered these passionate words about loans and envy:

> It's not good what the people do. It's not good what they do. . . . Some arrive and offer a little fertilizer and they receive it. They receive the fertilizer. . . . They only consume, like when they received the fertilizer last year and didn't pay. There are those who are defiant.
>
> *Brent*: Ah hah, the fertilizer that the church lent.
>
> *Cipriano*: Yes! . . . I don't say "give me money" and then don't return it. I have never asked for money, and therefore they are angry to see me, because. . . . I'm always with my business even if I have little money, but I'm marching forward with it, to clean my fields. . . . I harvest corn to pay my helpers, but I don't trick the people, and therefore the others get mad, as if I were the bad person. That's why they are angry to see me.
>
> *Brent*: There is always envy.
>
> *Cipriano*: There is *envy*. There is *envy*. . . . They don't think about *things*. And that's why they don't get ahead . . . with envy nothing abounds.

Cynical attitudes among Ch'orti's regarding the repayment of loans or keeping one's word are notable. Other gringos and I have been swindled on "loans" by Ch'orti's posing as friends or the needy. As gringos are thought to have interminable amounts of money, many are asked for gifts first, and loans second. From me, some Ch'orti's have requested pens, papers, dishes, groceries, and, if feeling particularly lucky, my computer, cassette recorder, lantern, Coleman camp stove, and a visa and ticket to the United States. Multitudes have asked for pocket change for chicha, while others have asked me to buy watches, cameras, and typewriters. One inebriated man told me that he needed Q15 for his sick boy in the hospital, but I discovered in the hospital registry that he had lied. I once sincerely told a friend that I would consider giving him Q2,000 (about $350) for his college education if I found employment after receiving my doctorate, but he said Q5,000 would be more appropriate. When I donated a typewriter to a Ch'orti' agency, I was told that what they really needed was a computer. One of the leaders eventually sold the typewriter and kept the money. The wives of two close friends even grossly overcharged me on goods they produced. The case of the woman who tried to persuade me to marry her daughter was also an attempt to tap the gringo's "wealth." When it was clear that I would not be coaxed into marriage, she turned to accusing me of killing her puppy with the evil eye and insisting that I pay for it. Peace Corps workers, so eager to help, are favorite prey for "loans" as well. Lest one think that this is simply a Ch'orti' phenomenon, I have been swindled even worse by Occidente Mayas and Ladinos posing as friends.

It is tempting to explain or justify the culture of handouts and swindling, which competes with a stronger culture of work, by emphasizing the Ch'orti's' poverty and desperation, their necessary reliance on momentary tactics rather than long-term social strategizing and investment (cf. De Certeau 1984:35–39; Scheper-Hughes 1992:471–72). But as has been seen throughout this book, those with the greatest power and wealth in Guatemala are the most corrupt and cynical swindlers of all. It seems that those who have faith in Guatemala and Guatemalans, those who are truly altruistic, remain at the bottom of the socioeconomic ladder, whereas the amoral rogues advance. Even at the local level, in my personal experience the poorest of the poor are often those who are the most generous, sincere, and honest, while the "wealthiest" of the poor are more opportunistic. The explanation for this pervasive national culture lies in the legacy of colonialism and countercolonialism.

One could also justify or at least explain the culture of corruption as the Ch'orti's getting their "fair share." Socially, they play the supporting roles as voters for Ladino political candidates, as the audience for town speeches, as buyers and suppliers for the merchants, and as curious bystanders at town events. For some townspeople, they serve as the "swine" who remind them that, even though have not reached white First World status, things could be worse. For the priests and pastors, Ch'orti's are the raw material with which to build the earthly Kingdom of God. For anthropologists like myself, for whom it is easier to criticize than constructively engage problems, Ch'orti's are raw material for building academic careers. However, as discussed, when Ch'orti's swindle these outsiders, the biggest victims are not the outsiders but their own neighbors, as all alliances and aid are cut as a result.

Indeed, among Ch'orti's themselves, envy and the suspicion of others' envy are major problems. Many projects have been sabotaged by Ch'orti's who feel threatened by others' success (e.g., Palma Ramos 2001:102) or believe it has been achieved by corruption. Ch'orti's, in fact, are more apt to blame each other, rather than others, for their poverty and marginality. It is particularly painful to endure one's neighbor's success when one has internalized the national contempt for one's own ethnic group. Victims of contempt can ease their pain by acting contemptuously towards neighbors like themselves. One friend, for example, was disgusted and ashamed that his neighbors had contracted cholera, as the Ladino health promoters emphatically instructed that cholera was transmitted among dirty Ch'orti's through the ingestion of body waste. He gleamed when he recounted that a soldier struck an old man for refuting the health workers' explanation of cholera transmission. Later the same friend received a dose of his own medicine when another, who attended high school and was one of a few Ch'orti's to own a bicycle, disdainfully ridiculed him and his used BMX bike as he tried to ascertain how to pump up its bald tires. The temptation to put ambitious neighbors in their place is too enticing for some to suppress. Those in positions of power, like bilingual teachers, project leaders, and professionals, are ever vigilant in watching for envy. And for those who have the initiative to start a business, like an ice cream salesman from Pelillo Negro, it is best to sell in municipalities other than one's own because one's neighbors "don't understand." Even for those who have saved a few acres of trees for firewood, the possibility always exists that an envious neighbor will torch it, as happened in Pelillo Negro in 1993. As Petronilo ruefully concluded, with people as divided as they are by religion, envy, and feuds, it is miraculous that anyone would want to fund aldea projects.

The problems of a handout culture, swindling, and envy can be overcome with good leadership, but nowadays leaders are often suspected of ulterior motives. When Cresencio, for example, volunteered his time to make an adobe oven for a school kitchen in a neighboring community, some parents refused to let their children work on the project without pay. In his own community, neighbors rejected his development group's offer to build terraces free of charge on their land because they surmised that it would rob the soil of its fertility. In another project, accusations of favoritism eventually halted the construction of a development center and split the beneficiaries into two groups. In another community, distrust between one barrio and the rest of the aldea was always rife whenever a project was initiated. At one community project meeting, accusations of corruption were so rampant that the community demanded food in exchange for cooperation. In a potable water project meeting, after twenty minutes of accusations about who would benefit the most, participants began to accuse and counteraccuse each other of misappropriating bags of cement and wire from a preexisting latrine project, because 21 of 260 homes lacked sufficient materials for construction. In another aldea, the acceptance of a broccoli project by some families prompted a rash of stealing of sprinklers and broccoli, followed by a series of sorcery accusations.

Projects attempting to organize across communities fare even worse. When Carlos began organizing a cooperative for Ch'orti' artisans, others began to undermine the project by saying that leaders of cooperatives always launder funds, that cooperatives are dangerous because they threaten Ladino businesses, and that a cooperative would not be able to compete with the cheaper prices of nonmembers. The Academy of Maya Languages (see next chapter) faced similar skepticism when it began organizing in the Ch'orti' area, some pointing to the leadership's inability to account for funds and others arguing that their aldeas or campesinos were suspiciously underrepresented.

By now some readers may be outraged that I have portrayed Ch'orti's as contributing to their own problems. If one takes the theoretical stance that all is struggle, agency, and praxis, then I am misguided. If one takes the ethical stance that the poor, discriminated against, and oppressed are angelic, then I am blaming the victim. Some have congratulated themselves for criticizing Oscar Lewis along these lines—overreading his "culture of poverty" as a self-reproducing organism driven by aggression, short-sightedness, depression, and fatalism—despite his tremendous strides in bringing the corrosive aspects of poverty to the First World's attention (Lewis 1959, 1966). I have tried to leave no opportunity for such misreading here, emphasizing that self-destructive practices are rooted in broader sociopolitical and economic contexts, and that what is destructive at the community level is sometimes practical at the individual level. The competing culture of work must also be kept in mind. Nor do I wish to insinuate that Ch'orti's, development projects, and state services are condemned to failure by historical circumstances. If projects take Ch'orti' cultures and social pressures into consideration, they will have a much higher success rate. If development promotes the senses of inclusion, pride, motivation, and hope, then these are successes in their own right, as will be seen in the next chapter.

EIGHT

The Ch'orti' Maya Movement

One does not have to lose one's pride.
Uno no tiene que perder su orgullo.
— Ch'orti' ex-recruit

Our blood is always Ch'orti'.
Kach'ich'er Ch'orti' sieeempre.
—Benjamín, former Ch'orti' Radio announcer

We will no longer be known as indigenous
peoples, but as Ch'orti's.
—Rigoberto, Ch'orti' leader

Richard Adams (1996) has identified a pattern of indigenous ethnic abandonment in Guatemala. In townships where Ladinos, or non-Mayas, constitute over 15% of the population—as is the case throughout the Ch'orti' region—distinctive indigenous culture and identity tends to be abandoned rapidly. The Ch'orti' predicament offers some explanations. Ladinos by definition occupy the role of mediator between local politics and the state, and between local and global markets. As the indigenous subsistence lifestyle has been undermined, Mayas are compelled to become dependent on the market and therefore the Ladinos, but Mayas have little experience in Ladino culture. Ladinos take advantage of Maya vulnerability by artificially cheapening Maya labor, products, and persons. Moreover, Mayas have faced repression whenever they have organized to counteract Ladino tactics. Many have chosen simply to abandon their indigenous ethnicity as best they can, especially in situations where Ladinos are present. Some even take the Ladino ideology of indigenous inferiority and backwardness to heart, feeling that they were foolishly naive to believe that they were at the center of the world, because they are really at the margins of the global market. They base their identity in new options such as religions, the army, and consumerism. Others, including those who have tried to become Ladino but found themselves excluded by racism, have taken everyone by surprise by uniting to forge a new, positive Maya identity. I was fortunate to be present when this movement gained momentum in the Ch'orti' region in 1992.

While many development projects have inadequately dealt with problems of ethnic identity and even exacerbated them, the Maya Movement attends foremost to ethnic pride. Some development experts like Kleymeyer (Kleymeyer, ed. 1994) see "culture," or historical self-recognition, as essential for the proud identity, optimism, self-esteem, vitality, unification, and courage needed to motivate marginalized peoples. In the words of indigenous leader Jorge Arduz, "to be productive, man has to value himself, which means being able to understand where he stands in society and history" (Breslin 1994:46). Valuing indigenous knowledge and reconstructing their history through autoethnography, radio, plays, musical performances, craft fairs, poetry, local museums, and native language courses can produce the "cultural energy" (Kleymeyer, ed. 1994) necessary for sustained development, rather than letting it crumble as soon as the project personnel leave the area. After all, indigenous peoples have the greatest investment in and knowledge of the places they inhabit (Kleymeyer 1994:197).

The Maya Movement

It is difficult to pinpoint when the Maya Movement started, as many pathbreaking events in Maya organizing occurred in western Guatemala in the twentieth century (Fisher 1996; Bastos and Camus 2003). R. Adams (1996:20) writes that the political opening of 1945–60 provided many Mayas the opportunity to abandon their Indian identity, but when they realized soon thereafter that the Ladino alternative was hollow, the seeds of indigenous activism were planted (see Fisher 1996). One could argue that Catholic Action Network in the 1960s–70s, which united Mayas under the rubric of liberation theology and grassroots development, was in a sense a pan-Maya movement even though its methods ultimately led to the adoption of Western cultures (Bastos and Camus 1996:20–22). Starting in 1972, "Indigenous Seminars," or conferences on Maya languages, also united Mayas, especially schoolteachers, while the Francisco Marroquín Linguistic Project (which researches, publishes, and teaches Maya languages) was being formed (Bastos and Camus 1996:24–25). Such ethnic organization was severely repressed during the massacres of 1979–83.

As the army sought to placate international investment in the mid-1980s by diminishing the repression and allowing democratic elections, some popular organizations courageously emerged and joined with the overall resistance movement. They demanded the rights of widows (CONAVIGUA), relatives of the disappeared (GAM), the displaced (CONDEG), the forcibly recruited (CERJ), and others severely affected by the violence, and were thus regarded as subversives by the army (Bastos and Camus 1996:9). None of these groups had explicitly ethnic or Maya objectives, but their memberships were largely Mayas, as Maya men, women, children, and elders were the main victims of repression (Bastos and Camus 1996:70–71, 81). Their ethnic consciousness, in fact, had been raised by the army's attack on themselves and their means of cultural regeneration (Bastos and Camus 2003:94). Meanwhile, the guerrillas claimed to be the defenders of the Mayas (Bastos and Camus 2003:72–73), although they themselves attacked the Tojil Indian Movement, the first multifaceted Maya movement in the 1980s, which included the Ajpub' military branch (Bastos and Camus 2003:65–66). In 1990 the popular organizations united with international indigenous groups in the Campaign of 500 Years of Resistance, procuring Guatemala as a site for the 1991 II Continental Encounter of 500 Years of Indigenous and Popular Resistance and initiating the campaign to have Rigoberta Menchú named for the 1992 Nobel Prize for Peace. They united under the Maya Coordination Majawil Q'ij, or "New Dawn," which integrated the popular organizations' sociopolitical agenda with an indigenous one, as the recovery of traditions and promotion of Maya religious ceremonies and marimba celebrations became important (Bastos and Camus 1996:59–61, 96–98, 2003:93, 101).

Meanwhile, other Mayas, feeling disenfranchised by the popular resistance movement, were more quietly organizing around the issues of ethnic autonomy and language preservation, emphasizing "cultural" rights over human rights (Bastos and Camus 1996:124–25, 168, 2003:99). The first and most important of these groups was the Academy of Maya

Languages, established in 1990 by the Guatemalan congress (Bastos and Camus 1996:102). The mission of the Academy is to train university-educated Maya linguists, promote scientific investigation of Maya languages, stimulate the growth of Maya languages and cultures, teach Maya literacy, publish Maya texts, normalize the use of Maya languages in national society, and provide technical assistance to the state. The state's concern was that the gradual abandonment of Maya languages and cultures was a loss for science and the cause of a destabilizing national identity crisis. Other important "cultural" organizations included the Center of Maya Research and Documentation (CEDIM), Cholsamaj, Association of Maya Writers (AEMG), Kaqchikel Coordination for Integrated Development (COCADI), Center for Maya Cultural Studies (CECMA), and other groups interested in Maya studies and publishing. These groups united to form the Council of Maya Organizations (COMG), the "cultural" counterpart of the "popular" Majawil Q'ij (Bastos and Camus 1996:106–9).

The different tendencies of "popular" and "cultural" groups became starkly apparent in the II Continental Encounter of 500 Years of Indigenous and Popular Resistance held in Quezaltenango, Guatemala, in 1991. One hundred thousand indigenous people united in a march, but COMG felt excluded from the leadership of the event and was angered that general human rights issues overshadowed ethnic ones. Demetrio Cojtí, a leading intellectual of COMG, accentuated the differences between the "cultural" and "popular" Mayas, considering the latter Marxist and not authentically Maya (Bastos and Camus 1996:55, 173–74; cf. Ekern 1998; Stoll 1998:259). For Cojtí (1997:51–52, 70–71), a truly Maya movement must strictly focus on ethnicity over other types of discrimination, like gender and socioeconomic class. He classified Mayas into three general tendencies: 1) proletarians interested in human rights and class issues; 2) the educated middle and lower classes who have a more developed ethnic consciousness but lack cultural authenticity; and 3) campesinos, who are the most authentically Maya but most in need of consciousness-raising. In defining indigenous authenticity, he employed the International Court of Justice's concept of a group of people feeling solidarity based on place, race, religion, language, and traditions.

Despite these differences, the so-called popular and cultural Maya umbrella organizations united in October 1992 to form the Mesa Maya (Maya Table) to participate in the peace negotiations. The Mesa Maya, like other sectors in the Coordinating Committee of Sectors in Civil Society (Coordinadora de Sectores de la Sociedad Civil), felt that their interests at the negotiating table were not represented by either the guerrillas or the army (Bastos and Camus 1996:52–53, 175–76, 2003:98). This Maya coalition soon splintered but then united again in 1994 with a stronger ethnic agenda (Cojtí 1997:113–14) to form the Coordination of Maya People's Organizations of Guatemala (COPMAGUA), which led to a flurry of peace negotiations resulting in the momentous 1995 Accord on Identity and Rights of Indigenous Peoples. The accord, which comprised nearly half of all provisions in the overall Peace Accords, states that Guatemalan society has historically been based on discrimination of indigenous peoples, and indigenous identity and rights—linguistic, proprietary (including archaeological sites), spiritual, dress, scientific, educational, media, administrative, political, and territorial—are the most fundamental issues in the country. Though a momentous step towards the inclusion of Guatemala's marginal majority into the national political process, there were few details on how the accord would be implemented.

Ch'orti's into Mayas

Indigenous pride and unity, according to one priest in 1993, is the key to reversing Ch'orti's' major problems:

> Look, in the first place—in my opinion, you know?—there are
> things that must be changed. The Ch'orti' has lived closed in his
> world. They have lived closed in their worlds, and few are those
> who are acquainted with their culture—even those of us who
> live in Jocotán, San Juan Ermita, and Olopa. The mestizos, the
> townspeople, don't know a thing! That's the truth. Nothing!
> And not only don't they know nor understand the Indian,
> what's more, they exploit him. They exploit him. The big
> problem for the Indian in Guatemala generally is that they're
> not organized! There's no organization. The day when the
> Ch'orti's and Guatemalan Indians organize themselves, will be
> the day the country changes. But there's so much individualism.

Indeed, little solidarity exists from barrio to barrio, aldea to aldea, and township to township. Ch'orti' friends and acquaintances even typically turn obliquely away when campesinos from other aldeas strike up conversations with me. But ethnic unity has slowly been undergoing a resurgence. Some Ch'orti's began to value their language and culture due largely to academics and churches. Protestant Bible translation starting in the 1930s, Fought's (1972) study in the 1960s, foreign linguistic initiatives in the 1970s like the founding of the Francisco Marroquín Linguistic Project, and the Catholic Radio Ch'orti' were critical for promoting the value of the language. By the early 1990s Radio Ch'orti' had devised its own language workbook using the Popol Vuh for examples, and had considerable success teaching Ch'orti' to nonspeakers in aldeas like Nochán, Las Pomas, Muyurcó, and Tierra Blanca, where campesinos began writing Ch'orti' songs. Timoteo articulated Ch'orti' pride in 1993 to stir up fellow campesinos at an Olopa political rally: "My language is worth a lot, gentlemen, my Ch'orti' language, because we still have the Radio Ch'orti' in Jocotán, we are in solidarity with our fellow Ch'orti's in Jocotán."

Much more than linguistic pride, the Radio Ch'orti' awakened Ch'orti' ethnic consciousness. Perhaps to the church's chagrin, the Radio Ch'orti' began to have an ethnic edge to its programs. In 1993 Benjamín, a broadcaster of a show on ancient Maya culture, provided me with my only Ch'orti' version of the Spanish invasion:

> What I know is that a long time ago when the other people [Spanish] hadn't arrived, I know that my grandparents told that the land wasn't like it is today. Yes. They worked whatever land they wanted, and little by little they worked, and the same for the river and streams like those of Tunucó and San Juan, where they made canals to plant corn and beans, so that if it didn't rain, they irrigated. That's how they used to do it . . . when it was the dry season they irrigated. That's how they worked long ago, but that's because there were no landowners; they didn't have them before, you know?
>
> But then the other people arrived, and the people were displaced, running if they could, and some were killed, and they left the land while those who we today call Ladino stayed on this land, and we the people went to the mountains over there . . . while the others stayed here. And they went inside the mountain forests to live and hide so they wouldn't be killed, after which the church was built and the people started working here in town again, but they were brought here. They were brought so that the church could be built. And they worked and learned as well about Our Father and that his name is Christ. They were also shown "the next language," Spanish, and they

learned. But it didn't stick with them, or they didn't find
themselves in it. They didn't like it. That's how they did it
before . . . and they lived but they weren't happy because they
were made to go without clothes; there were no clothes because
they used to plant cotton here as well to make their clothes,
but they no longer could work in it because they were seen
and captured to work for just one person, and they worked
long ago, and that's what the five hundred years is all about.

 And we are seeing today that from our perspective our kin
are proliferating here in town, in the mountains, and in the
forests, but the townspeople are not. They don't proliferate.
That is why we are losing our language today, they say. It's
disappearing, everything that our kin knew, like how they used
to pray to Our Father, all is becoming lost. Today the Catholic
religion stands, that's what is proliferating today, as are the
Evangelicals, but what our grandfathers knew is already lost,
it is no longer, like how they used to invoke the power of Our
Father, and they prayed for things as well. . . . Yes, the rituals, all
of that is lost today, it is disappearing, but we're also seeing
today that our kin are learning to write, while before they
were never taught. They never knew how to write, they never
understood the written page, and today they are learning. And
we're seeing today as well that we're already learning to write
our language too by using the other writing, but we're seeing
that we can write our language too, and we're learning to write
it. Well, that's what our grandfathers knew a long time ago.

Benjamín was likely the same radio announcer who explained to
Palma Ramos's (2001:63) research team why he broadcast a program on the
ancient Maya: "We feel here that we're Ch'orti', we come from the same
branch, and we have the same ideas. In the language it's clear that we have
a lot of words that are the same in other Maya languages. For example, for
dog we say '*tzi*' and almost every ethnic group and Maya language it's said
the same." Such an attitude of camaraderie with other Mayas is revolutionary because Ch'orti's have never seemed to identify with them. They often
refer to the Occidente Mayas as cobanes, and consider them exotic with
their different clothing and languages. Yet, the potential for unifying with
them has always existed, as they share similar languages, traditions, and
the stigma of being "Indians." Some Ch'orti's have mentioned friendships

made with Occidente Mayas on the plantations, and they are impressed with their lack of ethnic shame. Félix's son, for example, who had recently returned from army service, contemplated,

> I have seen many cases in which townspeople belittle one who is here from the aldea, but some say that one must feel proud, and an Indian must feel proud. . . . One does not have to lose one's pride. And as many people here say about the Occidente, as you say, right? They feel *proud*, you know, to know the language that they have because they haven't left it. . . . One has to feel proud like that, because much of what is the people's custom, of what is indigenous, much has been lost, you know. And those who are "the new people" right now have already changed a lot in regards to clothing, you know, something like that, but not before.

In 1992, in the middle of my extended fieldwork stay, "a revolution in thought and action on par with the life of Jesus," as one activist put it, began when Occidente Mayas in the Academy of Maya Languages and Majawil Q'ij began to organize in the Ch'orti' area. They attracted Ch'orti' bilingual teachers, development leaders, radio personnel, and religious leaders to their workshops, who in turn recruited Ch'orti' campesinos in their communities. Like a religious conversion, hundreds of Ch'orti's generally overcame their traditional distrust of outsiders and suspicions of embezzlement by local leaders, and were taken by the idea that ashamed "Indians" should appreciate their languages, cultures, and histories by unifying under "Maya" ethnicity (cf. Bastos and Camus 2003:18).

The "cultural" Academy of Maya Languages promoters—often professionals who impressively dressed in suits, used sophisticated language, and yet embraced their indigeneity—stressed that Maya imagery must be changed from that of "idolaters, savages, loafers, idiots, idlers, conformists, fools, brutes, *tixudos*, pigs, sandal-wearers, etc." to that of "the original people of this continent." They argued that Maya ethnic identities must be preserved for "a reason for being," "the intrinsic need for difference," "to resolve the Maya identity crisis," and because Maya traditions are morally superior to Western ones. For Mayas, the Earth is a nourishing mother who should be respected rather than exploited, Maya languages do not privilege masculinity over femininity, and Mayas traditionally respect their elders. Such discourse is echoed by national Maya leader Raxché (1996:80), "after five hundred years of aggression the effects can still be felt: each day we lose more of our profound respect toward Mother Nature, respect toward our elders, and reverence toward our dead. Each day we dehumanize ourselves more, a result of alienation from our worldview." The Occidente Maya leaders struck a chord with their Ch'orti' audiences by blaming the abandonment of central elements of Maya traditions, like language, surnames, history, cosmovision, music, dress, crafts, and the number system on foreign economic, political, and economic impositions. Explanations of cosmovision, ethnicity, human rights, and the Spanish invasion whetted Ch'orti' appetites for more knowledge, and leaders promoted literacy to combat centuries of discrimination. The workshops were also cathartic in that tense issues characteristically suppressed, like the clash between the older and new generations, men and women, and the army and guerrillas, were brought to the table and debated face to face.

The "popular" Majawil Q'ij began a series of even more energetic and political workshops in Jocotán during the week of the Columbian Quincentenary in 1992. Contrary to criticisms that Majawil Q'ij was simply a guerrilla puppet organization that privileged class warfare over ethnic autonomy, in the Ch'orti' region Majawil representatives emphasized respect for Maya culture, ethnic identity and unity as well as human rights, and did not rule out alliances with non-Mayas like myself. In fact, the Ch'orti's had largely rejected one of Majawil Q'ij's principal backers, the Campesinos Unity Committee (CUC), in the 1970s (Bastos and Camus 1996:64), perhaps due to their experience of repression in the campesino leagues in the 1960s, but many now enthusiastically embraced Majawil's ethnic goals. They called for equal political representation, "a true democracy," and demanded the rights to health care, education, housing, work, better salaries, and technical assistance because Mayas have been serving the state for centuries but have received little in return. They called for not just state services, but Maya inclusion in the state; not just more education, but Maya schools; not just the discussion of Maya rights in the peace process, but representation by Mayas; not just funds for promoting Maya languages, but the nationalization of Maya languages; not just recognition of the suffering caused by the Spanish invasion, but an official apology from the Spanish government; and not just state support for Maya museums, but financing for the manufacture of disappearing Maya crafts.

Among the many themes for which Majawil found an enthusiastic Ch'orti' audience was religion. Majawil introduced Occidente Maya concepts of the four directions, the four colors, and the four elements (fire, water, earth, and air), masculine and feminine complementarity, animism, and copal-burning Maya "priests," which were immediately recognizable to Ch'orti's. The very discussion of indigenous spirituality in public forums was electrifying.

Majawil's treatment of history was also exhilarating. The promoters explained the Maya calendar and the background of the Spanish invasion, including how divisiveness between various Maya polities weakened resistance. They told how colonial institutions enabled the exploitation of Maya labor and lands, comparing reducciones (forced concentrations) with the army's model villages. They described independence from Spain in 1821 as a power grab by the greedy American-born Creoles, stressing that the real independence movement was waged by K'iche' rebels Atanasio Tzul, Lucas Aguilar, and Manuel Tot. They depicted President Barrios (1871–85) as a thug who suppressed the use of Maya names and dress. When one young Ch'orti' blamed the elders for never teaching them any of this, a Majawil promoter corrected him: it is the fault of the Creole/Ladino educational system and mass media.

Majawil's representation of contemporary Guatemalan politics fell on fertile ground as well. They accused politicians of deceiving Mayas by buying their votes, the congress of corruption, and national human rights commissions of passivity. They urged Ch'orti's to unite with labor unions, student groups, and even international organizations truly interested in Maya rights, and to follow the news, while scolding two Ch'orti' leaders for saying that national politics is of no concern to them. One of the most effective political activities consisted of sending two Ch'orti' representatives to recently returned refugee settlements in Playa Grande in May 1993. For whatever reasons, many Ch'orti's had doubted the horrific stories of massacres in the Occidente, but the outraged emissaries reported that refugees were unable to farm alone for fear of army sniper fire and aerial bombardments, such as that of May 14, 1993. Army helicopters flew over regularly accusing the refugees of subversion and closely guarded mature coca and marijuana fields. Most stirring for the emissaries were the realizations that refugees are "just like us" but "the army treats them like animals," and that foreign human rights workers show solidarity by sharing danger with the refugees.

Reflecting their background in the resistance movement and their experience of repression, Majawil leaders did not shy away from criticizing the army and the oligarchy. They called for a reduction in the size and power of the army, the abolition of Civil Defense Patrols, and redistribution of wealth. They condemned the army for massacring and stealing from thousands of Mayas, while guerrillas, though fighting against injustice, were criticized for placing Maya communities in danger of army attack. At times they seemed to place a thin Mayanist veneer over more popular human rights goals. To paraphrase their charter, they intended to give voice to the voiceless, proclaiming "enough with displacement, with poor working conditions and salaries, and with military repression," thereby reversing five hundred years of discrimination, oppression, and exploitation of themselves and "Our Mother Earth." In December 1992 at a rally to commemorate Rigoberta Menchú's Nobel Prize and the International Year of Indigenous Peoples, one coordinator urged, "it's time that we end the slow death caused by hunger and misery; the marginalization and discrimination that we suffer; the forced or involuntary disappearances, tortures, massacres, and extrajudicial executions, as well as forced army recruitment and the Civil Defense Patrols." One of the most popular activities in 1993 was the singing of revolutionary songs, and two of the most popular were "Campesino, Learn to Read" and "It's Not Enough to Pray."

Majawil and Academy activities were cathartic in that they encouraged Ch'orti's to employ new concepts and sharper insights in criticizing others and themselves. Ordinarily, Ch'orti's are extremely cautious about criticizing Ladinos and the army, and some advised me to use only the word *ajchinam* (townsperson) when mentioning Ladinos, but they were emboldened by the meetings. When asked why the Spaniards came to America, many shouted "to enslave," "to wipe out our race," "to rob land," and "to rape women," and some argued that Ch'orti's are still slaves today. Others defined Ladinos as the offspring of Indian women raped by Spaniards, or claimed that the introduction of liquor was a Spanish plot. On October 12, 1992, when the church had arranged a celebration of the Columbian Quincentenary, I happened to pass a friend carrying his turkeys, sick with "the accident" (avian polio or smallpox), to sell in town before they died. With tears of frustration in his eyes he snapped, "while we're dying of hunger and disease, they are celebrating!" Ch'orti's rejected the Ladino classification of Ch'orti' as a "dialect" as well as their distinction between "civilized" and "Indian." Some participants overcame their fear to report that Camotán Ladinos were robbing their lands at gunpoint, which the coordinators assured them was occurring in the Occidente as well. They repeated that the national anthem misrepresents Guatemala to be a free country, and that schools teach government propaganda rather than "the truth," like the Popol Vuh does. When the coordinators rhetorically asked whether Ladinos served in the army, many replied "no, they are never forcibly recruited or serve as soldiers." One ex-recruit revealed that a Ladino contracted the army to kill many innocent families in Camotán. When the discussion reached whether they should obey unjust army commands, an ex-recruit who served in the 1940s said he would rather die. Nevertheless, it was both Majawil and the Academy's policy to welcome Ladino participation at events, and some teachers did attend and began learning Ch'orti'.

Gringos such as the priests, Protestants, and me were not immune to attack either. We were criticized for making money from Ch'orti' secrets, for appropriating authority over the Ch'orti' language, for the United States' loose morals in regards to divorce, and for our overall arrogance. According to Majawil promoters, gringos depict Mayas as monkeylike Indians with tails and feathers, appropriate Maya studies, monopolize the archaeological ruins, and carry artifacts out of the country. My professional justification for attending Jocotán's Ladino-organized Folklore Festival and the Columbus Quincentenary celebration was resentfully discounted by some. At the same time, foreigners' participation at the meetings was deeply appreciated and added an air of importance to events. Whenever I attended seminars and workshops, I was always asked to introduce myself in Ch'orti'—always followed by a resounding applause—and to participate in group activities.

Identifying common targets of criticism helped unify Ch'orti's of different aldeas and townships. Most participants had literacy and more than average education in common, but less educated and therefore less confident participants were encouraged in meeting exercises to shed their embarrassment. For example, at an Academy meeting in 1997, teenage participants were merely asked to come to the front of the room and give their name and aldea. Each young female participant had to be urged for minutes to go through the ordeal, after which she received an ovation. Though Ch'orti's of other townships are still considered strange, as in the case of teenage girls from Jocotán who scrutinized young men from Olopa as if they were from another planet, by the end of weekend seminars the once ashamed and insecure participants begin to feel comfortable with each other.

Perhaps the most frequent targets of criticism were the Ch'orti's themselves. A few leaders who lived in town were criticized for succumbing to the dominant culture and buying televisions or bowing to Protestant linguists. When western Mayas spoke about respecting elders, a few older men took the opportunity to criticize the educated youth for arrogantly forgetting their communities and their customs. One young man admitted that he never knew the importance of "paying" the earth. Prior to the meetings, I had few clues about women's feelings on gender, except that they some-times reject their parents' marriage arrangements, often jealously control household finances, and in rare instances take birth control pills behind their husbands' backs. Thus, their attacks on men in meetings devoted to gender were revelatory, as was some men's flippant dismissal of them. At one meeting two female coordinators—a K'iche' and a Pokomam—divided the women and men into gender-segregated groups to list their contribu-tions to the family and the community. Beyond listing obvious duties like cooking and childcare, the women's groups complained that domestic tasks prevent their public participation, husbands and fathers come and go as they please while not permitting women to leave home or attend school, and men do not appreciate the sacrifices of giving birth. The coordinators supported the women's complaints, and the K'iche' man scolded:

> [T]he women are always ashamed, and the men treat them like children, but there's no reason to be afraid. What do the men say when their children walk far from home? They say, "here comes the car," or "here comes a toad," or "here comes the gringo" [asking my pardon], and they scare the women the same way. The women should have their own permanent groups, their own cooperatives with their own store. The women should have the same liberty to drink and dance as the men. . . . [laughs] They shouldn't marry and have kids so soon, and many have told me that they don't know why they married. Women must vote. We can't marry and have kids so young, it's now the fault of both parents. The gringos are going to the moon and dividing up the Earth, but you can't unite to vote someone into congress.

As Maya demands were being met at the national level in the Peace Accords, the Academy and Majawil set up regional Ch'orti' offices. The first Ch'orti' Academy Executive Council was founded in 1993 and is elected every three years. In the beginning, it emphasized teaching Ch'orti' and Ch'orti' literacy and attracted a broad range of students, including Ladino teachers. Rural literacy promoters earned about $27 per month to teach roughly ten students apiece for a purported twenty hours a week, and classes were soon held in eighteen aldeas.[1] Guatemala's National Coordination for Literacy (CONALFA) complemented the Academy's literacy program in 1996, employing an additional twenty-one bilingual literacy promoters in Olopa, Camotán, and Jocotán at a salary of about $30 per month. The Academy has held intermunicipal poetry contests and regularly met with education officials, concerned citizens, and representatives of nongovernmental organizations (NGOs) to discuss the integration of Ch'orti' language and culture in the educational curriculum. From the late 1990s to 2003, it was devoted to publishing texts, largely abandoning instruction. In 2004 the focus returned to teaching, but this time with trained and better-paid teachers rather than part-time aldea instructors.

Majawil (then under the title Maya Unity and Consensus Tribunal, or IUCM) established the Ch'orti' Maya Regional Coordination in 1994 (eventually known as COMACH), which defined its goals as 1) rescuing culture, 2) bolstering indigenous identity, 3) promoting bilingual education, and 4) protecting rights and dignity. Though the IUCM trained Ch'orti' leaders to a minor extent, most of its assistance came in the form of funding for seminars, offices, transportation, and wages of the executive committee and rural promoters. The COMACH executive council was divided into a women's committee, an elders' committee, a land recovery committee, and an education (Ch'orti' literacy) committee. By 1998, thirty-eight promoters were working in twenty-nine aldeas of Jocotán, Olopa, Camotán, San Juan, and Chiquimula, and were earning $30 per month teaching Ch'orti' literacy, history, "social studies," and "cultural geography" (place names, herbal medicine, etc.) four afternoons per week to 1,120 registered aldea students.[2]

---

1. Participating aldeas have included: Limón in Camotán; Tuticopote Abajo, Tuticopote Arriba, and Roblarcito in Olopa; and Oquen, Escorial, Guareruche, Pelillo Negro, Las Flores, Tierra Blanca, Pacrén, Tunucó Abajo, Suchiquer, Amatillo, and Canapará in Jocotán.

2. Jocotán: Tierra Blanca (4); Guareruche (2); Pelillo Negro (2); Suchiquer (2); Pacrén (1); Candelero (1); Matazano (1); Los Vados (1); Guaraquiche (1); Canapará (1); La Arada (1). Registered students = 538.

   Olopa: Guayabo (3); Tituque (2); Sectorcafetales (1); El Chucte (1); Piedra de Amolar (1); Rodeo (1); El Tablón (1); Valle Nuevo Rodeo (1); Laguna Cayur (1); Talquezal (1); Las Pomas (1). Registered students = 392.

   Camotán: Shupá (2); Shalaguá (1); Brasilar (1); El Volcán (1). Registered students = 140.

   Chiquimula: Nueva Esperanza (1). Registered students = 30.

   San Juan Ermita: San Antonio Lajas (1). Registered students = 20.

The average age of the promoters was thirty-seven, with the youngest at twenty and the oldest at sixty, including three women, and they had an average educational level of 4.1 years of schooling, much higher than the general population, where 68% of households (297/436) had a total of only one year of education or less in 1993.

Much of the COMACH teachings involved the underlying theme of overcoming intimidation to defend one's rights. Pedro, director of cultural activities until 1996, explained what he meant by "rights":

> [B]ecause they never respect our rights in the municipal
> tribunal. For example, if I'm the mayor and an Indian arrives
> and is at the head of the line, but I see one of my acquaintances,
> I say "ah good, come on forward." They always call forward their
> Ladino friends, and one may have walked for hours, days, to
> pay for a birth certificate. So they pay no heed to the fact that
> I was there first. So we go to the communities and write and talk
> about it, and the people say "ah, well you've already learned,"
> and they remain thinking "that's the way it happens, isn't it."
> We ask them "is it the truth, or not?" "It's the truth," they say,
> "Ah, yes it is, just like that." In whatever store it was always like
> that. So we've been fighting against that; that's what we've been
> working on.

The UN Human Rights Mission (MINUGUA) also began holding many well-attended human rights workshops in conjunction with COMACH in 1994. At one meeting, Ch'orti's were quick to understand the violation of rights by the army and the guerrillas, but MINUGUA emphasized that the police or judges can violate human rights as well. The visual materials and exercises MINUGUA provided, including coloring books for children and poster scenes to be interpreted by participants, were very effective in reaching many semiliterate Ch'orti's.

In 1996–97 the Rigoberta Menchú Foundation and the United Nations Program for Development paid and trained several Maya representatives, including Pedro among the Ch'orti's, to explain the Accord on Identity and Rights of Indigenous Peoples to Mayas in rural Guatemala. Pedro gave seminars on the accord in Camotán, Jocotán, San Juan, and Olopa to over two hundred participants from forty-one aldeas. Attendants from Olopa admitted that they knew nothing about the accord until the seminar, and in Camotán some campesinos had to ask "what is the URNG [the guerillas]?," "who are the criollos [Creoles] and the indígenas?," and "did the Spanish live here before us?" Some equated any mention of human rights or the Peace Accords with the guerrillas, especially in Camotán and San Juan, where Maya activism was still weak.

Upon explanation of the accord and the elicitation of questions and comments, some women complained that they are poorly treated by men, they do not control their own work, they are paid little, and the few that find jobs are fired when they become pregnant. They demanded that fathers should not be allowed to prevent children from attending school, that teachers' hours be documented, and that schoolchildren should not be forced to sell raffle tickets. In Camotán particularly, all agreed that "fear must be abandoned," "discrimination should be denounced," and people should organize themselves and elect a representative to protect their identity and rights under the accord. In Jocotán, where much activism had already taken place, the attendants were clearest in their understanding of the accord's importance in overcoming discrimination by public institutions, manipulation by Ladino political parties, teacher irresponsibility and insensitivity, Ladino attempts to dispossess them of their lands, and Ladino accusations that spiritualists are sorcerers.[3] When the participants were asked to draw up a list of demands to the state, the lists were remarkable for people who before had wanted nothing to do with the state (see chart 1, p. 286).

In the late 1990s Ch'orti' campesinos remained highly motivated by the Maya Movement, and ethnic pride was strong. When Majawil arranged

---

3. *Sobre la lucha contra la discriminación: nos han maltratado diciendono indios, en todas las instituciones públicas, por cualquier trámite que necesitamos hacer no nos atienden por ser indígenas, nos humillan y nos ofenden en todas partes, nunca han respetado nuestra dignidad como seres humanos. Manifiestan también que el acuerdo les parece importante porque al cumplirse verdaderamente ellos tienen ya una base para poder defender sus derechos.*

La participación en los asuntos políticos y sociales del país: a ellos no se los permiten porque los consideran ignorantes que no sirven para nada, solamente los utilizan los partidos políticos para llegar al poder y después se olvidan totalmente de ellos, dicen ser engañados por los ladinos.

El idioma: dicen que los ladinos se burlan y se ríen de ellos cuando los escuchan hablar en su idioma, sin embargo aclaran también que se sienten orgullosos de ser indígenas y de ser bilingues, tenemos buen color, nos alimentamos de hierbas, nos mantenemos sanos y fuertes vivimos en ambiente sin contaminación y sin tanta violencia y maldad.

for a Maya priest from western Guatemala to hold a ritual in Jocotán, hundreds of campesinos arrived to witness the event. Many showed little or no hesitation to speak the language with Ladinos present, and Spanish-speaking campesinos who once mocked me for speaking Ch'orti' confidently sprinkled phrases into everyday discourse. Aldeas that had not heard Ch'orti' spoken in over a century, like San Antonio Lajas, San Juan, were eagerly learning the language. At one aldea seminar in Guayabo, Camotán, in 1990, coordination promoter Rigoberto explained, "we will no longer be known as indígenas, nor as the poor or dark-skinned people, but instead as speakers of Ch'orti'." When I introduced a young Ch'orti' man to an elder who knew little of the Maya Movement, I was impressed at the former's reverence for the latter. The elder, with cataracts at the time, could not see the young man's respect, and he lamented that nobody was interested in the elders' knowledge or in "pure Ch'orti'" anymore, but the young man strongly but politely contradicted him.

When I was hitching a ride to Olopa in 1997, a young Ch'orti' man accompanied me and offered to buy me a soda pop, a very generous campesino gift. We had attended a Maya meeting the day before and he was excited that I was a student of Ch'orti' culture and spoke the language. He flagged down a pickup for the both of us and procured a ride, but the driver, with a pistol in his belt, gruffly asked whether I was his guerrilla commander. The Ch'orti' man brushed it off as a joke. Despite the presence of a listening Ladino passenger in the back of the truck, he relentlessly tapped my knowledge of Ch'orti' history and politics on the hour and a half trip to Olopa.

En educación: los ladinos nos han dicho que nosotros los indios nacimos para cargar y trabajar y no para estudiar, y por eso muchos maestros de nuestras comunidades van a trabajar a veces sólo uno o dos días a la semana, además ellos también han contribuido a que se haya perdido en gran parte nuestra identidad porque nos exigen que les pongamos a nuestras hijos uniformes que ellos quieren, y que no hablemos en Ch'orti' diciendonos que no sirve.

En cuanto a nuestra cultura: se ha perdido porque nuestras autoridades nos han obligado a olvidarnos de ellas amenazándonos y tratándonos de brujos, lo que en algunas comunidades se realiza se hace en forma secreta porque existe temor.

Con respecto a la tenencia de tierras: han habido autoridades que han querido despojarnos de nuestras tierras siendo comunales hasta ahorita no lo hemos permitido.

Chart 1: Needs Expressed by Ch'orti' Area Campesinos, 1997

1. Land
2. Communal indigenous lands
3. Interest-free credit for agriculture
4. Technical training in agriculture
5. Better seeds
6. Technical support for soil conservation
7. Reforestation projects
8. Improved environment
9. Lower prices for fertilizer
10. Pesticide applicators
11. Tool/equipment aid
12. Markets for crafts and agricultural produce
13. Lower prices for staples
14. Employment
15. Fair salaries
16. Home improvement
17. Stoves
18. Potable water
19. Latrines
20. Electrification
21. Education
22. More capable teachers and health workers
23. Bilingual schools
24. Bilingual high schools
25. Indigenous scholarships
26. Time for children to study
27. Parental control over school hours
28. School meals
29. A typing school
30. Aldea pharmacies
31. Affordable medicine
32. Eradication of malaria
33. Food for the elderly
34. Veterinarians
35. Aldea meeting houses
36. Roads and paths
37. Bridges
38. Transportation, vehicles
39. Irrigation works
40. Aldea radios
41. Aldea sewing workshops
42. Aldea carpentry and masonry workshops
43. Aldea bakeries
44. Aldea corn mills
45. Support for traditional music
46. A Ch'orti'-Spanish dictionary
47. A local Rigoberta Menchú Foundation office
48. Promotion of Ch'orti' clothing
49. Reinforcement of beliefs about celestial movements
50. Laws protecting women from exploitation by the Folklore Festival
51. Equal treatment for Indians in hospitals
52. Teaching of indigenous spirituality by the elders
53. Reconstruction of ceremonial centers
54. Oratories
55. The construction of rural Evangelical temples
56. Soccer fields and recreational centers
57. Direct access to international funding
58. Women's participation
59. Political participation
60. Prohibition of armed security forces in the aldeas
61. An investigation of illegal arms possession
62. Elimination of terrorists
63. Indictment of corruption

The Maya Movement at the Crossroads

Even as the Peace Accords were signed in late 1996, the united front of Maya organizations was showing fissures. Perhaps due to the oligarchy's economic interests, the difficulties defining indigeneity, and lack of public backing (Holiday 2000:79), contentious issues remained unresolved and irreconcilable between the Mayas, the state, and the guerrillas, including collective and historical land rights, traditional forms of leadership, and political autonomy (Warren 2001:149; Bastos and Camus 2003:152). Due in part to international pressure, the PAN government collaborated with COP-MAGUA in forming eight commissions (Educational Reform, Officialization of Languages, Participation at All Levels, Spirituality and Sacred Places, Women, Rights, Constitutional Reforms, and Land Rights) to implement the Accord on Identity and Rights of Indigenous Peoples. While many new groups were splintering from the guerrilla-aligned organizations (Warren 2001:158), the COPMAGUA representatives on the commissions tended to remain aligned with them. These "popular" Mayas had more negotiating experience and felt that the middle class "cultural" Mayas were not true Mayas because they were not campesinos. The guerrilla influence in COPMAGUA was resented by many, but not the PAN government, with whom they shared the legacy and political capital of the Peace Accords. Ultimately, the representatives gradually abandoned the broader COP-MAGUA and Mayanist goals as they became entrenched in their commission employment (Bastos and Camus 2003:133, 154–55, 157, 165–66, 188, 262).

The PAN government, representing the oligarchy, was willing to accept credit for negotiating the Peace Accords but was not strongly committed to carrying them out. For example, the Secretariat of Peace, in charge of bringing government projects and policy in line with the Peace Accords, was a minor office, and the new Fund for Indigenous Development (FODIGUA) was made a suboffice of the National Peace Fund (FONAPAZ) and staffed with inexperienced administrators (Bastos and Camus 2003:169, 123). The government also retracted an income tax in favor of raising the regressive sales tax from 7% to 10%, cynically calling it the "peace tax" (IVA-Paz) (Bastos and Camus 2003:170). Underhanded PAN party and guerrilla collusion severely weakened Article 203 of the constitution, originally meant to address Maya autonomy (Bastos and Camus 2003:197). Mayas on the commissions were at a distinct disadvantage in negotiations due to lack of experience, qualifications, contacts, money, and access to government data, as well as being vulnerable to the political pressure (Bastos and

Camus 2003:175). Despite these setbacks, the commissions were invaluable introductions to government process, policymaking, and party politics for Maya leaders (Bastos and Camus 2003:185).

In May 1999 the PAN government's poor leadership in pursuing implementation of the accords resulted in only 18% of the voting population turning out for a national referendum on integrating the Peace Accords into the constitution (*Prensa Libre* 5/16/99, 5/18/99; *Cerigua* 5/20/99:1). The Supreme Electoral Tribunal had prevented government entities from campaigning on behalf of the accords, and in the final two weeks before the referendum, right-wing groups funded savvy attacks on the accords that preyed on the prejudices of middle class Guatemala City voters, claiming among other things that the constitutional changes would mean the balkanization of the country (Bastos and Camus 2003:206, 208; Holiday 2000:81). Ultimately, the low voter turnout reflected the population's lack of identification with either the guerrillas or the PAN party, and the "no" vote carried the day (Bastos and Camus 2003:171, 205; cf. Bocek 2000:4).

Within months after the failed referendum, PAN lost the national elections in a landslide to the proarmy, antioligarchy (and perhaps anti-Creole) FRG government of former dictator General Ríos Montt. Only in the Ch'orti' region, Guatemala City, and one other department (Petén) did the FRG not receive twice the votes of PAN (Bolaños 1999). Though PAN's achievements included an increase in paved highways by 75%, electric lines by 50%, access to telephone lines by over 200%, and investments in health and education, its structural adjustment policies, in which presidential friends were sold the public telephone company, drew outrage (Holiday 2000:79, 81). No doubt the PAN's mishandling of the Peace Accords was at least partially behind the defeat (Bastos and Camus 2003:212). The new FRG government, after fooling many with its rhetoric of multiculturalism, slowed implementation of the Peace Accords, diminished the size of the government, and committed unprecedented corruption (Bastos and Camus 2003:216, 224).

As for COPMAGUA, northern European donors, who had previously given little oversight to spending, called it to account for itself. COPMAGUA was given an ultimatum to design a plan for the future, but this created internal rancor and two of the "cultural" components, the Academy and the COMG, quit the coalition due to COPMAGUA's guerrilla leanings. After an audit of COPMAGUA's seventeen regional satellite offices, including the Maya Ch'orti' Coordination, funding was cut in 2000 (Bastos and Camus 2003:190–91, 216, 218, 220, 232). This setback, on a general level, was due to

Mayas simply not being ready to become part of the state, and their lack of bureaucratic and accounting skills necessary to interact with international donors and national politicians (Warren 2001:155–56; Cojtí 1997:146, 254). Not only were the "cultural" and "popular" leaders at odds, neither were they in touch with the rural Maya masses (cf. Cojtí 1997:94; Nelson 1999:132, 301; Bastos and Camus 2003:279, 313, 316).

The Ch'orti' Movement Returns to Earth

Campesinos of Jocotán and Olopa were euphoric about the Peace Accords in the late 1990s. Membership in COMACH continued to grow. International peace funds were applied to road construction projects employing multitudes of Ch'orti's and diminishing travel time from Jocotán to the small city of Chiquimula from one hour to twenty minutes. Almost all aldeas were now accessible by pickup, and thanks to incipient migration to the United States and high coffee prices, some campesinos began to own pickup trucks. Ladinos were eager to tell me that, thanks to Peace Accord donations and special attention by the PAN government, many aldeas were finally receiving basic infrastructure like electricity, roads, potable water, and telephone projects. Dozens of new Fe y Alegría Catholic schools and parent-governed schools (PRONADE) were built.

The longer I stayed, though, the more the old problems reared their heads. Population still grew unchecked, and some acquaintances had died of preventable health problems or were murdered. In 1998 coffee prices fell dramatically. Ch'orti's pressed me for large loans of $1,000–$2,000. Electricity, telephones, and potable water were only available to a fraction of households with the money, labor, and confidence to participate in their installation. The campesinos in charge of some projects were trusted by Ladinos but despised and envied by their fellow campesinos. The schoolteachers were grossly underpaid considering their travel to and from aldeas, some automatically failed all students of parents who reported their absences from work to the school superintendent, and many parents continued to refuse to send their children to school. FON-APAZ donations of food and building materials were distributed only to PAN party affiliates, who were then told that they were gifts from PAN (which may explain why the Ch'orti' area voted for PAN in higher percentages in 1999). The newly trained, well-paid police force was more professional but was imposing harsh penalties on chicha vendors and pickup drivers who carried dangerous numbers of passengers. Their operating costs would be sharply cut under the "law and order" FRG government. Hurricane Mitch struck in October 1998, causing considerable erosion and landslides on steep, cleared slopes.

The Ch'orti' Movement began to show problems of its own. Much competition existed for the few high salaried posts. In COMACH, only the president received a salary sufficient for full-time employment of Q700–Q1,250 (about $115–$200) per month, while the rural promoters and teachers' salaries of Q225–Q300 (about $35) per month were insufficient if they really followed the rigorous teaching schedule. For those working in the main offices in Jocotán, low staff salaries meant the inability to afford rent, necessitating walking several hours to and from aldea homes every day or sleeping in the office. Meanwhile, the salary of the Academy president in Jocotán rose to $700 per month, about triple what a campesino family earns per year, while resentful staff and rural promoters' salaries remained around $35 per month. Many have wondered whether Occidente Mayas receive higher priority. One rumor had it that at Academy national conventions, the national directors are given rooms at the most expensive hotels, while the local representatives must pay for their own room and board. At the local level, suspicions of corruption have been incessant, and a few leaders have been removed from office for embezzlement. Some of the suspicions are related to Ch'orti's' inexperience in bookkeeping and paperwork. One man said he quit COMACH because he spent more time accounting for pennies than doing outreach. Another side of the salary problem is commitment to the movement. One friend who claims to value the Ch'orti' language, refused to teach it for the Academy four afternoons per month because the salary ($14 per month) was too low. In fact, even when the salaries were doubled, many teachers, who may not have been qualified to teach to begin with, abandoned their posts. Another activist told me that if he found ancient Maya artifacts, it would be unthinkable to donate them as patrimony to a museum if he could sell them for the equivalent of a twenty-five-pound bag of corn.

The emphasis on educated leadership, especially in the Academy, has also spawned resentment and, at minimum, apathy by campesinos. Some say that Academy leaders only sit in town and get fat rather than reach out to uneducated campesinos. In one extreme case, a man with some university education, known for his arrogance, was macheteed by a poor campesino. His brother, also with some university education and a leader in the Academy, retaliated with other family members by hacking the poor man's father and burning his house down, and then exercised their educational and monetary capital by having the poor family impris-oned. The Ch'orti' MINUGUA representative for the aldea, envious of the educated family, accused the Academy leader of heading a criminal band. The MINUGUA representative then falsified a petition and sent it to the national office to request the Academy leader's removal. The organization sent a representative to investigate the matter, rebuked the leader pub-licly, but left him in his post.

I witnessed several occasions where younger, educated Ch'orti's con-descended toward campesinos. At one meeting an attendance sheet was passed around, and I showed the man next to me where to sign, but after signing he immediately turned to the older, barely literate man next to him and ridiculed him repeatedly for not knowing where to sign. At the same meeting another demanded that a campesino define "technical assistance" (*asistencia técnica*) and then declared his attempt unsatisfac-tory. Sometimes Ch'orti' leaders have shown little respect for the audi-ence or the topics discussed, as they passed notes, giggled, and walked in and out of the presentations, for which they were commonly criticized during the participants' evaluations. The leaders themselves castigated the general assembly for being unsanitary and undisciplined throughout the meetings. K'iche' representatives were disappointed that elders did not participate as they did in other Maya groups, but the young men insisted that the elderly do not respect them or understand "scientific studies" (*estudios científicos*). One educated leader who was said to have referred to himself as "a philosopher" refused to work with campesinos.

Another major problem has been communication. There are virtually no telephones in the rural areas, and cell phones do not pick up signals in the mountains. In order to pass messages from the town office to the aldeas, such as to confirm or cancel meetings, one must either be fortu-nate enough to find a campesino from that aldea in town, or travel into the mountains by hitching rides and walking, which can take an entire day. It takes only one unannounced meeting cancellation for campe-sinos, who travel hours to attend, to abandon their membership. When seminars and workshops do conform to their original schedules, they often run long to take advantage of attendance. Campesino participants, not used to sitting and focusing in chairs for long periods, have difficulty paying attention to long-winded lecturers who may have little experi-ence. When participants are given the opportunity to evaluate the semi-nars at the end, they turn the tables by accusing the leaders of lack of attention, general lapses in seriousness, and tardiness.

22. *COMACH Ch'orti' classes to Spanish-speaking campesinos,*
    Shalaguá, Camotán.

Hostility by the army and Ladinos has also dissuaded some from participating. Some Ladinos have been quite vocal in condemning "human
rights" as protection for guerrillas, terrorists, and criminals, and some say
the Maya Movement is dangerous. As criminal violence has increased,
Ladinos and Creoles have attacked "human rights" for presumably tying
the hands of the security forces. Any social problem, in fact, is blamed on
human rights. One Ladino claimed that his friend, out of restraint, beat a
campesino with his pistol rather than shooting him, but because of
human rights he still had to spend five months in prison. All the while,
extrajudicial killings of political leaders and human rights workers by the
army and paramilitary groups rose during the FRG government (2000–
2003). Even during the PAN government, an $11 million increase in military spending was budgeted for 1998, only a year after the Peace Accords
were signed (*Cerigua* 12/4/97:2).

A COMACH seminar on Maya cosmovision in 1999, led by a COP-
MAGUA coordinator, exemplified these problems. About sixty campesinos
from several aldeas of various municipios attended, and after two days of

training, they were asked to explain Maya cosmovision and how it is maintained. Answers included healing, respect for nature, the moon, sun, stars, trees, rain, culture, art, language, dress, dances, religion, medicinal plants, crops, animals, and togetherness. The coordinator was frustrated by the slow progress, and replied that the lists were good but explained little. The participants defensively responded that they did not have enough time to prepare. The coordinator then scolded that the Ch'orti's had lost their cosmovision, their beliefs in the end of the world are Christian lies, and their slash and burn agriculture, chemical pesticides, and litter are ruining the land. He also defended his open campaigning in support of the referendum on the Peace Accords, breaking the taboo of mixing the movement with politics. Some Ch'orti's identified the major obstacle in recovering their cosmovision as the dissolution of the elders committee due to unannounced meeting cancellations. The elders by and large are semiliterate and uncomfortable in the seminar settings. One young man blatantly said that the elders committee needed an "educated" leader, at which point the middle-aged COMACH president scolded, "the elders know more than the youth!"

When northern European funders gutted COPMAGUA's budget in 2000, COMACH virtually ceased to operate. However, a year before, the Austrian Cooperation for Development had begun a study of the history of Ch'orti' communal lands, and in 2001 founded a binational Guatemalan-Honduran Ch'orti' project, Proyecto Ch'orti' (PROCH'ORTI'), to mark their traditional territory, title their lands, and ultimately promote Ch'orti' management of their forests. PROCH'ORTI' employed the staff of COMACH and with support from international donors, including Oxfam, FLACSO (Facultad Latinoamericana de Ciencias Sociales), the Spanish Cooperation for Development, and the Jocotán Catholic Parish, it equipped the project with a four-wheel drive vehicle, computers, an office, telephone service, engineers, and legal counsels. From the start, the project ran into difficulties. The titling of aldea lands was fraught with difficulties because contiguous aldeas perceived that they would be losing lands to their neighbors. In one instance, campesinos shot several times at a surveyor trying to measure the lands of a neighboring aldea. Another problem was leadership competition between Ch'orti's and the Ladino professionals until COMACH split from PROCH'ORTI' in 2002. On the positive side, COMACH was provided much technical help in agronomy and founded a successful cooperative for women's crafts, but by 2005 it was on the verge of closing because its principal funder, Oxfam Australia, closed its operations in the Americas, while the Ladino-staffed PROCH'ORTI' continues to operate.

While the hopes and excitement brought by the Maya Movement in the early 1990s have diminished, and many projects have long been abandoned, the movement continues and has had long-term effects. In an area known for voter apathy, Ch'orti' townships voted in higher percentages than the national average in the 1999 referendum, and they voted overwhelming in favor of the Peace Accords. The Maya Movement has reduced apathy about community organizing and politics, for which Guatemala was worst in the Caribbean Basin in 1992 (Portes 2001:235). While government control has oscillated between the oligarchy and the army, the Maya Movement has made transnational alliances that have transcended the nation-state and politically united Mayas (Portes 2001:238; Warren 2001:161; cf. Brysk 1996). This new visibility, self-esteem, and motivation has garnered respect from the Creole/Ladino population (Casaús 2001:227).

An event in Pelillo Negro in 1995 demonstrates the newfound courage. Several Ladinos from state offices visited the aldea to celebrate the inauguration of an aldea road project. The local military commissioners on patrol, perhaps at the behest of the Ladinos, tried to dispossess a drunk campesino of his machete, even though he was threatening no one. In fact, it is common etiquette for campesinos to abandon their machetes when in Ladino public spaces. Many other campesinos defended the drunk's "rights," and in the resulting tussle, the commissioners were overpowered. The commissioners threatened army retaliation. MINUGUA was invited to ease the tension, and the local army lieutenant scolded the commissioners for carrying machetes themselves. Had such a dispute occurred in during the 1960s–80s, assassinations would certainly have followed.

Across the border in Copán and Ocotepeque, Honduras, Chortí (spelling used in Honduras) activism has been more militant and oriented towards land. Self-identified Chortís from both townships have demanded land and rights to proceeds from the Copán Archaeological Park. Nonethnic local movements began in the 1970s when campesinos demanded a minimal amount of land on which to live, to which the state and landowners responded with assassinations and imprisonment. In Copán, one landowner family controlled much of the township, and in 1986 Honduran troops were sent to quell Chortí demands for land, but the dispute continued to simmer. In Ocotepeque, informants recount that rich ranchers with state support began to seize virtually all the valley lands at the turn of the century, much of which remains unused today. The locals have been fighting legally to recover the land ever since.

In 1994 the campesino activists were contacted by Honduran anthropologists and Lenca leaders in the Confederation of Autonomous Honduran Peoples (CONPAH) to organize as indigenous peoples, and were encouraged when the government signed the ILO #169. They formed CONIMCHH (Confederación Indígena Maya Chortí de Honduras) and soon began to reclaim their ethnic heritage t land. As their demands were met with violence and government stonewalling, the intensity of the conflict heated up, including two marches on Tegucigalpa in 1997.

In July 1996, I rode a bus next to a friendly Ladino who was at once an Evangelical preacher, Copán hotel owner, and owner of three and a half acres of coffee. He told me that unlike in Guatemala, with its hands tied by human rights laws, vigilantes were taking care of crime in Honduras. I asked him how the vigilantes sorted the criminals from the innocent. He replied, "we never make mistakes." I forgot about our conversation until I heard of assassinations and the imprisonment of thirty-six Chortí protestors in 1996, and then the April 1997 assassinations of CONIMCHH leader Cándido Amador by Ladino landowners in Copán. The literate and savvy Amador, who had once been a tour guide in the Copán Archaeological Park, was not an original founder or office holder in CONIMCHH, but his public courage and distinctive long hair made him an easy target for assassination. After his assassination, fifteen hundred Chortís marched on the town of Copán Ruinas, sending townspeople to hide behind locked doors. They also blocked the suspected assassin from entering his land and twice uprooted his crops. A few weeks later, Oviedo Pérez was assassinated, presumably for refusing to provide information about CONIMCHH. A few weeks after that, Pedro and I walked to Carrizalón, Copán, to investigate. No campesinos acknowledged our presence. We approached two boys to ask where the aldea leaders lived, but they eerily said they knew nothing. We only received cooperation when we managed to find a leader who was a distant relative of Pedro's.

The assassinations and government foot-dragging motivated two marches on Tegucigalpa in 1997. Copán and Ocotepeque Chortís were joined by other Honduran indigenous peoples. They invaded the Costa Rican embassy, demanded asylum, and, when it was refused, staged a month-long hunger strike. On Columbus Day they joined Lencas in destroying the Statue of the Navigator (Columbus) national monument. The Lencas, who have also had several leaders assassinated and much land stolen by non-Lenca landowners, renewed protests in January 1998, when four hundred US troops were stationed on their land on a "humanitarian mission" (*Latinamerica Press* 1/22/98:7). The state subsequently signed a treaty promising to buy twenty thousand manzanas (about thirty-five thousand acres) for Ch'orti's, but only bought six thousand. After more reneging by the government, in August 2000 the Honduran Chortís once again blocked the entrance to Copán Archaeological Park. This time the townspeople, supported by the police and a military helicopter, attacked the protesters with tear gas and clubs, injuring two hundred peacefully protesting campesinos.

The Honduran government has argued that these so-called Chortís, who especially in Ocotepeque have European and African features like blue eyes and kinky hair, are not authentic, and has threatened to genetically test their teeth for Native American features. CONIMCHH members, however, point to their cultural heritage, including their respect for the forest, worship of saints, enactment of traditional dance dramas, use of herbal medicine, subsistence maize agriculture, consumption of various types of tamales, and continued occupation of Antigua Ocotepeque after the county seat was moved in the 1930s (see Fought 1972:96–99). In contrast to Guatemala Ch'orti's, they distinguish themselves by class from "the rich" (*los ricos*), not the "Ladinos." The government has counteraccused the Copán Chortís of being Guatemalan immigrants with no ancestral rights to Honduran territory. By 2005, the government was refusing to buy the promised lands because it simply did not have the money.

Indigenous Maya Ch'orti's

I . . . only that I tell you, that we're thinking that everything
today is being lost, we need put our heads together again, right?
Nen . . . jaxtaka inwa're't pues, que war kab'ijnu que
tunor xe' koner war asatpaaa, uk'antwa' kak'opi watar
otronyajr u't, verdad?

—Benjamín

I set out on this project searching for indigeneity in eastern Guatemala with the foundation of Wisdom's and Girard's works in the 1930s and 1940s. Obviously, much has changed since then, causing me to question not only whether these campesinos are still indigenous, but also the very idea of "indigenous," just as other scholars have. Some strictly apply the term only to those people with a localized, non-Western worldview and subsistence lifestyle. They ask such questions as: If traditions are most likely reproduced when taken for granted and embodied in subconscious routines (Pouillon 1997:19; Lenclud 1997:48; Hervik 1999:124–27), and indigenous movements *consciously* try to "rescue" traditions, are they really indigenous? When people organize beyond local communities and ally with international brokers who espouse such Western concepts as "rights," have not localized indigenous cultural systems been forever shattered? Other academics who err on the side of deconstruction claim to do away with the concept of indigenous authenticity altogether because it is arbitrarily defined and applied, and lends to essentialism, romanticism, exoticism, and nostalgia. So-called indigenous movements are practicing conscious identity politics, exoticizing themselves to garner political and economic capital. Such positions lead Maya leaders like Irma Otzoy (1997:9) to decry that First World academics, very powerful arbiters of indigeneity, can say "with complete comfort and frankness that the Indians of today are not true Indians," while the indigenous people live with the consequences. How can these positions—one a highly strict application of indigeneity, and the other seeking to deconstruct it altogether—be tempered to comprehend the situation of people like the campesinos in the Ch'orti' area? The answer lies partly in renovating the concepts of culture and by extension tradition.

Strict definitions of indigeneity, popularly and academically, tend either to restrict the application of "culture" to some spheres and not others or to approach it as a coherent, integrated, encapsulated system. Popularly, culture is often restricted to non-White people, as if whites had colorless science and rationality and non-Whites had irrational, colorful, exotic culture. Also, some (including the indigenous themselves) conflate cultures with "peoples" or ethnic groups, as if thoughts, behaviors, material settings, and sentiments were innate forces, racial characteristics, or superorganic phenomena. Thus, one encounters such infelicitous phrases as "X culture has resisted . . ." or "Y culture has achieved . . ." (Turner 1993:411–15; Kottak 1997:20–21). Such conflation of people and culture also leads to confusing applications of culture strictly to nations, ethnicities, or civilizations, such that French, Hawaiian, or Maya cultures overshadow contradictory or incongruent cultures within these societies, such as those of the household, community, work, or school. Academically, some ethnographers, especially those of indigenous societies, conceive of cultures as self-regulating functional systems, as generative, coherent mental structures, or simply as an integrated, encapsulated "complex whole," with accompanying models of culture-as-body, machine, or computer (cf. Friedman 1994:67–77).

If one thinks of culture as shared understandings, routines, material settings, and sentiments, people produce as many distinctive but overlapping cultures as the types of ongoing social relationships in which they engage. One can share distinctive jokes, eating habits, spaces, memory, etc., in the home, at work, at school, with friends, within nation-states, or transnationally. Ethnographers themselves create cultures with informants. If individuals are the loci of many different social spheres of cultural production and these social spheres are rife with competition and inequality, then cultures can be contradictory and dynamic, something obscured when cultures are thought of solely as peoples, nations, or encapsulated, functioning entities. If one expects culture to be synonymous with peoples or an integrated system, then people are either indigenous or they are not. People either perpetuate a functioning system or whole called "indigenous culture," or they do not.

Such all-or-nothing approaches are problematic for indigenous peoples who have suffered an onslaught of pressures. They must adapt and adjust culturally to the pressures of globalization or be exterminated, and yet such adaptation and adjustment disqualifies them from the protection, rights, and remuneration of being indigenous. Arbiters of authenticity, with out-moded notions of culture, demand exact continuity, cohesiveness, and political passivity regardless of the circumstances and discourage any indigenous cultural development, like gender reform (Sieder and Witchell 2001; Pyburn 1998; Linnekin 1996:154; Nelson 1999:131, 134, 302–4, 358; Ramos 2000; Wilson 1995; Rappaport and Dover 1996:27, 35; Hale in Fischer 1999:491–92). Perhaps it is not surprising that such an untenable approach tends to be exercised by interested parties, such as the same promoters of globalization, like big business interests in Guatemala (e.g., Nelson 1999:317, 321). They are often willing to recognize indigeneity and accompanying rights until their economic interests are compromised, upon which they decry the lack of indigenous authenticity. But even some indigenous themselves, trapped in the outmoded holistic concept of culture, are overly critical of themselves for not reproducing selected aspects of the ancestors' culture.

At the other extreme, some bent on deconstructionism try to rise above such debates by discarding authenticity altogether. They rightly recognize that people perpetually coconstruct their realities, but this can lead them to claim that all traditions are equally invented or imaginary (cf. Friedman 1994:66–77; Poullon 1997:20; Harkin 1997). Indigeneity, according to this approach, is not based on real historical differences between colonizers and colonized, but on the practical, self-interested inventions of the so-called indigenous and non-indigenous, such that all indigenous movements are seen as having no legitimate historical foundations (see Watanabe 1995; Warren 1992:204–9; Briggs 1997). Thus, the only way to identify who is "indigenous" is to observe who is making politics as indigenous peoples. In the end, deconstruction is limited to the conscious politics of identity while attention to cultural differences is deemphasized (for views and counter-views, cf. Hervik 1999:104, 115, 124–25, 191–94; Bastos and Camus 2003:303; Sieder and Witchell 2001:59–60; Nelson 1999:270, 301–3; Handler and Linnekin 1984; Hawkins 1984; Pyburn 1998; Warren 1998:70–74; Mauzé 1997; Rogers 1998; Friedman 1994:141; Watanabe 1995; Briggs 1997; Metz 2001a).

Not just anyone makes politics or could effectively make politics as indigenous peoples because it is widely recognized, even by deconstructionists, that the concept of indigeneity is rooted in real historical conditions marked by traditions, "race," and identities (Nelson 1999:5; Mauzé 1997:12–15). While no society can claim to reproduce unaltered traditions (Brysk 1996), only when using a "discourse bent on accentuating discontinuity" do enduring traditions seem impossible (Friedman 1994:13). Evidence of traditions abounds in Mesoamerica (and everywhere else). Household beliefs and rituals have especially ancient roots (Gossen 1996a; Montejo 1997), and archaeologists and epigraphers have used data from contemporary indigenous cultures to interpret effectively texts over one thousand years old. Mayas themselves recognize the mannerisms and phenotypes of other Mayas regardless of clothing, language group, or context.[1] The rapid unification of disparate Guatemalan communities in the Maya Movement is inexplicable if the newly self-identified "Mayas" did not share some history and traditions (Casaus 2001:224–25). Although much emphasis has been given to *mestizaje* and hybridization, in the end mestizos and Mayas recognize a basic difference between themselves (Beverley 2001:230). This is not because Mayas share a primordial essence that determines their behaviors, but because they reproduce mutually recognizable traditions and share similar histories as colonized peoples. Recognizing the historical foundations of tradition is not to deny identity politics, only to say that caution must be taken so as not to portray *all* indigeneity as purely a political matter of strategic identity (Watanabe 1992:x; Hervik 1999:116).

The most useful, incisive approaches neither overemphasize cultural continuity nor identity politics, but historically and ethnographically investigate the complex, overlapping realms of cultural, political, legal, and economic indigeneity as distinguishable from national or transnational cultures (e.g., Simard 1990:342–45). The reproduction of distinctive culture regarding language, cosmological principles, and kinship, for example, can be key aspects of indigeneity (Casaús 2001:224; Cojtí 1997:70–71).

Some scholars have drawn up cultural continuum models from most distinctively indigenous to most globally integrated (e.g., Mayberry-Lewis 1997), and while such two-dimensional models simplify, they are useful

---

1. Some Maya colleagues and friends have provided anecdotes recounting how they have correctly identified other Mayas even without obvious distinguishing features like language and dress, and Nelson (1999:214) reminds that Ladinos also claim to "know them when they see them."

to think with. Friedman (1994) provides a particularly attractive model because it encompasses indigenous movements and their critics and uses culture, "race," and strategic identity as operating principles. He explains the explosion of identity movements since the 1970s as a loss of faith in modernization, a multiplication of histories and identities that reverse the modernist hegemonic expansion and cultural homogenization (1994:78, 142). Modernist identity for Friedman involves the detachment of the self-controlled ego from larger social networks like kin, family, and community. As autonomous actors, moderns realize themselves as purely disciplined, rational, atomized capital, repressing cultural particularities and natural instincts. He identifies three types of reactionary movements to modernism. Tribal societies, or the Fourth World, are societies never brought under modernist hegemony and therefore still take for granted the correctness of distinctive locally based cultures. A second type involves tribal societies modernized enough to call their centrality into question and know the benefits of individualism, but they remain enmeshed in traditional webs of social relations, continue to practice aspects of their now "marginal" culture, and still remember a more unified way of life. The third type entails groups that have been fully modernized to the extent that their identities are based not on cultural distinctions as much as symbols of "racial," "ethnic," or "national" differences. These movements remember no alternatives to modernity and tend to reproduce the modernist consumerism they seek to escape (1994:87, 97–100, 126). The contradictions of modernism also lead to undisciplined postmodernity, a "return" to the libido, selfishness, unrestrained creativity, spontaneity, and imagined tribalism (1994:92, 95). Postmoderns tend to confront identity in two ways: 1) acute awareness of their own lack of group identity and cynicism about all identity claimed by others, i.e., deconstructionism; and 2) narcissistic consumerism (1994:191, 238).

Far from discounting tradition, Friedman recognizes its importance especially for both tribal societies and partially modernized, semitribal societies. He opposes "a modernist retrenchment of anthropologists and cultural theorists [Hobsbawn and Ranger 1983; Linnekin 1983; Thomas 1989; Gellner 1983]" who express a concern for traditional purity that even the founders of anthropology did not have, and who "have tended to see modern traditionalism as unauthentic, a modern invention that deviates from the true past by virtue of the politically motivated circumstances of its creation" (1994:12–13, 125, 136, 144). Invention must be recognized, but it also must be grounded in particular histories:

Invention is thus grounded in historical conditions and
necessarily in a social and existential continuity. This
continuity is systematically overlooked in a discourse bent
on accentuating discontinuity. The particular combination
of elements that are integrated in a cargo cult, a Kastom
movement, a religious sect or a nationalist or ethnic revolt
can only function if they resonate with the experiences of
the subjects that participate in them. (1994:13).

"Culture is supremely negotiable for professional culture experts, but for
those whose identity depends upon a particular configuration this is not
the case. Identity is not negotiable. Otherwise it has no existence" (1994:140).

Friedman's model transcends essentialism and deconstructionist
cynicism by recognizing varying degrees of indigeneity. Culturally, indigeneity means alterity from modernism and postmodernism, and his
tribal and semimodern tribal societies are the most indigenous. The fully
modernized indigenous are those whose distinguishing features regard
simply race, often place, and strategic invention. Other scholars point to
different operating principles than Friedman's modernist individualism
but recognize punctuated moments of cultural change and indigenous
erosion. Niezan, for example, recognizes that

[A]t some point in the colonization of indigenous nations,
a tremendous disparity between the technology and
organizational powers of dominant and dominated peoples
makes itself felt ... when social and technological powers
are associated with direct assaults on indigenous identity
and esteem through the inherently contradictory vehicles
of racism and assimilation, indigenous societies become
infected with cultural malaise—a widespread sense of
wounded pride, violated honor, and lack of self-esteem.
(2003:12, 19)

Ch'orti' Survival, Survival of Ch'orti's

When the campesinos of the Jocotán Parish and their ancestors have
changed so much over the past 30, 100, and 480 years, to what extent are
they semimoderns with memories of a distinctive integrated lifestyle, or

simply a discriminated against "race" who have been fully modernized? Local Ch'orti' culture has been undermined from within and without over the past century. Their subsistence economy has been under great stress while they have had more access to national and global cultures, and thus more information and options for how to interpret and lead their lives. Access to modern antibiotics and lack of cultural access modern contraception have boosted their population tremendously and put overwhelming pressure on the land. Their political consciousness was stirred by the extraordinary brutality of the Ubico regime, and then nourished by the Arévalo and Arbenz administrations, which introduced electoral democracy, education, modern health care, and agricultural development. Since the 1960s, they have been evangelized intensely by Catholics and Evangelical Protestants. During las ruinas, they were subject to the horrors of global geopolitics. Yet even in the twenty-first century, campesinos in the Ch'orti' region continue to reproduce distinctive cultures and even longstanding traditions, especially in the realms of values, the household, and agriculture (cf. Wilson 1995:318 for Q'ekchi-speakers). This is partly due to the continued faith, especially by the elders, that subsistence agriculture with all its social and religious features is the correct way to live. Elders and some youth still take for granted ancient histories, remedies, cosmologies, and linguistic expressions. Contrary to Ladino cultures, Ch'orti's are accustomed to judge strangers on whether they share food or not, especially tortillas. To give without expecting anything in return is considered a high virtue, and sharing food distinguishes humans from animals, and the saved from the damned (López 2003; López and Metz 2002). Values like reciprocity and humility and notions about the body, sickness, the life cycle, and leadership—whether traditional or not—sharply contrast with Ladino cultures. Overall, campesinos of the Ch'orti' region are more religious, and divine destiny is a concept used especially to explain births, deaths, misfortunes, and one's natural abilities.

Ch'orti's have one foot in a local subsistence lifestyle, and one in modernity, which is not a comfortable place to be. Were Ch'orti's included as equal and respected citizens in a multicultural Guatemalan nation, then they might well give up their indigeneity and would have no need for indigenous organizing. But most have no electricity, read no newspapers, attend no schools, and have limited access to modern health care. Racism and ethnocentrism reinforce an invisible wall between town and aldea social circles. Like Mayas throughout Guatemala (Casaús 2001:229, 234; Pop Bol 2001), campesinos with "Indian" characteristics are subconsciously presumed to be more ignorant, dirty, and immature than those with European features.

Is Maya activism a semimodern movement contributing to the preservation of at least some distinctive indigenous culture, or is it a modern movement unwittingly using global cultures in a futile fight against globalization (Watanabe 1995)? Maya organization at the national and international levels is clearly new, and indeed has been motivated by a cultural crisis with roots in poverty, oppression, and new opportunities in a more integrated, less local world. It is no surprise that we see such disputes about authenticity as "cultural" Mayas condemning "popular" Mayas for being contaminated by Western humanism, while "popular" Mayas accuse the "cultural" Mayas of being elitist and detached from Maya campesinos (cf. Bastos y Camus 1996:168, 174, 183–84, 193; Sieder and Witchell 2001:66; Ekern 1998:76–77; Warren 1998:48; Cojtí 1996; Nelson 1999:20–21; Stoll 1998:206–11). Maya activists complain that Mayas in general are losing respect for nature, exterminating all animals, burning the forests, and dropping the language. Such paradoxes, including the use of Western concepts and Spanish as a lingua franca, have not escaped activists, but most are like Friedman's semi-moderns who remember, value, and practice an alternative lifestyle to some degree rather than parodying it. While the Maya Movement is distant from local community cultures in some ways (see Bocek 2000), it was astounding how quickly Ch'orti's and other "semimoderns" were taken by it (Metz 1998; Warren 2001:157; cf. Bastos and Camus 2003:321).

Some Ch'orti' traditions as well as their experiences of "modernization"—population growth, unjust land distribution, environmental degradation, evangelization, political violence, Western education, corruption, partial national integration, ongoing discrimination, increasing crime, and identity crises—are shared with Mayas of western Guatemala, Chiapas, Yucatán, Belize, and Honduras (e.g., Carlson 1997; Carmack 1995; Watanabe 1992; Wilson 1995; *Latinamerica Press* 1/22/98 for Honduras; Nash 1973; cf. Eber 1995). A unified, nationalized Maya identity emphasizing different values and more autonomy is a logical alternative. At the same time, there will always be postmodern "Maya" cynics who will seek to take advantage of the identity crisis for their own personal benefit.

The Future

I have been in the Ch'orti' area every year since 1990 to visit old friends and acquaintances, hear the news, and find answers to elusive questions.

Are development and national integration, as partial as they are, contributing to a more fulfilling quality of life? Would Ch'orti's feel more satisfied surrendering their ethnic identity, abandoning their new Maya one, and dissolving into the "mestizo" or "Ladino" Guatemalan nation as so many others have done? Was the decade of Maya activism in the 1990s a dramatic shift in Guatemalan history on par with the 1520s, the 1830s, the 1880s, or 1944–54?

In 1993, when I asked interviewees how their communities would fair in twenty years, most did not have a clear concept of the distant future (cf. Gillen 1952:198), and I had to rephrase the question in several ways. Once we understood each other, some, like Macaria, Selma, Gerarda, Joaquina, Tereso and Paulina, thought of the future strictly in terms of their own children and viewed it positively because they will learn how to work and provide for their parents. Others looked to education as their salvation. María remarked that though there is less land today, her kids were going to school and would therefore be able to fend for themselves. Cheo said simply that the future is education. Raul, who sent his eldest boy to school, saw a brighter future because of it. In 2005 his son worked in a gas station outside the Ch'orti' area and was desperately trying to immigrate to the United States. Juliana, a women's development leader, was particularly positive about how national integration was influencing Ch'orti' cultures, especially in regards to machismo and respect:

There is more today I think because, like we women, there is
a respect among us women, with the women as with the men.
There is respect with the men because long ago when they
passed us they only laughed. But today no, because we too are
passing, already accustomed. We say "good morning" or "we
want to go." "OK," they say. Even though we only say a word as
we pass, there is respect, as they don't just fart and laugh as we
walk by. I think there's been a change. There's been a change
because today there's more respect in the minds of the children;
they play at school and they're always hearing advice. I see that
there's plenty of advice that they are given, too, and the same
with the father of the family. They are teaching the children that
there must be respect because, because if they respect another,
whether it's their mothers or not, or if not, their fathers, there
has to be respect. And they give the advice to the kids that they
too have to grow up respectful. They respect people, but why?

Because the father of the family or mother of the family gave advice to their kid that they must respect an elder, a grandfather or grandmother, because their experience is greater. Because an elder should not hear a little kid making fun of them, because, because an elder's time must end. And when one's strength ends one must remain old, but a kid must be respectful because if one's life is also long, one will be treated the same, just as they are seeing the elders over there. So the father of the family indeed must give advice to his kids.

Yes, I see that there's a change in kids today, because long ago there was less respect; there was less before. Today, we understand or participate in the church. The catechist gave us good advice that one must be respectful. Why do we go and listen to God's message? So that there's *respect*. Or if we see that someone is angry with us, we can't be, because we see that one is angry with us, and we are as well and our tongues return the same, or we listen to what they are telling us and we say the same too. Because they always tell us that God doesn't want that. And God told us that he wants us to like each other all the same, because with God we're all the same. It's not that we say that there are a multitude of gods, but always that only one God left family in the world, and God wants to see us doing a good thing. But if we hit each other a lot, they yell at us or make fun of us, and our tongues return the words, and the feud or the anger grows. So they tell us that that's not the way it should be.

Others responded that there would be no twenty years. Others still, like Paulo and Vicenta, Mercedes, and Selma said that life will continue as it always has. Fidel gave a common response when he quipped that he does not know about the future, but he is prepared to emigrate for his kids' sake if the drying trend continues. Tancho, in his late teens, stated that people must start to work together and stop burning their lands or there would be nothing left. Jorge opined that the future lies in land management and ethnic strength. The more the people learn to care for the land and appreciate their Ch'orti' heritage, the better the future will be. Eighteen-year-old Miguel heard that God wants to start the world again, but if not, the future will be better as more people learn to read and write in Ch'orti'. Benjamín, an employee of the Radio Ch'orti' (laid off soon thereafter), agreed that hope lies in ethnic continuity:

We're thinking that everything today is being lost, we need to come and gather our thoughts again, right? So that we don't let everything disappear from our kin who still live here and from those who we know have left Jocotán to live on the coast, in the Petén, right? . . . Because we are seeing that the rest, like those who come and speak Q'eqchi', they all live over there but continue to speak their language, just as one here speaks our Ch'orti' language. We are where we are, just as we speak our language, which is why I say we are kin, right? And I know too that long ago they spoke our language and prayed to God too, and everything they knew was good, right? They weren't ashamed to speak it, and we all lived here, and we lived and entered Copán Ruins. Then the Spanish arrived here, and they came and lived in Jocotán . . . and they settled the rivers and valleys here. And so today we are seeing that we have yet to leave all our language because we still live here, we have already been born here to conserve everything. Like, like our ancestors lived long ago, like they used to think, like they used to pray to God, like they used to pray for rain, like they used to pray for food, everything of God, that's how we must pray as well, because it's as if we think God is angry with us, as they like to say.

Most Ch'orti's take the issue of their indigeneity for granted, but Benjamín provided me with an analysis of Ch'orti'-ness. One is Ch'orti' by "blood" (race) and by choosing to accept the status, as some have Ch'orti' blood but identify themselves as Ladinos. Other Ch'orti's argue that membership must include language, dress, rural habitation, and milpa farming, but he disagreed because he himself dressed as a Ladino and once lived in town. Language is the best marker for identifying a Ch'orti', he conceded, but, regardless of traditions, "our blood is *always* Ch'orti'" (*Kach'ich'er Ch'orti' siempre*).

APPENDIX I: Dwellings Materials in Three Ch'orti'
Communities, 1992–1993

		Pacrén n=177		Pelillo Negro n=245		Tuticopote Abajo n=103		Ave.
Households w/ only 1 hut		45	25%	134	65%	43	42%	42%
Walls	Palm	116	66%	42	17%	0	0%	30%
	Thatch	0	0%	121	49%	0	0%	23%
	Wattle and daub	18	10%	58	24%	22	21%	19%
	Adobe brick	13	7%	12	5%	1	1%	5%
	Sticks and leaves	30	17%	2	1%	78	76%	21%
Roof	Palm or thatch	145	82%	234	95%	99	96%	91%
	Laminated metal	32	18%	11	5%	4	4%	9%
Floor	Dirt	171	93%	244	100%	103	100%	99%
	Cement	6	3%	1	0%	0	0%	1%

APPENDIX II: Corn and Bean Agricultural Expenses per Manzana (ma.), 1992–1993

	CORN			BEANS		
	Unit Cost	Amount	Total Cost	Unit Cost	Amount	Total Cost
Seed (if needed)	$.58/lb	16 lbs	$9.28	$.19/lb	150 lbs	$28.50
Fertilizer	$.11/lb	800 lbs	$88.00	$.16/lb	300 lbs	$48.00
Labor for planting	7 mds*	$1.75/md	$12.25	$1.75/md	16 mds	$28.00
Weeding: Labor	9 mds	$1.55/md	$13.95	$1.55/md	16 mds	$24.80
Weeding: Herbicide	$37.30/ ma.†		$37.30			$37.30
Labor for harvest	50 *cargas*§	$.39/ carga	$19.50			$19.50
Materials (bags, machetes, etc.)			$9.70			$9.70
TOTAL COSTS	w/ herbicide		$176.03			$171.00
	w/ labor for weeding		$152.68			$158.50
	w/ one's own weeding labor		$138.73			$133.7

		CORN	BEANS
Tuticopote Abajo	**Harvest**	$495 ($11/m. x 45 q.)‡	$432 ($27/q. x 16 q.)
	Net (w/ herbicide)	-$176 = **$319**	-$171 = **$262**
	Net (w/ hired weeders)	-$153 = **$342**	-$158 = **$274**
	Net (weeding by oneself)	-$139 = **$356**	-$134 = **$298**
Pelillo Negro	**Harvest**	$198 ($11/q. x 18 q.)	$216 ($27/q. x 8 q.)
	Net (w/ herbicide)	-$176 = **$22**	-$171 = **$45**
	Net (w/ hired weeders)	-$153 = **$45**	-$158 = **$48**
	Net (weeding by oneself)	-$139 = **$59**	-$134 = **$82**
Pacrén	**Harvest**	$220 ($11/q. x 20 q.)	(do not plant)
	Net (w/ herbicide)	-$176 = **$44**	
	Net (w/ hired weeders)	-$153 = **$67**	
	Net (weeding by oneself)	-$139 = **$81**	

*md=man-day(s)   † ma.= AUTHOR   § *cargas*=loads   ‡ m.=manzas; q.= quintas

310

APPENDIX III: Requests for Service at the
Hospital Betania, Jocotán*

	1972 (serving approx. 40,000)	**1991** (serving approx. 60,000)
Gastrointestinal	1,921	1,421
Malnutrition	1,331	158+§
Respiratory infection	1,001	889
Tuberculosis	417	79
Injury	337	93
Cardiovascular	187	–
Urinary	103	341
Gynecology/pregnancy	81	479
Skin	34	493
Neurology	–	178
Ear, nose, throat	–	156
Other (medicine, eyes, etc.)	718	2,026
Total	6,130	6,313

*The 1972 data was tabulated by Buysse and Alvarez (1974:204),
and the 1991 data by the hospital.
§ Diagnosis of malnutrition is not clear from the records, and many
may be located in the "other" category.

Mortality Patterns in Olopa and Jocotán

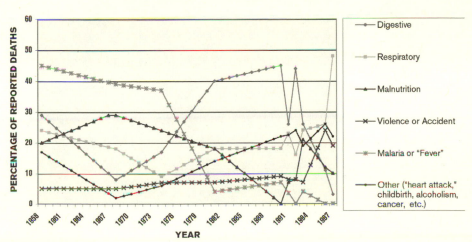

311

APPENDIX IV: Population Of Jocotán Ch'orti'-Speaking Aldeas where Data Is Complete*

	1979	1990	1992	2001
Conacaste	272	511	490	332
Guaraquiche	647	1,041	1,516	808
Guareruche*	799	1,030	1,076	3,137
Matazano	1,214	1,372	1,315	2,310
Oquén*	698	1,276	1,715	2544
Pacrén*	606	838	945	1,282
Pelillo Negro*	1,098	1,363	1,334	1,926
Rodeito	502	664	633	1,015
Tatutú	393	631	596	832
Tierra Blanca	559	762	752	1,142
Tontoles	686	777	850	1,233
Tunucó Abajo*	949	1,159	901	867
Total	**8,423**	**11,424**	**12,123**	**17,428**

* The 1979 data were taken from National Census, and the 1990, 1992, and 2001 data, with the exception of the 1992 data for Pelillo Negro and Pacrén that I collected, were taken by the Jocotán Health Center. In those aldeas marked with a *, Ch'orti' is spoken by virtually all residents. This list is not comprehensive due to incomplete records for other Ch'orti'-speaking aldeas.

References

ADAMS, RICHARD N.

1970   *Crucifixion by Power*. Austin: University of Texas Press.

1988   Conclusions: What Can We Know about the Harvest of Violence? In *Harvest of Violence: The Maya Indians and the Guatemalan Crisis*, ed. Robert M. Carmack, 274–92. Norman: University of Oklahoma Press.

1990   Ethnic Images and Strategies in 1944. In *Guatemalan Indians and the State: 1540–1988*, ed. Carol A. Smith, 141–62. Austin: University of Texas Press.

1996   Un siglo de geografía étnica: Guatemala 1893–1994. *Revista USAC* (2):7–58.

AMNESTY INTERNATIONAL

6/9/05   Guatemala: Hundreds of Women Murdered while Authorities Fail to Act. http://www.politics.co.uk/press-releases/amnesty-international-hundreds-women-murdered-in-guatemala-$8706987.htm

ARCHIVO GENERAL DE CENTROAMÉRICA (AGCA)

1696–97   Exp. 39,667, Ramo A1.24.20, Leg 4648. Chiquimula de la Sierra.

1802   Exp. 4858, Ramo A3–16, Leg 243. Estado que manifiesta las cantidades que al ramo de tributos...

1810   Exp. 49,630, Ramo A1–1, Leg 5859. El Pbro. Baltasar Escobar, Parroco de Jocotán...

1812   Exp. 7876, Ramo A1–4, Leg 380. Diligencias instruidas sobre el contagio...

ARIAS, ARTURO

1990   Changing Indian Identity: Guatemala's Violent Transition to Modernity. In *Guatemalan Indians and the State: 1540–1988*, ed. Carol A. Smith, 230–57. Austin: University of Texas Press.

ARIAS DE BLOIS, JORGE

1982   Mortality in Guatemala Towards the End of the Nineteenth Century. In *The Historical Demography of Highland Guatemala*, ed. Robert M. Carmack, John Early, and Christopher Lutz, 155–68. Albany: Institute for Mesoamerican Studies, SUNY.

ASTURIAS, MIGUEL ANGEL

1985   *El señor presidente*. 6th ed. San José: Editorial Universitaria Centroamericana.

AVANSCO/PACCA
   1992   Growing Dilemmas: Guatemala, the Environment, and the Global
          Economy. Guatemala.

BASTOS, SANTIAGO, AND MANUELA CAMUS
   1996   *Quebrando el silencio: Organizaciones del pueblo maya y sus
          demandas.* Guatemala City: FLACSO.
   2003   *Entre el mecapal y el cielo: Desarrollo del movimiento maya en
          Guatemala.* Guatemala City: FLACSO & Cholsamaj.

BEVERLEY, JOHN
   2001   What Happens When the Subaltern Speaks? In *The Rigoberta
          Menchú Controversy*, ed. Arturo Arias, 219–36. Minneapolis:
          University of Minnesota Press.

BILSBORROW, RICHARD E., AND PAUL STUPP
   1997   Demographic Processes, Land, and the Environment in Guatemala.
          In *Demographic Diversity and Change in the Central American
          Isthmus*, ed. Anne R. Pebley and Luis Rosero-Bixby, 581–623. Santa
          Monica, CA: Rand.

BLACK, GEORGE
   1984   *Garrison Guatemala.* London: Zed Books.

BOCEK, BARBARA
   2000   Guatemalan Indigenous Views of Politics and the Peace Process.
          Active Voices: Testimonial Narratives: Guatemala and Beyond.
          http://www.cs.org/AVoices/articles/LevelFour-Bocek

BODLEY, JOHN H.
   1997   *Cultural Anthropology: Tribes, States, and the Global System.*
          Mountain View, CA: Mayfield.
   2000   *Cultural Anthropology: Tribes, States, and the Global System.*
          Mountain View, CA: Mayfield.

BODMAN-SMITH, JANE P.
   2002   Sponsoring State Terrorism: U.S. International Security Assistance
          for Guatemala and Human Rights Abuses, 1960–1996. Master's thesis,
          University of Kansas.

BOLAÑOS, ROSA MARÍA
   1999   TSE confirma: Portillo 68.32, Berger 31.68. *Siglo Ventiuno*, edición
          electrónica, 28 de diciembre.

BOLANOS, MARGARITA, AND JANE ADAMS
   1994   Seis décadas de la antropología norteamericana en Centroamérica,
          1930–1990. Paper presented at the Primer Congreso Centroamericano
          de Antropología, San José, Costa Rica.

BOURDIEU, PIERRE
1977   *Outline of a Theory of Practice.* New York: Cambridge University
        Press.

BOWEN, ELEANOR SMITH
1954   *Return to Laughter: An Anthropological Novel.* New York:
        Anchor Books.

BRESLIN, PATRICK
1994   Identity and Self-Respect. In *Cultural Expression and Grassroots
        Development*, ed. Charles David Kleymeyer, 39–56. Boulder, CO:
        Lynne Rienner.

BREWER, STEWART W.
2002   Spanish Imperialism and the Ch'orti' Maya, (1524–1700): Institutional
        Effects of the Spanish Colonial System on Spanish and Indian
        Communities in the Corregimiento of Chiquimula de la Sierra,
        Guatemala. PhD diss., SUNY-Albany.

BRICKER, VICTORIA R.
1973   *Ritual Humor in Highland Chiapas.* Austin: University of Texas Press.
1981   *The Indian Christ, the Indian King: The Historical Substrate of Maya
        Myth and Ritual.* Austin: University of Texas Press.

BRIGGS, CHARLES L.
1997   The Politics of Discursive Authority in Research on the "Invention of
        Tradition." *Cultural Anthropology* 11(4):435–69.

BRINTNALL, DOUGLAS E.
1979   *Revolt Against the Dead: The Modernization of a Mayan Community
        in the Highlands of Guatemala.* New York: Gordon and Breach.

BROSNAN, GREG
2001   Starving Peasants Descend on Guatemalan Town. Jocotán,
        Guatemala: Reuters, September 7.
2002   Hunger Tightens Grip on Guatemala's Children. Reuters,
        February 20.

BRYSK, ALISON
1996   Turning Weakness Into Strength: The Internationalization of Indian
        Rights. *Latin American Perspectives* 23(2):38–57.
2000   *From Tribal Village to Global Village: Indian Rights and International
        Relations in Latin America.* Stanford, CA: Stanford University Press.

BURGOS-DEBRAY, ELIZABETH, AND RIGOBERTA MENCHÚ
1984   *I . . . Rigoberta Menchú.* London: Verso.

BURNETT, VIRGINIA GARRARD

1988   Protestantism in Rural Guatemala, 1872–1954. *Latin American Research Review* 24:127–43.

BUYSEE, PATRICIO, AND EDMUNDO ALVAREZ

1974   Estudio de la Diócesis de Jocotán. Jocotán, Guatemala, unpublished manuscript.

CAMBELL, LYLE, AND TERRENCE KAUFMAN

1985   Mayan Linguistics: Where Are We Now? *Annual Review of Anthropology* 14:187–98.

CAMBRANES, J. C.

1985   *Coffee and the Peasants in Guatemala.* Stockholm: Institute of Latin American Studies.

CARLSON, ROBERT S.

1997   *The War for the Heart and Soul of a Highland Maya Town.* Austin: University of Texas Press.

CARMACK, ROBERT

1981   *The Quiche Mayas of Utatlan: The Evolution of a Highland Guatemala Kingdom.* Norman: University of Oklahoma Press.

1995   *Rebels of Highland Guatemala: The Quiche-Mayas of Momostenango.* Norman: University of Oklahoma Press.

CARMACK, ROBERT, ED.

1988   *Harvest of Violence: The Maya Indians and the Guatemalan Crisis.* Norman: University of Oklahoma Press.

CARMACK, ROBERT M., JANINE GASCO, AND GARY H. GOSSEN, EDS.

1996   *The Legacy of Mesoamerica: History and Culture of a Native American Civilization.* Upper Saddle River, NJ: Prentice Hall.

CASAÚS ARZÚ, MARTA ELENA

1998   *La metamorfosis del racismo en Guatemala.* Guatemala: Cholsamaj.

2001   La renegociación de las identidades étnicas a raíz de los Acuerdos de Paz en Guatemala. In *Los derechos humanos en tierras mayas: Política, representaciones, y moralidad*, ed. Pedro Pitarch and Julián López García, 209–42. Madrid: Sociedad Española de Estudios Mayas.

CERIGUA WEEKLY BRIEFS

5/8/97   More Guatemalans Reading, 4.

6/12/97   Environmental Future Bleak, 4.

7/31/97   UNFPA: Lack of Reproductive Health Care Causes Hundreds of Deaths Annually, 4.

10/23/97   Gains of October Revolution Defended, 1.

11/13/97   Registration Drive Launched for Next Elections, 3.

12/4/97   ASC: New Budget Not Made for Peace, 2.

12/4/97   Community Radio Fights to be Heard, 4.

1/15/98   Macroeconomic Gains Elude Majority, 3

3/5/98   Violent Crime Unchallenged, 3.

4/2/98   4,500 Banana Workers Strike in Protest of Firings, 1–2.

4/23/98   Candidates for By-Elections Set, 3–4.

5/7/98   Indigenous Women Accuse State of Genocide, 3–4.

5/14/98   ECLA Advises More Taxes on Wealth and Greater Social
Spending, 4.

5/20/99   Guatemalans Vote "No" on Constitutional Changes, 1.

6/3/99   Women's Health Day Sparks Call for Greater Government Effort, 2.

7/29/99   Guatemala City Third in LA for Violence, 2.

7/29/99   Guatemala Still Trails in Development, 4.

8/26/99   Birth Control Gaining Ground, electronic edition.

CHAPIN, MAC

1989   The 500,000 Invisible Indians of El Salvador. *Cultural Survival
Quarterly* 13:11–16.

COJTÍ CUXIL, DEMETRIO

1996   The Politics of Maya Revindication. In *Maya Cultural Activism in
Guatemala*, ed. Edward F. Fisher and R. McKenna-Brown, 19–50.
Austin: University of Texas Press.

1997   *El movimiento maya (en Guatemala)*. Guatemala: Cholsamaj.

COMISIÓN PARA EL ESCLARECIMIENTO HISTÓRICO (CEH)

1999   *Guatemala: Memoria del silencio*. Capítulo 1: *Causas y orígenes del
enfrentamiento armado interno*. Guatemala: Office of Services for
United Nations Projects.

1999   *Guatemala: Memoria del silencio*. Capítulo 2a: *Las violaciones de los
derechos humanos y los hechos de violencia*. Guatemala: Office of
Services for United Nations Projects.

1999   *Guatemala: Memoria del silencio*. Capítulo 2b: *Las violaciones de
los derechos humanos y los hechos de violencia*, vol. 2. Guatemala:
Office of Services for United Nations Projects.

1999   *Guatemala: Memoria del silencio*. Capítulo 3: *Consecuencias y
efectos de la violencia*. Guatemala: Office of Services for United
Nations Projects.

1999   *Guatemala: Memoria del silencio*. Capítulo 4: *Conclusions y recomen-
daciones*. Guatemala: Office of Services for United Nations Projects.

1999   *Guatemala: Memoria del silencio*. Anexo 1: *Casos ilustrativos*.
Guatemala: Office of Services for United Nations Projects.

1999   *Guatemala: Memoria del silencio*. Anexo 2: *Casos presentados*.
Guatemala: Office of Services for United Nations Projects.

CONKLIN, BETH A.

1997 Body Pain, Feathers, and VCRs: Aesthetics and Authenticity in Amazonian Activism. *American Ethnologist* 24(4):711–37.

CORTÉS Y LARRAZ, PEDRO

[1768–70] 1958 *Descripción geográfico-moral de la Diócesis de Goathemala.* Sociedad de Geografía e Historia de Guatemala, vol. 20, tomo 1. Guatemala: Biblioteca "Goathemala."

CRÓNICA

7/95 Guatemala en números, 11–14.

CULLATHER, NICHOLAS

2004 *CIA Guatemala: Operación PBSuccess.* Guatemala: Tipografia Nacional.

DARY, CLAUDIA

1986 *Estudio antropológico de la literatura oral en prosa del Oriente de Guatemala.* Guatemala: Editorial Universitaria de Guatemala.

1994 Ladino: Apuntes para la historia de un término. *Ethnos* (2):1–10.

DARY, CLAUDIA, SILVEL ELÍAS, AND VIOLETA REYNA

1998 *Estrategias de sobrevivencia campesina en ecosistemas frágiles.* Guatemala: FLACSO.

DAVIS, SHELTON H., AND JULIE HODSON

1983 *Witnesses to Political Violence in Guatemala: The Suppression of a Rural Development Movement.* Boston: Oxfam America.

DE CERTEAU, MICHEL

1984 *The Practice of Everyday Life.* Berkeley: University of California Press.

DE LA CADENA, MARISOL

1995 "Women Are More Indian": Ethnicity and Gender in a Community near Cuzco. In *Ethnicity, Markets, and Migration in the Andes: At the Crossroads of History and Anthropology,* ed. Brooke Larson and Olivia Harris, 329–50. Durham, NC: Duke University Press.

DIENER, PAUL

1978 The Tears of St. Anthony: Ritual and Revolution in Eastern Guatemala. *Latin American Perspectives* 5(3):92–116.

DÍAZ POLANCO, HÉCTOR

1997 *Indigenous Peoples in Latin America: The Quest for Self-Determination.* Trans. Lucia Rayas. Boulder, CO: Westview.

DIRKS, NICHOLAS B., GEOFF ELEY, AND SHERRY B. ORTNER, EDS.

1994 Introduction. In *Culture/Power/History: A Reader in Contemporary Social Theory,* ed. Nicholas B. Dirks, Geoff Eley, and Sherry B. Ortner, 3–45. Princeton, NJ: Princeton University Press.

DOCUMENTOS HISTÓRICOS DE LA PARROQUIA DE
SANTIAGO JOCOTÁN, DEPARTAMENTO DE CHIQUIMULA
1978   Jocotán, Guatemala, unpublished.

DOVER, ROBERT V. H., AND JOANNE RAPPAPORT
1996   Ethnicity Reconfigured: Introduction. *Journal of Latin American Anthropology* 1(2):2–17.

DOWNING, TED
2001   Why Comment on the World Bank's Proposed Indigenous Peoples Policy? *Anthropology News* 42(9):23–24.

EARLE, DUNCAN
2001   Menchú Tales and Maya Social Landscapes: The Silencing of Words and Worlds. In *The Rigoberta Menchú Controversy*, ed. Arturo Arias, 288–308. Minneapolis: University of Minnesota Press.

EARLY, JOHN D.
1982   *The Demographic Structure and Evolution of a Peasant System: The Guatemalan Population.* Boca Raton: University Presses of Florida.

EBER, CHRISTINE
1995   *Women and Alcohol in a Highland Maya Town: Water of Hope, Water of Sorrow.* Austin: University of Texas Press.

EKERN, STENER
1998   Las organizaciones mayas de Guatemala: Panorama y retos institucionales. *Mayab* 11:68–83.

ELKIN, HENRY
1963   The Northern Arapaho of Wyoming. In *Acculturation in Seven American Indian Tribes*, ed. Ralph Linton, 207–58. Gloucester, MA: Peter Smith.

ELMENDORF, MARY
1976   *Nine Mayan Women.* New York: Schenkman.

ENGLE, PATRICE, ELENA HURTADO, AND MARIE RUEL
1997   Smoke Exposure of Women and Young Children in Highland Guatemala: Prediction and Recall Accuracy. *Human Organization* 56(4):408–17.

EUROPEAN UNION
1998   Council Resolution of 30 November 1998. http://europa.eu.int/comm/external_relations/human _rights/ip/res98.pdf

EVANS-PRITCHARD, DIEDRE
1987   The Portal Case: Authenticity, Tourism, Traditions, and the Law. *Journal of American Folklore* 100(397):287–96.

FALLA, RICARDO
    1971   Juan el gordo: Visión indígena de su explotación. *Estudios Centroamericanos* 26(268):98–107.

FAVRE, HENRI
    1984   *Cambio y continuidad entre los Mayas de México*. Mexico: Instituto Nacional Indigenista.

FELDMAN, LAWRENCE H.
    1975   Riverine Maya, the Torquegua, and Other Chols of the Lower Motagua Valley. Museum Brief 15. Columbia: University of Missouri.
    1982   *Colonial Manuscripts of Chiquimula, El Progreso, and Zacapa Departments, Guatemala*. Columbia: Museum of Anthropology, University of Missouri.
    1983   Un reconocimiento de los recursos de Centroamérica en manuscritos chorti. In *Introducción a la arqueología de Copán, Honduras*, 144–94 Tegucigalpa: Proyecto Arqueológico Copán, Secretaria de Estado en el Despacho de Cultura y Turismo.
    1985   *A Tumpline Economy*. Culver City, CA: Labyrinthos.
    1989   In Back of the Beyond: Colonial Documentation for a Rural Backwater. In *New Frontiers in the Archeology of the Pacific Coast of Southern Mesoamerica*, ed. Frederick Bove and Lynette Heller, 242–56. Anthropological Research Papers 39. Tempe: Arizona State University.

FELDMAN, LAWRENCE H., ED.
    2000   *Lost Shores, Forgotten Peoples: Spanish Explorations of the South East Maya Lowlands*. Durham, NC: Duke University Press.

FISHER, EDWARD F.
    1996   Induced Culture Change as a Strategy for Socioeconomic Development: The Pan-Maya Movement in Guatemala. In *Maya Cultural Activism in Guatemala*, ed. Edward F. Fischer and R. McKenna Brown, 51–73. Austin: University of Texas Press.
    1999   Cultural Logic and Maya Identity. *Current Anthropology* 40(4):473–99.

FISHER, EDWARD F., AND R. MCKENNA-BROWN, EDS.
    1996   *Maya Cultural Activism in Guatemala*. Austin: University of Texas Press.

FOLEY, DOUGLAS
    1995   *The Heartland Chronicles*. Philadelphia: University of Pennsylvania Press.

FOSTER, GEORGE M.

1965   Peasant Society and the Image of Limited Good. *American Anthropologist* 67(2):293–315.

1994   *Hippocrates' Latin American Legacy: Humoral Medicine in the New World.* Langhorne, PA: Gordon and Breach.

FOUCAULT, MICHEL

1994   Two Lectures. In *Culture/Power/History: A Reader in Contemporary Social Theory*, ed. Nicholas B. Dirks, Geoff Eley, and Sherry B. Ortner, 200–221. Princeton, NJ: Princeton University Press.

FOUGHT, JOHN

1969   Chortí (Mayan) Ceremonial Organization. *American Anthropologist* 71:472–76.

1972   *Chorti (Maya) Texts (I).* Philadelphia: University of Pennsylvania Press.

FOWLER, WILLIAM R., JR.

1983   Distribución prehistórica e histórica de los pipiles. *Mesoamérica* 4(6):348–72.

FOX, JOHN W.

1981   The Late Postclassic Eastern Frontier of Mesoamerica: Cultural Innovation along the Periphery. *Current Anthropology* 22(4):321–34.

FRIEDLANDER, JUDITH

1975   *Being Indian in Hueyapan: A Study of Forced Identity in Contemporary Mexico.* New York: St. Martin's Press.

FRIEDMAN, JONATHAN

1994   *Cultural Identity and Global Process.* Thousand Oaks, CA: Sage.

FUENTES Y GUZMÁN, FRANCISCO ANTONIO DE

[1699] 1933   *Recordación Florida: Discurso historial y demostración natural, material, militar y política del reino de Guatemala.* 3 vols. Guatemala: Biblioteca "Goathemala."

GALEANO, EDUARDO

1980   *Las venas abiertas de América Latina.* Mexico: Siglo XXI.

GALINDO, JUAN

1945   Informe de la comisión científica formada para el reconocimiento de Copán, por Decreto de 15 de enero de 1834. *Anales de la Sociedad de Geografía e Historia.* 20(3):217–28.

GANN, THOMAS WILLIAM FRANCIS, AND
JOHN ERIC SIDNEY THOMPSON

1931   *The History of the Maya from the Earliest Times to the Present Day.*
        New York: C. Scribner's Son.

GARCIA DE PALACIO, DIEGO

[1576] 1985   *Letter to the King of Spain.* Trans. and with notes by Ephraim
        G. Squier [1859] and Alexander von Frantzius and Frank E.
        Comparato. Culver City, CA: Labyrinthos.

GELLNER, ERNEST

1983   *Nations and Nationalism.* Ithaca, NY: Cornell University Press.

GEORGE, SUSAN

1992   *The Debt Boomerang: How Third World Debt Harms Us All.*
        Boulder, CO: Westview.

GIBSON, CHARLES

1952   *Tlaxcala in the Sixteenth Century.* New Haven, CT: Yale
        University Press.

GILLEN, JOHN

1952   Ethos and Cultural Aspects of Personality. In *Heritage of Conquest,*
        ed. Sol Tax, 193–222. Glencoe, IL: Free Press.

GIRARD, RAFAEL

1949   *Los chortís ante el problema maya.* 5 vols. Mexico: Antigua Libreria
        Robredo.
1962   *Los mayas eternos.* Mexico: Libro México Editores.
1977   *Origen y desarrollo de las civilizaciones antiguas de América.* Mexico:
        Editores Mexicanos Unidos.

GIRÓN PALACIOS, FELIPE ANTONIO

2001   "Los huitecos no hablamos así": Una etnografía del Oriente de
        Guatemala. Tesis de Maestría, Universidad de San Carlos,
        Guatemala.

GLEIJESES, PIERO

1989   La aldea de Ubico: Guatemala, 1931–1944. *Mesoamérica* 17:25–59.

GOLDIN, LILIANA R., AND BRENDA ROSENBAUM

1993   Culture and History: Subregional Variation Among the Maya.
        Comparative Studies in Society and History 35(1):110–32.

GOSSEN, GARY

1974   *Chamulas in the World of the Sun.* Cambridge, MA: Harvard
        University Press.

1993 The Other in Chamula Tzotzil Cosmology: Reflections of a Kansan in Chiapas. *Cultural Anthropology* 8(4):443–75.

1996a The Religions of Mesoamerica. In *The Legacy of Mesoamerica: History and Culture of a Native American Civilization*, ed. Robert M. Carmack, Janine Gasco, and Gary H. Gossen, 290–320. Upper Saddle River, NJ: Prentice Hall.

1996b Maya Zapatistas Move to the Ancient Future. *American Anthropologist* 98(3):528–38.

GREEN, LINDA

1994 Fear as a Way of Life. *Cultural Anthropology* 9(2):227–56.

GRIEB, KENNETH J.

1979 *Guatemalan Caudillo: The Regime of Jorge Ubico.* Athens: Ohio University Press.

GUZMÁN-BÖCKLER, CARLOS

1975 *Colonialismo y revolución.* Mexico: Siglo XXI.

GUZMÁN BÖCKLER, CARLOS, AND JEAN-LOUP HERBERT

1970 *Guatemala: Una interpretación histórico-social.* Mexico: Siglo Veintiuno Editores.

HADDEN, GERRY

2002 Central America Faces Severe Food Shortages. National Public Radio report, April 9.

HALE, CHARLES R.

1996 *Mestizaje*, Hybridity and the Cultural Politics of Difference in Post-Revolutionary Central America. *Journal of Latin American Anthropology* 2(1):34–61.

HANDLER, RICHARD, AND JOCELYN LINNEKIN

1984 Tradition, Genuine or Spurious. *Journal of American Folklore* 97:273–90.

HANDY, JAMES

1984 *Gift of the Devil: A History of Guatemala.* Boston: South End Press.

1990 The Corporate Community, Campesino Organizations, and Agrarian Reform: 1950–1954. In *Guatemalan Indians and the State, 1540 to 1988*, ed. Carol A. Smith, 163–82. Austin: University of Texas Press.

HARKIN, MICHAEL

1997 A Tradition of Invention: Modern Ceremonialism on the Northwest Coast. In *Present Is Past: Some Uses of Tradition in Native Societies*, ed. Marie Mauzé, 97–111. New York: University Press of America.

HARRIS, OLIVIA

1995 Ethnic Identity and Market Relations: Indians and Mestizos in the Andes. In *Ethnicity, Markets, and Migration in the Andes: At the Crossroads of History and Anthropology*, ed. Brooke Larson and Olivia Harris, 351–80. Durham, NC: Duke University Press.

HAWKINS, JOHN

1984 *Inverse Images: The Meaning of Culture, Ethnicity, and Family in Postcolonial Guatemala*. Albuquerque: University of New Mexico Press.

HERVIK, PETER

1999 *Mayan People Within and Beyond Boundaries: Social Categories and Lived Identity in Yucatan*. Amsterdam: Harwood Academic.

HILL, JONATHAN D., ED.

1988 *Rethinking History and Myth: Indigenous South American Perspectives on the Past*. Urbana: University of Illinois Press.

HOBSBAWN, ERIC, AND TERRENCE RANGER

1983 *The Invention of Traditions*. New York: Cambridge University Press.

HOLIDAY, DAVID

2000 Guatemala's Precarious Peace. *Current History* (February):78–84.

HORIZONT 3000 AND PROYECTO CH'ORTI'

2004 *Esta tierra es nuestra: Compendio de fuentes históricos sobre denuncias, medidas y remedidas, composiciones, titulaciones, usurpaciones, desmembraciones, litigios, transacciones y remates de tierra (Años 1610–1946), Departamento de Chiquimula*, tomo 4. Guatemala: Horizont 3000 and Proyecto Ch'orti'.

HORST, OSCAR H.

1998 Building Blocks of a Legendary Belief: The Black Christ of Esquipulas, 1595–1995. *The Pennsylvania Geographer* 36(1):135–47.

1998 The Evolution of the Ethnic Character of the Municipio of Esquipulas, Guatemala. Paper presented at the annual meeting of the American Anthropological Association, Philadelphia.

HOUSTON, STEVEN, JOHN ROBERTSON, AND DAVID STUART

2000 The Language of the Classic Maya Inscriptions. *Current Anthropology* 41(3):321–56.

HULL, KERRY MICHAEL

2003 *Verbal Art and Performance in Ch'orti' and Maya Hieroglyphic Writing*. PhD diss., University of Texas at Austin.

HUNT, EVA
1977   *The Transformation of the Hummingbird: Cultural Roots of a Zinacantecan Mythical Poem*. Ithaca, NY: Cornell University Press.

INTERNATIONAL LABOR ORGANIZATION (ILO)
2003   Convention No. 169: Its nature and fundamental principles. http://www.ilo.org/public/english/employment/strat/poldev/papers/1998/169guide/169guide.htm

INSTITUTO NACIONAL DE ESTADÍSTICA (INE)
1964   *Censo de población*. Guatemala.
1996   *Censo de población*. Guatemala.

JENKINS, JANICE H.
1991   The State Construction of Affect. *Culture, Medicine, and Psychiatry* 15(2):1–39.

JENKINS, JANICE H., AND MARTHA VALIENTE
1994   Bodily Transactions of the Passions: *El Calor* among Salvadoran Women Refugees. In *Embodiment and Experience: The Existential Ground of Culture and Self*, ed. Thomas J. Csordas, 163–82. New York: Cambridge University Press.

JOCOTÁN MUNICIPAL ARCHIVES
Jocotán, Guatemala.

JONAS, SUSANNE
1974   Guatemala: The Land of Eternal Struggle. In *Latin America: The Struggle with Dependency and Beyond*, ed. Ronald H. Chilcote and Ronald H. Edelstein, 93–219. New York: John Wiley and Sons.

JUARROS, DOMINGO
[1808–18] 1936   *Compendio de la historia de la ciudad de Guatemala*. Guatemala: Tipografía Nacional.

KANE, STEPHANIE
1994   *The Phantom Gringo Boat: Shamanic Discourse and Development in Panama*. Washington, DC: Smithsonian Institution Press.

KAUFMAN, TERRENCE
1974   *Idiomas de Mesoamérica*. Seminario de Integración Social Guatemalteco 33. Guatemala: Editorial José Pineda Ibarra.

KEARNEY, MICHAEL
1996   Introduction. *Latin American Perspectives* 23(2):5–16.

KEEGAN, JOSEPH
1994 Dying Young in Olopa: An Analysis of the 1992 Mortality Records for Olopa, a Guatemalan Municipality. Master's thesis, SUNY-Albany.

KING, J. C. H.
1997 Marketing Magic: Process, Identity and the Creation and Selling of Native Art. In *Present Is Past: Some Uses of Tradition in Native Societies*, ed. Marie Mauzé, 81–96. New York: University Press of America.

KIZCA, JOHN
1993 *The Indian in Latin American History: Resistance, Resilience, and Acculturation*. Wilmington, DE: Scholarly Resources.

KLEIN, CECELIA F.
2003 The Devil and the Skirt: An Iconographic Inquiry into the Prehispanic Nature of Tzizimime. http://www.ejournal.unam.mx/cultura_nahuatl /ecnahuatl31/ECN31002.pdf

KLEYMEYER, CHARLES DAVID
1994 The Uses and Functions of Cultural Expression in Grassroots Development. In *Cultural Expression and Grassroots Development*, ed. Charles David Kleymeyer, 17–36. Boulder, CO: Lynne Reinner.

KLEYMEYER, CHARLES DAVID, ED.
1994 *Cultural Expression and Grassroots Development*. Boulder, CO: Lynne Reinner.

KOTTAK, CONRAD PHILLIP
1997 Teaching the Introductory Course. In *The Teaching of Anthropology*, ed. Conrad Phillip Kottak, Jane J. White, Richard H. Furlow, and Patricia C. Rice, 13–21. Mountain View, CA: Mayfield.

KUFER, JOHANNA, HARALD FORTHER, ELFRIEDE POLL, AND MICHAEL HEINRICH
2005 Historical and Modern Medicinal Plant Uses—The Example of the Ch'orti' Maya and Ladinos in Eastern Guatemala. *Journal of Pharmacy and Pharmacology* 57:1127–52.

LA FARGE, OLIVER
1947 *Santa Eulalia*. Chicago: University of Chicago Press.

LA NACIÓN
12/31/96 Despiden 1997 con ambiente de paz. San José, Costa Rica. http://nacion.co.cr/diciembre/31/guatemala.html#2

LANDA, FRAY DIEGO DE

1941 *Relación de las cosas de Yucatán*. Trans. and ed. Alfred M. Tozzer.
Cambridge, MA: Peabody Museum of Archeology and Ethnology.

LATINAMÉRICA PRESS

1/22/98 Indigenous Activists Protest, 7.

LAUGHLIN, ROBERT M.

1977 *Of Cabbages and Kings*. Smithsonian Contributions to Anthropology,
no. 23. Washington, DC: Smithsonian Institution.

LENCLUD, GERARD

1997 History and Tradition. In *Present Is Past: Some Uses of Tradition in
Native Societies*, ed. Marie Mauzé, 43–64. New York: University
Press of America.

LEWIS, OSCAR

1959 *Five Families: Mexican Case Studies in the Culture of Poverty*.
New York: Basic Books.

1966 The Culture of Poverty. *Scientific American* 215(4):19–25.

LINNEKIN, JOCELYN

1983 Defining Tradition: Variations on Hawaiian Identity. *American
Ethnologist* 10:241–52.

1991 The Politics of Representing Scholarship. *Contemporary Pacific*
Spring:172–77.

1996 Indigenous Sovereignty Scenarios in Latin America and Hawaii:
Parallels and Possibilities. *Journal of Latin American Anthropology*
1(2):152–65.

LÓPEZ DE CERRATO

1549–1551 Guatemala 128. Seville: Archivo General de Indias.

LÓPEZ GARCÍA, JULIÁN

1993 Comidas de mayas chortís y ladinos del oriente de Guatemala.
PhD diss., Universidad Complutense, Madrid.

2003 *Símbolos en la comida indígena guatemaltéca: Una etnografía
de la culinaria maya-chorti*. Abyayala.

LÓPEZ GARCÍA, JULIÁN, AND BRENT E. METZ

2002 *Primero dios: Etnografía y cambio social entre los mayas ch'orti's
del oriente de Guatemala*. Guatemala: FLACSO, Oxfam,
Plumsock, & COMACH.

LOVELL, W. GEORGE

1982   Collapse and Recovery: A Demographic Profile of the Cuchumatan
       Highlands of Guatemala (1520–1821). In *The Historical Demography
       of Highland Guatemala*, ed. Robert M. Carmack, John Early, and
       Christopher Lutz, 103–20. Albany: Institute for Mesoamerican
       Studies, SUNY.

1988   Surviving Conquest: The Maya of Guatemala in Historical
       Perspective. *Latin American Research Review* 2:25–57.

LOVELL, W. GEORGE, AND CHRISTOPHER H. LUTZ

1997   The Maya Population of Guatemala. In *Demographic Diversity and
       Change in the Central American Isthmus*, ed. Anne R. Pebley and
       Luis Rosero-Bixby, 117–32. Santa Monica, CA: Rand.

LOW, SETHA M.

1989   Gender, Emotion, and *Nervios* in Urban Guatemala. *Health Care for
       Women International* 10:115–39.

1994   Embodied Metaphors: Nerves as Lived Experience. In *Embodiment
       and Experience: The Existential Ground of Culture and Self*, ed.
       Thomas J. Csordas, 139–62. New York: Cambridge University Press.

LUBECK, JOHN.

1989   *Método moderno para aprender el idioma Chortí: Una gramática
       Chortí*. Guatemala: Instituto Lingüístico de Verano.

LUTZ, CHRISTOPHER H.

1988   Guatemala's Non-Spanish and Non-Indian Population: Its Spread
       and Demographic Evolution, 1700–1821. Paper presented at the
       Guatemalan History and Development Conference, University of
       Guelph, Ontario.

1999   Evolución demográfica de la población no indígena. In *Historia
       General de Guatemala*, tomo 3. Guatemala: Asociación de Amigos
       del País.

LUTZ, CHRISTOPHER H., and W. GEORGE LOVELL

1990   Core and Periphery in Colonial Guatemala. In *Guatemalan Indians
       and the State: 1540–1988*, ed. Carol A. Smith, 35–51. Austin: University
       of Texas Press.

LYONS, BARRY J.

2001   Religion, Authority, and Identity: Intergenerational Politics, Ethnic
       Resurgence, and Respect in Chimborazo, Ecuador. *Latin American
       Research Review* 36(1):7–48.

MACÍAS, JULIO CÉSAR

1999   *La guerrilla fue mi camino*. San Salvador: Editorial Piedra Santa
       Arandi.

MACLEOD, MURDO

1973   *Spanish Central America: A Socioeconomic History, 1520–1720.*
        Berkeley: University of California Press.

1982   An Outline of Central American Colonial Demographics: Sources,
        Yields, and Possibilities. In *The Historical Demography of Highland
        Guatemala*, ed. Robert M. Carmack, John Early, and Christopher
        Lutz, 3–18. Albany: Institute for Mesoamerican Studies, SUNY.

CONDORI MAMANI, GREGORIO, AND ASUNTA QUISPE HUAMÁN

1996   *Andean Lives: Gregorio Condori Mamani and Asunta Quispe
        Huamán.* Ed. Ricardo Valderrama Fernández and Carmen Escalante
        Gutiérrez. Trans. Paul H. Gelles and Gabriela Martínez Escobar.
        Austin: University of Texas Press.

MARTÍNEZ PALÁEZ, SEVERO

1970   *La patria del criollo: Ensayo de interpretación de la realidad colonial
        guatemalteca*, 6th ed. San José: Editorial Universitaria
        Centroamérica.

MAUZÉ, MARIE

1997   On Concepts of Tradition: An Introduction. In *Present Is Past: Some
        Uses of Tradition in Native Societies*, ed. Marie Mauzé, 1–15. New York:
        University Press of America.

MAXWELL, JAMES

1974   A Model of Culture Change. In Master's thesis, chapter 13. Antigua:
        CIRMA archives.

MAY, RACHEL

2001   *Terror in the Countryside: Campesino Responses to Political Violence
        in Guatemala, 1954–1985.* Research in International Studies, Latin
        America Series, no. 35. Athens: Ohio University Center for
        International Studies.

MAYBERRY-LEWIS, DAVID

1997   *Indigenous Peoples, Ethnic Groups, and the State.* Needham Heights,
        MA: Allyn & Bacon.

MCCLINTOCK, MICHAEL

1985   *The American Connection: State Terror and Popular Resistance in
        Guatemala.* London: Zed Press.

MCCREERY, DAVID

1988   Land, Labor and Violence in Highland Guatemala: San Juan
        Ixchoy (Huehuetenango), 1893–1945. Paper presented at the
        Guatemala History and Development Conference, University of
        Guelph, Ontario.

METZ, BRENT

1998 Without Nation, Without Community: The Growth of Maya Nationalism Among Ch'orti's of Eastern Guatemala. *Journal of Anthropological Research* 54(3):325–49.

2001a Representación colaborativa: Un gringo en el movimiento Maya-Ch'orti'. In *Los derechos humanos en el área Maya: Política, representaciones y moralidad*, ed. Pedro Pitarch and Julián López, 311–40. Madrid: Sociedad Española de Estudios Mayas.

2001b Politics, Population, and Family Planning in Guatemala: Ch'orti' Maya Experiences. *Human Organization* 60(3):259–74.

MINTZ, SIDNEY W.

1985 *Sweetness and Power: The Place of Sugar in Modern History*. New York: Viking.

MONDLOCH, JAMES

1982 Syncretismo religioso maya-cristiano en la tradición oral de una comunidad quiché. *Mesoamérica* 3(3):107–23.

MONTEJO, VICTOR D.

1997 Pan-mayanismo: La pluriformidad de la cultura maya y el porceso de autorrepresentación de los mayas. *Mesoamérica* 33(June):93–123.

MORAL, RAÚL DEL

1983 El chontal de Tabasco y el chortí de Guatemala. In *Antropología e historia de los mixe-zoques y mayas*, 347–53 Mexico: Universidad Nacional Autónoma de México.

1988 Introducción al sistema verbal del chortí de Guatemala. In *Estudios de cultura maya*, vol. 17, 397–421. Mexico: Universidad Nacional Autónoma de México.

MORLEY, SYLVANUS

1920 *The Inscriptions of Copan*. Publication 219. Washington, DC: Carnegie Institution.

MOSQUERA, ANTONIO

1982 *Los chortís en Guatemala*. Guatemala: Editorial Universitaria (San Carlos).

NASH, JUNE

1973 Death as a Way of Life: The Increasing Resort to Homicide in a Maya Indian Community. In *To See Ourselves as Others See Us: Anthropology of Modern Social Issues*, ed. Thomas Weaver, 346–54. Glenview, IL: Scott, Foreman.

1995 The Reassertion of Indigenous Identity: Mayan Responses to State Intervention in Chiapas. *Latin American Research Review* 30:7–41.

NELSON, DIANE M.
1999   *A Finger in the Wound: Body Politics in Quincentennial Guatemala.*
       Berkeley: University of California Press.

NICK, ELIZABETH
1975   Social Factors Related to Knowledge about and Use of Fertility
       Control in a Traditional Mayan Village in Guatemala. Master's thesis,
       Florida Atlantic University.

NIEZEN, RONALD
2003   *The Origins of Indigenism: Human Rights and the Politics of
       Identity.* Berkeley: University of California Press.

OAKES, MAUD
1951   *Beyond the Windy Place: Life in the Guatemalan Highlands.*
       New York: Farrar, Straus and Young.

OAKLEY, HELEN
1966   Chorti. In *Lenguas de Guatemala*, ed. Marvin Mayers, 331–53.
       Publicación no. 20. Guatemala: Seminario de Integración Social
       Guatemalteca.

OFICINA DE DERECHOS HUMANOS DEL ARZOBISPADO DE GUATEMALA
(ODHAG)
1998   *Guatemala: Nunca* más. Vol. 1: *Impactos de la violencia.* Guatemala:
       Proyecto Interdiocesano de Recuperación de la Memoria Histórica
       (REHMI).
1998   *Guatemala: Nunca* más. Vol. 2: *Los mecanismos del horror.*
       Guatemala: Proyecto Interdiocesano de Recuperación de la Memoria
       Histórica (REHMI).
1998   *Guatemala: Nunca* más. Vol. 3: *El entorno histórico.* Guatemala:
       Proyecto Interdiocesano de Recuperación de la Memoria Histórica
       (REHMI).

OLOPA MUNICIPAL ARCHIVES
Olopa, Guatemala.

ORDUNA, FRANCISCO DE
1530   Información del señor capitán e juez de residencia, Francisco de
       Orduna. *Actas de Cabildo de Guatemala,* tomo 1. Archivo General
       de Centroamerica A1.2.2–11763–1768.

OTZOY, IRMA
1997   Fantasía y desdén: Imágenes y contestación. *Mesoamérica*
       33(June):1–14.

PALMA RAMOS, DANILO A.
  2001   Así somos y así vivimos: Los ch'orti'. Guatemala: Universidad Rafael
         Landivar.

PAUL, LOIS
  1974   The Mastery of Work and the Mystery of Sex in a Guatemalan Village.
         In *Women, Culture, and Society*, ed. Michelle Zimbalist Rosaldo and
         Louise Lamphere, 281–99. Stanford, CA: Stanford University Press.

PÉREZ, HECTOR
  1997   Estimates of the Indigenous Population of Central America (16th to
         20th Centuries). In *Demographic Diversity and Change in the Central
         American Isthmus*, ed. Anne R. Pebley and Luis Rosero-Bixby, 97–115.
         Santa Monica, CA: Rand.

PÉREZ MARTÍNEZ, VITALINO, ED.
  1996   *Leyendas Maya Ch'orti'*. Guatemala: Proyecto Linguístico Francisco
         Marroquín.

PITARCH, PEDRO
  2004   The Zapatistas and the Art of Ventriloquism. *Journal of Human
         Rights* 3(3):291–312.

PLANET ARK
  2002   Central America Drought Worsens Hunger, UN Says. Rome:
         http://www.planetark.org/avantgo/dailynewsstory.cfm?newsid=3D179=58,
         September 30.

PLATAFORMA DE SOLIDARIDAD CON CHIAPAS, OAXACA, Y GUATEMALA
DE MADRID
  5/13/05   Análisis sobre los últimos ataques efectuados en Guatemala con-
            tra defensores de los derechos humanos.
            http://www.nodo50.org/pchiapas/guate/noticias/ddhh.htm

POHL, MARY, AND LAWRENCE H. FELDMAN
  1982   The Traditional Role of Women and Animals in Lowland Maya
         Economy. In *Maya Subsistence: Studies in Memory of Dennis E.
         Puleston*, ed. Kent Flannery, 295–311. New York: Academic Press.

POP BOL, AMANDA
  2001   Huérfanos en derechos: El caso Rax Cucul. In *Los derechos humanos
         en tierras mayas: Política, representaciones, y moralidad*, ed. Pedro
         Pitarch and Julián López García, 245–72. Madrid: Sociedad Española
         de Estudios Mayas.

PORTES, ALEJANDRO

2001 Theories of Development and Their Application to Small Countries.
      In *Globalization on the Ground: Postbellum Guatemalan Democracy
      and Development*, ed. Christopher Chase-Dunn, Susanne Jonas, and
      Nelsom Amaro, 229–40. Oxford: Rowman and Littlefield.

POUILLON, JEAN

1997 The Ambiguity of Tradition: Begetting the Father. In *Present Is Past:
      Some Uses of Tradition in Native Societies*, ed. Marie Mauzé, 17–42.
      New York: University Press of America.

PRENSA LIBRE

3/20/96   Disparan contra vivienda del alcalde de Jocotán, 25.
5/16/99   Consulta: Apatía y desinformación. www.prensalibre.com.gt
5/18/99   No se modifica la Constitución. www.prensalibre.com.gt

PROYECTO DESARROLLO RURAL PARA PEQUEÑOS
PRODUCTORES EN ZACAPA Y CHIQUIMULA

1991 Informe final del sondeo. Documento 003, Ministerio de
      Agricultura, Ganadería, y Alimentación/FIDA/Gobierno de
      los Países Bajos/OPEP/PMA/Gobierno de Guatemala.

PYBURN, K. ANNE

1998 Consuming the Maya. *Dialectical Anthropology* 23:111–29.

QUIZAR, ROBIN, AND SUSAN M. KNOWLES-BERRY

1988 Ergativity in the Cholan Languages. *International Journal of
      American Linguistics* 54(1):73–95.

RAMESH GOVINDARAJ, GNANARAJ CHELLARAJ, AND
CHRISTOPHER J. L. MURRAY

1997 Health Expenditures in Latin America and the Caribbean.
      Social Science and Medicine 44(2):157–69.

RAMÍREZ VARGAS, MARGARITA

1995 Cofradías de Quezaltepeque. *Prensa Libre* (June 10):10–11.
      Colección: Conozcamos Guatemala.

RAMOS, ALÍCIDA RITA

2000 Anthropologist as Political Actor. *Journal of Latin American
      Anthropology* 4(2)–5(1):172–89.

RAXCHÉ

1996 Maya Culture and the Politics of Development. In *Maya Cultural
      Activism in Guatemala*, ed. Edward F. Fisher and R. McKenna-Brown,
      74–88. Austin: University of Texas Press.

REDFIELD, ROBERT
1941   *The Folk Culture of Yucatan*. Chicago: University of Chicago Press.
1953   *The Primitive World and Its Transformations*. Ithaca, NY: Cornell
       University Press.

REINA, RUBEN
1966   *The Law of the Saints*. Indianapolis, IN: BobbsMerrill.

ROBLES, ARODYS
1997   Use of Contraception and Knowledge of Health Technologies.
       In *Demographic Diversity and Change in the Central American
       Isthmus*, ed. Anne R. Pebley and Luis Rosero-Bixby, 367–402.
       Santa Monica, CA: Rand.

RODAS, ISABEL
1995   A la búsqueda de la diversidad del ladino. *Estudios* (2):53–82.

ROGERS, EVERETT M.
1973   *Communication Strategies for Family Planning*. New York: Free Press.

ROGERS, MARK
1998   Introduction: Performing Andean Identities. *Journal of Latin
       American Anthropology* 3(2):2–13.

ROSALDO, RENATO
1980   *Ilongot Headhunting, 1883–1974: A Study in Society and History*.
       Stanford, CA: Stanford University Press.

ROYS, RALPH LOVELAND
1965   *Ritual of the Bacabs*. Norman: University of Oklahoma Press.

RUBIO SÁNCHEZ, MANUEL
1976   *Historia del añil o xiquilite en Centro América*. 2 tomos. San
       Salvador: Ministerio de Educación, Dirección de Publicaciones.

SANDERS, WILLIAM T., AND CARSON MURDY
1982   Population and Agricultural Adaptation in the Humid Highlands of
       Guatemala. In *The Historical Demography of Highland Guatemala*,
       ed. Robert M. Carmack, John Early, and Christopher Lutz, 23–34.
       Albany: Institute for Mesoamerican Studies, SUNY.

SANTISO-GALVEZ, ROBERTO, and JANE T. BERTRAND
2004   The Delayed Contraceptive Revolution in Guatemala. *Human
       Organization* 63(1):57–67.

SCHEPER-HUGHES, NANCY
1992   *Death Without Weeping: The Violence of Everyday Life in Brazil*.
       Berkeley: University of California Press.

SCHIRMER, JENNIFER

1999   *Las intimidades del proyecto político de los militares de Guatemala.*
       Guatemala: FLACSO.

SCHUMANN DE BAUDEZ, ISABELLE

1983   Agricultura y agricultores de la region de Copán. In *Introducción
       a la arqueología de Copán, Honduras*, 196–228. Tegucigalpa:
       Proyecto Arqueológico Copán, Secretaria de Estado en el
       Despacho de Cultura y Turismo.

SCOTT, JAMES C.

1976   *The Moral Economy of the Peasant: Subsistence and Rebellion in
       Southeast Asia.* New Haven, CT: Yale University Press.

1985   *Weapons of the Weak: Everyday Forms of Peasant Resistance.* New
       Haven, CT: Yale University Press.

SEXTON, JAMES D., AND CLYDE M. WOODS

1982   Demography, Development, and Modernization in Fourteen
       Highland Guatemalan Towns. In *The Historical Demography of
       Highland Guatemala*, ed. Robert M. Carmack, John Early, and
       Christopher Lutz, 189–202. Albany: Institute for Mesoamerican
       Studies, SUNY.

SIEDER, RACHEL, AND JESSICA WITCHELL

2001   Impulsando las demanda indígenas a través de la ley: Reflexiones
       sobre el proceso de paz en Guatemala. In *Los derechos humanos en
       tierras mayas: Política, representaciones, y moralidad*, ed. Pedro
       Pitarch and Julián López García, 55–82. Madrid: Sociedad Española
       de Estudios Mayas.

SIMARD, JEAN-JACQUES

1990   White Ghosts, Red Shadows: The Reduction of North American
       Natives. In *The Invented Indian*, ed. James A. Clifton, 335–67.
       New Brunswick, NJ: Transaction.

SLUKA, J.

1989   Living on Their Nerves: Nervous Debility in Northern Ireland.
       Health Care for Women International 10:219–44.

SMITH, CAROL

1984   Local History in Global Context: Social and Economic Transitions
       in Western Guatemala. *Comparative Studies in Society and History*
       26(2):193–228.

1987   Culture and Community: The Language of Class in Guatemala.
       In *The Year Left*, 2, ed. Michael Davis et al., 197–217. London:
       New Left Books.

SMITH, CAROL, ED.

1990 *Guatemalan Indians and the State: 1540–1988*. Austin: University of Texas Press.

STAVENHAGEN, RODOLFO

2001 Derechos humanos y derechos culturales de los pueblos indígenas. In *Los derechos humanos en tierras mayas: Política, representaciones, y moralidad*, ed. Pedro Pitarch and Julián López García, 373–89. Madrid: Sociedad Española de Estudios Mayas.

STEPHENS, JOHN L.

1969 *Incidents of Travel in Central America, Chiapas, and Yucatan*, vol. 1. New York: Dover.

STOLL, DAVID

1993 *Between Two Armies in the Ixil Towns of Guatemala*. New York: Columbia University Press.

1998 *Rigoberta Menchú and the Story of All Poor Guatemalans*. Boulder, CO: Westview.

2001 Derechos humanos, conflicto de tierras y memoria de la violencia en el país ixil del norte del Quiché. In *Los derechos humanos en tierras mayas: Política, representaciones, y moralidad*, ed. Pedro Pitarch and Julián López García, 103–23. Madrid: Sociedad Española de Estudios Mayas.

TAUSSIG, MICHAEL

1980 *The Devil and Commodity Fetishism in South America*. Chapel Hill: University of North Carolina Press.

1987 *Shamanism, Colonialism, and the Wild Man*. Chicago: University of Chicago Press.

TAX, SOL

1952 *Acculturation in the Americas, Proceedings and Selected Papers*. New York: Cooper Square.

TAX, SOL, ED.

1952 *Heritage of Conquest: The Ethnology of Middle America*. Glencoe, IL: Free Press.

TEDLOCK, DENNIS

1993 *Breath on the Mirror: Mythic Voices and Visions of the Living Maya*. San Francisco: Harper.

TERGA, RICARDO

1980 El valle bañado por el río de plata. *Guatemala Indígena* 15(1–2):1–100.

THOMAS, N.
1989 *Out of Time: History and Evolution in Anthropological Discourse.*
Cambridge: Cambridge University Press.

TORRES MOSS, JOSE CLODOVEO
1994 *Apuntes para la historia de Jocotán.* Guatemala.

TOZZER, ALFRED M.
1907 *A Comparative Study of the Mayas and the Lacandones.* New York:
MacMillan.

TURNER, TERRENCE
1993 Anthropology and Multiculturalism: What Is Anthropology That
Multiculturalists Should Be Mindful of It? *Cultural Anthropology*
8(4):411–29.

TZIAN, LEOPOLDO
1994 *Mayas y ladinos en cifras: El caso de Guatemala.* Guatemala:
Editorial Cholsamaj.

UNITED NATIONS DEVELOPMENT PROGRAMME (UNDP)
2003 Who Are Indigenous Peoples?
http://www.undp.org/cso/ip/faq.html. October 3.

US DEPARTMENT OF HEALTH AND HUMAN SERVICES
1997 Vital Statistics Report Shows Significant Gains in Health, Press
Release, September 11. http://www.hhs.gov/news/pres/970911a.html.
2000 Death: Final Data for 1998. *National Vital Statistics Reports*
48(11):1–106.

VAN MAANEN, JOHN
1988 *Tales of the Field: On Writing Ethnography.* Chicago: University of
Chicago Press.

VAN OSS, ADRIANN C.
1986 *Catholic Colonialism: A Parish History of Guatemala, 1524–1821.*
New York: University of Cambridge Press.

VAUGHAN, C. LINCOLN
2002 "There is Another Story that Is Told": A Tale of Maya Chortí in
Western Honduras and Their Precarious Positions in Maya
Ethnography. Master's thesis, London School of Economics.

VEBLEN, THOMAS T.
1982 Native Population Decline in Totonicapan, Guatemala. In *The
Historical Demography of Highland Guatemala,* ed. Robert M.
Carmack, John Early, and Christopher Lutz, 81–102. Albany:
Institute for Mesoamerican Studies, SUNY.

VOGT, EVON Z.
1969   *Zinacantan: A Mayan Community in the Highlands of Chiapas.*
        Cambridge: Belknap Press.
1976   *Tortillas for the Gods: A Symbolic Analysis of Zinacanteco Rituals.*
        Cambridge, MA: Harvard University Press.

WAGLEY, CHARLES
1949   *The Social and Religious Life of a Guatemalan Village.* Memoirs
        of the American Anthropological Association, no. 71. Menasha,
        WI: American Anthropological Association.
1957   *Santiago Chimaltenango.* Guatemala: Seminario de Integración
        Social Guatemalteca.

WALTERS, GARRY REX, AND LAWRENCE H. FELDMAN
1982   On Change and Stability in Eastern Guatemala. *Current
        Anthropology* 23:591–604.

WARD, VICTORIA M., JANE T. BERTRAND, AND FRANCISCO PUAC
1992   Exploring Sociocultural Barriers to Family Planning Among Mayans in
        Guatemala. *International Family Planning Perspectives* 18(2):59–65.

WARREN, KAY
1989   *The Symbolism of Subordination: Indian Identity in a Guatemalan
        Town.* Austin: University of Texas Press.
1992   Transforming Memories and Histories: The Meanings of Ethnic
        Resurgence for Maya Indians. In *Americas: New Intrepretive Essays*,
        ed. Alfred C. Stepan, 25–56. New York: Oxford University Press.
1993   Interpreting *La Violencia* in Guatemala: Shapes of Mayan Silence
        and Resistance. In *The Violence Within: Cultural and Political
        Oppression in Divided Nations*, ed. Kay B. Warren, 25–56. Boulder,
        CO: Westview Press.
1998   *Indigenous Movements and Their Critics: Pan-Maya Activism in
        Guatemala.* Princeton, NJ: Princeton University Press.
2001   Pan-Mayanism and the Guatemalan Peace Process. In *Globalization
        on the Ground: Postbellum Guatemalan Democracy and
        Development*, ed. Christopher Chase-Dunn, Susanne Jonas, and
        Nelsom Amaro, 145–66. Oxford: Rowman and Littlefield.

WASSERSTROM, ROBERT
1976   Revolution in Guatemala: Peasants and Politics under the Arbenz
        Government. *Comparative Studies of Society and History* 18:443–78.

WATANABE, JOHN M.
1992   *Maya Saints and Souls in a Changing World.* Austin: University of
        Texas Press.
1995   Unimagining the Maya: Anthropologists, Others, and Inescapable
        Hubris of Authorship. *Bulletin of Latin American Research* 14(1):25–45.

2001 With All the Means that Prudence Would Suggest: "Procedural Culture" and the Writing of Cultural Histories of Power about 19th-Century Mesoamerica. *Journal of Latin American Anthropology* 5(2):134–75.

WEAVER, FREDERICK STIRTON
1999 Reform and (Counter)Revolution in Post-Independence Guatemala: Liberalism, Conservativism, and Postmodern Controversies. *Latin American Perspectives* 26(2):129–58.

WILLIAMS, MIKE
2002 Deadly Drought Grips Central America: As Malnutrition, Disease Stalk Region's Children, Calls for Aid Shipments Grow. *Austin American-Statesman*, April 26.

WILSON, RICHARD
1995 *Maya Resurgence in Guatemala: Q'eqchi' Experiences*. Norman: University of Oklahoma Press.

WISDOM, CHARLES
1940 *The Chorti Indians of Guatemala*. Chicago: University of Chicago Press.
1952 The Supernatural World and Curing. In *Heritage of Conquest*, ed. Sol Tax, 119–41 Glencoe, IL: Free Press.
1961 *Los Chortis*. Guatemala: Seminario de Integración Social.

WOLF, ERIC R.
1957 Closed Corporate Peasant Communities in Mesoamerica and Central Java. *Southwestern Journal of Anthropology* 13(1):1–18.

WOODWARD, RALPH LEE
1985 *Central America: A Nation Divided*. New York: Oxford University Press.
1993 *Rafael Carrera and the Emergence of the Republic of Guatemala, 1821–71*. Athens: University of Georgia Press.

WORLD BANK
2001 Draft Operational Policies (OP 4.10) Safeguard Provisions, Identification of Indigenous Peoples. http://lnweb18.worldbank.org/ESSD/sdvext.nsf/63ByDocName /PoliciesDraftOP410March232001

WYCLIFFE BIBLE TRANSLATORS
1996 *El nuevo testamento en chortí-español*.

YASHAR, DEBORAH J.
1998 Contesting Citizenship: Indigenous Movements and Democracy in Latin America. *Comparative Politics* 31(1):23–42.

INDEX